Population and Society in Britain 1850-1980

Population and Society in Britain 1850-1980

Edited by
THEO BARKER and **MICHAEL DRAKE**

New York University Press • New York *and* London

New York University Press
Washington Square
New York, N.Y. 10003

**Library of Congress Cataloging in
Publication Data**
Main entry under title:

Population and society in Britain,
1850–1980.

   Includes bibliographies and index.
   1. Great Britain — Population — History —
Addresses, essays, lectures.   2. Great
Britain — Social conditions — Addresses,
essays, lectures.   I. Barker, T. C.
(Theodore Cardwell),
1923–   .   II. Drake, Michael.
HB3583.P597   1982   304.6′0941   82–6437
ISBN 0-8147-1043-3   AACR2

Contents

Introduction

THEO BARKER AND MICHAEL DRAKE

Social history has taken a long time to escape from its political history origins. Even today much of the teaching about changing social conditions in Britain since the 1840s concentrates upon Acts of Parliament, party programmes and the work of particular politicians. According to this view of the past, social progress during the nineteenth century was due almost entirely to Factory Acts and to Public Health and Trade Union legislation, and during the twentieth to the national insurance measures, school meals and old age pensions brought in by the Liberals before 1914 and to other welfare legislation thereafter, particularly since 1948.

Nobody would deny the relevance of this legislation; but many other developments have also contributed to social change and improvement which need to be fitted into this now outdated black and white picture. The very process of economic growth, to which the State contributed little in the nineteenth century and to an increasing, though much disputed, degree since the First World War, itself had a generally ameliorating effect upon most people, though some sections of society then (as always) gained more than others at various points in time. As Social History has evolved as a branch of the broader discipline of History, especially during the past two decades, so these other, non-political features have been further explored. During the 1970s, for instance, important new works appeared which have told us much more about the nature of the class structure in Victorian society. Studies of the lower middle classes, and especially of clerks, have shown how many of these Pooters, earning little, if any, more than skilled workers, were often much worse off than this artisan *élite* because of their need to spend more on rent and in keeping up appearances generally.[1] Much research has been carried out, too, on organized religion's role in spanning the classes, and on Victorian attempts to exercise social control.[2] The very rich, too, have been counted and named.[3] The beginnings of the spread of leisure from the well-to-do and middle classes to wage earners, as the working week became shorter, have also been studied. With the advent of the Saturday half holiday from the 1860s onwards, organized sport became more popular and, with growing real earnings, more of the working classes, as well as the middle classes, could afford to take some annual holiday having saved for it throughout the year. More historians have been studying recreation and seaside towns: a book about Blackpool, whence Lancashire workers flocked in increasing numbers from the 1890s, makes particularly good reading.[4]

The greater relevance and richness of this new Social History, more penetrating in its treatment and often full of revealing insights, has brought about greater specialization and has attracted to the subject many new and enthusiastic recruits. Some of them have taken to supplementing traditional sources of information by the interviewing of older people, and this Oral History, often full of pathos, has helped to fill in many gaps about the day-to-day concerns of life which ordinary folk rarely committed to paper.[5] Various new societies emerged during the 1970s to cater for these new enthusiasts: the Oral History Society, for instance, and the Social History Society, founded by Professor Perkin. The former publishes its own journal,[6] and there is also a *Journal of Social History*, published independently of the Social History Society. The *Economic History Review* and the Economic History Society's series of *Studies in Economic and Social History* also carry material written by the new social historians. The *International Journal of Social History* has had a much longer existence. In America there are journals devoted to the study of women's history and family history.

Historical demography provides the oldest of approaches to Social History. Census material, and occasionally even details of age and occupational structure, sometimes found their way into the earlier teaching of the political historians. Indeed, the late Professor D.V. Glass, to whom this present volume owes its existence for he was originally invited to edit it, pointed out that the beginnings of a persistent interest in the history of population antedated the founding of population studies itself.[7] As was to be expected, the recent new wave of Social History drew much of its strength, and even more of its rigour, from this long-standing interest in historical demography. The Cambridge Group for the History of Population and Social Structure, the leading figures among which have been Dr Laslett, Professor Wrigley and Dr Schofield, set on foot a number of valuable research projects and enlisted much regional and local support. At the LSE Professor Titmuss, as well as Professor Glass, made very significant contributions in this field, especially in his Millicent Fawcett Lecture on 'The position of women: some vital statistics' in which he chided psychologists, psychiatrists and sexologists for neglecting demographic trends and went on to show how the fall in family size in western societies had been the major liberator of women. 'At the beginning of this century', he pointed out, 'the expectation of life of a woman aged 20 was 46 years. Approximately one-third of this life expectancy was to be devoted to the physiological and emotional experience of childbearing and maternal care in infancy. Today (his lecture was published in 1958) the expectation of life of a woman aged 20 is 55 years. Of this longer expectation only about 7 per cent of the years to be lived will be concerned with childbearing and maternal care in infancy'.[8]

The present volume aims to introduce present generations of university students in the social sciences, and also the not inconsiderable numbers of the general public who are also interested in these vital matters, to the role of demographic change since the mid-nineteenth century in explaining some of the topics of present-day social concern. Rapid population growth before the later nineteenth century, for instance, increased the demand for school building and teacher training and, together with larger families and urbanization, contributed to overcrowding and slum conditions. Subsequent slower growth eased the pressure on schools and schooling and made the larger investment in education from the later nineteenth century more effective than it would otherwise have been. Slower population growth also eased overcrowding, although it did not reduce the demand for an increase in the number of separate dwellings. As the larger pre-1914 cohorts passed through the population, so the elderly, not the young, preponderated among the dependants whom those of working age had to sustain.

Bountiful supplies of labour were, of course, available for some time after very rapid population growth had ceased, and, so long as this even greater labour force could find employment, there was growing effective demand for the goods and services it produced. In due course, however, slower population growth reduced the ever-increasing supply of labour. For a time, this gap was made good by fewer people of working age emigrating; but, then, with full employment after the Second World War and no remaining reserves to be drawn in from the agricultural sector, active immigration had to be encouraged. As Mr Holmes tells us in his chapter, the Irish came over to work in numbers unknown since the nineteenth century; and by 1978 immigrants from the New Commonwealth and Pakistan, together with their children, totalled (according to official estimates) 1.9m., or 3.5 per cent, of the British population. By then, however, the Malthusian spectre of population outrunning resources had again reappeared after the quadrupling of oil prices in 1973 and subsequent increases in costs of all sorts. By 1981 these newcomers from across the seas found themselves prominent among the increasing number of unemployed.

The relationship between population and resources is complex, as Mr Oxborrow emphasizes in the first contribution to the volume which in many ways strikes its keynote. Reduced resources can contribute as much to unemployment as can excess population. It so happened that before 1914, when there were vast areas of the world still waiting to be developed and millions of able people prepared to move to these still underdeveloped areas in the United States, South America, the British Empire and elsewhere, massive unemployment was avoided despite unprecedented population increase. The First World War destroyed this international equilibrium. In the world crisis of the early 1930s, unemployment in Britain climbed to an even higher proportion of the labour force than it has reached in 1981. Yet this, as Mr Oxborrow points out, was after Britain had lost 750,000 men in the First World War who would otherwise have formed part of the interwar labour force, and, in addition, after a further 1.5m. people had emigrated over the previous 20 years.

The relentless increase in the numbers of children in Britain, though growing at a slower pace after the later nineteenth century, is the aspect of population growth which Professor Hair explains and examines. Instead of children growing up in families averaging four or more, many of whom lost parents (and certainly grandparents), before reaching adulthood, others being obliged to leave home while still quite young because there was no longer any room for them there, children nowadays grow up in greater comfort in smaller households, though they now more often lose parents by divorce, not by death. Professor Hair points out that, even in the mid-nineteenth century, surprisingly few children under 14 had to go out to work (and then it was usually those who were nearly 14); but many of them were kept doing jobs in and around the home. Parents, on their side, were already making considerable sacrifices to enable their children to attend school, not necessarily on a full-time basis, but enough to enable them to grasp the rudiments of education. Dr Roberts, in her study of working wives in Barrow, Lancaster and Preston between 1890 and 1940, also puts much emphasis on the family economy, every member, young or old, being expected to pull his or her own weight. She uses interviews with the elderly, as well as more traditional sources, to show that emancipation for working-class women before 1914 consisted of being freed from having to go out to work. Few wives of skilled workers took outside employment unless it was in shops (in which they often had a share). Married women who went out to work did so because their husbands earned too little, and the wives' earnings were essential for the family's subsistence.

More children survived from the mid-nineteenth century and more infants survived from the 1890s. It was this reduction in death rates at earlier ages, rather than greater longevity of adults, which mainly explains the increase in life expectancy at birth from 40.5 years for men and 43.0 years for women in 1861 to over 70 in the 1960s. As Dr Winter points out in his contribution to this volume, 'the increase in life chances' among Europeans has probably been greater since the mid-nineteenth century than the total gains had been over the previous millenium. There was less grief — and more certainty of children's survival, which in turn explains to a large extent the spread of family limitation which Dr Roberts also touches upon in passing. Better diet, rather than better medical care or medical knowledge seems to have made the main contribution to the decline of tuberculosis and the other killer diseases. Professor Oddy chronicles this nutritional improvement by referring both to reports on the health of schoolchildren, who grew much taller in this period, and to particulars of army medical examinations. Only three out of every nine men of military age were passed as perfectly fit and healthy by the National Service Medical Board in 1917-18 after the flower of youth had already been recruited; and of the remaining six, three were physical wrecks and a fourth was declared a chronic invalid. Comparable details collected as a result of conscription in the Second World War and after it while conscription lasted — six million case studies — await the courageous at the Public Record Office.

All our authors are at pains to stress the unreliability of much of the statistical evidence, and to explain why this should be so. None more than Mr Wall, of the Cambridge Group for the History of Population and Social Structure. He concentrates mainly on the censuses, and especially on the recent ones, the General Household Survey of the Social Survey Division of the Office of Population Censuses and Surveys and the Family Expenditure Survey of the Department of Employment to examine changes in the structure of the British household since 1851. He finds that the number of households in which relatives lived with the family changed little in the hundred years between 1851 and 1951 (it fell from just over 20 per cent to 15 per cent); but between 1951 and 1971 it has fallen much more steeply, to 7.7 per cent, a phenomenon he goes on to explore and explain.

The essays in this volume show not only how central the demographic experience is to all our lives, but also how radically much of that experience has changed over the last century or so. Knowing just how and when it has changed and what its impact has been over this period provides us with a perspective to many of our current concerns, without which our understanding of them must remain sadly deficient. It is hoped then that social scientists, of all descriptions, together with those many members of the general public who share their interests, will find in these essays a valuable contribution to their studies.

Notes

[1] Geoffrey Crossick (ed.), *The Lower Middle Class in Britain, 1870-1914* (1977); Geoffrey Crossick, *An Artisan Elite in Victorian Society. Kentish London 1840-1880* (1978); Gregory Anderson, *Victorian Clerks* (1976).

[2] A. D. Gilbert, *Religion and Society in Industrial England. Church, Chapel and Social Change, 1740-1914* (1976); Stephen Yeo, *Religion and Voluntary Associations in Crisis* (1976); John Stevenson, *Popular Disturbances in England, 1700-1870* (1979); A. P. Donajgrodzki (ed.), *Social Control in Nineteenth Century Britain* (1977).

[3] W. D. Rubinstein, 'The Victorian middle classes, wealth, occupation and geography', *Economic History Review*, November 1977; W.D. Rubinstein, 'Wealth, elites and the class structure of modern Britain', *Past and Present*, August 1977; W.D. Rubinstein (ed.), *Wealth and the Wealthy in the Modern World* (1980)

[4] John K. Walton, *The Blackpool Landlady. A Social History* (1978) See also Peter Bailey, *Leisure and Class in Victorian England. Rational Recreation and the Contest for Control, 1830-1885* (1978); Hugh Cunningham, *Leisure in the Industrial Revolution* (1980); H. E. Mellor, *Leisure and the Changing City, 1870-1914* (1976).

[5] See, for example the writings of the doyen of oral historians, George Ewart Evans especially *Ask the Fellows Who Cut the Hay* (1956); *The Days We Have Seen* (1975) and *From Mouths of Men* (1976); Michael Winstanley, *Life in Kent at the Turn of the Century* (1978); Thea Thompson, *Edwardian Childhoods* (1981). As an introduction to oral history, see Paul Thompson, *The Voice of the Past* (1978).

[6] Edited from its inception by Paul Thompson and published from the Sociology Department, University of Essex.

[7] Introduction to D. V. Glass and D. E. C. Eversley (eds.), *Population in History* (1965); See also Peter Laslett, D. E. C. Eversley and W. A.

Armstrong, *An Introduction to English Historical Demography* (ed. E. A. Wrigley 1966); Peter Laslett (ed.), *Household and Family in Past Time* (1972); and E. A. Wrigley (ed.), *Identifying People in the Past* (1973); E. A. Wrigley and R. Schofield, *The Population History of England 1541-1871: a Reconstruction.*

[8] Richard M. Titmuss, *Essays on 'The Welfare State'* (1958), 91-2. This lecture has been reprinted in M. W. Flinn and T. C. Smout (eds.), *Essays in Social History* (1974).

Acknowledgement

The editors and Richard Wall wish to thank John Hunt, Research Cartographer, The Open University for preparing the figures appearing on pages 70-80.

Unemployment

JOHN OXBORROW

'Class of 80 facing the dole' was the headline for an article in *The Guardian* newspaper (21 July 1980). The 'class of 80' is the 'baby boom' generation. The number of births in the UK reached a peak in 1964, which was one of only two years since 1921 when they exceeded a million. An immediate reaction to these figures might be that if there were fewer school leavers, they would have more chance of getting a job. A glance back through the figures for unemployed school leavers at mid-summer each year would offer some support for this. There is a prominent dip in 1972, corresponding to the raising of the school leaving age to 16.[1] But it is easy enough to offer an example in the opposite sense. In the First World War about three quarters of a million British males of working age were killed. Between 1911 and 1931 there was a net loss of population of nearly one and a half million by migration. This did not prevent very high levels of unemployment in interwar Britain. The 'class of 80' may be suffering to some extent from being a large class, but other factors are much more important in determining their employment prospects. W. B. Reddaway comments that if one asks a class of first year undergraduates about the effects on unemployment of a falling birth rate, '. . . probably the majority will reply that unemployment will be reduced because there will be a smaller number of people seeking jobs; most of the rest will say it will be increased, because there will be fewer people to buy' and all of them will hesitate on the issue if pressed.[2]

Most views on the population/unemployment relationship can be discussed in terms of a simple model involving the total available labour force, employment, output and labour productivity. By definition, output is equal to employment times labour productivity. Discussion is often in terms of the rates of change of the variables rather than their absolute values. For example, assume that labour productivity is increasing at 2 per cent per year.

Assume also that output is increasing at 1 per cent per year and is limited to this rate of increase by some factor external to the model. Then it follows that employment must decline at 1 per cent per year. If the total number of persons seeking employment is, say, constant, then clearly unemployment will increase. This is the case where productivity gains are 'destroying jobs'. If output were to increase at the same rate as productivity, then the growth of productivity would not destroy any jobs. Rather, other things being equal, it would raise living standards. Most views which have been held on this issue can be discussed in terms of the supposed interactions between the variables and the limitations which it is assumed will apply to the growth of output. It is a subject which has often aroused strong views. It is, as G.P. Hawthorn comments in an incisive survey, 'a topic peopled with vigorous optimists and gloomy pessimists'.[3] Later in this chapter we shall look at the pessimists and the optimists in turn. First however it is necessary to consider the first term in the model; what was called above the total available labour force or 'those seeking employment'.

Who wants to work? Measuring the labour force

Labour productivity determines the labour input necessary for any given output. But the necessary labour input can be applied in many different forms. The available employment opportunities can be spread over all or nearly all those seeking work by adjusting working hours. In economies in the early stages of industrialization, or in economies with large agricultural sectors or a high proportion of self-employed workers, there is commonly more under employment than overt unemployment. This can be thought of as adjusting the productivity term in the model or alternatively it can be viewed as a reduction in labour input by what amounts to part-time working. In highly industrialized modern economies there is more commonly complete and overt unemployment for a proportion of the labour force. This is what is normally meant by the term unemployment in modern discussion. Historically this conception of unemployment arises concurrently with the industrialization and urbanization of the country. In Britain examples of the use of the word in the modern sense can be found as early as the 1840s, but it was not introduced into formal economic discussion until 1888 (by Alfred Marshall). The first attempt at a formal definition was made by J. A. Hobson in 1895.[4]

If unemployment is used in this modern sense, it might seem that its definition is straightforward. It is the difference between the numbers seeking work and the numbers actually working. In practice this is a very difficult number to pin down, because of both conceptual and data collection problems. What is ideally needed is a survey, using a very tight definition of what is meant by 'wanting to work' and 'available for work'. There is no survey of this sort at all in Britain prior to 1971. The commonly quoted figures for unemployment make use of data collected, since 1921, under the unemployment insurance scheme, or of census data. The differences which can result are illustrated by the figures given for unemployment in two authoritative sources for the year, say, 1932. From the London and Cambridge Economic Service's *The British Economy Key Statistics 1900-1970* the answer is 22.1 per cent but Angus Maddison's *Economic Growth in the West* (1964 appendix E) gives 13.1 per cent. When there are problems of this order in defining the variable, caution is obviously in order in discussing its causes.

Space does not permit a full discussion of these definitional problems. One issue in this area which calls for at least a brief mention is that of activity rates. At different points in time a larger or smaller proportion of the population in any age or sex group may seek employment. Economic development and rising incomes tend to reduce male activity rates in the younger and older age groups. This is because education is lengthened while pension schemes make retirement from work financially possible. On the other hand female activity rates rise in the later stages of development. This is perhaps due to the downward trend in the birth rate, the increased availability of work in services often considered specially suitable for females, and, to some extent, the liberalization of law and convention regarding female employment. The increase in female activity rates in Britain since 1950 has been the most important single factor acting on labour supply.[5] To give an example from a period for which fairly good statistics are available: in the UK between 1969 and 1978 females aged 15-64 declined in numbers by about 100,000, but the number in employment rose by 925,000. The number of females in this age group registered as unemployed rose five and a half times, by 350,000. The rate for this age group rose from 49.7 per cent to 57.4 per cent.[6] Activity rate changes here swamp the actual change in the population. In western industrial countries increases in female activity rates since 1950 are general, though there are considerable variations between countries. The British figures are distinguished by the unusually high proportion of females who work part-time. Activity rates cannot be calculated with much confidence for earlier periods, though changes seem to have been much slower. The female proportion of the labour force was much the same in 1921 as it was in 1951 and perhaps not very much different from typical nineteenth-century figures. But figures for before 1948, when universal national insurance was introduced, need to be treated with scepticism.[7]

'Gloomy pessimists'

Thomas Malthus is the father of all gloomy pessimists in this area.[8] Malthus's famous essay had six editions between 1797 and 1826 and must be among the most quoted and influential works in social science. J. J. Spengler comments 'although the course of events in the century and a half succeeding the appearance of the sixth edition of the essay has altered the dimensions of the population problem, it has not altered its essential character'.[9] An important element in any Malthusian approach is the assumption that output will be limited by the availability of some input, other than labour, into the productive system. The input which concerned Malthus was agricultural land and he did not think that other raw materials would pose a problem. This is understandable enough in early nineteenth-century Britain. Agriculture was still the largest single industry; food is obviously vital to human survival and the land area of Britain was obviously finite. The possibilities at that time for importing food were slight; neither the sources of supply nor the means of transport existed. Malthus guessed in 1797 and knew by 1826 that the population was increasing rapidly. A second element in the argument was that any increase in the productivity of land brought about by technical progress would simply lead to a further increase in population, via temporarily higher living standards. Thus although there might be an oscillation over time in population and living standards, the latter would be repeatedly forced back to subsistence level by the pressure of population. The size of the population would be kept in check by the disease and 'misery' implied by this low level of living. Any surplus population would be starved out of existence.

The power of population is so superior to the power in the earth to produce subsistence for men that premature death must . . . visit the human race. The vices of mankind are active and able ministers of depopulation . . . but should they fail . . . gigantic inevitable famine stalks in the rear and with one mighty blow levels the population with the food of the world.[10]

Malthus's reputation owes much to his policy proposals, especially for the abolition of the poor law. Such ideas aroused the fury of Marx and will certainly seem illiberal to many modern readers. But much of his analysis is persuasive. It was influential in political and economic thought, though not without modification, through the middle of the nineteenth century. J. S. Mill's *Principles of Economics* was the leading text in its field for many years after its publication in 1848. It was thoroughly permeated by Malthusian ideas. M. Blaug remarks that Mill thought every conceivable policy must be judged in terms of its effects on the birth rate.[11] Mill wrote in his autobiography that Malthus's great population principle was a banner and point of union among the utilitarians.

This great doctrine, originally brought forward as an argument against the indefinite improvability of human affairs, we took up with ardent zeal in the contrary sense, as indicating the sole means of realizing that improvability by securing full employment at high wages to the whole labouring population through a voluntary restriction of the increase of their numbers.[12]

Birth control is the only route to full employment. Another comment from Mill catches the essence of the Malthusian approach:

The niggardliness of nature, not the injustice of society, is the cause of the penalty attached to over-population ... it is in vain to say, that all mouths which the increase of mankind calls into existence, bring with them hands. The new mouths require as much food as the old ones, and the hands do not produce as much.[13]

The basic Malthusian fear is that there will not be enough of something, specifically land as far as Malthus himself was concerned, to employ the labour force. This fear was prominent at the beginning of the period under consideration. Never entirely absent, it rises to prominence again at the end. But then it was extended to cover the fear of running out of a wide range of materials; not only food (which has continued in some areas to be in surplus) but fuel, minerals and fibres. As Spengler puts it: 'It is the finiteness of a now more broadly defined biosphere that sets limits to how large a population may become and yet remain compatible with man's long run welfare.'[14] Between about the 1870s and the 1960s these Malthusian fears were largely in abeyance. During this period the limitations which had seemed so constrictive to Malthus were removed. Britain, which had seemed such a small country to him, was able to draw food and raw materials from all over the world and provide employment for a population ten times that of 1800 at a greatly increased standard of living. Technical progress raised the productivity of agricultural land. The development of industry and the cumulation of capital provided opportunities for employment and the growth of output on a scale which Malthus could hardly have dreamed of. This was the age of the 'frontier'; a period in which the world seemed to offer possibilities for more or less indefinite expansion, both geographically and technically.[15] More of everything could always be found, 'out there', over the horizon. But in the late 1960s many observers started to discern the return of the Malthusian nightmare, and this time in a form from which there was no easy escape. A few western industrial countries could transcend their own limits by exploiting the rest of the world's resources. But, as the first photographs from space served to dramatise, the world as a whole was finite.

The late 1960s saw a spate of publications arguing about the finiteness of the world's resources on these lines. Their impact however was nothing compared with that of the 1973 oil crisis. This seemed to herald the first real fulfilment of such predictions. Indeed the quadrupling of oil prices in 1973 may well prove to have been the end of the 'frontier' era in economic history. From 1850 to 1973 there was one statistic which appeared to prove Malthus decisively wrong. This was the figure for the terms of trade between primary produce and manufactured goods. Throughout this period, the trend, with some interruptions, was for primary produce to get cheaper relative to manufactured goods.[16] This must be strong evidence of the absence during this period of any constraint on employment arising from physical shortages of inputs. But although it is still early in the day for generalizations, it could well be that the trend of relative prices was permanently reversed in the early 1970s. It was not only oil prices that rose at that time but those of many other raw materials as well.

The substantial rise in unemployment in Britain and most other industrial countries since 1973 has not however been directly caused by any physical shortage of inputs. Raw materials and fuel have continued to be available, but at higher real prices. The rise in unemployment has been the result of balance of payments problems and of inflation brought about by the higher import prices and of the policy reactions to these developments. The rise in oil prices was of great importance, but there was not, except for a few weeks, a 'shortage' of oil, in the sense that oil could always be had, at a price. The price was high because of the success of the cartel instituted by OPEC. But it may be asked, what was it that enabled OPEC to be successful when nearly all earlier attempts at rigging the market by primary producers had failed (apart from those involving industrial countries' own agricultural output)? The answer must be that the rise in world population combined with the spectacular rise in per capita consumption had placed a severe strain on the world's energy resources. Energy did not run out in any simple sense. But what the world did run out of was large, easily and cheaply exploitable new sources of energy. This contrasts sharply with experience during the 'frontier' phase.

During the 1950s and 1960s the industrial west had grown at record rates on the basis of a flood of cheap oil. If any oil producer tried to restrict output, as Persia did from 1950-1953, supplies could easily be replaced from elsewhere.[17] In the 1960s large new producers entered the market, for example Libya and Nigeria. But in 1973, when OPEC struck, there was no new source to turn to in the short term, either geographically or technically. And so the cartel worked. The inflation and balance of payments problems which its success created in industrial countries have led to increased unemployment. In a broad sense the crisis had a Malthusian element in it.

There are many 'vigorous optimists' who would strongly dispute this conclusion. A great deal of the pressure on energy and other natural resources could be said to derive from the rise in per capita consumption rather than from the rise in population. This is a two-edged argument. The higher the level of consumption per person, the greater the effect of any change in the number of persons. For instance, between 1951 and 1973, UK energy consumption increased from 236 million tons of coal equivalent per year to 353 million tons per year. The per capita consumption increased from 4.70 to 6.32 tons per year, or by 34.5 per cent. Over the same period the population increased by 11.2 per cent. But if the population had not increased at all, then annual consumption would have increased by 81.5 million tons a year instead of 117 million tons; an increase 30 per cent less than actually occurred.[18]

Again, there has been no shortage of optimistic assertions to the effect that the technological or even the geographical frontier is not over. Just as the early nineteenth-century political economists failed to foresee the technical changes that were to falsify their views, so today's 'pessimists' may be failing to take adequate account of tomorrow's technical progress.[19] The present author inclines to a pessimistic view. The easy options are likely to be taken first and most of them have been. North Sea oil and nuclear power are each in their way examples of the very difficult areas that it is now necessary to explore if the broadly defined Malthusian limits are to be pushed back again. But the only sure judgement is that the future is difficult to predict.

Optimists

Three aspects of the history of the last 100 years or so will be covered under this heading. The first will be described as the neoclassical phase. The second aspect is 'secular stagnation' and the third is the phase of rapid economic growth from the Second

World War to the oil crisis.

The neoclassical phase

Quite early in the nineteenth century it became clear that the gloomy classical view of the relationship between demographic and economic variables did not fit some of the evidence. The discrepancy emerges clearly in the work of Phelps Brown and Hopkins, who made a brave attempt to chart the real value of a wage series over the enormous time span of seven centuries.[20] As they themselves make clear, there are reservations about accepting their data as an indicator of real wages in general. But their results seem plausible when related to other accounts of the economy over much of this period. Their graph shows a high point for real wages at the end of the fifteenth century, and a low point at the end of the sixteenth. It then rises until the middle of the eighteenth century and then turns down again. If we grant ourselves a little poetic licence and imagine Malthus reading the relevant issue of *Economica* in about 1800, he would probably have been quite pleased. 'Look' we can imagine him saying, 'there in the late fifteenth century is the peak which results from the reduction in the population in the Black Death. Then the population starts to rise again and we can see the resulting low point, which induced the Elizabethans to start that wretched poor law. Population growth in the late seventeenth and early eighteenth century was quite slow and agricultural improvement, which you know cannot go on for ever, did raise real wages. But look at the present trends. Population is rising more rapidly than ever before and we can see all too clearly the effect on living standards. We are clearly heading for a crisis'. But let us now move forward to the view as seen from about 1900. After a period of awful hesitation in the first four decades of the nineteenth century, when it seemed that Britain stood at the brink of the crisis Malthus expected, the graph turns decisively upwards. But not because population growth was checked. In Ireland the Malthusian crash did indeed take place. The famine of 1846 and the subsequent high levels of emigration brought a drastic reduction in population. But in Britain, after the 1840s, the figures are amazing in relation to previous experience. Despite population growth at a sustained 1 per cent per annum, wages rise steadily and there is no evidence of any secular increase in the level of unemployment. The economy was finding jobs for the rising population and at ever higher real wages. By 1880 the Phelps Brown-Hopkins graph has, after a lapse of four centuries, again passed its high point of the 1480s.

Commenting on their figures, the authors write:

Do we not see here (the low point of 1597) a Malthusian crisis, the effect of rapid growth of population impinging on an insufficiently expansive economy; such as perhaps we see also in the fall that set in again around 1750, until this time a commercial and industrial revolution came to save Britain from the fate of Ireland?

The 'commercial and industrial revolution' broke the relationship, in those countries which succeeded in industrializing, between population change and the economic situation. It did so by technical progress and trade. We now move into a period in which the most important constraint on output is effective demand. The constraints envisaged by the classical economists, of land and food supply and, by 'latterday' Malthusians, of energy and raw materials, fade into the background. Hence it followed that the economy could provide employment for all who wanted. And although there were fluctuations in activity, on the whole it did.

Economic and social thought soon began to reflect the new situation.[21] The emerging industrial and urban society was far more complicated than its predecessors. The division of labour was finer and the links between producer and consumer much longer. The financial system developed a matching complexity. Saving and investing, and owning and managing were now more often separated. But none of this had been planned, in Britain anyway. It appeared that the best model of this economy was that of a self adjusting system, too complicated perhaps to ever analyze fully, but whose main links and feedbacks could be understood. The new assumptions were that, providing the labour market was working properly, real wages would depend on productivity, which would in turn depend on investment and technical progress. Real wages had risen and could rise further. Employment had been and could in the future be found for all who wanted it, though the problem of trade fluctuations needed attention. From 1890, Alfred Marshall's *Principles of Economics* was the leading text. A quotation illustrates the change. 'If real wages were forced down by the difficulty of obtaining food, the working class could relieve themselves of the pressure of diminishing returns by reducing their numbers. But they cannot do so now, because there is no such pressure'[22] The level of employment would be determined by the level of demand. And the level of demand would be self adjusting, since the process of production itself generated the necessary demand through the payment of wages, salaries and profits. These ideas led to the view that, if there was unemployment, a principal cause must be institutional failings in the labour market. Thus economists in this period had little to say about unemployment, which increasingly came to be regarded as a problem of social administration.

Politically, unemployment was a matter of mounting concern. But it was increasingly regarded as being due to the 'injustice of society', or at least the defective organization of society, rather than the 'niggardliness of nature'. William Beveridge emerged as a leading authority on the topic. In his *Unemployment: A Problem of Industry* published in 1909 he briefly but firmly dismissed over-population as a cause of unemployment:

It is clearly possible, theoretically, for there to be more men in a country than can find living room there. To the English economists of a past generation this appeared to be a practical and urgent danger in the country that they knew ... today economists view the matter very differently. The fear of over-population is dispelled or at least postponed to a remote future.[23]

The most important evidence for this was, he argued, the rise in real wages. If there was a pressure of population on the labour market, this would have been reflected in a fall in real wages. But there was no doubt that unemployment existed and was being increasingly recognized and discussed as a problem in terms of its modern definition. The main strands in the diagnosis offered by Beveridge and his contemporaries were: firstly that some of the population were so uneducated and mentally and physically defective as to be unemployable; secondly that the labour market was defective and needed to be improved by such things as labour exchanges and thirdly that some unemployment was due to the trade cycle. Temporary gluts were acknowledged as a possibility and could be dealt with by various relief and make-work schemes. Later Keynes was to overturn the neoclassical assumption that demand was self-adjusting within a reasonable time period.

Keynes engaged in a controversy with Beveridge in the early 1920s. Keynes had referred in his controversial best-seller *The Economic Consequences of the Peace* to the population of Britain as 'excessive' and wrote of its dependence for survival on a 'complicated and artificial organization'. Beveridge used his presidential address to the economics section of the British Association for a fierce refutation of these ideas. 'Over-population' was a possibility, he argued, only in extreme circumstances, such as those following the dismemberment of the Austro-Hungarian Empire.

Vienna remains a head grotesquely too large for the shrunken body of German Austria, manifestly over-populated and as unable to support its former members ... as would be Monaco if the nations gave up gambling or Gibraltar if they gave up war. It is over-populated not through exhaustion of its natural resources ... but because the world outside has changed too suddenly[24]

Later in the article he wrote confidently: 'The problems of unemployment and over-population are distinct; they are two problems not one'. The press was pleased with Beveridge. *The*

Guardian wrote: 'At the British Association Sir William Beveridge effectively laid the bogey and convinced most of us that there are no grounds for Malthusian pessimism'.[25] Keynes had indeed picked the wrong moment for such comments. The movement of the terms of trade in favour of manufactured goods was carried even further in the inter-war years. The late 1920s and 1930s saw a mounting glut of food, minerals and fuel. Primary producers everywhere, whether British coal miners or Australian sheep farmers, struggled with falling prices and surplus capacity. In the 1931 edition of *Unemployment* . . . Beveridge had little hesitation in confirming his denial of any connection between the mounting problem of unemployment and the population factor. Politicians, we may note in passing, often do not keep up with academic thought. At the same time as Beveridge was editing the new edition of *Unemployment* . ., the man actually faced with the problem, the Prime Minister, Ramsay MacDonald, committed to his diary the despairing Malthusian comment: 'The simple fact is that our population is too great for our trade'.[26]

Secular stagnation

There was, then, no shortage of materials; indeed by the 1930s the world was awash with them. There was no shortage of 'needs'; there were plenty of ill-fed, ill-clothed and ill-housed people who would be very happy to consume more than they did. What was in short supply was effective demand. This was what caused unemployment; the neoclassicists had erred in assuming an automatic match, but it was within the power of governments to make the necessary adjustments. And these adjustments could be achieved within the existing economic and social framework. These, in brief outline, were the conclusions reached by J. M. Keynes by 1936. Keynesianism is now, in 1980, again the subject of controversy, after being the accepted view for 30 years. This controversy cannot be covered here, but it should be said that the present writer is 'Keynesian' in that he believes that Keynes' analysis of unemployment was correct in all essential points.

From the point of view of the 'population factor', there is one aspect of the Keynesian revolution which demands attention. It is the strand of thought known as 'secular stagnation'. The word secular is used to distinguish a long term rise in unemployment as opposed to the fluctuations in unemployment due to the trade cycle. Keynes himself offered some support to this approach, but its main originator is usually considered to be the American economist and early convert to Keynesianism, Alvin Hansen. The argument is straightforward. It reflects the switch of emphasis

from the supply side factors which had preoccupied earlier commentators, to the demand side of the equation to which Keynes,
and the facts of the situation, so strongly pointed. The striking
thing about the nineteenth century had been the way in which
there was a reasonably good match between effective demand and
productive capacity. But one major factor which had contributed
to the level of demand was investment. Keynes' diagnosis of the
failure of effective demand to reach adequate levels in the inter-war
years rested on the absence of any necessary match between intended levels of saving and investment. If intentions to save
exceeded intended investment, unemployment would result.
Generally in the nineteenth century, investment had reached the
levels necessary for approximately full employment. Why was
this? At least partly because of the growth of population. Entrepreneurs, knowing that they had an expanding market for their
goods, decided to extend their factories and build new ones. But
population growth was now slowing down. Keynes wrote in 1937
that 'we know much more securely than we know almost any other
social or economic factor relating to the future . . . that we shall be
faced in a very short time with a stationary or declining
population'.[27] And it followed that the businessmen of the future
would not be making those investments which in the past had
anticipated the steady growth of population. It was possible that
there would be a sufficient flow of new technology to stimulate
investment up to the required level, the level that is where it would
employ all the savings that social convention and habit would tend
to generate. But Keynes thought that the maximum likely growth
of output per head that could be tolerated for long without social
disruption was about 1 per cent per annum. This would be insufficient to provide outlets for all the savings people would probably
want to make. There was likely to be a problem therefore in
keeping effective demand up to the level of full employment.
Basically it was that, in the absence of rapid population growth to
stimulate investment, intended savings were likely to be excessive
and lead to unemployment.

The reader may by now be wondering what justification there is
for including this idea under the general heading of 'Optimists'. It
may well seem that we have now come full cycle in our discussion.
From the classical view that employment would be limited by
supply side problems generated by a rising population, we have
moved to the opposite pole where the fear is that employment will
be limited by demand side problems arising out of a stationary or
falling population. From some points of view secular stagna-
tionism is pessimistic. It is labelled as optimistic here because

Keynes thought that, although there was a problem, it could be solved. Monetary and fiscal policy, and possibly some more far reaching changes in the government's role in the economy, could achieve the required result. Hansen's status as an optimist is more doubtful. His analysis was basically similar to that of Keynes. In the USA an even larger proportion, about 60 per cent, of nineteenth-century investment had arisen because of the need to provide for a growing population. This rapid expansion of the population had been associated with an equally rapid expansion of the geographical frontier westwards. By 1939 the frontier was closed, population growth by natural increase was slowing to a halt and immigration had been virtually suspended by legislation in the early 1920s. Thus the only route to providing an adequate level of demand was for the government to greatly increase its level of current expenditure. Not unexpectedly for an American, this was a possibility Hansen regarded with great suspicion.

As so often in economic life, we are confronted by a dilemma. Continued unemployment on a vast scale, resulting from inadequate private investment outlets, could be expected sooner or later to lead straight into an all-round regimented economy. But so also, by an indirect route and a slower process, might a greatly extended programme of public expenditures[28]

The ending of rapid population growth had removed, Hansen seems to be suggesting, one of the major elements which had tended to stabilize the employment situation in the nineteenth century. The only alternative agency which could now ensure full employment was the government. The idea of government performing such a role was not one likely to endear itself to many Americans at this time.

From the Second World War to the oil crisis

This is in many ways a remarkable period. Most of the advanced industrial economies grew at rates wich must be considered amazing in the perspective of previous history. Between 1952 and 1971, Japan, Germany and France grew at 8.44, 4.72 and 4.23 per cent per annum per capita respectively. Britain's per capita growth over this period was 2.24 per cent, faster than in earlier periods but much slower than her main competitors, other than the USA .[29] This relatively slow rate of growth soon became the dominating topic for economic discussion in Britain. Unemployment in Britain was very low taken as a national average, though some regional rates were still a cause for concern. Unemployment was low in most other industrial countries. In this new situation the focus of attention with respect to the population factor shifted again. Many commentators now discerned a labour shortage.

It had been observed that in the industrial sectors of advanced economies, a rapid growth of employment in manufacturing industry was associated with a rapid growth of labour productivity, and hence of course with the growth of output.[30] The fast growing countries, which did not include Britain, all had access to elastic supplies of labour and could rapidly increase employment in manufacturing. These supplies of labour did not derive from high birth rates. Birth rates turned up after the war, but this did not effect employment until the 1960s, by which time differences in growth rates were well established. Rather they came from two sources, immigration and agriculture. All the fast growing countries had at the start of this period large and relatively inefficient agricultural sectors. As these contracted, so the farm workers moved into industry. And most fast growing countries recruited substantial additions to their industrial labour forces from abroad. By 1974 there were about 2.25 million migrant workers in West Germany and 1.5 million in France.[31] In contrast the net inflow of migrants to Britain between 1951 and 1976 was 280,000 and, after allowing for the indirect effects of this inflow, the population aged 15-64 was only 696,000 larger in 1976 than it would have been in the absence of all migration, outwards or inwards, since 1951.[32] And British agriculture was already too small an employer by 1950 to contribute significantly.

In terms of the previous discussion and of course especially with respect to Malthusian thinking, the idea that the rapid increase of the labour force raises labour productivity is paradoxical. At the same time as these ideas were being expounded in the west, other western economists were developing pessimistic views about the 'third world' population situation. Here the very rapid growth of population was seen in fairly straight Malthusian terms as a threat to prospects for employment and for improvements in the social and economic situation.[33] The inverse relation between growth of per capita product and population growth which is implied by the pessimistic approach was only very weakly confirmed, with many exceptions, when detailed studies were made.[34] This does not of course mean that birth control programmes were not desirable on more general social grounds.

The apparent paradox between the situation in advanced and developing countries is fairly easily explained. In 'capital rich' advanced countries an elastic supply of labour for industry stimulated investment and technical progress and reaped the benefits of economies of scale. The availability of capital and, in this period, of energy and raw materials prevented the influx of labour being much of a threat to employment. This was especially the case in

Europe since during downturns in economic activity, many immigrants went home again. In contrast, capital in developing countries was desperately scarce. Rates of population growth were twice and sometimes three times those of the British industrial revolution. And many developing countries when compared with nineteenth-century Britain were deficient in political stability, literacy and entrepreneurial abilities. In these circumstances many of them appeared to be avoiding the 'fate of Ireland' only with difficulty and western food aid.

The 'labour shortage' view of the role of the population factor in Britain and Europe in this period does share something with the views of the secular stagnationists. The economy may perhaps be easier to manage when investment is stimulated by an elastic labour supply for manufacturing industry. The British industrial labour force did not grow rapidly, and, although the British economy grew at a substantial rate and had low unemployment, it was notably difficult to manage. It was increasingly subject to balance of payments problems and industrial relations were poor and deteriorating. When the oil price shock hit the western world in 1973, Britain found it particularly difficult to cope with, compared with, say, Germany, where a relatively smooth adjustment was made to the new conditions. It may be that the rather poor British performance owes something to our slow rate of economic growth and this in turn may owe something to the slow rate of growth of the labour force in industry. Possibly, but not probably. It must be stressed that the causes of slow British growth are complex and controversial. Many economists would now argue that the key constraint was the balance of payments, which exhibited special features peculiar to Britain, or some other aspect of the British situation such as her industrial relations system. But the labour shortage idea has had its adherents. Selective employment tax in 1966 was designed to squeeze labour out of the service sector and make it available for industry, where it was hoped it might initiate growth at European rates. Other commentators have regretted the restrictions on immigration imposed in 1962 due to the social problems it was thought to be generating.[35] From the point of view of the discussion in this chapter, the labour shortage idea does complete a neat 'full house' of theories. We have now seen every factor proposed as the crucial constraint; land, raw materials and energy, demand and now labour.

Conclusion

Looking back over the period since the industrial revolution, the outstanding impression is the way in which, over the long term, employment opportunities have kept pace with the rise in population. Phelps Brown and Browne comment: 'However fast and cumulatively the numbers seeking work increased, there was no cumulation of unemployment and over any long span of years, the number of vacancies increased in the same proportion as that of applicants'[36] The population factor has been largely accommodated within the other variables of the economic system. This is despite frequent expressions of anxiety that it was likely to be a major problem in one direction or the other.

The accommodation which has been achieved has required a quite high degree of social flexibility. Children in industrial societies cannot and do not expect to be able very often to do the same type of jobs as their parents. All industrial societies show a considerable though far from complete transmission of social status from parents to children. But each new generation is fed into a constantly changing spectrum of occupations through increasingly elaborate and formalized systems of education. Given that population growth, after a rise in the birth rate in Britain (and most other industrial countries) in the 1950s and 1960s, is tending once again towards zero, fears are often expressed about the continuance of this flexibility.[37] The degree of flexibility required may need to be all the greater, if, as is sometimes forecast, the growth of labour productivity increases because of new technology. Fluctuations in the birth rate may create problems of a similar type. On the upswing there tends to be scarcity of educational and training facilities and perhaps difficulties in absorbing school leavers into employment. As the bulge passes into the labour force, schools and teachers are left redundant and in need of redeployment. Even here it is easy to overstate the importance of the demographic effects. According to one calculation, out of the total inflow into the teaching profession in England and Wales between 1961 and 1971, only 8 per cent was needed to match demographic growth. By far the largest proportion of the inflow was needed simply to replace teachers leaving the profession (77 per cent), leaving 15 per cent for reduction of class sizes and increased attendance.[38] The author of this study comments that in his view the abrupt contraction of the teacher training colleges in the mid-1970s arose much more from the 'unwise increase in their capacity' rather than from demographic factors.

Often more sweeping assertions are made about the effects of the ending of rapid population growth. A French demographer remarked that a 'stationary population would be a population of old people ruminating over old ideas in old houses'[39] This is not persuasive, although as we have seen, a growing population may well be a stimulus to investment. As for creativity and inventiveness, children are not particularly creative and high rates of population growth produce a high proportion of children under 15. The lowest level of dependants of non-working age is given by a net reproduction rate of 0.9, i.e. in a slowly declining population. It is sometimes not realized that there is little difference in the proportion of dependants over a wide range of growth rates, lower growth rates merely substituting old dependants for young ones.[40] Sweezy and Owens calculated the probability of a population producing a Nobel prize winner in physics in terms of its age structure and the age distribution of actual physics Nobel prize winners. This showed the probability at a broad maximum over a wide range of growth rates between zero and plus 1.5 per cent a year, and falling off rapidly above plus 2 per cent and below minus 0.5 per cent.[41] It remains true that a stationary population with a high rate of labour productivity growth would have to adapt itself to increased levels of adult re-training and education.

In Britain in 1980, the prospects for employment are considered gloomy. They are often presented in terms of a given and currently still rising labour force competing desperately for employment opportunities which are being constantly eroded by technological change. But when confronted with this pessimism, the student should return to the simple model introduced at the start of the chapter. Employment equals output divided by labour productivity. Throughout the history of industrialization, gains in labour productivity have always presented both a threat and a promise; a threat of reduced employment but a promise of higher living standards. If they in fact result in reduced employment rather than in higher output, one needs to ask, why? Of course at the level of the individual firm or even industry, a cut in employment may be inevitable. It is here that the need for re-training and so on already discussed manifests itself. But if productivity gains are used to cut employment in the economy as a whole, then the question stands. The answer could be the 'niggardliness of nature'; it could be that we really have come up against the limits of the supply of energy and raw materials needed to raise output any further. But alternatively it could be the 'injustice of society' or, if not exactly the 'injustice' then the defects of our institutions and the errors of our policies. To the present writer, the possibilities of resource scarcities in the future suggest every reason to welcome the cessation of population growth, as a matter of prudence at least. But unemployment is not currently created directly by either resource scarcities or any other aspect of the population factor.

Notes

[1] A. J. H. Dean, 'Unemployment among school leavers: an analysis of the problem', *National Institute Economic Review*, November 1976.

[2] W. B. Reddaway, *The Economics of a Declining Population*, 1939, p. 48.

[3] G. P. Hawthorn, 'Some social consequences of growing numbers', in L. R. Taylor (Editor), *The Optimum Population for Britain*, 1970, p. 60.

[4] J. Harris, *Unemployment and Politics*, 1972, p. 4.

[5] 'Female activity rates', *Department of Employment Gazette*, January 1974, p. 8.

[6] Calculated from *Annual Abstract of Statistics*, HMSO, 1980 edition, pp. 14 and 146.

[7] 'The fall in the labour force between 1966 and 1971', *Department of Employment Gazette*, December 1973, p. 1084.

[8] Not all commentators regard Malthus as 'pessimistic' and the heading is intended to provide a framework. K. E. Boulding comments that Malthus's message is one of hope since it 'reveals the nature of one dragon which must be slain before misery can be abolished'. *Collected Works*, vol. 2, 1971 p. 142.

[9] J. J. Spengler, (Editor), *Population Problems in the Victorian Age*, 1973, editor's introduction, no page number.

[10] T. R. Malthus, *An Essay on the Principle of Population*, 1978, Pelican Classics reprint, 1970, pp. 118-9.

[11] M. Blaug, *Economic Theory in Retrospect*, 3rd edition, 1978, p. 231.

[12] ibid.

[13] J. S. Mill, *Principles of Political Economy*, Peoples' Edition, 1891, p. 118.

[14] Spengler, op. cit. introduction.

[15] K. E. Boulding, 'The economics of the coming spaceship earth' in H. Jarret, (editor), *Environmental Quality in a Growing Economy*, 1966, p. 3.

[16] W. A. Lewis, *Economic Survey 1919-1939*, 1949, p. 195 and London and Cambridge Economic Service, *The British Economy Key Statistics 1900-1970*, p. 14.

[17] P. Odell, *Oil and World Power*, 3rd edition, 1974, chapters 2 and 4.

[18] Calculted from *Digest of UK Energy Statistics*, HMSO, 1980, table 2.

[19] See for instance C. Freeman and M. Johoda (editors), *World Futures*, 1978, chapter 2.

[20] E. H. Phelps Brown and S. V. Hopkins, 'Seven centuries of the prices of consumables compared with builders' wage rates', *Economica*, vol 23, November 1956, p. 296.

[21] G. Stedman Jones, *Outcast London*, 1971, p. 9.

[22] A. Marshall, *Principles of Economics*, 1890, p. 691.

[23]   W.H. Beveridge, *Unemployment: a problem of industry*, 1909, p.6.

[24]   W. H. Beveridge, 'Population and unemployment', *Economic Journal*, December 1923, p. 447.

[25]   *The Guardian* quoted by J. M. Keynes in 'Reply to Sir William Beveridge', *Economic Journal*, December 1923.

[26]   D. Marquand, *Ramsay MacDonald*, 1977, p. 537.

[27]   J. M. Keynes, 'Some economic consequences of a declining population', *Eugenics Review*, April 1937.

[28]   A. H. Hansen, 'Economic progress and declining population growth', *American Economic Review*, March 1939, pp. 12-13.

[29]   Calculated from United Nations Yearbook of National Account Statistics, 1969, vol. II, table 7 and 1972, vol. III, table 7. Compound annual rates of growth of per capita product.

[30]   This is 'Verdoorn's law'. The original article is in Italian and was published in 1949. See N. Kaldor, *Causes of the Slow Rate of Economic Growth of the United Kingdom*, 1966, p. 10.

[31]   *OECD Observer*, no. 104, May 1980, p. 24.

[32]   C. Walker and M. Gee, 'Migration: the impact on the population', *Population Trends*, no. 9, autumn 1977, p. 24.

[33]   For an example see A. Coale and E. Hoover, *Population Growth and Economic Development in Low Income Countries*, 1958.

[34]   United Nations, *Determinants and Consequences of Population Trends*, 1973, vol. I, pp. 533-5.

[35]   M. Lipton, 'Manpower and growth', *Aspect*, December 1963, p. 38. C. P. Kindleberger, *Europe's Postwar Growth*, 1967, chapters 2 and 4. Kaldor (see note 30), said to be the originator of Selective Employment Tax, also supported such theories for a time.

[36]   E. H. Phelps Brown and M. H. Browne, *A Century of Pay*, 1968, p. 324.

[37]   H. Wander, 'Zero population growth: theory and reality', in T. J. Espenshade and W. J. Serow (editors), *The Economic Consequences of Slowing Population Growth*, 1978, p. 66.

[38]   W. B. Reddaway, 'The economic consequences of zero population growth', *Lloyds Bank Review*, April 1977, pp. 24-5.

[39]   Quoted in A. Sweezy and A. Owens, 'The impact of population growth on employment', *American Economic Review*, Papers and Proceedings, May 1974.

[40]   H. Wander, 'The working population' in Council of Europe, *Population Decline in Europe*, 1978, p. 55.

[41]   Sweezy and Owens, op. cit.

Further reading

W. B. Reddaway, *The Economics of a Declining Population*, Macmillan, 1939. This has acquired almost classic status in the literature. Clear and readable, though rather disappointing on employment and unemployment.

A. Sweezy and A. Owens, 'The impact of population growth on employment', *American Economic Review, Papers and Proceedings*, May, 1974. A very useful survey of the economic issues.

Cmd 7695 (1949). Royal Commission on Population, Papers vol. vi Report of the Economics Committee, HMSO. The report of the Economics Committee is a very well written survey of a range of economic issues, including a balanced discussion of the effects of falling or zero rates of population growth on growth and employment.

T. J. Espenshade and W. J. Serow, (editors), *The Economic Consequences of Slowing Population Growth*, Academic Press, 1978. A useful set of essays on various aspects of the population question, including one (by L. Neal) on the 'secular stagnation' thesis.

A. Scaperlanda, 'Hansen's secular stagnation thesis once again?', *Journal of Economic Issues*, vol. xi no.2 June, 1977. An interpretation of recent increases in unemployment rates in terms of the secular stagnation hypothesis. Mainly refers to the USA.

J. J. Spengler, 'The economist and the population question', *American Economic Review*, vol. 56 no.1 March, 1966. A wide ranging, though rather diffuse review of the population question as seen by economists since 1800.

A. P. Thirlwall, *Growth and Development* second edition, Macmillan 1978. Although concerned mainly with developing countries, there is a very clear chapter on the population problem.

R. A. Easterlin, *Population, Labour Force and Long Swings in Economic Growth*, Columbia University Press, 1968. An extremely detailed and complicated presentation of what has come to be called 'the Easterlin hypothesis', concerning inter-related rhythmic cycles in birth rates and economic change. The same author's *Birth and Fortune: The Impact of Numbers on Personal Welfare* 1980 was published too recently for consideration in this chapter.

United Nations, *The Population Debate: Dimensions and Perspectives* vol. I, United Nations, 1974. Detailed, long and not easy to read, this report of the United Nations conference in Bucharest covers most aspects of the interactions between demography and social and economic conditions.

E. H. Phelps Brown and M. H. Browne, *A Century of Pay*, Macmillan, 1968. The majority of this work is concerned with wage rates and their share in the national product of five industrial countries, including Britain. The concluding chapters however include some interesting reflections on the relationships between population growth, employment and income.

Children in society 1850-1980

P. E. H. HAIR

This essay sketches certain quantifiable aspects of the history of British childhood in the period between 1850 and 1980 — the numbers, mortality and family-distribution of children, and the process of direction of children into labour and schooling. Quantitative data on these matters, largely unavailable for earlier centuries, began to become available in the mid-nineteenth century and has since become increasingly full, detailed, accurate and complex; though of course even today the data is not so complete that it tells the historian all he wants to know.[1] Usefully delimited by this condition of data availability, the period 1850-1980 nevertheless benefits from being studied in historical perspective, not least as regards its demography.

The history of British population comprises two periods of dramatic change separated by four centuries of relatively minor fluctuation. The explosion and subsequent collapse of an agricultural and rural population in the period 1100-1350 is known only in outline; but the explosion and subsequent controlled deceleration of an increasingly industrialized and urbanized population after 1750 can be and has been closely studied. It is true that our understanding of childhood during the first century of the latter movement is seriously hampered by lack of quantitative data and by the thin, partial and often patently tendentious evidence of non-quantitative sources. Yet it would be absurd to consider the numbers, mortality and family distribution of British children after 1850 without taking some note of those broad (and plausibly evidenced) trends of the previous century which produced the conditions of 1850. After all, the century after 1750 generated children to an extent which made the numbers in 1850 startlingly different from those at any of the earlier mid-centuries between 1350 and 1650.

The concept and therefore the chronological definition of 'childhood' vary as between cultures and periods (it was left to later nineteenth-century societies in western Europe and north America to discover 'adolescence'). For simplicity, this essay will follow the chronological definition adopted in the major part of the historical data. Unless exceptionally specified as being 'under 17' (aged 0-16), the children discussed in this essay were individuals under the age of 15 (ages 0-14).

It is often kindly pointed out that quantitative data does not tell us about what is unquantifiable. This essay certainly does not claim to depict more than a few aspects of past British childhood. Yet the quantitative data must have some bearing on what can be reasonably asserted about the unquantifiable. Those unhappy with conclusions from quantitative data sometimes prefer to invoke their own subjective judgements on 'the quality of life'. I shall conclude the essay by briefly considering whether what we have learned about British childhood from quantitative data requires to be set against a 'quality of life' assessment.

Numbers of children

The outline of the demography of British childhood since 1850 here presented aims to offer a few general conclusions, to identify a few critical areas of uncertainty, and, perhaps most important, to indicate to the general reader the extent of the quantitative data and its limitations.

It is highly likely that since 1750 the number of children in Britain has increased decade by decade, almost without exception. The experiences of the two regions here taken to constitute 'Britain', England and Wales on the one hand, and Scotland on the other, have been similar though with significant minor differences.[2] Since 1750 the increase in the number of children has been very considerable, perhaps more than three-fold; but the increase in the period under study, from 1850 on, which we can measure more or less exactly, has been proportionately much less, having been only about 50 per cent.[3] From what we know about the post-1850 period we can infer some of the demographic trends of the century before 1850; and it would seem likely that the increase in the number of children was not only steeper in the mid-nineteenth century than it was to be thereafter, but that a relatively steep increase was equally the experience of the earlier nineteenth century and of much of the later eighteenth century. This sharp decade-by-decade increase was a factor in contributing to the social mentality of the decades immediately after 1850, a factor which the mid-and-later twentieth century, lacking this experience may fail to allow for when attempting to understand Victorian social behaviour. Since the sharp increase was, almost certainly, not new in 1850, British society at the beginning of our period was already accustomed to the pressure of 'excess' numbers each decade. On a longer view, however, for a century and a half (or so) after 1750, British society had to cope with many more children each decade, a national problem it had not faced in the previous four centuries. And the increase was particularly sharp and therefore socially disturbing during the nineteenth century. 'Suffer little children to come unto me' may have been a favourite Victorian text, but the Victorian era was the first in British history to find itself forced to take thought about a flood of children.

In the twentieth century the increase slowed down, with marked deceleration at times, even to the extent of the 1920s and 1930s recording a slight dip in numbers, though later decades resumed the slow increase. However, recent indicators strongly suggest that the present decade, the 1980s, will be a final turning-point. The decline will be decisively resumed and the 1980s will mark the end of a 200-year era of British history, an era of virtually continuous growth in child population. Yet a *caveat* is necessary. Within the long-term trend of increase in child population, short-term fluctuations have been so common that contemporaries have generally failed to predict either set of trends with any exactitude. (Hence, the claims sometimes made that a communal 'social policy' closely tailored to child population trends should have been, has been, or was being developed seem a little unrealistic.) The prediction above, that numbers will now decline, may turn out to be similarly based on false or inadequate assumptions, for instance, on the assumption of the persistence and dominance in Britain of the traditional genetic stock.

That the number of children increased decade by decade after 1750 is highly likely but not certain, for the following reason. Children were only separately counted on a national basis, first (and incompletely) in the 1821 census, and then in decennial censuses from 1841 (omitting 1941 the wartime year when no census was taken).[4] Thus, full and regular enumerations of child populations are only available from 1841 — just as detailed national figures for numbers of births and for child mortality are only available from 1838 for England and Wales and from 1855 for Scotland. For the demography of childhood in the century before 1850, as indeed to a large extent for the overall demography of that century, we therefore have to make do with very ingenious yet somewhat speculative estimates, derived in the main from the limited amount of hard evidence that can be drawn from parish registers and listings. Thus we may fairly reasonably deduce a continuous increase in the number of children in England and Wales from the continuous increase in baptisms shown in the admittedly much-less-than-satisfactory parish register totals; the Scottish evidence is, alas!, a good deal thinner. Still, we cannot seriously doubt that the number of British children was regularly increasing during the century immediately before 1850. Thereafter we can be more definite. From 1841 the printed census returns give us moderately exact figures for numbers of children by ages, tabulated in five-year spans; and from 1851 they give ages tabulated by individual years up to age five, with estimated (or later, enumerated) figures for individual years following up to age 16. Since these statistics were prepared separately for England and Wales and for Scotland the overall experience of child population increase can be analyzed in terms of two regions and various age-spans.

So much for the data − or in some areas − the lack of it. The figures for numbers of British children of all ages (0-14) are as follows. In 1850 there were 7.3 m. children (See Appendix Tables 3a and 3b). Arguably the number had risen steadily from 1750, when it may well have been less than half that in 1850. By 1980, the number was just over 11 m., half as many again as in 1850. But this was only a modest increase for a period of 130 years, and it is very telling that the total had been floating around the figure of 11 m. since 1880. Scotland, though providing a small component of the British total, pulled downwards throughout: its child population increased less steeply than England's in the nineteenth century and declined more decisively in the mid-and-later twentieth century. All told, the number of children living in Britain between 1850 and 1980 was of the order of 100 m. As we shall shortly see, of this number at least one tenth died as children, without reaching adulthood.

The overall increase in child population just outlined becomes more meaningful to the social historian when we dissolve out the blunt concept of 'child' and refocus on specific age-groups of children. The data allows us to generalize with fair ease about 'infants' (children in their first year), 'toddlers' (children aged 1-4) and 'children of school-age' (children aged 5-14 − disregarding for the moment that in the nineteenth century schooling often stopped earlier and that in recent decades the term has applied to children aged 5-15 and aged 5-16). Between 1841 and 1971, the trends in numbers of children at these ages was, very broadly, the same as the overall trend, that is, numbers rose, at first steeply, then less and less steeply, until they levelled off and even declined. But this pattern, this curve, varied chronologically as between age-groups, very significantly.

To begin with infants. The number rose 1841-1881, but thereafter more or less levelled off, with a serious dip 1931-1951, then recovered until it fell away in 1971. In contrast, the number of children of school age not only rose 1841-81 but continued to rise, though less steeply, until 1911. It then dipped slowly until 1951, when it recovered to reach a new high in 1971 — though it must fall sharply in the 1980s. Thus, whereas there were more children of school age in the 1970s than ever before in British history, the largest number of infants occurred in the late decades of the nineteenth century. (But since infant mortality was then high, the total of completed infant-years was less than that in later decades, less for instance than in the 1960s). The pattern for numbers of toddlers was different again. The number rose sharply from 1841 to a peak in 1891-1911, and after a dip rose again to the same peak in 1951-71. These differences in age-group trends have been partly the logical result of general factors working up through the ages, particularly the effect of family limitation by contraception, which kept down the number of births from the 1880s; and partly the rather less predictable results of differential reductions in age-specific mortality. To family limitation and child mortality we shall be returning shortly.

How were these numbers of children distributed throughout British society? Distribution by families will occupy a section of this paper. But otherwise the distribution need not be discussed at length — its features are often of importance for local history but of limited significance at the national level. The close natural balance of numbers between the sexes averaged throughout the nation contrasted with the imbalance maintained in a few districts, particularly in earlier decades, when girls or boys in their mid-teens were drawn away from home into districts specializing in more-or-less single-sex industries, such as textiles (especially cotton), domestic service or mining. But as long as children remained at home boys and girls were found in almost equal numbers. The geographical distribution of children changed greatly over time, but only shadowed the distribution of parents. That is, more and more children came to live in towns and in new industrial districts, in the nineteenth century in London, central and northern England, and central Scotland, in the present century in London and southern England. New industrial districts attracted young adult immigrants, men and women, and thus generated babies in large numbers: the high proportion of infants and toddlers in the total population often persuaded innocent visitors that the local adults were unduly prolific.

Mortality of children

The almost simultaneous beginning of census-counting of children and of secular registration of deaths enables child mortality to be assessed quantitatively from the 1850s. The overall trend is very clear: a constant decline.[5] The rate and timing of the decline varied between age-groups and between social groups, but these significant variations should not direct attention away from the major feature; a decline in mortality despite a growth in numbers. This was a phenomenon most likely new in world history; though it must be immediately added that more rapid improvement occurred in the present century when numbers increased less steeply, a shift back towards the more common historical phenomenon, 'More mouths, less cake'. The figures may be presented briefly thus. Of 1000 children born in each of the years 1850, 1900 and 1950, there died in childhood, without reaching the age of 15, respectively about 300 in 1850, about 230 in 1900, about 40 in 1950. This reduction of child mortality, so drastic as to approach elimination, forms the thematic centre point of this essay; and many might consider it the same in relation to the social history of Britain in this period.

Now let us look at the age-specific mortality of infants, toddlers and school-age children (5-14). Throughout the period there has been no change in relative positions, the pattern being a traditional and universal one: older children survive better than toddlers and toddlers than infants. (The most dangerous hours and days of life have always been and probably always will be those immediately after birth). However throughout the period deaths of infants, toddlers and older children have all been reduced very sharply. The mortality of older children fell off from the time the records begin, around 1850; that of toddlers fell off from about 1870; and that of infants fell off from about 1900. Thus the Victorians succeeded in saving lives of toddlers and older children, but it was left to the twentieth century to reduce infant mortality. And since child mortality is heavily weighted by infant mortality, this means that the former was reduced more strikingly after 1900 than it was before. It is tempting to argue, speculatively, that infants could not be saved until two pressures within the family had been relieved, by the slackening of births and by the removal of older children to school, both processes having gained ground in the late Victorian decades. Infant mortality stood at around 160 (deaths per 1000 live births per annum) between 1850 and 1900, so that one in six of babies died in the Victorian era; but by the 1950s it had fallen to under 30 — the improvement since 1900 having been sharp and steady in each intervening decade, including the 'distressed' 1920s and 1930s.[6] Toddler and school-age mortalities fell from around 35 and seven (deaths per 1000 living per annum) respectively in the 1850s, to around 20 and three in the 1900s, and to around 1.0 and 0.4 in the 1950s. Thus, at the beginning of the period one in seven of toddlers died during the four years of toddlerhood, and one in 14 of older children during the remaining years of childhood: today the rates are so slight as to be almost accounted negligible.

Mortality as between 'social classes' was not investigated closely until the present century, but there is vast scope in the riches of later-nineteenth century demographic data for investigating differences between regions, rural and urban areas, sections of towns, and to some extent occupations. As a result of such investigations to date, we can be reasonably certain that children at all ages have, throughout the period, tended to survive best in upper-class homes, next in lower middle-class and 'decent' working-class homes, and worst in exceptionally 'deprived' homes — in homes with unskilled or unemployed family heads, in slum homes, in one-parent homes, in homes where one or both parents were sick or mentally or emotionally incapable, or socially irresponsible (and it was worst of all for children if they were born bastards). Since the exceptionally deprived formed a minority of the nation, mortality in these 'black spots' was often well above the national average. These social gradients in mortality continue to exist to the present day, with only limited diminution. But the pace of overall decline in mortality has been such that the most privileged child mortality of one generation has tended to be higher than the least-privileged of the next — though it may be conceded that this process can hardly continue indefinitely.[7]

If reduced child mortality spread from the top, so did contraception, which, though it had made inroads among the more privileged working classes by 1900, apparently in the main by awkward self-control methods (a testimony to considered family responsibility among the parents involved), had still left untouched most of the nation. No doubt the continuance of relatively high child mortality and hence of uncertainty about completed family size among less privileged groups inhibited the development of any pressure for deliberate family limitation. But child mortality and the spread of contraception were not everywhere tightly linked since each was also affected by social factors not economically determined. (The modestly prosperous coalminers of the North East, an ingrown and socially-conservative group, resisted contraception until the inter-war depression.) How, for instance, was child mortality affected by the topographical environments of countryside and town? On account of its historical implications, this is a question not to be lightly answered.

The 1850s marked the watershed between a British population largely rural and a British population largely urban and industrial. Hence it is misguided to assess the child mortality of the century immediately before 1850 by pointing to estimates of the child mortality of a minority of industrializing districts. (And it is even more misguided to assess pre-1850 industrial mortality by inferring it from tenuously relevant crude rates, for instance, by inferring phenomenally high infant mortality in Manchester, Liverpool and Glasgow solely from a high proportion among burials of those of infants — without noting that the immigrant structure generated more births, hence more dead infants, irrespective of industrial-urban living conditions.[8]) However, in the absence of exact statistics for the century leading up to 1850, it is common for historians to draw a black-and-white picture of child mortality fearfully increasing as industrialization spread, and to justify this on the grounds that in the second half of the nineteenth century rural mortality tended to be lower than urban mortality, as it certainly did.

But there are grounds for doubting whether this procedure is justified. First, because rural mortality itself improved after 1850, and the presumed change in rural conditions which caused this prevents us assuming that rural experience after 1850 can stand in for rural experience before that date; secondly, because parish register studies indicate that very high infant mortality rates existed and persisted in certain rural localities during the earlier modern centuries[9]; and thirdly, because the post-1850 statistics show mortality gradients across rural as well as across urban areas, with significant regional and local differences. The existence of child mortality black spots in post-1850 urban areas did not prevent the general improvement of urban child health (the balance between country and town so rapidly tipped in favour of the latter that by the end of the nineteenth century national averages were heavily weighted by urban experience.) What then of the rural black spots detected both after 1850 and before? Were they as exceptional as the urban ones? Or instead do they testify to, or are typical of, the general rural experience of the past? It is not at all easy to say which view is right. The experience of child mortality in the century immediately preceding 1850 is therefore still in the main an unsettled issue.

It is unlikely that child mortality increased sharply with the onset of Industrial Revolution after 1750; it is not very likely that it increased markedly between 1750 and 1850; and it is just conceivable that rural mortality was so high before 1750 that the decline in child mortality after 1850 actually began a number of decades earlier. However perhaps the most plausible view is that the appearance of urban black spots, as industrialization advanced, tended to cancel out gains in rural or petty-urban health; and therefore that in the century before 1850 child mortality on average in Britain remained fairly stationary. If this last conclusion is correct, we can again see 1850 as initiating a new chapter in British social history. Marked decline in child mortality was another novel phenomenon in British history and therefore, like the marked increase in numbers which began somewhat earlier, was for contemporaries unexpected, unplanned and at first unrealized.

Children in families

It is a little far-fetched to discuss children without considering the adults who produce them, that is, without seeing the children in families. Unfortunately, whereas we have exact demographic data on children as individuals — hence the earlier discussion of numbers and mortality — for most of the period little data was produced, or at least published,[10] on the more complex matter of children in families. We have often to rely on sample surveys reporting past experience rather than on contemporary data; and in general the elaborate evidence we have for the second half of the period is lacking for the first half. The historical discussion in this section is therefore often speculative.

Trends in child population size and total population size are naturally inter-related, both synchronically and over time. In the case of Britain 1850-1980, the general trend for both populations has been upwards, steeply so in the nineteenth century, less and less steeply so in the present. The deceleration of the increase operated sooner for children, to some extent logically, but in fact also because adult mortality declined — adults lived longer so there were more of them to count. The result of the different paces in trends is striking. The *proportion* of children in the total population has declined smartly during the period. Between 1841 and 1891 the proportion was rather over one third (around 36 per cent), but between 1931 and 1961 it was just under one quarter (around 23 per cent).[11] (See Appendix Tables 3a and 3b). Thus the mid-and-later twentieth century has notably fewer children to adults than had the Victorian period. What caused this? Briefly, adults have increased, children been limited. Mortality has fallen for all adults, hence the vast majority of parents now live to see their children into adulthood. Further, in the present century the number of elderly and retired persons has greatly increased, so that the majority of children now know at least half of their grandparents throughout most of their childhood — yet another novel feature in world demographic history. But at least as important as the better survival of adults has been the adults' reluctance to produce 'excess' children, that is, long-term reduction in family size.[12]

Whereas well over 70 per cent of couples who married in the 1870s (and who survived until the woman was past childbearing) produced four or more children, over 70 per cent of those married in the 1920s and later (and who survived similarly) produced fewer than four. Completed family size is of course affected negatively by child mortality, and large Victorian families were whittled down to some extent in this way. Indeed, it may be surmised that it was only when child mortality visibly fell that parents wholeheartedly went in for producing a minimum rather than a maximum of children, knowing that all the smaller number would almost certainly survive. Again, in the case of some Victorian families the prevailing adult mortality killed off one parent and prevented child-bearing being completed by that couple; and perhaps it was fear of this which led to rapid childbearing after marriage. Despite these qualifications, the stark contrast remains: the typical mid-Victorian completed family contained not less than four children, with almost equal frequencies of between four and ten children: the typical mid-and-late twentieth century completed family contains under four children, with almost equal frequencies of between three and nil children, and families of eight or more children are very uncommon. Of course there have been regional, economic and social (e.g. religious) gradients in this movement, typified perhaps by the fact that family size is only just beginning to fall among poor Catholics in North West England and West Scotland.

What was the social and psychological significance of this change, above all for the children concerned? Once again it would help if we knew more about the demography of childhood in earlier centuries. The popular view that because Victorian families were large there were more children around in Victorian Britain than ever before or since is probably untrue as regards 'before' though true as regards 'since'. The incomplete census returns of 1821 suggest a proportion of children in the population rather higher than the 36 per cent of the mid-Victorian period, and there is fairly sound evidence (including Gregory King's age-distribution sample for *c.*1695) for supposing that the proportion stood at about 40 per cent in the earlier modern centuries. Therefore, although we can be certain that the Victorians would have found it difficult to envisage the paucity of children in our recent society, the comparative abundance of children in theirs probably did not strike them as novel or curious. Nevertheless, it can be argued that there was something new in the distribution of Victorian children, and that this demographic factor needs to be taken into account in assessing Victorian and post-Victorian society, as does the sheer increase in numbers. The novelty lay in the containment of these abundant numbers of children within stable and long-term families.

At first sight it is difficult to reconcile the declining child mortality of Victorian society with the even higher proportion of children in earlier societies — that is, without invoking implausible suppositions, such as that child mortality shot up before it declined, or that pre-Victorian parents produced more children. The explanation is instead to be found, most probably, in a higher adult mortality in earlier periods. While Victorian parents reproduced no more briskly than their ancestors, they sometimes reproduced longer, because fewer parents died; and this, taken with the decline in child mortality, meant that they finished up with larger surviving families than ever before. On the other hand, if pre-Victorian parents tended to die more rapidly, both during the child-bearing period and after it, then, even allowing for a child mortality no lower than that in 1850, the proportion of children in the population might well finish up higher. Two suppositions could follow from this (slightly speculative) analysis. One is that Victorian parents, finding themselves, because of their own and their children's better survival, with families actually or potentially larger than those of their ancestors, turned to forms of birth control to provide the family limitation which nature and mortality had provided earlier. The second supposition is that the children of pre-Victorian times were less frequently contained throughout childhood in stable long-term families. Though there is much less evidence for this than for Victorian and post-Victorian family patterns, what we do know does not contradict the supposition.

Whereas mid-and-later twentieth-century children expect to grow up knowing throughout childhood not only both parents but also some of their grandparents, the children of the centuries before the nineteenth regularly knew none of their grandparents, frequently knew only one of their natural parents (though this one was often united to a step-parent) and not uncommonly knew no parents. That is, there were large numbers of orphans (including many without grandparents and some without any relatives), foundlings and homeless children, one-parent families and step-parent families.[13] Now the Victorian family fell between these extremes. As it became demographically possible, for the first time in British history, for most surviving children throughout childhood to live with parents and even to be in contact with some grandparents (an important figure in Victorian urbanization was the child-minding granny),[14] the concept of the normality of a long and stable family life was realized. Children were distributed more exclusively within long-term family units, and the long-term family unit became more exclusively the normal social unit. The Victorians and their immediate successors appreciated the new norm of a long and stable (and introverted) family life, they publicized, idealized and romanticized it, they pressed its sanctions a little tediously in all directions, and also, being only human, they at times revolted against it. But in the decades since, and despite shifting demographic reality, the Victorian norm has powerfully influenced family life in all classes.

Looking at the period in historical context, we can detect (a) a *growth* generally in average completed family size and specifically in the proportion of families with four or more children suriving childhood, a process whose beginnings are difficult to date but which was most likely well under way before 1850, and which continued until probably the 1890s; followed by (b) a sharp *decline* in average completed family size and in the proportion of large families, levelling out and fluctuating slightly in recent decades. Of course in the nineteenth century there was, at any time, a large number of incompleted and smaller families, because in a period of rapidly growing population there are more marriages in the early stages of family formation than in the later. Further, in the nineteenth century older children continued to be exported from the home, perhaps in increasing numbers as their siblings survived, and then in decreasing numbers as less siblings were born, so that trends in numbers of children actually present at home are difficult to assess. But there can still be no doubt about the contrast between the Victorian child who generally grew up in a home with several if not many siblings, and the mid-and-later twentieth century child who generally grows up, if not as a single child, then as a child with only one or at the most two siblings. Many of the implications of this change are too far-reaching or too close to ourselves to be sure about, but some are worth considering.

The sympathy generously spilt by historians on the nineteenth-century male adult worker, beset by industrialization, urbanization and poverty, might be more shrewdly expended on his wife. The irony of improving national health was that it left the Victorian mother with a burden her ancestresses had not known, a string of children in the home, and particularly, when toddler mortality fell, an excess of toddlers under her feet. Compared with her ancestresses, the Victorian mother had fewer child-deaths to get over but more child-years to endure. In so far as the older girls had to look after the younger children, these responsibilities began even before marriage. It may well be that attention to insatiable toddler demands, giving less time for care of the baby puling in the cradle, helps to explain why infant mortality fell late — and only after birth control had helped to space out the excess toddlers.

As for the children themselves the Victorian child tended to grow up in close association not only with siblings of ages close to its own but with siblings of the other sex, points which may have made post-childhood socializing easier and less narcissistic than that of later times. (As family size declined, adolescence had to be invented.) It is debatable whether children gain more in security, balanced individualism, and enterprise in a large family than they do in a small one; but it is certain that the Victorian child witnessed and even participated in, for better or worse, the adult crises of normal humanity which the mid-and-late twentieth-century child tends to miss as a child — birth and nursing, serious illness and death, courtship and marriage.

The upbringing of children: work and schooling

Two major aspects of the upbringing of children in our period, the cost of upbringing and the mode of socialization, can usefully have some light thrown on them by analysis of the available quantitative data. The data specifically refers to the direction of children to work and/or to schooling, two powerful elements in the overall cost to the nation and to the family, and two important forms of socialization. Let us begin by laying down the supposition that because Victorian parents tended to have to support larger numbers of children than is the case with their descendants or was the case with their forebears, the cost of upbringing loomed larger over the family budget than it had ever done before or was to do since. To this it might be riposted that the Victorians had one advantage on the positive side of the budget — their children from an early age were sent out to work and earn. How much truth is there in this last generalization? To inquire what proportions of children of various ages under 15 were in fact at work during the period we turn to the censuses, which from 1851 counted children 'in specified occupations' — we shall call these the 'occupied' children.

Because the numbers had become negligible or nil, the census did not bother to count up the occupations of children aged under 10 separately after 1871 and at all after 1881, of children aged under 14 after 1931, and of children aged under 15 after 1951. The number of occupied children aged between five and nine was always very small. In 1851, out of 2.2 m. children of this age-group in Britain, only 85,000 or 3.5 per cent were occupied; and the proportion fell in 1861 and 1871. Even if in this case we allow a very high margin of error in the returns, there cannot be any reasonable doubt that the vast majority of children under ten did not undertake any regular gainful employment, not even at the beginning of the period. Children therefore normally began work when they were ten or over. The proportion of children aged 10-14 who were occupied was 30 per cent in 1851, and then fell off, decade by decade, to 17 per cent in 1901. More boys were gainfully occupied than girls, roughly half as many again, for instance, 37 per cent of boys were so occupied in 1851, 22 per cent of girls.[15] Thus, even in 1851 the majority of this age-group were not occupied. Distribution within the age-group probably followed the pattern revealed in 1911, when only 2 per cent of children aged 10-13 were occupied, but 17 per cent of children aged 13 and 52 per cent of children aged 14; and in 1921, when only 5 per cent of children aged 12-14 were occupied but 52 per cent of children aged 14-16. All this confirms the commonsense expectation, that children were more frequently sent out to work as they grew older. To sum up, while there was a general trend throughout the period in the direction of reducing the proportion of children at work, so that the period concluded with no children at work (at least full time or legally), it would be quite incorrect to suppose that the period began with all children, or even most children, at work. It was only in the case of the oldest children, those 14 and over, that the majority worked (the vast majority of boys, not quite so many girls). Turning to younger children, while work began at all ages from five on, only tiny proportions of children ever worked before nine; and although increasing proportions worked at 10, 11, 12 and 13, it is unlikely that even at the beginning of the period the majority of children were working before the ages of 11 and 12.

Very little is known with any quantitative exactitude about child employment before 1850. However an important clue is afforded by analysis of the occupations of children in the later decades of the nineteenth century (in England and Wales). In 1851 the industries employing most children were agriculture (100,000, mainly boys), textiles (100,000 boys and girls), and domestic service (70,000 mainly girls). Agriculture fell off after 1871, but domestic service and textiles (becoming predominantly cotton and girls gaining over boys) increased until 1891. (From 1901, the total number of children in employment began to decline.) But the industries mentioned account for less than half the occupied children in either 1851 or 1891: where were the rest? In fact, agriculture (and other rural industries) and domestic service accounted for about one third of child labour in the later nineteenth century; textiles and the heavy industries (coalmining and iron-manufacture especially) accounted for rather more than one third; but the remainder, almost a third, was distributed over a very large number of trades (e.g. 11,000 boy shoemakers in 1851, 17,000 girl milliners in 1891) and humbler vocations (e.g. 40,000 errand boys in 1851, 17,000 drapers' shop-boys in 1891). Only the middle group represented the booming industries of Industrial Revolution, and over half the children worked in traditional pre-industrial occupations. It can be inferred that child labour was not the product of industrialization and that large numbers of children were employed in agriculture, domestic service and trades long before 1850. Given the increase in population it is not unlikely that the number of children in employment increased with industrialization, but whether the proportion increased is uncertain. Although a short-term increase during the century before 1850 is not implausible, the modest proportion of children employed in 1851 makes it likely that the long-term trend during the previous century was the same as that after 1850, downwards.

The above view gains some slight support from fragmentary data on the ages at which children began work before 1850. In the early 1840s samples of children in various industries were surveyed and interviewed about entry-age.[16] Because only children already at work were interviewed and because the surveys concentrated on younger children, the average entry-ages of these samples were not only much lower than the overall average entry-age of 1851 stated above but also somewhat lower than the true average entry-ages *c.*1840; nevertheless comparison of these entry-ages suggests one conclusion. The average entry-ages of children (both boys and girls, sometimes calculated separately) in Birmingham pin-making and metal trades, Nottingham lace-making, Lancashire print-works, Yorkshire worsted manufacture, and coalmining throughout Britain (coalfields calculated separately) fell between 8.0 and 9.8 years; and for London trades the average was 10.8 years. But in farming in Dorset the average entry-age was only 7.8 years. Thus the most traditional industry had the lowest average entry-age. Another straw in the wind is that when 74 coalminers who had begun work before 1810 were interviewed *c*. 1840, they gave entry-ages averaging 7.5 years, lower than the average entry-age of children who began in coalmining *c*. 1840. Finally, the surveys *c*. 1840 show that children were then beginning work at all ages between five and 14. The surveys made a point of hunting for children who had begun work at a very early age. For instance, among the 15,000-20,000 children employed in coalmines throughout Britain, one child of four was met, and out of 3,000 children interviewed about a dozen claimed to have begun work when they were four. Entry seriously began at five, and of those surveyed about 10 per cent had begun at five or six; about 60 per cent at seven, eight or nine; and about 30 per cent at ages beween ten and 14. The true figures were probably near the reversal of the last two.

Two important points emerge from this discussion. One is that entry to child employment was staggered. In the nineteenth century — and presumably throughout earlier centuries — the proportion of children at work was unequal between ages and between the sexes at the same ages, and it was therefore unequal between families and within families. Some children went to work early, most did not; some children stayed at home till late, most did not. The reasons in individual cases were no doubt the family's economic, social and moral circumstances at a particular time. The family budget, the birth order, the sex of the child, and local work opportunities must all have played a part. But the final decision was normally taken within the family. (Therefore to discuss 'the exploitation of children' solely in terms of the experience of a handful of workhouse orphans is peculiarly misleading.) In complete contrast to this Victorian state of affairs is that of the egalitarian but regimented mid-and-late twentieth century, when all children are directed in precisely the same way at precisely the same ages — away from employment and into schooling, en bloc, between the ages of five and 14, 15 or 16. In this direction of its children, the family has no say.

The second point also has ideological content. Historians contemplating past childhood often appear to share the supposition of the post-1850 censuses, that an 'occupied' child can always be clearly distinguished from a child not occupied. Thus 'at work' is conveniently contrasted with 'at home' (as in preceding paragraphs). Yet we know of course that in earlier centuries much industrial work was done literally at home.[17] The problem becomes acute when we consider the labour of girls — the 1881-1901 censuses tied themselves in knots trying to decide whether girls who 'helped at home' full-time should be counted under the occupational head of 'domestic service'. Throughout the earlier part of the period older girls helped to keep the wheels of industry turning, and mothers from distraction, by full-time baby-minding and other domestic duties, either for out-at-work parents and relatives, or just for hard-pressed mothers and aunts, without being gainfully employed. Again, it is highly likely that among the over 90 per cent of children aged 5 — 9 and 70 per cent aged 10 — 14 who counted in the census as 'not occupied' there were large numbers who did little or not-so-little jobs around and about the home, and sometimes further afield — running errands, carrying meals to fathers at work, shopping for parents and neighbours, helping tradesmen, and perhaps even lapsing into being gainfully employed for odd hours or odd weeks (for instance, in agriculture, at harvest-time). The tasks were perhaps mainly for social convenience but as contemporary economists pointed out, they contributed to family budgets and the national economy. Thus, just as the nation's children, as they grew up, cumulatively moved towards total employment, so individual children moved gradually towards being 'occupied'. The notion that children were normally transferred in one stage from an idyllic nursery existence at home to the harsh world of the factory work-bench or the mill production-line is absurd, though middle-class reformers at the time often talked as if they believed this.

Labour being the universal lot, Victorian children were trained to accept labour from an early age, in order that when they became adults they might exist independently, as the society of the day (not unreasonably in terms of its own circumstances) demanded. Children were therefore socialized through labour. But this was done at various paces — justly or unjustly for the individual child. That some children went out to work early is certain, yet whether they were 'worse-treated' thereby than, say, their sister who stayed at home and did house-work, is hardly possible to say. Children themselves had mixed views: according to the interviews in the reformers' Blue Books, while some children complained about work, there were others who delighted to leave the baby-ridden atmosphere of home. Those left at home were never interviewed. Since Victorian children were indoctrinated to expect labour to at least the extent that mid-and-later twentieth century children are indoctrinated to believe that all child-labour is wicked, it is likely that most Victorian children were not unduly distressed by either the prospect or the reality of going out to work, even when the conditions of labour were such that their mere telescopic contemplation induces mild hysteria in latterday reformers, politicians and historians.

The period saw both the virtual elimination of gainful employment for children, and the triumph of schooling, that is, the
emergence of universal, compulsory, regular, full-time, extended-
term schooling. Neither process was as dramatic as commonly
represented, and the connections between the two forms of direction and socialization of children are more complex than sometimes suggested in political and economic histories.[18] It was not
merely a matter of political will and legislative ukase, outlawing
the one, sanctifying and commanding the other; nor was it merely a
matter of economic reflexes, with poverty compelling parents to
send children to work at the beginning of the period, and riches,
acquired by sound Victorian capitalism and imperialism, enabling
child labour to be progressively dispensed with. For we have seen
that even in 1851 many children under 15 were not 'occupied';
hence, the legislative veto on child employment, as it developed
step by step (mainly in 1833, 1842, 1844 − 5, 1847, 1860 − 2, 1864,
1867 and 1874) meant, as far as the younger ages were concerned,
say, up to 10 or 11, only that a minority of that age group within the
nation was brought into line with the majority. Even when it came
to the turn of the children of older ages up to 16, who were excluded
not so much by direct veto as by direction into schooling, what
would certainly have been a major social revolution had it occurred in mid-Victorian times, was much less so later, because
children at those ages had already come to be less exclusively
at work.[19] In other words, parents preceded reformers in deciding
for more schooling. As we shall shortly see, schooling extended
widely long before effective state intervention, yet was in large part
paid for directly by parents. Thus, in mid-Victorian times many
parents not only kept at least some of their children away from
early work, foregoing the economic advantage, but also sent them
instead to school for at least some part of their childhood, to the
further disadvantage of the family budget. Their motives we shall
shortly examine.

The category of the early occupational censuses relating to
school children (often headed 'scholars') is somewhat indeterminate and ill-defined. To remind the reader of this, we shall coin the
term 'schooled' to describe the children enumerated.[20] It is likely
that almost all schooled children were actually attending a school,
though less likely that all were attending regularly; it is unlikely
that most had attended or would attend for more than a few years
of childhood; and it is conceivable that some had only a slight
record of attendance in the past and little prospect of future
attendance. But though we would do well to set our sights low

regarding the school experience of schooled children as a category, we can still accept that these children had at least some acquaintance with the three Rs and were, in the opinion of their parents, to be sharply distinguished from illiterates. Up to 1871 schooled children were counted by the censuses: thereafter more specific (though for long less than fully satisfactory) Education Department statistics quantify schooling. What we learn from these figures is that during the third quarter of the nineteenth century far more children under 15 were schooled or were school-children than were at work. In 1851, when only 3.5 per cent of children aged 5 − 9 were 'occupied', 58 per cent were 'schooled'; and whereas only 30 per cent of those aged 10 − 14 were occupied, 41 per cent were schooled.[21] By 1871 the proportions occupied had fallen but the proportions schooled had risen to 68 per cent and 53 per cent. Because figures for other individual years of age are not available in the printed censuses, it is not possible to say what proportion of children were 'never-schooled'. But if schooled children were on average at school for not more than two or three years, then the schooled proportion must have been very high and the never-schooled very low. This was the conclusion of the Newcastle Commission in 1861; that most children were schooled.

It would seem that, confronted by two avenues of extra-domestic socialization for their children, work and schooling, most Victorian parents wisely hedged their bets by choosing both. By the age of 14, very few children had *never* been gainfully employed full-time; and very few had *never* had any form of schooling, even though up to the 1880s most schooling required fees from parents. Educationally speaking, at the time there may well have been little to choose between these two forms of training for adult life (the equation of education with schooling is of course a twentieth-century preconception); and most parents, unconstrained either way by legislation and state power, had an element of choice in relation to individual children in individual years. However the options for parents when socializing their children were of course not confined to work and school; most socializing is still done at home, before and between extra-domestic socializing, and a Victorian child, after infancy and toddlerhood, could be neither at work nor at school but could continue at home, sometimes for all its childhood. It is patent that this option was deliberately chosen for a number of girls, and particularly for older girls. No doubt parents chose in terms of what was best for the family as well as what was best for the child. From the child's viewpoint, it was not unreasonable for parents to argue that inasmuch as in the past the predominant career for females had been in the home, for girls training in the home was more important than any other training; though this view turned out to be misguided and unprogressive. From the point of view of the family, over against economic and educational considerations there were the considerations which arose from demographic change. With the Victorian home bursting at the seams with children, particularly those tiresome toddlers, the hard-pressed mother could be child-helped in two ways; first, by keeping the more responsible children at home to assist, and secondly by exporting from the home, and hence from minute-by-minute responsibility during many hours of the week, a proportion of the other children, either to work or to school. The child-minding function of both employment and schooling tended to be overlooked by highminded reformers, as it still is by highminded historians.

The legislation to reduce child-labour and to promote schooling is the standard fare of history textbooks. But contrary to what is inferred in these, and generally by historians of education and childhood, constraints on child-labour existed before state intervention. Lack of jobs for children in specific industries and localities was one constraint (there were perhaps fewer child-jobs in the new industries than in the traditional ones); but another, probably a major one, was the will of parents, directing children to school or keeping them at home, for the reasons indicated. Quantitatively, the excluding legislation had limited effect, since relatively few children followed the occupations selected by the legislators, and only a small proportion of these numbers were excluded. For instance, the 5000 or so young children who were excluded from coalmining by the famous 1842 act cannot have been more than about 1 per cent of the total occupied child population (if we may judge by the 1851 figure) — though perhaps about 5 per cent of those aged 5 - 9 — or more than about 0.1 per cent of the total child population. The danger of writing the history of nineteenth-century childhood solely in terms of chimney-sweepers, trappers and coalminers, cotton-factory-piecers and such tiny minority groups — while ignoring the vast majority of children who were in agriculture, in trades, in less dramatic occupations in new industries, at school or at home — is obvious. The legislation that did have substantial quantitative effect was that compelling children to attend school, beginning in the 1870s. In stages over the next one hundred years the extension of compulsory schooling killed off all regular full-time labour for children.

Although quantitative evidence about mass voluntary schooling is limited to the nineteenth century, the extent of literacy at the end of the eighteenth century (documented in parish register signatures, confirmed by the explosion of mass ephemeral publishing) suggests that long before 1850 British society was advancing towards acceptance of the desirability of general knowledge of the three Rs, at least for males. (Scottish historians would argue that this attitude was nothing new North of the Tweed). It is fair to doubt whether adequate skills with even the two Rs were normally acquired in dame schools or by light exposure to Sunday schools. But it is reasonably certain that, at least as early as the 1830s, a substantial part of the child population, in the countryside and perhaps even more in the industrial towns, was successfully acquiring the three Rs, that is, full literacy and the elements of arithmetic; and that this was being achieved by regular schooling at moderately well-run day or evening institutions, for periods of some two to three years, often during the age-span five to nine.[22] Although these institutions were supplied by non-government (albeit establishment and middle-class) bodies such as the churches, the attendance of individual children was generally made possible by the economic support of their parents. Fees were in pennies but added up to some degree of sacrifice on the part of average parents. A minority of parents went further and supported selected children, perhaps selected by sex, birth-order, intelligence and motivation, for longer periods of schooling.

Compulsory schooling from the 1870s was therefore less of a discontinuity than has often been supposed, though it was certainly more than a mere topping-up of the previous voluntary system. Its novelty lay less in its getting a larger proportion of children to school than in its developing insistence that the objectives of schooling demanded standard years of attendance from each child, irrespective of ability, and a length of years much greater than previously common. This degree of regimented socialization was administratively convenient, perhaps essential; it fulfilled the state-interventionist beliefs of some reformers; and it provided a context for the equation of education with formal schooling. But it must also have improved the quality of the output of the schooling system, difficult though this is to measure objectively. The mere extension in the proportion of children regularly at school is often asserted to have effected, or at least influenced, political and social change, and this is plausible, though it has seldom been demonstrated convincingly in detail because those who have asserted this for the period after the 1870s have been unwilling to apply the same argument to the earlier period. One interesting conjecture is that schooling encouraged better personal hygiene and medical self-care, and therefore contributed to the fall in mortality in the home which affected parents, older children, toddlers and — eventually — infants.

That the number of children at school has progressively increased over the last two hundred years is of course in the first instance a reflection of the increase in child population. The extent to which compulsory schooling steepened the previous rising trend is controversial, but twentieth-century legislation has certainly kept it rising, by extending the period of compulsory schooling (to age 13 in 1918, to age 14 in 1947, to age 15 in 1972).[23] It can be confidently stated that never in history had as many children under 16 been at school in Britain as there were in the 1970s. But because of the latter-day fall in the proportion of children in the population, and the uncertainty about the size of the school population in the middle quarters of the nineteenth century, we cannot be quite as confident that today's schools provide for a significantly larger share of the total population than ever before. However if we count not merely enrollment at school but regularity and length of attendance, then the total of school-years almost certainly increased throughout the nineteenth century and certainly has increased since, at a rate of increase exceeding that of the child population. In this sense, Britain is more schooled than ever before; and there has been constant extension throughout our period. (But the inevitable decline of school population during the 1980s may be yet another indication that the period is closing.)

Because schooling is now largely undertaken by the state, its overall cost can be calculated with fair ease — the capital cost of buildings and equipment, the recurrent cost of teachers and other employees — as can therefore the tax-cost to the individual average family. However the loss of labour and enterprise to the productive economy, not only of children but of adults, like the economic and educational value gained by training the next generation at school which (one hopes) out-balances the loss, cannot of course be easily or perhaps even sensibly quantified. In 1850 the cost of schooling was borne partly by voluntary bodies but largely by parents, and hardly at all by the state; and for this reason alone, estimates of the contemporary cost to the average family and to society of schooling are, like estimates of the economic value to family and society of child labour, difficult to make — and those attempted to date are not altogether convincing. But what has become clear by study of the problem of costing is that, though we cannot quantify the partly-countervailing elements in the cost of upbringing children to the point where we can lay down a clear period trend in cost to society and family, the factors involved are so complex, and the data so limited, that it would be arrogant to have other than an open mind on the degree of change in the extent to which society and family have over-ridden immediate cost considerations when planning the socialization of children.

Quantitative analysis has disclosed certain trends in the history of British childhood since 1850 — broadly, increase in numbers, decline in mortality and average numbers of children per family, decline in child labour and increase in schooling. Certainly these trends do not cover all aspects of childhood, even perhaps all significant aspects. Nevertheless, any discussion involving British children in this period which ignores these trends does so at its peril. For instance, any history which discusses Victorian child-labour must surely consider them all, since (as shown) they inter-relate. However a common ploy of historians is not so much to ignore the quantitative evidence as to set over against it warmly-documented individual instances which are said to indicate, in controversion of the arid statistics, the true 'quality of life' at the time. What those who argue in these terms perhaps fail to appreciate is that quantitative analysis, like other forms of evidential analysis, cannot produce knock-down conclusions on a subject as elusive as the quality of life, and therefore cannot be controverted. What our quantitative analysis does do, however, is to raise questions which throw doubt on whether there is much substance in the concept of 'quality of life'. Suppose, for instance, that because toddler mortality falls, a number of late-Victorian children who would have otherwise died before the age of five live on to die of tuberculosis in their teens. What possible conclusion can we reach about changing quality of life, either for the children or their parents? How confident can we be that the quality of life for an individual has improved because he went to school from 10 to 14 instead of to work? Does a child benefit by not meeting death in the family? By knowing more grandparents? By having a bed to himself — in a family to himself? Who can assess the quality of life as between the teenagers of 1850 facing the prospect of a sickly adult life in a smoke-polluted environment and those of 1980 facing the prospect of either long healthy years or instant nuclear holocaust? Each age has a quality of life, no doubt, but each to each is not only largely incomparable but largely incomprehensible.

Throughout this essay doubts have been raised about familiar preconceptions, sometimes a shade sharply, because childhood being a sentimental subject the history of childhood can easily turn into a sentimental chronicle of progress, hence a smug glorification of the present. But to gain comfort in the present by knocking the past betrays both the pursuit of truth and our own human fore-bears. To be fair to the past is the best guarantee that we will be fair to the future. If history exists to warn us to be as critical about the present as about the past, quantitative analysis' special contribution to history is to advise us to form muted judgements on both. For statistical evidence has this advantage over literary evidence — the limits and limitations of data are more self-evident.

Notes

[1] The period is largely covered in two works of quantitative historical survey: D. C. Marsh, *The changing social structure of England and Wales 1871-1961,* 1965; A. H. Halsey, ed., *Trends in British society since 1900,* 1972. Unfortunately neither work deals separately or at all fully with children. Both works supply exact references for statistical data and Halsey in particular is well-provided with lists of official sources: both are therefore cited below, to save multiplying official references. A work not henceforth cited is I. Pinchbeck and M. Hewitt, *Children in English society, II, From the eighteenth century to the Children's Act,* 1973, which is grossly mistitled, since it deals almost exclusively with minorities of especially deprived children and with social welfare legislation. Further, its understanding of the past is severely limited by its ubiquitous tone of maiden-auntly shock.

[2] In this section of the essay an attempt is made to present figures for Britain, but the 'tedious separatism of Scottish statistics' causes a lapse back in later sections to (mainly) statistics of England and Wales only. For the demographic experience of Scotland, though this is poorly documented before the 1850s, see the excellent survey and guide by M. Flinn et al., *Scottish Population History from the Seventeenth Century to the 1930s,* 1977.

[3] Numbers of children since 1851 can be traced through the censuses but are more conveniently found in B. R. Mitchell, *Abstract of British Historical Statistics,* 1962, Table 4, and B. R. Mitchell and H. G. Jones, *Second Abstract of British Historical Statistics,* 1971, Table 3. Also there are handy summary tables in March, op. cit., p. 24, repeated and extended in Halsey, op. cit., p. 33.

[4] For details of printed nineteenth-century census reports, see M. Drake, 'The census 1801-1891', in E. A. Wrigley, ed., *Nineteenth Century Society: Essays in the Use of Quantitative Methods for the Study of Social Data,* 1972.

[5] For a very striking graphic presentation of child mortality trends, see Figure 5.3 in E. A. Wrigley, *Population and History,* 1969, p. 166: this is mainly based on *Registrar General's Statistical Review for 1962,* part I, p. 6, table 4. See also Halsey, op. cit., pp. 336-338, Tables 11.2 and 11.3, based on official sources which are cited. Infant mortality rates from 1838 and 1855 and child mortality rates from 1938 are tabulated in Mitchell, *Abstract* and *Second abstract,* Table 12 and Tables 10-11.

[6] After 1950 infant mortality continued to fall and by the 1970s was around 17.

[7] For instance, social class I in 1930-32 had a rate of 33 (infant deaths per 1000 births), higher than the rate of 21 achieved by classes IV-V in

1964-1965: Halsey, op. cit., p. 343, Table 11.9.

[8] But for genuine high infant (and child) mortality in Glasgow before 1850, see Flinn, op. cit., pp. 378-379.

[9] See R. E. Jones, 'Further evidence on the decline in infant mortality in pre-industrial England: North Shropshire 1561-1810', *Population Studies*, 34, 1980, pp. 239-250; and other recent studies cited and summarized in this article.

[10] The unprinted source behind the printed census return, the enumerator's book, is now being widely and intensively studied for information on the family: see M. Anderson, 'The study of family structure', in Wrigley, *Nineteenth Century Society*; and a pioneering investigation of Preston in 1851, M. Anderson, *Family Structure in Nineteenth Century Lancashire*, 1971. At Preston about 90 per cent of children were living with parents, though in a sample from near-by villages only about 80 per cent (pp. 54, 85).

[11] For tables summarizing census data on proportions of children, see Marsh, op. cit., p. 25, repeated and extended in Halsey, op. cit., p. 33. In 1971 the proportion was slightly higher than that stated for 1931-1961.

[12] The best discussion of changing family size, with illuminating tables, is in Wrigley, *Population and History*, pp. 185-191. See also Marsh, op. cit., pp. 41-47, and Halsey, op. cit., pp. 28-29, 54-57. All tend to be based on the 1911 census fertility inquiry, the 1946 family census (*Royal Commission on Population*, vol. VI, 1954), and the fertility tables of the 1961 census report.

[13] On orphans and step-parenthood, see P. Laslett, *Family Life and Illicit Love in Earlier Generations*, 1977, 'Parental deprivation in the past', pp. 160-173; J. R. Holman, 'Orphans in pre-industrial towns — the case of Bristol in the late seventeenth century', *Local Population Studies*, 15, 1975, pp. 40-44.

[14] Anderson, *Family Structure*, pp. 74, 141-144.

[15] For the view that early censuses may overstate the number of occupied children (because of faulty recording by enumerators), see P. M. Tillott, 'Sources of inaccuracy in the 1851 and 1861 censuses', in Wrigley, *Nineteenth Century Society*, specifically p. 124.

[16] The material in this paragraph is from an unpublished doctoral thesis, P. E. H. Hair, 'The social history of British coalminers 1800-1845', Oxford, 1955.

[17] The early censuses did in fact require householders and enumerators to record the occupations, not only of children who worked away from the home, but also of those who worked on other than domestic duties at home. However it may be doubted whether all children occupied at home were so recorded, partly because of the lack of instructions regarding what constituted 'occupation'. Given that numbers of children worked spasmodically in domestic industries, that this might be regarded as not occupied because not full-time or regular, and that the census did not inquire into part-time working, it would seem likely that whereas part-timers who worked away from home tended to be recorded as 'occupied', those who helped in occupations at home tended to be not so recorded. But

this view may be wrong. The extent to which 'occupied' included or excluded part-timers requires further investigation but for lack of evidence may never become clear. This is one of many grey areas in the quantitative assessment of nineteenth-century child-labour, and nothing in the text of this essay should be read as indicating confidence in the capacity of the published data to establish other than the broadest trends.

[18] The argument of this section is in keeping with the approach presented in T. W. Laqueur, 'Growth of English elementary education 1750-1850', in L. Stone, ed., *Schooling and Society*, Baltimore, 1976.

[19] According to the Robbins Report, cited in Marsh, op. cit., p. 218, the proportion of children aged 14 in full-time schooling rose from 2 per cent in 1870 and 9 per cent in 1902 to 38 per cent in 1938.

[20] There is advantage in concentrating the argument on these early census figures, since the census treated 'occupied' and 'schooled' as mutually exclusive categories. Later on, census figures for children at work and Education Department figures for children at school overlap, because of educational part-timers, that is, children both at work and at school. The essay indicates the broad trend and avoids this statistical complication. However it may be noted that among those enumerated in the early censuses as occupied there must have been some who had previously been at school, therefore the proportion of schooled under-estimates the proportion of ever-schooled.

[21] For a discussion of schooling statistics, see B. I. Coleman, 'Education in mid-century', in Wrigley, *Nineteenth Century Society*; and see also, in the same volume, Tillott, op. cit., pp. 122-124. The school surveys of 1818, 1833, and 1851 are less informative about child attendance by ages than are the census returns. The 1851 census instructed householders to record as 'scholars' those children above five 'daily attending school' — but this essay assumes that this instruction was not rigidly adhered to. The census distinguished a small number of children who were receiving tuition, not at school but at home: this category has been ignored. The census also recorded a number of children under five as 'schooled' (12 per cent of the age-group in 1851, a high figure). Again, our discussion ignores these children. Though of much interest in the history of nursery schooling, we cannot believe that schooling for toddlers meant the same as schooling for older children.

[22] On the quantitative aspects of schooling before the 1870s, see the controversial articles (usefully reprinted in M. Drake, *Applied Historical Studies*, 1973, pp. 53-119), E. G. West, 'Resource allocation and growth in early nineteenth century education', *Economic History Review*, 2nd. ser., XXIII, 1970, pp. 66-95; J. S. Hurt, 'Professor West on early nineteenth century education', *ibid.*, XXIV, 1971, pp. 624-632; E. G. West, 'The interpretation of early nineteenth century education statistics', *ibid.*, pp. 633-642.

[23] Usually expressed as leaving-ages of 14, 15 and 16, meaning that children could leave school at some convenient administrative date after these birthdays.

Further reading

E. A. Wrigley, *Population and History*, Weidenfeld and Nicolson, 1969. Disguised as an elementary introduction to historical demography, this book includes an original discussion of nineteenth- and twentieth-century changes in mortality and fertility across industrial western Europe (chapter 5). Child mortality and family size in Britain since 1850 are depicted in neat and bold diagrams and tables. The best starting-point for novices.

Rosalind Mitchison, *British Population Change Since 1860*, Macmillan, 1977. Up-to-date bibliography and useful background reading. The brief text is particularly good on methodological problems, but rather harps on the wrongs of women and has too little to say about family size and the social issues most relevant to childhood.

Ivy Pinchbeck and Margaret Hewitt, *Children in English society, Vol. II, From the Nineteenth Century to the Children's Act*, Routledge and Kegan Paul, 1973. Not about 'children in society' on any broad view but about the development of reformist and *dirigiste* 'child welfare' attitudes and legislation: see my footnote 1. On its narrow topics, the book is authoritative if blinkered.

J. S. Hurt, *Elementary Schooling and the Working Classes 1860-1918*, Routledge and Kegan Paul, 1979. This work, a sound and penetrating discussion of the social issues surrounding the imposition of universal schooling, sometimes expressed quantitatively, indicates how far the 'history of education' is now broadening out from a simple, institutional, linear-progressive model. Hurt concludes that 'almost one century after Forster's Bill had become law, some parents still acquiesced in rather than accepted the legal requirements that had changed the pattern of family life that dated back to a pre-industrial society'. Though unfortunately not available to me when the present essay was being drafted, the book is recommended as the best starting-point for reading on the schooling aspect of childhood.

Pamela Horn, *The Victorian Country Child*, Roundwood Press, 1974, and *Education in Rural England 1800-1914*, Gill and Macmillan 1978. In these books, and in a number of less easily accessible articles, the author draws attention to the life of the rural child. The writings excel in pointing to the range of published and unpublished sources but sadly the historical approach is in the outdated fashion of the Hammonds. Select quotations are deployed to prove the Bad Old Days and quantified assessment is limited.

E. A. Wrigley, ed., *Nineteenth Century Society: Essays in the use of Quantitative Methods for the Study of Social Data*, Cambridge University Press, 1972. The essential introduction to quantitative census data for the critical student or the researcher. Although there is no separate essay on childhood, the essays by Drake, Anderson, Tillott and Coleman are very relevant. The work serves to demonstrate to what a limited extent the received generalizations about the social history of the period have been constructed from, or have been checked against, even *published* quantitative data.

Michael Anderson, *Family Structure in Nineteenth Century Lancashire*, Cambridge University Press, 1971. Actually about Preston in 1851, this historical analysis draws its evidence from unpublished census data (enumerators' books) and is pioneering. A little overburdened with sociological chatter but the questions raised touch on most aspects of family life, including childhood. This work points the way forward. Yet it deals with only one town in one census — it therefore warns us how much similar analysis remains to be done before we can confidently gain a rounded view of the late nineteenth-century family.

Peter H. Lindert, *Fertility and Scarcity in America* Princeton University Press 1978. The most recent, elaborate, and sensible attempt to cost post-1850 Anglo-Saxon children. Mainly treating the USA, it successfully proves the range of data — and the range of assumptions — the exercise demands. It is therefore useful for reminding historians about important questions concerning past British childhood (e.g., was there a relationship between late nineteenth century family size and child earnings?) that apparently are now unanswerable.

Carol Dyhouse, 'Working class mothers and infant mortality in England 1895-1914', *Journal of Social History*, 12, 1978. This stimulating article offers useful comment and bibliography on the infant welfare movement; and it exposes the anti-female, anti-working-class bias of contemporaries who blamed high infant mortality on maternal ignorance and mothers going out to work. Only a faint whiff of the voguish opposite bias surfaces in this article. Nevertheless critical readers may not be entirely convinced that the myths assaulted were totally without foundation in fact.

William Brass and Mohammed Kabir, 'Regional variations in fertility and child mortality during the demographic transition in England and Wales', in John Hobcraft and Philip Rees, *Regional Demographic Development*, Croom Helm, 1979. Distinguished demographers conclude from a highly technical discussion that 'a direct influence of child mortality on fertility cannot be detected' by analysis by regions. Mortality fell unevenly, fertility evenly. Presumably whereas the former was determined by local socio-economic circumstances, the latter was determined by more widespread social attitudes. Where do we go from here?

Postscript While the present volume was at press, E. A. Wrigley and R. S. Schofield's *The population history of England 1541-1871* Edward Arnold 1981 appeared (but has not yet been subject to critical review). Readers who may wish to check my speculations about pre-1850 child population against the suggestions of Wrigley and Schofield are directed to the following passages. Their back projection exercise suggests that the proportion of children in the population was fairly steady during the early nineteenth century but grew throughout the eighteenth century, Gregory King's age-distribution figures being wrong (pp. 216-218). Reconstitution studies of 12 non-random parishes suggest that child mortality rates were lower 1750-1800 than they were 1700-1750 (p. 249); and the figures given would mean that toddler mortality began an overall decline long before 1850 but that infant mortality rose somewhat during the early nineteenth century, with the result that child mortality in 1800 and child mortality in 1850 were much the same.

Regional and temporal variations in the structure of the British household since 1851

RICHARD WALL

It is often asserted that large and complex households occurred more frequently in past societies than present ones: that now people live in nuclear families or alone whereas previously they would have joined the households of others as parents, brothers, sisters or more distant relatives. In practice, as will be demonstrated later, the inclusion of such relatives in the household was as common in Britain in 1951 or even 1961 as it had been in mid-nineteenth-century Britain. Merely to note the proportion of households with relatives would, however, not be enough. It is necessary to establish in which sort of households relatives were located. Accordingly, the analysis has been extended to cover the significant variation in the composition of the household by social class and by region. The latter aspect has been much neglected although as is shown by an examination of the 1971 census the regional pattern is a striking one with a higher proportion of households containing relatives in the west of the country than in the east. In this paper, therefore, particular attention will be focused on this pattern, noting its relative durability and the possibility of associations with the economic and social characteristics of individual regions.

Concepts and definitions: the household of the enumerator and the enumerated

An overwhelming proportion of the present-day population of Britain lives in households and the importance of the household as a social and housing unit is widely recognized. The General Household Survey of the Social Survey Division of the Office of Population Censuses and Surveys (OPCS) and the Family Expenditure Survey of the Department of Employment (GHS and FES) now supplement the decennial census with an annual breakdown of household composition. Nevertheless the shape and composition of the contemporary household are still shrouded in obscurity. There are many reasons for this. Both the FES and the GHS are surveys and depend on voluntary co-operation. There is in consequence a certain, and variable, non-response rate. The GHS with a higher success rate than the FES still achieve only 76 per cent complete returns in 1976 and a further 10 per cent of partial returns. If the non-responders could be assumed to be typical of the general population this would not matter but this seems unlikely. A report of 1969 showed that the response rate to the FES declined as rateable value increased. It was also found that small households were the least likely to co-operate although as outright refusals appear to have been accorded a household size of one (representing the person refusing) there seems to be room for a certain amount of conjecture regarding the degree of bias that enters the surveys from this source.

It is not altogether surprising, therefore, that researchers have tended to turn first to the decennial census rather than to the surveys. Information on household composition was first collected in 1851 for a handful of far from representative districts but the experiment was not a success, and after 1861 interest appears to have lapsed until 1951 when a special set of tables was introduced apparently in response to expressed requests by sociologists. Further sets of tables appeared in 1961, 1966 and 1971. The difficulty with them is that it has been found impossible to keep either definitions or the level of detail constant, as on each occasion an attempt has been made to avoid the mistaken approaches of the previous census. It also has to be said that the various classification schemes that have been tried have tended to obscure rather than illuminate the structures they were trying to describe. In 1951 the Registrar General favoured a system in which the household was divided into a primary family unit and an optional 'remainder' section. The former consisted of the head, and where present, spouse, child (including siblings, children of servants and parentless children), near relatives (including siblings aged 16 and over unless married, or widowed with children of their own, and ancestors whether married or not) and domestic servants. The 'remainders' absorbed all other household members and were analyzed according to whether they contained family nuclei of their own (i.e. at least one married couple or parent-child group). Households could consist of a primary family unit only or be 'composite', that is, contain a primary family unit and a 'remainder'. The system was not repeated but it cannot be said that later attempts have been much more successful at providing a neat, clearly understood categorization of types of household and this despite the fact that the majority of present-day households are exceedingly simple in structure. In the 1971 volume, there were as many as 52 separate categories of household making compression inevitable if the result is not to be a hopelessly confused picture.

On the other hand it is all too often the case that compression removes vital pieces of information. The categorization schemes employed by the FES and GHS, for example, have the advantage of greater brevity but see the household from one point of view only. One of the FES schemes, for example, in the code book to the 1973 survey, runs to 28 types based only on combinations of adults and children, with child defined as any unmarried person under the age of 18 rather than in terms of relationship to the head of household as in the case with the decennial census. More widely used is the scheme adopted by the GHS of individuals under 60, small adult, small family, large family, large adult, older small, and individual aged 60 and over. However although it provides a neat enough portrayal of households at particular stages of their developmental cycle from formation to dissolution, like the FES scheme it does not attempt to show the relationships between co-residents. It does not therefore succeed in throwing much light on why people choose to live together. For this purpose it is necessary to fall back on the decennial census and promote one's own rearrangement of the 52 household types. Inevitably this involves focusing on one particular aspect of the household to the exclusion of others as in the present paper where the focus is on the presence in the household of relatives of the household head.

The focus on relatives could, though, be attacked on two counts. First, it is generally accepted that the 'extended family' as a co-residential group, has been virtually eliminated from present-day Britain and involved no more than a minority of households even in the nineteenth century. However, although relatives form only a small part of the household it has already been intimated that there is a significant variation in the frequency with which households contain relatives both in terms of social class and by region. The argument is that this reflects different attitudes towards the wider family . The second and more difficult problem arises from the failure of the census to provide a complete and consistent count of households with relatives. Even the 1971 census which is the best suited to our purpose is not entirely satisfactory in this respect. Grandchildren living with their grandparents in the absence of the intervening generation are treated in all tabulations as though they were offspring. There is also a minor loss amongst the more complex households (consisting of two or more married couples or parent-child groups) where it is impossible to ascertain how many of these involve a relationship other than that of direct descent.

With the earlier censuses the problems are greater. In the case of 1961 it is impossible to identify households with lone ancestors if persons unrelated to the household head were also present. A lone ancestor, it should be noted, is the census term for the resident ancestor of the head or one of his or her direct descendants not belonging to a family in their own right. Also in the 1961 volume we find a distinctly chilly warning in regard to comparisons between 1951 and 1961. 'Undoubtedly', says the report on household composition, 'a limited number of the figures can be regarded as approximately comparable if reasonable assumptions are made about the smallness of certain marginal groups of persons who might be included in one tabulation but not another. The purpose of these paragraphs is to stress that any such comparisons should only be made with caution after careful study of the definitions used in each method of classification'. From our point of view the important differences between 1951 and 1961 are first that in the former year only those persons resident *and present* on census night were included and secondly that the definition of child embraced widowed and divorced children of the head unaccompanied by children of their own who in later censuses were classed as relatives (widowed or divorced children of the head with children of their own are always taken to be relatives). On the other hand a number of siblings of the head (those under the age of 16) were included amongst the count of children in 1951 and as relatives in 1961 and later. Such changes in definitions affect our count of the proportion of households with relatives in a number of different ways. Sometimes they tend to be self-cancelling, sometimes the effect is difficult to predict as with the change from a *de facto* to a *de jure* style census between 1951 and 1961. Since visitors are excluded from consideration on both occasions the result inflated the number of relatives recorded in 1951, other factors being equal, but can one be sure that all chance relatives in the household in 1951 were dutifully recorded as visitors?

It is necessary to introduce such detailed points because they determine the level of confidence that can be accorded to the calculation of the proportion of households with relatives for each of the census years. The lack of consistency in the definition of relatives is of less importance when we wish to determine whether it is always the same areas of the country which are associated with 'high' or 'low' proportions of households with relatives. The only assumption made here in comparing one census with another is that the change in definition from census to census has not cut out a particular household type common to one part of the country but not to another. Analysis of a sample of the 1851 enumerators' schedules suggests that there may indeed have been at that stage some rather subtle variations in the composition of the kin group from region to region but it seems unlikely that many of the various types of relatives might have been missed had the rules of later censuses for observing such households been applied.

Attention is directed to 1851 in particular as it is with this year that assessment of regional variation in household structures becomes practical (earlier materials occurring too sporadically across time and space for this purpose). It provides a point of comparison for both the degree and direction of the regional variation a century later. However, the sample 1851 schedules have yet to be fully processed, and for information on the *proportion* of households with relatives it is necessary to rely on the figures published in the 1851 and 1861 Reports. These figures, it must be remembered, relate to a far from representative selection of settlements. They contain in particular a too large urban element, with sections of the country omitted, areas from Wales appearing only in 1861 and Scottish ones never, but the figures can be compared for general consistency with extensive, if somewhat disorganized, work based on the 1851 enumerators' schedules undertaken more recently (summarized in Wall, 1979).

Before we start to look in detail at the pattern of household composition, the level of census accuracy ought to be examined from a wider perspective. So far we have considered only the question of the detailed classifications of households and not the problems of under-enumeration. The latter is of particular concern when the information on households is obtained from a sample and not the complete population (1951, 1 per cent, 1961-71, 10 per cent) and when the drawing of the sample was in the hands of the enumerator and not the census office (as in 1961). Along with the *Guide to Census Reports Great Britain 1801-1966* (1977, p. 274) we do not expect perfection in any census but 'follow up' surveys and comparisons between the results of sample and general censuses where these cover the same ground demonstrate that the level of inaccuracy, particularly as regards household composition, can be surprisingly high. For example, for 1961 it is estimated that the number of one-person households was under-stated by between 8 and 9 per cent. The important point is that it is particular *types* of household that are likely to go under-recorded.

The *Guide to the Census Reports,* having spent some time trying to discover the reasons for this, eventually decided that the chief cause lay with enumerators who had departed from the strict sampling system by avoiding households that were going to be 'difficult' or 'unusual' either because they were large, or contained immigrants or the elderly, who would experience problems with the more complicated form used in the sample. Since the enumerators in rural areas were more likely to be aware of the nature of an individual household before calling on it than their urban counterparts, this 'explained why the discrepancy was greatest in rural areas'.

Another type of problem arises because of the failure of the staff at census headquarters, the enumerator and the householder filling in the schedule, to agree on the definition of household. This is by no means a simple matter in that it is possible to think of the household in terms of the physical space it occupies, its function and its social meaning and emphasizing one of these at the expense of another can alter the number of units that are identified as households. For example a group of persons may occupy a defined living space but not pool their incomes or adopt a common housekeeping. They will certainly not always acknowledge a common authority in the form of a 'household head', the appearance of whom on census forms as a reference point from which to calculate relationships within the household has on occasion sparked off the destruction of the questionnaire. Such problems as these are of course very well known and great efforts have been made to keep to a standard definition of common housekeeping. However, if the rules regarding co-residence change, for example if more people start living together but catering separately, as can be the case with friends sharing flats, then the definition of household may have to change. Indeed the Office of Population Censuses and Surveys has considered, but not yet implemented, a redefinition of the household on the basis of the use of a communal living room.

The various surveys to which we have referred, the FES and GHS also get into difficulties with definitions. On the other hand they have one advantage over the decennial census in that as they keep track of the same household over a period of months quite elaborate rules can be formulated to determine whether an individual qualifies for membership of a particular household. These rules take into consideration how many nights the individual resided in the household, in conjunction with his marital status and the closeness of his relationship to the household head. At the same time the question of household definition can be handled in an almost cavalier way in the commentaries on the results of the surveys. Thus the FES defines a household as a group of people living at the same address and having meals prepared together and with common housekeeping, while the GHS prefers a group living at the same address and *catered for by the same person for at least one meal a day*. This leaves the reader to wonder whether a real difference is intended or whether it is simply the case of trying to avoid too much detail which can make for a long and involved text. The different objectives of the surveys, particularly in the case of the FES with its emphasis on income and expenditure seems likely to give rise to further discrepancies in the identification of households.

The principal problem in this area, however, arises from the presence of lodgers (the subletting of part of a family's living space to other families, or more usually to individuals, who provide their own food). This was recognized as long ago as the 1831 *Population Return*. Indeed a housing report that appeared after the end of the Second World War (Block, *Estimating Housing Needs*, 1946, p. 30), concluded that its definition of a household had not been improved upon, and that the various difficulties which it occasioned were still unsolved. The same could doubtless be said today. Part of the problem undoubtedly arises from the fact that although the census authorities have tried to count lodgers as separate households, at least since 1831, neither the enumerators nor the householders who fill out the schedules have been able to visualize them as such, with the consequence that lodgers have to varying degrees been credited to the principal households who provide them with house room. As residential units have gradually acquired more living space with the general advance in the standard of living, it seems reasonable to hypothesize that it should be rather easier to agree on lodgers as 'separate' today than was the case in the past. Even so, it was reported to a conference in Cambridge in November 1977 by a spokesman for OPCS that a special survey of students in lodgings had shown that the 36 recorded housholds should really have been 98 representing about a 1 per cent undercount of existing households.

For earlier periods it is difficult to get a precise estimate of the number of 'lodgers' and others that might have constituted distinct households. Block in *Estimating Housing Needs* (p. 77) calculated 3,445,000 potential candidates for one-person households in 1931 against the recorded total of 689,000 but he makes it clear that the difference was only in part to be accounted for by under-enumeration of households. The remainder were genuinely attached to other households although, according to Block, they would have liked separate dwellings. The relative weights to be accorded these two factors could not be determined. This comment apart, it appears we have to go right back to the two special analyses of household composition in the Reports on the censuses of 1851 and 1861. At this time lodging was apparently exceedingly common (although the bias in favour of urban areas is a factor here) and if we were to follow the advice of the 1851 Report that 'many of the "single lodgers" and "widowers" or "widows" are occupiers of parts of houses' and should be classified as householders it would be necessary to add 20,378 extra households to the recorded total of 48,985. When Alan Armstrong resurveyed these data in the early 1970s he therefore provided two sets of figures, one including all the sole widowed, bachelors and spinsters and even married couples as the equivalent of households and the other excluding them all (i.e. classing them as lodgers).

To this sort of problem there is no 'right' solution, but lodgers clearly do not constitute full households even though they cater separately. Their living space is generally more circumscribed and more often shared with other people than is the case of those recorded households who have to share facilities with other households. There is a similar logic to the 1961 redefinition of the household which resulted in those residential units not having exclusive use of at least one room no longer counting as households. Where the option exists, therefore, we would probably be justified in trying to classify a lodger or 'lodging group' without a distinct living space as an attachment to a household rather than as a separate household. Even when all that is available are the numbers of households and lodgers we might still for the mid-nineteenth century want to attach them to existing households. This after all is how the enumerators of the time seem to have seen them and it also squares with current interpretations of pre-industrial English household structure. It is important, however, that the implications of such an argument are fully realized. In effect we should be overlooking groups in the nineteenth century whose equivalents in the twentieth century are more readily accredited with the title of 'household'. There are also implications for the estimate of the proportion of households with relatives because the structure of lodging groups is very much simpler than that of households. Not to count lodgers as forming households 'raises' the proportion of households with relatives in the average (median) settlement in the special analysis of 1851 from 13.4 to 20.2 per cent, which set alongside our best estimate for the country as a whole a century later implies a quite considerable fall in the frequency of living with relatives by 1951 (the median was then 15.0 per cent, see figure 5). However, had we taken the 'official' advice proffered in the 1851 Report and equated lodgers with

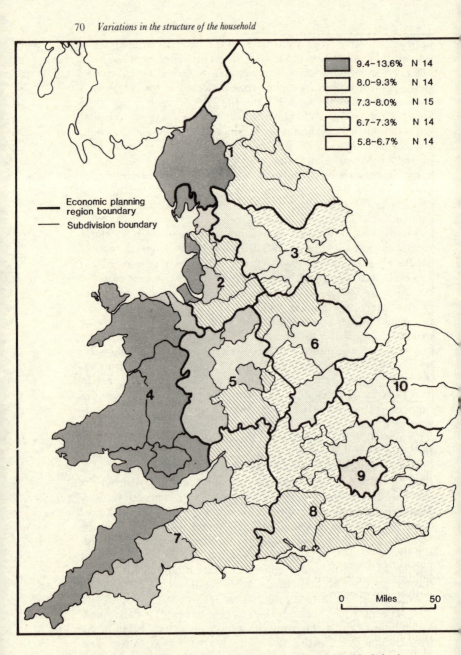

Figures 1(a) and (b) *Great Britain 1971. Proportion of households with relatives in subdivisions of economic planning regions (definitions of 1971).*

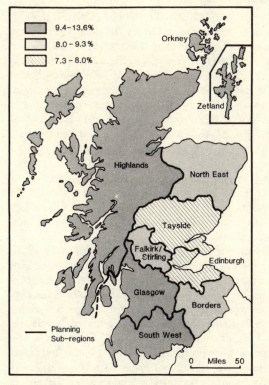

Figure 1(b)

households then we could produce an 1851 figure that was below that of 1951 and very little removed from that of 1961 (the median for the areas into which the country was divided for the purposes of figure 2 is 12.8).

Round the regions

For the moment let us put this issue to one side, and consider the question that, as intimated above, should be considerably easier to elucidate, the degree of regional variation in this aspect of household structure. Figure 1 makes it very clear that in 1971 households with relatives were concentrated into particular parts of the country. The regional variation is the more striking because of the crudeness of the figures which are available for no units smaller than sub-divisions of economic planning regions. For the purposes of figure 1, these regions have been divided into five arbitrary groups, each containing about 20 per cent of the areas, according to the rank order of the proportion of households with relatives.

These groups can be termed respectively the areas of relatively high extension, medium high, medium, medium low and low and the pattern produced is one of high areas to the west and low areas to the east. From a high in western Scotland, Wales, the south west and the north west the proportion of households containing relatives declines almost inexorably as one moves eastwards and is least noticeable in Yorkshire, the east Midlands and East Anglia. There are a few exceptions: the Greater London and Birmingham areas, for example, and it will be noted that the proportions for Scotland are in general above those for England. The overall trend, however, is very clear, although since the gradations in the proportions are very slight involving, even in the west, only a small minority of households, it is not a characteristic that would strike a newcomer to a particular area. It is perhaps for this reason that it has previously escaped attention.

In the search for an explanation both the age structure and the economic and social structure of the various regions must be kept in mind. I have demonstrated in a recent paper how the presence of what are termed 'no family' households, that is households lacking either a married couple or a parent-child group, are associated with areas in which there are at the same time a high proportion of elderly persons. This particular explanation, however, is less plausible in the case of households with relatives. In the first place, while several of the classic retirement areas with their large proportions of elderly persons do seem to be favourable to this sort of household, other such areas, particularly in the south east, do not. In the latter one finds a relatively high proportion of old people, a relatively high proportion of whom live alone or with just a spouse, whereas in Wales and the west there are similar proportions of the elderly, but comparatively few of them living alone. The second reason for thinking that age structure is not the key factor is that it is possible to replicate the regional pattern almost exactly, using a quite different sub-set of households: one family households containing children. This removes from consideration those households most likely to reflect the preponderance of old people (no family households). A child is defined by the Office of Population Censuses and Surveys not in terms of age but in terms of relationship to the household head, including some grandchildren in addition to never married sons and daughters (see above). Relatives are certainly rarer in households which contained children than they were in households in general. This one might well expect given that such households contained by definition a parent-child group and might well lack the resources to lodge an extra relative. It could also be argued that the heads of such households were at a particular phase of the life cycle when they might expect to have fewer relatives alive (parents at any rate) with whom they might co-reside. It is particularly interesting, therefore, that the same sort of *regional* pattern emerges from this set of figures as from the other. (The second set of figures is not reproduced here but has appeared in map form covering England and Wales only in my article 'The historian and data tapes', *Social History Society Newsletter* 3(1) Spring 1978.) At the same time it has to be admitted that the attempt to control for the effect of age structural variation is only partially successful. This is principally, though not entirely, because child is not defined in terms of age, and it is to be hoped that future censuses will provide fuller and more direct data to enable one, for example, to measure the presence of relatives by the age of household head.

Similar difficulties surround the possible links between the proportion of households with relatives and the economic and social structure of the particular area. At first sight such links seem unlikely. One does not have to be particularly familiar with Wales to know that central Wales and the north Wales coast differ from each other and from the south Wales valleys yet all end up with approximately similar proportions of households with relatives. Similarly, although a number of conurbations stand out as having above average proportions of these households, Merseyside, Birmingham and London for example, suggesting that housing costs, or the lack of suitable housing, causes families to 'huddle up', it is equally possible to point to other conurbations such as Tyneside and west Yorkshire where this is not the case.

Uncertainty arises because there is no information on the social class of the households *within each area* that contain relatives. Nationally it is known that these households are most common amongst the unskilled (social class V) and decrease in proportion as one ascends the social hierarchy. This, it is worth emphasizing, completely reverses the hierarchy of pre-industrial times when the most complex households in terms of kin composition were almost invariably commoner amongst the wealthier groups. Whether this hierarchy persisted in some of the regions that might be regarded as rather more traditional in outlook is as yet unknown.

Social classes are not, of course, homogeneous entities. The term as used here is an OPCS construction from a combination of some 17 socio-economic classes (see the list in table 3 p. 96, and, to avoid possible confusion between the social classes and socio-economic classes, in this paper the latter will be referred to as groups and not as classes). The 17 socio-economic groups are in '

turn based on what are necessarily sometimes rather fine judgements, again by OPCS, about employment status and the standing
of particular occupations. Not surprisingly the groups and their
principal sub-divisions (no finer breakdown is available) suggests
a more complex picture than the five class division introduced
above. Where a particular socio-economic group, such as employers with small establishments, spans a series of classes, the
general class hierarchy (the lower the social class the more households with relatives) was sometimes broken. For example, employers placed in social classes II and III were rather more likely
to live with relatives than were those accorded only the status of
semi-skilled and unskilled (classes IV and V) although the reverse
was generally the case. The absolute level is also higher than the
average for households in class II (9.1 per cent against 7.8 per
cent).

Other examples could be found suggesting that socio-economic
group rather than social class provides the surer guide although it
might be necessary to modify this if data at the level of the occupational group were to hand. It is also true that certain of the
socio-economic categories are, from the present point of view,
distinctly unhelpful. There can be no surprise, for example, that
farmers on their own account, using no labour other than family
labour, are more likely to have relatives living with them than
other farmers; indeed the farmers using familial labour head the
list of groups most likely to have relatives present. Similarly the
mobility of members of the armed forces, and the mobility and
perhaps the poverty of students provide natural constraints to
their taking in relatives. Together with the economically inactive
they were the three groups least likely to do so. Other differences
cause far more consideration. Professional people are below
average in the proportion of households with relatives. So, too, are
agricultural workers, particularly in relation to other socio-
economic groups deemed by OPCS to be of the same social class,
and the factors that might be appropriate in the case of professionals seem scarcely likely to fit agricultural workers. The conventional interpretation would see the low frequency with which
professionals live with their relatives as a natural consequence of
their own mobility, and symptomatic of the severance of kin ties
that social and geographical mobility induces, though the case for
the dislocation of kin ties as a result of social advancement has
sometimes been overstated. The household patterns of agricultural workers are even more difficult to interpret than those of the
professionals. In contrast to the professionals, they have been little
studied in recent years as they have shrunk to a fraction of their

former importance in the national economy. All that can be said is that it seems unlikely that mobility is the factor behind the low proportion of agricultural workers' households with relatives. Alternatively it might be argued that the ready availability of suitable housing made co-residence less necessary (see below) but a possible superfluity of housing for poorly paid workers in East Anglia scarcely seems likely.

Such speculation tends to be endless and much of the relevant information is in any case simply not available. This applies equally to the question of the relationship between the socio-economic variation and the east-west differences which were such a marked feature of the map of household composition in 1971 (figure 1). As with social class there is no direct evidence on the variation in household composition by socio-economic group within regions and the only recourse is to fall back on indirect evidence. For example, Wales has an above average proportion of farmers not employing outside labour as does the south west. On the other hand in East Anglia, which also has an above average proportion of farmers, the balance between those using non-familial labour and those who do not is quite different and there are many more agricultural labourers than in the west. The lack of households with relatives in the south east could be explained by the marked concentration of professionals in the region. It would be premature, though, to claim that it is the presence of farmers using familial labour in Wales, of agricultural workers in East Anglia and of professionals in the south east that accounts for the differences between these regions in the proportion of households with relatives. The link between socio-economic group and the proportion of households with relatives has been established on a national basis and the pattern in a particular region or sub-region need not be the same.

To proceed further, therefore, it is necessary to switch direction yet again by taking into consideration the historical base to the regional patterns of 1971. How long had they been in existence? Might there be a tradition of staying with relatives in particular areas perhaps built up by a set of circumstances in the past, long since disappeared? These could be as old as the social structures to which they now apparently attach or even older. They might even be part of a division that distinguished the areas subject to Celtic influence from the rest of the country.

To test this proposition let us look at the regional pattern as it appears from the censuses of 1851, 1951 and 1961, beginning with the last as in definitions and detail it comes closest to those of 1971. Nevertheless there is a certain loss of information in that for

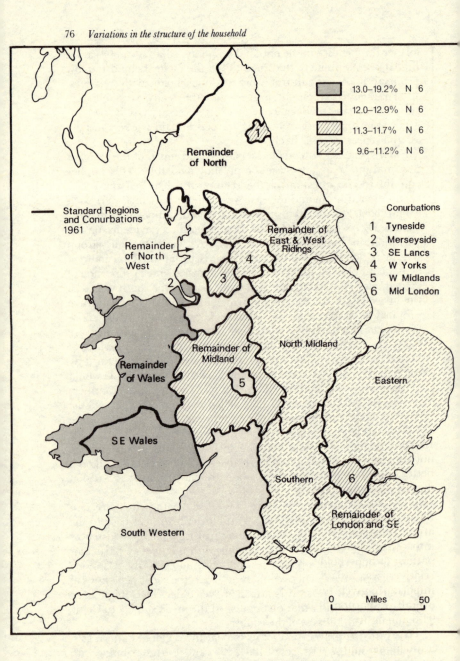

Figure 2(a) and (b) *Great Britain 1961. Proportion of households with relatives in standard regions, subregions and conurbations (definitions of 1961).*

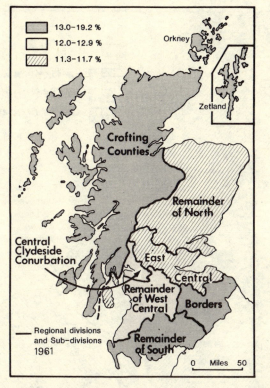

Figure 2(b)

England it is possible to distinguish conurbations and regions but not sub-regions. For Wales and Scotland the situation is a little better but comparison with 1971 is again made difficult by the fact that the boundaries of the sub-regions are differently drawn. The result is 24 analysis areas divided into four categories according to the proportion of households with relatives compared with the 71 areas spread over five categories for 1971. Taking all these factors into consideration, however, it would appear that in 1961 the pattern of household complexity as measured by the presence of relatives, was broadly the same as in 1971, a fact of considerable importance given the dramatic change that had occurred in the overall proportion of households with relatives (see table 1, pp. 91-3 and figures 1 and 2).

To proceed further back in time it becomes necessary to move to a still higher unit of aggregation as for 1951 regional level data only is available. For the purposes of comparability the figures for 1961 and 1971 have been reproduced at regional level yielding 12 areas

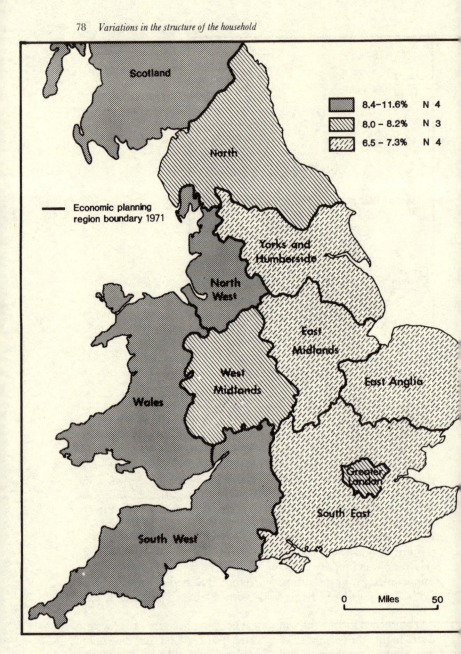

Figure 3 *Great Britain 1971. Proportion of households with relatives in economic planning regions (definitions of 1971).*

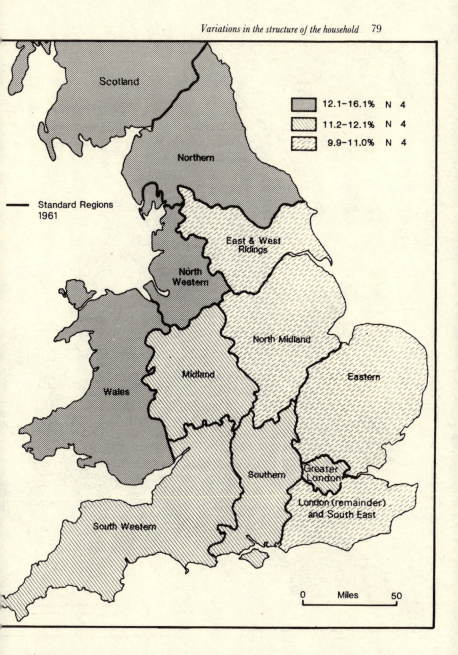

Figure 4 *Great Britain 1961. Proportion of households with relatives in standard regions (definitions of 1961).*

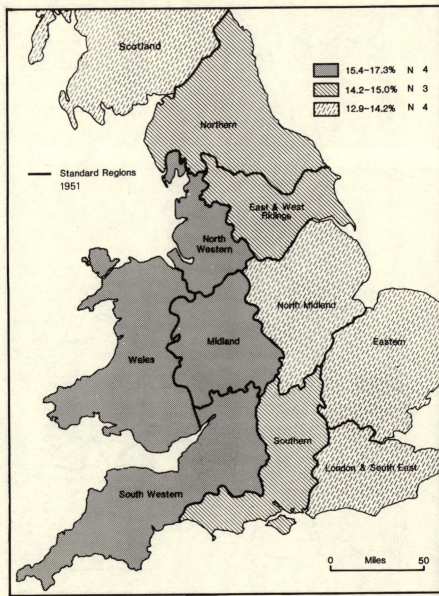

Figure 5 *Great Britain 1951. Proportion of households with relatives in standard regions (definitions of 1951).*

in 1961 and 11 in 1971. The loss of information that results from using regional rather than sub-regional data may be judged by comparing figure 3 with figure 1. The former completely misses, for example, the above average proportion of households with relatives in north-west England. It is unfortunate, too, that even at regional level changes in boundaries between censuses make it impossible to preserve strict comparability. In 1951, for example, there is no separate figure for Greater London and the southern region projects westwards to include Dorset while between 1961 and 1971 the southern region disappears altogether, to be replaced by a circular area around London which absorbs, as well as the old south-east, a sizeable section of the eastern region. For 1951 there is also the totally different categorization system of primary family units and 'remainders' with which to contend (see above).

As far as it is known no previous attempt has been made to summarize the 1951 figures in terms of the total number of households with relatives. It is appropriate, therefore, to say something very briefly about the methods that have yielded the results in figure 5. The totals of households with relatives have been produced by summing the number of primary family unit households with near relatives, and two sorts of composite households — with family nuclei formed by the presence of the son or daughter of the head, or with other relatives. Two great assumptions have had to be made. The first is that the proportion of composite households with relatives and related nuclei, which is available only on a national basis, is applicable to all regions. Secondly, although the total number of the composite households with nuclei and relatives is known, the number containing both relatives and nuclei is not and the assumption was made that composite households without nuclei were at equal risk to contain these additional relatives. Needless to say the margin for error is considerable.

Despite all these problems, however, the 1971 pattern of rather more households containing relatives in the west than in the east seems to hold up. There is just one exception, and it is a sufficiently important one to preclude a general claim about regional differences having been maintained throughout the post-war period. In 1951 Scotland was one of the areas where households with relatives were least frequent. By 1961 it had already moved into the top category (ranking third of the 'regions') and a decade later came second only to Wales. It is important to realize that it is not a case of the proportion of households with relatives having increased in real terms in Scotland, rather that the relative decline has been less marked here than elsewhere.

To move back a further century, however, is to introduce a

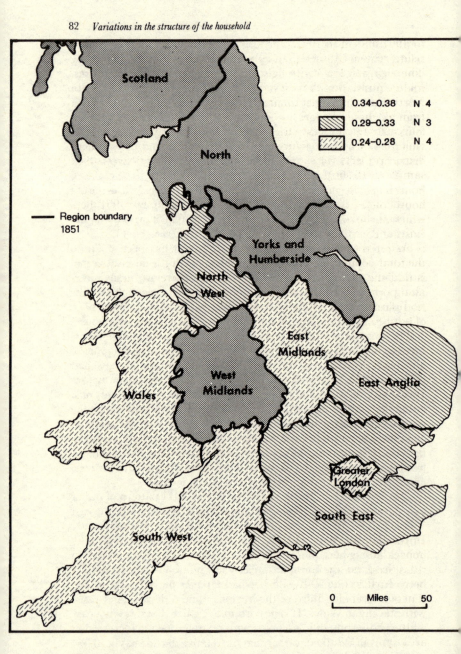

Figure 6 *Great Britain 1851. Proportion of households with relatives in economic planning regions (definitions of 1971).*

totally different regional picture (figure 6). In 1851 the areas where relatives were least frequent included Wales and the South-West. The east, the low area of the mid-twentieth century occupied a middle position and relatives were most numerous in Scotland and North-East England. Admittedly these figures differ in two ways from all those previously considered. First, the source is a one in four sub-sample by Michael Anderson of enumerators' schedules which in turn constitute a 2 per cent sample of the enumeration districts of 1851. The regional figures are derived, therefore, from a sample of districts rather than, as elsewhere, from a sample of households. Secondly, the figures show the number of relatives per household rather than the proportion of households with relatives which at the time of writing was not possible to calculate from the existing computer tapes. This apparently rather obscure measure is preferred to the more straightforward proportion of relatives in the total population. One of the problems with the latter measure is that the changes in fertility exert such a powerful influence on total population size that calculations of, for example, the proportion of relatives in the population, are more likely to reflect the level of fertility than they are the frequency of relatives.

There is not the time here to explain the basis of the sampling method of Michael Anderson who has issued a number of guides to aid those wishing to use the collection for their own purposes and placed all the data on tape in the SSRC Survey Archive at the University of Essex. There is no reason to think, however, that either the sampling method or the use of the mean number of relatives per household would overturn the two very broad conclusions which are all that we would wish to draw from the 1851 figures: namely that the 1851 regional pattern was very different from that of a century later and that the twentieth-century patterns emerged very late in the process of industrialization.

How many households with relatives?

In the light of these findings the issue of how the proportion of households containing relatives has changed since 1851 can be reassessed. On the basis of the figures given earlier the difference between 1851 and 1951 is relatively modest (from 20.2 to 15.0 per cent of households with relatives), especially given the comparison with the change since 1951. By 1961 the proportion of households with relatives had fallen to 12.8 per cent and by 1971, an even sharper decline had occurred to 7.7 per cent. It may also be observed that between 1851 and 1951 the regional pattern altered while the proportion of households with relatives fell only modestly, but that between 1951 and 1971 the tendency was for regions to maintain an above, or below, average proportion of households with relatives, despite the fact that at the same time the frequency of living with relatives was being halved.

In considering the *proportion* of households with relatives it is important to remember that ideally one ought to make various adjustments to correct for the under or over-counting of relatives in particular censuses. The former seems the more likely but over-counting is technically possible depending on the definition of relative thought appropriate (in both 1961 and 1971 but not earlier widowed and divorced children without offspring of their own are counted as relatives). Under-counting of other household types, particularly one-person households, will also artificially raise the proportion of households with relatives. To carry out all these adjustments would be an exceedingly tedious task and lead in all probability to a result that was still highly questionable. Hence all the figures presented here are uncorrected. As an example of what such revision might entail, however, the following propositions may be considered. To the registered number of households with relatives in the censuses of 1951-1971 would need to be added those households with grandchildren residing with a grandparent in the absence of their own parents. The 1951 figures for households with relatives would also need inflating to account for certain siblings registered as children, for an over-counting on the 1961 definition of one person households sharing a room, and together with the 1851 figure for not having included as relatives ever-married children without offspring of their own. On the other hand the revised 1961 figure would need deflating because of the under-registration of one person households. Overall the effect would probably be to increase the registered decline in the proportion of households with relatives between 1951 and 1961 at the expense of that between 1851 and 1951 and 1961 and 1971. If we focus on the 1951 figure, however, there is no evidence yet available to suggest that the frequency of living with relatives was then much lower than it had been in the middle of the nineteenth century.

Another problem is what was happening to the proportion of households with relatives in the long interval between 1851 and 1951. Very little systematic work has been carried out on the enumerators' schedules of the 1861, 1871 or 1881 censuses and the remainder are closed under the hundred year rule. Ebery and Preston suggest 19.0 per cent of households with relatives in 1871 (this is the mean figure for a total of 20 non-random but economically and socially diverse settlements). There is also the special analysis of household structure carried out at the time of the 1861 census which yields a proportion of households with relatives averaging 16.3 per cent (the median value based on 14 settlements). This is quite an interesting figure in that the comparable figure for 1851, also for 14 settlements, was 20.2 per cent. This discrepancy could result from the choice of a different set of 14 settlements in each year but there is some evidence to suggest that it may have arisen rather from the census officials who worked on the special tabulations having adopted different definitions of the household. It is noticeable, for example, that the proportion of households headed by single persons 'fell' sharply, between 1851 and 1861 and that there were in 1861 fewer single people living alone and more households with visitors and boarders, all of which one might expect if the rules according household status to individual lodgers had been less rigidly applied. However, whether the difference between 1851 and 1861 is due to temporal, spatial or definitional factors, the main point is that the mid-nineteenth century 'estimate' of households with relatives moves closer to that of the mid-twentieth.

To plug the gap after 1881 caused by the closure of the censuses under the 100 years rule the only recourse at present is to fall back on such indirect measures as headship rates. This is not particularly satisfactory from the present point of view since headship rates (the proportion of persons heading households) are influenced not only by the presence of relatives in households and therefore not establishing their own households, but by a number of other factors. These include the number of non-relatives, the age at which children leave the parental home and, if age specific and marital status specific rates are not produced, by changes in age structure and in age at marriage and proportions marrying. Nevertheless headship rates do at least make it clear whether the pace of household formation altered between 1871 and 1951. There are in fact two studies that can be called upon. The first, by Block, is based on the ratio of adults to households. The lower the ratio, Block argued, the more adults had been absorbed into the households of others. This index reached its low point in 1921 having declined steadily from a high point in 1871; 1921 was therefore the 'crunch point' in terms of housing needs. The difference between the high and low points, however, was only 12 per cent implying a greater degree of continuity in the pace at which new households were formed than Block seems prepared to allow.

Continuity is certainly what is stressed by the authors of the second study published in 1971 (W. V. Hole and M. T. Pountney) which is based on the more widely accepted technique of headship rate and covers a wider period (1861-1966). They found that 1951 headship rates specific to age, sex and marital condition gave a very good guide to the number of households as far back as 1861. In other words the rules regarding the formation of new households had not changed throughout the period in terms of an individual's age, sex and marital condition, although two riders must be added, the first concerning 1921 and the second 1951 itself. 1921 is, as in Block's analysis, an exception, being the one occasion on which the number of households expected is in excess of the number actually recorded. This can be interpreted as further evidence of families having to share accommodation because of the drop in house building before and during the First World War. Otherwise, the number of households recorded in the censuses were always slightly in excess of their estimates derived from 1951 headship rates which tends to lend support to the widely canvassed suggestion that the housing shortage after the Second World War was still retarding the formation of new households in 1951. Of course, as Hole and Pountney are careful to make clear, none of this bears directly on the kin composition of the household. The general picture of stability which emerges, however, is one which it seems reasonable to think that relatives will conform to in the absence of any evidence to the contrary.

Towards an explanation

After 1951 and more particularly after 1961 the situation is clearly very different. It has already been established that the proportion of households with relatives was probably halved during this period. At the same time the 1951 headship rates become increasingly unreliable as a guide to the numbers of new households. Headship rates moved up sharply for married men under 40, for widowed women and there were more spectacular gains by single women and men.

As an example of the sort of increases that are involved, we may take the case of never-married women aged 60 and above. In 1951 no more than 46.7 per cent of these women headed their own households. By 1971, 68.3 per cent of such women did so.

It is important to recognize that there are two problems requiring a solution. The change after 1951 is certainly dramatic and it would be easy to give this all the attention, but equally if not more puzzling is the stability of the previous century or, to be cautious, the similarity between 1851 or 1861 and 1951, given the economic and social change engendered by the growth of towns, the development of the new types of employment and the decline of old ones such as working on the land.

Britain's recent experience, it will be no surprise, has not been unique. It is known that parallel developments in recent years have taken place in the rest of Europe, the United States and Japan although the pace of change has not always been the same and has at times eaten its way into quite different family systems. Some of these countries have rather better data at their disposal than it has been possible to assemble for Britain and it is worth listing the factors that have been advanced to explain the break up of the more complex households and the proliferation of one person households. To take the case of Japan, a recent study identified three critical factors behind a decline in households with relatives from 34.7 per cent in 1960 to 29.3 per cent in 1965 and 25.3 per cent in 1970. These were higher proportions employed resulting in geographical mobility and increased life expectancy after the war producing more small households consisting of aged persons.

Such explanations could be equally relevant to the British experience. It has already been demonstrated, for example, how the households of professionals in Great Britain, likely to have had the most experience of higher education and conditioned to mobility through the nature of their employment, were among the least likely to contain relatives. If we now take further guidance from the work that has been done on Britain based principally on headship rates, it can be seen that the various possible explanations can be grouped under four heads, demographic, housing, economic and behavioural. For example, the demographic explanation would be that the proportion of households with relatives has fallen only because increased life expectancy has added to the number of households least likely to contain relatives; added perhaps a totally new phase to the life cycle. Hole and Pountney say that it was demographic factors that had kept headship rates steady up to 1951, thereafter they appear to give greater weight to the second factor, housing. The relevance of housing seems patently obvious. If it is not available people will have to crowd together: conversely as slum clearance programmes are implemented and housing provided for elderly persons, so overcrowding falls and the headship rate of the elderly rises. In practice the relationship between new housing and new households is not so straightforward. After all it is not so much the total stock of housing that counts but the availability of a suitable house at the time that an individual wishes to form a household. There is also the problem that exercised Hole and Pountney so strongly: that the housing market has continued to provide houses suitable for 'families', indeed that the housing stock has in fact become more homogenous in terms of size, at the same time as the *household* has fragmented into smaller and smaller units. Not all of this is to be accounted for by an attempt to meet the demand for greater space in the home and the consequence has been an increasing disjuncture between housing provision and housing needs.

Neither is it particularly easy to settle the importance of economic and behavioural factors. The underlying assumption behind Block's study, for example, is that people have long valued privacy. Accordingly there would be no behavioural change when in the 1950s their wishes were, with rising incomes, translated into independent households and significantly, a recent study of trends in living arrangements in the United States (Michael et al. 1980) has singled out income as the chief factor behind the rise since 1950 in the number of young adults (25-34) and elderly widows (65+) living alone. The difficulty comes from the fact that living standards have risen generally if not consistently from the 1860s. Supporters of economic based arguments have therefore had to think in terms of a certain (but undefined) 'income threshold', set in the 1940s for the United States, in the 1950s perhaps, for Britain, when the rise in the living standards was first translated into separate living accommodation. The behavioural model also has to cope with the question of whose behaviour has changed; is it the decision of the person who would have taken in the relative, or that of the potential lodger-relative, or even a joint decision by the two (or more) persons not to co-reside? To take a particular example: are more of the elderly living alone because of the excellence of the state's social services or because their children are more tied than were past generations of children to their own concerns and do not wish any longer to open their homes to their parents? This is a question which research has not yet been able to solve although on it depends the whole issue of whether one should respond positively or negatively to an increase in 'living alone'.

To the general debate previously based for the most part on the analysis of headship rates this paper has added three new elements: a longer temporal perspective, and the links between the proportion of households with relatives and specific regions and socio-economic groups. Most of the earlier arguments, it will have been seen, were framed with the intention of explaining temporal change, yet the temporal perspective has often been short, and, even when historical evidence has been introduced, it has been considered very briefly, avowedly to allow more time for interpretation of the present. The full significance of the fact that many people lived alone in nineteenth-century Britain (in the sense that they were lodgers) has not therefore been fully appreciated. Viewed from this perspective, some of the rise after 1951 in one person households merely reflects the fact that people now have more living space at their disposal. It has been our contention that this constitutes a more dramatic development than any change that may have overtaken the frequency with which households encompassed relatives. It is important to make it clear, though, that the creation of these new households has, of course, influenced the proportion of households with relatives, even if it took no relatives out of the households with relatives, simply by expanding the total number of households. In addition, there can be no doubt that after 1961 the household has fragmented in more ways than could be accounted for by disappearing lodgers, although the process is certainly not fully understood. Income may indeed be the critical factor but in what circumstances it is expended on housing, and by whom, in a situation where they might otherwise co-reside, is far from clear. The decline in the proportion of households with relatives has also to be interpreted in conjunction with the association of the presence of relatives in the household with specific regions and socio-economic groups.

Both the variations by socio-economic group and by region in the frequency with which households contain relatives need, though, to be kept in perspective since the differences between individual socio-economic groups and regions are rather fine. Could there be a tradition of extended family living in particular areas? The balance of the evidence presented above is rather against it in that it is very difficult to conceive of factors which could link together the very diverse regions and the socio-economic groups which share the same pattern of taking in relatives. For example, what sort of bond should be looked for common to the people of mid-Wales and those of Merseyside?

One possibility worth considering is that there are variations between these regions in the type of relative taken into the household, variations that we have missed in this paper by focusing on relatives as a group. For want of detailed evidence it has been necessary to group all relatives together, but it is an open question whether it is the same process that brings into the household siblings, parents and married offspring. Admittedly a limited sort of breakdown for the 1971 figures can be carried out, separating for instance one-family households with relatives from no-family or two-family households. Some of this can be quite revealing. For example there is some sign that two-family households formed a higher proportion of the households with relatives in coalmining areas (the rank order of the sub-regions shows the five leading areas to include South Yorkshire and the Yorkshire coalfield, the Nottingham-Derbyshire coalfield and the Central and Eastern valleys of South Wales and West South Wales).

None of this, however, can compensate for the absence of precise information on relationship to the household head. When this is available, as in the analysis of the 1851 enumerators' schedules, it is possible to show that the regions varied not only in terms of the size of the kin element in the household but also in terms of the type of relative present, even down to such details as nieces rather than nephews in some areas and the reverse in others. This element of the household is certainly small and the relationship between the household and the degree of co-operation with the kin outside it, is of unknown quality. Nevertheless the taking into the household of relatives involves from any point of view a major commitment of resources and in identifying variations in the type of relative at regional level we are picking up an important aspect of the family system. If the same should hold true for 1971, it might seem that we have suggested a spurious unity in establishing the proportion of households with relatives as a defining characteristic of an area. On the other hand, all these 'extras' are bound to the households by ties of kinship. It is, therefore, meaningful to group relatives together under a general category of 'persons related to the head of the household', just as one might measure the number of servants per household despite the differences in their precise functions in the household.

The decision to look at all relatives is in any case forced upon us by the lack of relevant information and it is to be hoped that OPCS will, with the 1981 and later censuses, provide some of the tabulations that would be necessary. Preferably these should be produced at a lower level of aggregation than that of the region or sub-region which, although based in part on the planning region and therefore having some logic, is in many ways an unsatisfactorily large unit of analysis. Smaller areas, however, will inevitably mean smaller numbers and a whole battery of new techniques involving simulation of household structures in a given set of demographic and economic circumstances, will have to be developed to distinguish random variation from variation that implies a different set of norms regarding co-residence. There is also a need to consider carefully how far it is possible to infer from all this how household structures may evolve in the immediate future. Students of British headship rates are generally agreed that there is room for further rises, particularly at the younger ages and the latest surveys (General Household Survey 1980 containing data for 1978) are still showing a further fragmentation of households. However, it would be unwise to predict rapid change in the future simply on the basis of rapid change in the past. If it is income level in relation to the cost of 'adequate' housing that has sparked off the changes to the household of recent times, then we may find that if the economy takes a further nose dive, there is a halt to further fragmentation and, within some sections of the population, a resurgence of the extended family.

Table 1 *Households containing relatives: Great Britain 1851-1971 Regions.*

1851

Region	Mean relatives per household
North	0.37
Yorkshire-Humberside	0.34
North West	0.31
East Midlands	0.28
West Midlands	0.36
East Anglia	0.33
Greater London	0.26
Remainder of South East	0.29
South West	0.25
Wales	0.24
Scotland	0.38

1951

Region	Proportion of households with relatives
Northern	15.0
Yorks: East & West Ridings	14.2
North Western	16.3
North Midland	14.1
Midland	15.5
Eastern	14.2
London and South East	12.9
Southern	14.2
South West	15.4
Wales	17.3
Scotland	14.1

1961

Region	Proportion of households with relatives
Northern	12.1
Yorks: East & West Ridings	10.2
North West	12.4
North Midland	9.9
Midland	12.0
Eastern	9.9
Greater London	11.4
Remainder of South East	11.0
Southern	11.2
South West	12.1
Wales	16.1
Scotland	12.3

1971

Region	Proportion of households with relatives
North	8.1
Yorkshire-Humberside	6.9
North West	8.8
East Midlands	7.0
West Midlands	8.2
East Anglia	6.5
Greater London	8.0
Remainder of South East	7.3
South West	8.4
Wales	11.6
Scotland	9.1

Sources
1851. One in four sub-sample of 2 per cent sample of enumeration districts
(yielding 178 disctricts). Data in machine-readable form deposited by
Michael Anderson at SSRC Survey Archive, University of Essex. I am
grateful to Michael Anderson of the University of Edinburgh for granting
access to the data and to Ros Davies for further programming undertaken
at the SSRC Cambridge Group.

1951. Calculated from *Census of England and Wales 1951 Housing Report* Appendix A, tables A1, A5; and *Census of England and Wales 1951. 1 per cent sample tables*, part II, section VI, table vi:8

1961. Figures for England and Wales calculated from *Census of England and Wales 1961. 10 per cent sample. Household composition tables*, table 26, Households containing children, persons of pensionable age (distinguishing non-earners) and domestic servants by household type. Figures for Scotland calculated from *Census of Scotland 1961, 10 per cent sample. Household composition tables*, vol. IV, part II, table no. and title as for England and Wales.

1971. Figures for England and Wales calculated from *Census of England and Wales 1971. 10 per cent sample. Household composition tables*, table 13. Figures for Scotland calculated from *Census of Scotland 1971. 10 per cent sample Household composition tables*, table 26.

For details on the calculations and guidance on the delineation of the regions see the chapter by Wall above, and especially figures 3-6.

Table 2   *Number and proportion of households with relatives: Great Britain 1971 Economic planning sub-regions*

Region	Sub-region	Total households	Households with relatives	
			No.	%
North	Industrial North East			
	North	54,612	4,234	7.8
	South	29,802	2,259	7.6
	Rural North East			
	North	4,703	406	8.6
	South	9,538	718	7.5
	Cumberland & Westmorland	12,130	1,231	10.1
Yorkshire and Humberside	North Humberside	15,939	1,051	6.6
	South Humberside	10,422	754	7.2
	Mid-Yorkshire	14,466	1,022	7.1
	South Lindsey	5,269	332	6.3
	South Yorkshire	26,179	1,783	6.8
	Yorkshire Coalfield	25,981	1,605	6.2
	West Yorkshire	67,832	4,496	6.6
North West	South Cheshire	18,320	1,396	7.6
	South Lancashire	21,838	1,793	8.2
	Manchester	85,479	6,699	7.8
	Merseyside	55,992	5,659	10.1
	Furness	3,714	353	9.5
	Fylde	10,857	1,072	9.9
	Lancaster	4,333	402	9.3
	Mid-Lancashire	11,010	876	8.0
	North East Lancashire	17,051	1,301	7.6
East Midlands	Nottingham & Derby Coalfield	25,642	1,886	7.4
	Nottingham-Derby	35,021	2,212	6.3
	Leicester	24,870	1,782	7.2
	Eastern Lowlands	13,621	899	6.6
	Northampton	15,912	991	6.2
West Midlands	Central			
	North	19,384	1,304	6.7
	South	19,841	1,450	7.3
	Conurbation	78,439	6,755	8.6
	Coventry Belt	22,642	1,535	6.8
	Rural West	11,015	946	8.6
	North Staffordshire	17,251	1,429	8.3

Table 2 *Continued*

Region	Sub-region	Total Households	Households with relatives	
			No.	%
East Anglia	South East	13,118	879	6.7
	North East	21,326	1,331	6.2
	North West	10,536	716	6.8
	South West	12,257	713	5.8
South East	Greater London	266,874	21,472	8.0
	Outer Metropolitan			
	West	31,679	2,297	7.2
	North	37,883	2,416	6.4
	East	31,517	2,119	6.8
	South East	25,681	1,670	6.5
	South	20,691	1,470	7.1
	South West	25,752	1,878	7.3
	Outer South East			
	Essex	14,335	876	6.1
	Kent	22,148	1,597	7.2
	Sussex Coast	37,053	2,776	7.5
	Solent	55,819	4,278	7.7
	Beds & Bucks	9,976	673	6.7
	Berks & Oxon	16,671	1,173	7.0
South West	Central	24,812	1,917	7.7
	Southern	28,749	2,544	8.8
	Western	16,807	1,581	9.4
	North Gloucestershire	15,596	1,248	8.0
	Bristol-Severnside	31,654	2,545	8.0
	North Wiltshire	11,311	779	6.9
Wales	Central and Eastern Valleys	21,008	2,715	12.9
	West South Wales	15,503	2,117	13.6
	Coastal Belt	23,936	2,438	10.2
	North East Wales	7,594	632	8.3
	North Coast	4,294	395	9.2
	Remainder North Wales	7,749	788	10.2
	Central Wales	2,811	305	10.8
	South West Wales	7,623	925	12.1
Scotland	North East	14,829	1,315	8.9
	Highlands	8,896	1,186	13.3
	Tayside	15,557	1,151	7.4
	Edinburgh	34,531	2,746	8.0
	Falkirk	8,010	647	8.1

Table 2   *Continued*
Economic planning sub-regions

Region		Total Households	Households with relatives	
			No.	%
	Glasgow	79,531	7,636	9.6
	South West	4,866	492	10.1
	Borders	3,608	335	9.3
England		1,571,350	122,517	7.8
Scotland		169,828	15,508	9.1
Wales		90,538	10,471	11.6

Sources

10 per cent sample. Figures for England and Wales calculated from unpublished extension to *Census 1971 Household composition tables*, table 13, Households containing dependent children, persons of pensionable age and domestic servants by household type, available for the cost of reproduction from Customer Services, Census Office, OPCS, Titchfield, Fareham, Hants PO 15 5RR. Figures for Scotland calculated from Unpublished Table 644, Households containing dependent children, persons of pensionable age and domestic servants by household type, available for the cost of reproduction from General Register Office for Scotland, Ladywell House, Ladywell Road, Edinburgh EH 12 7TF.

Table 3   *Number and proportion of households with relatives by social class and socio-economic group: England and Wales 1971*

	Total Households	Households with relatives	
		No.	%
Social class			
I Professional, etc. occupations	71,127	3,964	5.6
II Intermediate occupations	288,619	22,413	7.8
III(N) Skilled occupations: non-manual	1,206,574	17,591	8.5
III(M) Skilled occupations: manual	501,629	42,193	8.4
IV Partly skilled occupations	266,350	25,259	9.5
V Unskilled occupations	107,771	11,327	10.5
Not classified	128,541	8,556	6.6
Socio-economic group			
1 Employers and managers in industry, commerce, etc: large establishments	59,219	4,238	7.2
2 Employers and managers in industry, commerce, etc: small establishments	129,377	9,656	7.5
3 Professional workers: self employed	13,540	784	5.8
4 Professional workers: employees	57,587	3,071	5.3

Table 3 *Continued*

	Total Households	Households with relatives	
		No.	%
5 Intermediate non-manual workers (auxiliary workers, artists, foremen and supervisors non-manual)	98,735	6,816	6.9
6 Junior non-manual workers	210,394	17,615	8.4
7 Personal service workers	33,790	2,999	8.9
8 Foremen and supervisors: manual	56,466	4,573	8.1
9 Skilled manual workers	382,886	31,248	8.2
10 Semi-skilled manual workers	187,038	17,600	9.4
11 Unskilled manual workers	103,662	10,573	10.2
12 Own account workers (non-professional)	68,064	5,457	8.0
13 Farmers: employers and managers	12,226	1,123	9.2
14 Farmers: own account	11,656	1,541	13.2
15 Agricultural workers	17,430	1,372	7.9
16 Members of armed forces	14,962	512	3.4
17 Inadequately described occupations	113,579	7,880	6.9
Retired	258,104	15,363	6.0
Students	5,256	178	3.3
Others economically inactive	86,021	2,391	2.8

Source

Calculated from *Census of England and Wales 1971*, 10 per cent sample, Unpublished table 621 U, Household by type and size and by social class and socio-economic class of chief economic supporter. Unpublished tables are available for the cost of reproduction from Customer Services, Census Office, Office of Population Censuses and Surveys, Titchfield, Fareham, Hants PO15 5RR

Further reading

M. Anderson, *Family structure in nineteenth century Lancashire*, Cambridge University Press, Cambridge, 1971. This remains the most thorough study of household and family structure in an English town of the nineteenth century (Preston in 1851). Its particular excellence lies in the theoretical perspective on the motives for co-residence.

W. A. Armstrong, 'A note on the household structure of mid-nineteenth century York in comparative perspective' in P. Laslett, and R. Wall, eds, *Household and family in past time*, Cambridge University Press, Cambridge, 1972, contains a comparison of various attributes of households in York in 1851 and pre-industrial England with a summary of the special analysis of household structure in 14 enumeration districts carried out in conjunction with the census of 1851.

A. Block, *Estimating Housing Needs*, The Architectural Press, London, 1946, surveys trends in household size and structure (using a ratio of adults to households) in England and Wales between 1861 and 1931 coming to the conclusion that one-person households had been consistently under-enumerated and that many people had been deprived of the possibility of forming households because of a lack of suitable accommodation.

T. K. Birch, 'The index of overall headship: a simple measure of household complexity standardized for age and sex', *Demography*, no.17(1), February 1980, pp. 25-37. The paper develops and tests an age-sex standardized measure of household complexity, defined broadly as the tendency of adults (other than spouses) to head households or to share households. Results are presented for 33 countries *c.*1960.

H. Doering, 'Die wirtschaftliche und sociale struktur der Drei-Gene-rationen-Familie. Bisherige Entwicklung und Künftige Gestaltungsmo-glichkeiten unter bevölkerungspolitischern Aspekt', *Materialien zur Bevölkerungswissenschaft*, Heft 14, Bundesinstitut für Bevölkerungsforshung, Wiesbaden, 1979. This is rather more comprehensive than its title suggests, containing many detailed tables on the structure of the household in West Germany since 1949.

W. V. Hole and M. T. Pountney, *Trends in population housing and occupancy rates 1861-1961*, Department of the Environment, Building Research Station, HMSO, 1971,discusses the relevance to the British situation of a number of factors that influence household composition, namely, kinship organization, demographic structure of the population, the financial re-sources of the group or individual and the availability of housing. 1951 headship rates are projected back to 1861 and forward to 1966 and compared with the actual numbers of households. There is also a useful comparison between the structure of the household in the 14 sub-districts originally undertaken in 1861 and in the 1 per cent sample for Great Britain in 1951.

A. E. Holmans, 'Housing tenure in England and Wales: the present situation and recent trends', *Social Trends*, 9, 1979, covers the period 1961-1976 and notes an increasing tendency of the elderly to live on their own and a substantial fall in the number of young married couples living with their parents, but does not offer a detailed breakdown of household membership.

W. F. F. Kemsley, *The Family Expenditure Survey. Handbook on the Sample, Fieldwork and Coding Procedures,* HMSO, 1969, is indispensable for anyone wishing to make use of the data collected as part of the survey.

P. Laslett, 'Mean household size in England since the sixteenth century' in P. Laslett and R. Wall, eds., *Household and Family in Past Time*, Cambridge University Press, Cambridge, 1972. An analysis of the main elements of the household in pre-industrial England which established that house-holds had not been particularly large or complex.

C. M. Law, and A. M. Warnes, 'The changing geography of the elderly in England and Wales', *Institute of British Geographers*, new series, no.1(4), 1976, pp. 453-71, charts the development of retirement areas since 1951.

R. T. Michael, V. R. Fuchs, and S. R. Scott, 'Changes in the propensity to live alone: 1950-1976', *Demography,* no.17(1), February 1980, pp. 39-56.

This suggests that the growth of income has been the primary cause of the increasing numbers of single men and women 25-34 and elderly widows living alone in the United States. Other variables found to effect positively the propensity to live alone included mobility, schooling level and for younger people, a liberal social climate identified by state legislation on abortion in 1970.

E. Nakano, and N. Ikenoue, 'A demographic analysis of the change of family type', *Jinko Mondai Kenkyu,* no.149. January 1979, pp. 1-15. The article is in Japanese with an English summary (translation of table titles on the copy, in the library of the SSRC Cambridge Group). The authors point to increased employment participation, greater opportunities in higher education and increased life expectancy as the causes of the simplification of household types in Japan since 1935.

Office of Population Censuses and Surveys, *General Household Survey 1976,* HMSO, 1978. In addition to the figures the survey includes some commentary on changes in household structure in England and Wales since 1971. It is fuller than the survey by Holmans (above).

Organisation for Economic Co-operation and Development, Centre for Educational Research and Innovation, Le Bras, H., ed., *Child and Family: Demographic Developments in the OECD Countries,* OECD, Paris, 1979. This is a comparative study of the composition of households and families based on census data from 20 countries, mainly for the 1970s but with some earlier material. It is particularly valuable because of its reproduction of various detailed tabulations that would otherwise have to be sought in the publications of the respective countries and for its notes on the way in which key definitions of the household vary from country to country.

M. Plessis-Fraissard, 'Households: a review of definitions, trends and forecasting methods', *School of Geography, University of Leeds, Working Paper No.164,* 1976 is an analysis based on headship rates for England and Wales showing stability of rates in the first half of the twentieth century, and important changes thereafter, caused by the increase of non-family households.

M. Stacey, et al., *Power, Persistence and Change. A Second Study of Banbury,* Routledge, 1975. This would appear to be the only study at the level of the individual community which has provided a detailed assessment of the extent to which the composition of the household has changed since 1950 and some reasons for the change.

R. Wall, 'Regional and temporal variations in English household structure from 1650', in J. Hobcraft, and P. Rees, *Regional Demographic Development,* Croom Helm, London, 1979, supplements the analysis by Laslett (see above). It documents variation in household structure in England between the seventeenth and nineteenth centuries and between five contrasting areas (London, Southampton, Shrewsbury, East Kent and East Wiltshire) *c.*1700.

The decline of mortality in Britain 1870-1950

J. M. WINTER

The decline of mortality in Britain in the period 1870-1950 was on a scale both unprecedented and dramatic. In roughly three generations, crude death rates (deaths per 1000 population per year) were halved, infant mortality rates (deaths per 1000 live births per year) were reduced by 80 per cent, and mortality at all ages due to infectious diseases was reduced by approximately 90 per cent. Another way of measuring this astonishing change is in terms of life expectation at birth, which in England and Wales in 1861 stood at 40.5 years for men and 43.0 years for women. Sixty years later, after the First World War, the 50-year mark was passed for women but not yet for men. Ten more years were added to life expectation at birth for both sexes by 1951. It was only in the 1960s that infants born in England and Wales were likely to survive to the Biblical lifespan of threescore years and ten.

The full effect of these changes in survival rates may be gauged by noting that in 1947, approximately 590,000 people died in England and Wales. Had the death rates of a century earlier prevailed, over half a million more would have died.[1] In 1950, 95 out of every 100 children born in England and Wales survived to the age of five. In 1860, only 70 did so.[2] The elimination over less than a century of much of this toll of suffering and bereavement is one of the most important chapters in the social history of this country. It is the purpose of this essay to describe the process of mortality decline and to discuss the complex interplay of forces which brought it about.

Mortality decline: dimensions and components

I International comparisons
Mortality decline was an international phenomenon. The increase

in life chances among Europeans since the middle of the nineteenth century was probably greater than the total gains made over the previous millenium. Everywhere in Western Europe the pace of improvement accelerated after 1900, and the gap in mortality experience between and among European nations narrowed. As Table 1 demonstrates, at the turn of this century, the rank order of the four major European countries in terms of life expectation at birth was England and Wales first, at about 45 years for men and 49 years for women, followed by France, Germany, and Italy. It is a chastening thought to observe that even after at least a generation of improvement in mortality rates, these nations were all at or below the level reached by Guatamala in 1963-5 and India in 1966-70. In Europe by the 1930s, Germany had taken the lead in life expectation at birth, registering approximately 60 years for men and 63 for women. England and Wales, Italy, and France followed in that order. These pre-Second World War improvements had brought life expectation in industrialized Europe to approximately the level reached by Tunisia in 1960 and Colombia in 1965. By the 1960s, the four major European nations virtually had converged in terms of mortality experience. Throughout this period, though, the Scandinavian countries and the Netherlands were consistently ahead of the rest of the Continent in terms of life expectation at birth. Despite such variations, it is clear that the decline of mortality in Britain was part of a wider process in which all European nations took part and from which all have benefited.[3]

Within Great Britain, aggregate mortality decline has meant a reduction in national variations. The one major exception to this rule is that in the nineteenth century, Scottish death rates were slightly lower than English and Welsh death rates, but higher after 1900. Probably originating in the comparatively late urbanization of central Scotland, this Scottish disadvantage in this century persists to the present day. The experience of Wales has not departed significantly from that of England, in part because the high mortality of coal mining regions was balanced by the low mortality of Welsh agrarian regions.

II Regional variations and uniformities in mortality patterns
Regional variations within England were significant throughout the period under review, but they diminished during the twentieth century. In 1859 Dr Farr published life tables based on the mortality experience of 63 districts, the death rate of each of which did not exceed 17.5. The crude death rate for England and Wales in 1861 was over 22. The selected villages and towns were denoted 'healthy' districts. It should cause no surprise that almost all were

Table 1   *Life Expectation at Birth in Selected Countries, 1900-1970*

Country	Date	Life Expectation at Birth Males	Life Expectation at Birth Females
England & Wales	1901	45.3	49.4
France	1898-1903	45.3	47.0
Germany	1901-1910	44.8	46.6
Italy	1901-1911	44.2	44.5
Guatemala	1963-1965	48.3	49.7
India	1966-1970	48.9	46.2
Germany	1932-1934	59.9	62.8
England & Wales	1931	58.2	62.4
Italy	1935-1937	55.3	57.5
France	1928-1938	55.1	60.3
Tunisia	1960	55.7	63.2
Colombia	1965	58.2	61.7
Norway	1967	71.3	76.9
Denmark	1967	70.7	75.4
Holland	1967	71.2	76.6
England & Wales	1960	68.2	74.1
Italy	1966	68.4	74.2
W Germany	1964-1965	67.6	73.5
France	1965	67.8	75.0

Sources

S. Preston, *Mortality Patterns in National Populations*, pp. 84-87; S. Preston, N. Keyfitz and R. Schoen, *Causes of Death: Life Tables for National Populations* (New York, 1972), pp. 224-67.

agricultural. A later study of these same areas showed that, unaffected by industrialization, these districts retained their 25 per cent advantage in death rates over the rest of England and Wales until 1901-10. By 1925, though, their lead had been halved. This implies not a deterioration in rural conditions, but rather a quickening in the pace of improvement in urban areas that had been particularly unhealthy in the nineteenth century.[4] There seems little doubt that urbanization and the flight from the land in the late nineteenth century acted as obstacles to more rapid rates of decline in mortality. By 1950, the urban environment in Britain had been significantly sanitized and offered city dwellers certain advantages in health care unavailable in the countryside.

One of the most striking features of recent research has been that within England, different regions experienced mortality decline as a unity. That is to say, in areas as distinct as Northumberland and Cornwall, all parts of each region showed the same downward trend over time.[5] Period rates of decline varied depending on how high mortality was in 1870. In general Northern and Western countries had higher death rates than Southern and Eastern counties in England, but within each region, there were no leading sectors. Within London too the downward trend in mortality rates has been remarkably uniform. In other words, boroughs with the highest and lowest death rates early in this century retained the same relative positions in the 1950s.[6]

The process of mortality decline, therefore, had distinctive international, national, and regional characteristics. Concentration on aggregate behaviour, defined geographically, while unavoidable and essential, should not obscure important variations in the mortality experience of different age groups, of the two sexes, of different occupational groups and different social classes. Any attempt to provide even a rough outline of these demographic developments must deal with each in turn.

III Age differentials

Mortality decline was restricted initially to children, adolescents, and young adults. The onset of aggregate decline in death rates in the 1870s can be ascribed almost entirely to improvements in the life chances of people aged 2-35. Twenty years later, older adults (aged 35-65) began to register significantly lower death rates. Finally, only after the turn of the twentieth century did infant mortality rates and death rates for the elderly begin to drop. It is hardly surprising that the more vulnerable groups at the extremities of age should lag behind in the process of mortality decline.

IV Sex differentials

Male mortality rates exceeded those of females throughout the period 1870-1950.[7] This sex differential rose significantly in the twentieth century; thus the gap has widened between male and female life expectation at birth and at all other ages. Here the British experience differed from that of countries which industrialized later, where mortality differentials were less favourable to women.[8] Since male foetal wastage rates and male neonatal mortality rates are apparently always greater than the equivalent female rates, part of the sex differential in mortality rates must be biological in origin. Within genetically determined parameters, though, sex differentials do reflect variations in conditions which affect males and females in different ways or to different degrees.

Women, of course, faced special risks in childbirth, in particular, a virulent haemolytic streptococcal infection classed under the heading of puerperal fever. Case fatality rates for this disease were extremely high and account for the stubborn persistence of maternal mortality rates at about four per 1000 live births until the mid-1930s, two generations after adult death rates began their descent and one generation after infant mortality rates began to drop. Treatment with prontosil, the first of the sulphonamide drugs, from 1936, finally enabled doctors to control this lethal disease.[9]

Even in the 1860s, maternal mortality was not a major component of the pattern of female mortality. Had all such deaths in childbirth been eliminated in 1861, it would have added only six months to the average female life span. The elimination of respiratory tuberculosis, on the other hand, would have added over four years to the average female life span.[10] Pregnancy and labour are, after all, natural rather than pathological events.

In the twentieth century, there were special reasons why at certain ages, the sex differential in mortality rates rose strikingly. The most important case is that of age groups from which the bulk of soldiers who fought in the 1914-18 war were recruited. In that war approximately 750,000 men were killed or died in uniform and over 1,200,000 were wounded or otherwise disabled.[11] The ratio of male to female mortality rates at late middle age during the interwar years and after was much greater than the equivalent ratios for the same age groups at the end of the nineteenth century. For example, the ratio of male to female death rates in 1896-1900 for the 45-64 and 65-75 age groups were 1.29 and 1.24 respectively. In 1948 the differential for these two age groups was 1.55 and 1.77 respectively.[12] Here we see an indication of the way that the Great War helped to produce a 'burnt-out' generation of men who were either disabled during the war or unfit to fight in it. Any study of population change in twentieth-century Europe is incomplete without the recognition of the magnitude of the impact of war on the male cohorts which bore its burdens during the conflict and in its aftermath. Because of improvements in medical care and in chemotherapy as well as a change in military strategy, there was no such shadow effect in Britain as a consequence of the Second World War.

V Occupational and class differentials

When we turn from variations in mortality patterns by age and sex to occupational and class differentials, we enter an area of much greater controversy. One dispute is over the effects of female employment on female mortality rates and on stillbirth and infant mortality rates. Some contemporaries blame working women for infant disease and death.[13] In more recent times, some scholars unaffected by the ideology of domesticity have found a statistically significant correlation between infant mortality rates and female employment rates.[14] Others have argued that the additional income generated by female labour kept women and children alive.[15] Probably both arguments hold true in different cases, depending on what sort of work women did and how low their family income was without the woman's contribution. It seems likely, though, that for many working-class women, any work, whatever the pathogenic risks associated with it, was better than none at all, since it enabled them to buy essential family food. High female employment rates in both World Wars were consistent with major improvements in infant survival rates.[16]

Another question on which it is difficult to provide a clear-cut answer is whether changes in occupational mortality affected the overall pattern of mortality decline. The major problem here is that it is virtually impossible to separate fully the effect of conditions at work from the effect of conditions at home on male and female mortality. There have been attempts, though, to calculate regression equations which are meant to specify rigorously the exact contribution of work and home environment to mortality rates. Thus, in a study of infant mortality in England and Wales in 1928-38, Woolf argued that female employment in manufacturing industry increased the infant mortality rates by 5.3 deaths per 1000 live births. The increase attributable to overcrowding was 13.8; to low wages, 10.3; and to unemployment, 8.0 per 1000 live births per year. The remainder formed a residual unaffected by adverse social conditions.[17] There were two strong reasons, though, why it is impossible to accept this argument. First, there are technical problems of multivariate analysis of highly intercorrelated statistical series, which vitiate the assumption that each variable has an independent influence on the infant mortality rate.[18] Secondly, even accepting for a moment the statistical basis of the case, the residual of 23 deaths per 1000 live births is not an irreducible minimum and has been halved in the years since the Second World War.

Other doubts about attempts to correlate occupation and mortality are raised by an examination of statistics on the death rates of the wives of men who worked in particular occupations. If work was the decisive factor in variations in mortality patterns, it should be possible to measure, as Percy Stocks argued, 'to what extent the mortality of men engaged in the occupation is affected over and above that of married women who share the general environmental handicaps or disadvantages of the group'. He showed conclusively that in many cases the mortality experience of working-class married women who did not work out of the home was very similar to that of their working husbands. From this he concluded that the direct effects of work are much less significant than the indirect effects of environment on changes in mortality rates.[19]

For these reasons it is not possible to sustain the argument that a change in the occupational structure of itself was responsible for the decline of mortality in Britain. There are other grounds too for rejecting this claim. It is well known that coal mining communities have high mortality rates at all ages. The secular decline in the death rate in Britain occurred, though, precisely in the period of maximum expansion of coal mining and related heavy industry.

None of the above is meant to suggest that manual workers registered lower death rates than did non-manual workers or the self-employed. The contrary is, of course, true, but we must look beyond the work experience itself in order to appreciate the demographic implications of social inequality in nineteenth- and twentieth-century Britain. In this context it is necessary to describe variations in mortality by social class.

Since the 1920s Registrars-General have employed a five-tiered taxonomy of social classes. While it is true that this framework is essentially a re-ordering of occupations, and an arbitrary one at

Table 2 *Legitimate Infant Mortality Rates, England and Wales, 1911, 1920-2, 1930-2 and 1939, with Respect to Excess Mortality in Social Class V compared to Social Class I*

	1911	1920-2	1930-2	1939
		Neonatal Mortality		
Class V	42.5	36.9	32.5	30.1
Class I	30.2	23.4	21.7	18.9
Excess	12.3	13.5	10.8	11.2
% Excess	40.7	57.7	49.7	59.3
		Post-neonatal Mortality		
Class V	110.0	60.1	44.5	30.0
Class I	46.2	15.0	11.0	8.0
Excess	63.8	45.1	33.5	22.0
% Excess	138.1	300.1	304.5	275.0
		Mortality at 6-12 Months		
Class V	50.0	24.6	19.4	10.4
Class I	18.3	5.8	3.6	2.3
Excess	31.7	18.8	15.8	8.1
% Excess	173.2	324.1	438.9	352.2
		Infant Mortality		
Class V	152.5	97.0	77.0	60.1
Class I	76.4	38.4	32.7	26.9
Excess	76.1	58.6	44.3	33.2
% Excess	99.6	152.6	135.5	123.4

Sources
R. Titmuss, *Birth, Poverty and Wealth* (1943), pp. 44-5; *Registrar-General's Decennial Supplement. England and Wales 1931. Part IIB. Occupational Fertility. 1931 and 1939,* Table Q1, p. 86.

that, into the categories independent (I), intermediate (II), skilled manual (III), semi-skilled manual (IV), and unskilled manual workers (V), these distinctions do have two major attractions. First, they suggest that people who earn a living in similar ways, such as carpenters and electricians, have important similarities in their way of life outside of work. Secondly, they correspond roughly to perceptions of relative social status in what was in 1870 (and remains today) the most class-conscious nation in Europe.

Through the use of this framework, we can see evidence of the demographic disadvantage of being born into a workingman's family in Britain in the period under review. As is clearly illustrated in Table 2, in 1911 the mortality rate of infants born to the families of unskilled workers was double that of infants born to professional men's families. Between 1911 and 1939 the aggregate infant mortality rate for England and Wales dropped from 130 to 51 deaths per 1000 live births per year. Yet over the same period, the advantage of Class I over Class V babies had not only been maintained but actually increased. This was only marginally true in the first month of life, when congenital abnormalities and prematurity cause most deaths. At aged 6-12 months, though, when most babies have been weaned and lose the protection of their mothers' antibodies infectious diseases predominate. At this period of life, the advantage in survival chances which infants of well-to-do families had over those of poorer families increased substantially. The gap narrowed slightly in the 1930s. Still, in the years 1911-39, the most deprived benefited least from improvements in conditions leading to a decline in infant mortality in the nation as a whole. Aggregate demographic improvement was consistent, therefore, with deepening demographic inequality in twentieth-century Britain.[20]

VI Mortality decline by cause of death

Thanks to the scholarship of Professor Thomas McKeown and his co-workers, we can establish precisely the contribution made by individual causes of death to overall mortality decline. McKeown distinguishes between deaths caused by micro-organisms and others. In the former case, he separates for analysis deaths attributable to micro-organism by vectors of transmission. Between 1848-54 and 1971, airborne diseases were responsible for over two-fifths of the reduction of deaths from all causes. Of all such infections, respiratory tuberculosis was by far the most important, alone accounting for over a sixth of the total mortality decline. Bronchitis, pneumonia, and influenza together accounted for a tenth of the overall decline, and a similar contribution was made by a mixed group of airborne infections comprising measles, scarlet fever and diphtheria, smallpox, and infections of the ear, nose, and throat. In the same time period, there occurred a decline in mortality due to water- or food-borne infections which added a fifth to the overall decline of mortality rates. In this category, half of the decline was registered in deaths due to cholera, diarrhoea, and dysentery, and the other half to non-respiratory tuberculosis, typhoid, and typhus. A third group of diseases due to infections transmitted in other ways, including convulsions, syphilis, appendicitis, and puerperal fever, accounted for over an eighth of the overall decline.

Conditions not attributable to micro-organisms behaved differently in the period under review. Not all declined. On the one hand heart disease and cancer at all sites have increased so significantly over the past century that we must admit that a real change, rather than merely a shift in diagnostic practice or in the age structure of the population, is involved. On the other hand, deaths due to prematurity, pregnancy, nephritis, and violence have all declined. Together with other more ambiguous causes, such as old age, about a quarter of the total decline in mortality can be attributed to a change in conditions not known to be associated directly with viral or bacterial infection.

In almost all cases, the decline of mortality began well before the introduction of relevant immunization and therapy. For instance, treatment of respiratory tuberculosis by streptomycin began only in 1948, 80 years after the onset of the decline in mortality due to this disease, the 'white plague' of the nineteenth century. In the overall period 1850-1970, streptomycin added only 3 per cent to the total reduction of deaths caused by respiratory tuberculosis. Most other diseases manifested a similar decline decades before specific medical treatment to counteract them was devised and applied. The exceptions are smallpox, for which vaccination and inoculation were available before 1850; puerperal fever, effectively controlled only after the introduction of prontosil in 1936; and appendicitis and related internal disorders, in which case surgical intervention was decisive in the antiseptic age. On balance, though, there is no evidence of synchronism, or of causation, between medical developments and demographic change in this period.[21]

Causes of mortality decline in Britain 1870-1950

Demographers, historians, and doctors have engaged in a number of inconclusive debates about the causes of mortality decline in Britain. Some have stressed nutritional improvements as decisive in the pattern of increasing resistance to infectious disease.[22] Others have pointed to medical or para-medical intervention as key components in the gradual lengthening of life expectation.[23] A third group of writers has emphasized the importance to improvements in public health of the growth of state and local authority support and supervision of health and welfare schemes and institutions.[24] Few suggest that any one factor is exclusively responsible for declining death rates,[25] but there is no consensus about the appropriate weight to be placed on the contribution of each. In this essay, we can only provide synopses of the literature and a few suggestions as to how medical intervention, health administration, and improvements in standards of living combined to permit the extension of life expectation in the period 1870-1950.

I Medical intervention

The most sustained attack on the argument that medical intervention was responsible for the decline of mortality has come from within the medical profession itself. Early in his medical training, Professor McKeown came to doubt the pretensions of those doctors who believed that most of their efforts made their patients any better. He harboured suspicions that there was 'an inverse relation between the interest of a disease to the doctor and the usefulness of its treatment to the patient'. Indeed, he mused, in a tone which reveals the harsh judgemental quality of his argument,

> if I were St Peter, admitting to Heaven on the basis of achievement on earth, I would accept on proof of identity the accident surgeons, the dentists, and, with a few doubts, the obstetricians; all, it should be noted in passing, dealing mainly with healthy people. The rest I would refer to some celestial equivalent of Ellis Island, for close and prolonged inspection of their credentials.[26]

McKeown has spent thirty years on this inspection, and has concluded that medical intervention has affected life expectation in ways that are either negligible or negative.[27] This is largely due to the fact that doctors have acted traditionally on the mistaken assumption that the course of disease depends more on their internal intervention than on those 'external influences and personal behaviour which are the predominant determinants of health'.[28] They have distorted their own importance in the process of mortality decline and have misled historians intimidated or dazzled by the mysteries of the medical profession.

McKeown's argument, while a useful rebuttal to the heroic tradition in the writing of medical history, is as much an overstatement as that which it is intended to displace. His case has its strengths. He has established beyond question that the decline of infectious disease in the nineteenth century antedated the isolation of infective agents and the development of therapeutic measures to deal with them. His position is supported by the fact that in the nineteenth century, and to a smaller extent in more recent times, the majority of the population of this country rarely saw a doctor, whose fee, attitude, and class situation frequently placed his care out of their reach.[29] Some doctors did, of course, vary their fees according to the ability of their clients to pay and some treated the poor for nothing. Poor Law inmates also received medical attention.

The main difficulty with McKeown's argument, though, is that he defines medical intervention too narrowly. He concentrates on the instrumental, chemical, and surgical weapons in the medical arsenal and finds them wanting before the appearance of the sulphonamides in the 1930s. There is much truth in this judgment, but medical intervention also encompasses advice on precisely those areas of personal behaviour and environmental control which McKeown sees as the real determinants of health. When a doctor advises a change in diet or the removal of unsanitary debris, he may very well improve the survival chances of his patients. Simply because doctors do not require a medical education to make such statements is no reason to conclude that such indirect medical intervention was unimportant in the process of mortality decline. The same case could be made for the beneficial effects of the work of nurses, midwives, and health visitors, who may lack the doctor's authority, but also may inspire at times less fear and less resistance to the measures they advocate and enforce. The role of medical and para-medical personnel in educating the population about hygiene and nutrition had a greater significance than McKeown is prepared to allow.

Even within McKeown's terms of reference, there were in the period 1870-1950 developments in medical treatment which may not have initiated but reinforced the process of the control and eradication of infectious and non-infectious disease. Most innovations came after 1900, but some appeared earlier. The improvements in surgical technique which followed the introduction of anaesthesia in the 1850s and of antiseptics in the 1870s saved the lives of some patients, although it may have endangered the lives of others able to survive without surgery.[30] In this century, important medical advances have been in part a function of what Sir Henry Dale called a 'revolution' in the active links between medicine and the experimental sciences, which transformed the relationship between the laboratories and the wards from aloofness to symbiotic collaboration.[31]

The three major areas in which breakthroughs have been made are in immunotherapy, in chemotherapy, and in the treatment of deficiency diseases. Agents of passive immunization were introduced for diphtheria just before the turn of the century and for tetanus on a large scale during the First World War. At the same time an antidysentery serum was developed and used with effect among men in uniform. Active immunization procedure dates from the pioneering work of Jenner and Pasteur, but was extended in this century for the treatment of typhoid, cholera, and tuberculosis. These diseases were in decline, as McKeown notes, long before these developments, but few would deny the importance of the role of immunization in preventing a serious recrudescence of these killer diseases during the political and economic upheavals of this century.

Chemotherapy, too, provided powerful checks against the reversal of gains made in survival rates since 1900. The discovery by Ehrlich and Shiga of the benzidine dye trypan-red in 1903 led to further research which yielded a remedy for trypanosomal sleeping-sickness. Ehrlich was responsible as well for the preparation of salvarsan, an arsenic compound effective in the treatment of syphilis. In the interwar years German scientists isolated a chemical anti-malarial compound, the use of which during the Second World War was crucial due to the occupation by Japan of areas of quinine supply. Since 1936, the use of the sulphonamides and penicillin have eradicated certain infectious diseases, and other drugs like streptomycin and aureomycin have proved effective against infections stubbornly resistant to sulphanylimide derivatives or penicillin.

Our knowledge of the nature of deficiency diseases has grown enormously in this century, and so has the armoury of drugs to deal with them. Treatment of some hormonal deficiencies had begun before 1900, but the major breakthrough was undoubtedly the isolation of insulin by Banting and Best in 1921. In the years which have followed many hormonal preparations have come into medical use in previously untreatable disorders. Similarly, since Mellanby's classic study of rickets, published in 1919, a whole field of vitamin deficiency research and treatment has opened up. As a result we have transformed our ideas about what constitutes an adequate diet.[32] If, as we shall suggest below, nutritional improvements were decisive in the process of mortality decline, then on these grounds too medical research and treatment cannot be dismissed as largely irrelevant to the control of disease and its ravages.

II Health administration

One hundred years separates the passage of the Public Health Act of 1848, and the birth of the National Health Service in 1948. In the intervening period to what extent did local or central administrative action contribute to the process of mortality decline? A full answer to this question is beyond the scope of this essay, but some elements of a reply are clear.

The first point that needs to be made is that the justly famous

Act of 1848 was an emasculated version of an earlier bill introduced the previous year, opposition to the comprehensiveness of which had led to its demise. The General Board of Health which emerged in 1848 had no compulsory powers and left to local authorities the real work of enforcement of sanitary reform. Without a Minister responsible for its actions and without a permanent salaried inspectorate, the Board was effectively impotent, both politically and administratively. In 1854 and 1855 these deficiencies were recognized and to some extent remedied in legislation. The most important aspect of the 1855 Act was the provision for the appointment of a government Medical Officer. The first man to hold this post was John Simon, who had been a successful Medical Officer of Health to the City of London in 1848-54 and who became the towering figure in sanitary reform and public health in the second half of the nineteenth century. In his long and distinguished career, he helped more than any other man to establish the crucial role of permanent medical advice in central government. In twenty years the Board of Health was transformed into the medical department of the Local Government Board and administered, in pursuance of the Acts of 1866 and 1875, a common and comprehensive sanitary code unrivalled in Europe.[33] The real work of sanitary improvement still had to be done by local authorities, which ensured the widest possible variation in the effectiveness of steps taken to provide clean water, regular scavenging, and reliable systems of sewerage disposal.

There is little doubt, nevertheless, that the decline of mortality due to water-borne infections is attributable to publicly enacted improvements in sanitation. Still it was not until the interwar years that water-carriage systems of sewerage disposal displaced privy middens or other conservancy systems in certain parts of the country.[34] Under such conditions it is hardly surprising that infant diarrhoea, transmitted by flies which feed on faeces, remained a scourge of infant health until the second decade of this century. In this context, steps taken to prevent the adulteration of food and protect the purity of milk helped check the spread of food-borne infections such as tuberculosis contracted from contaminated cow's milk.[35]

In other ways, too, the development of health administration helped ensure that the question of disease and the conditions which bred it were permanently in the political arena. In 1837 Dr William Farr was appointed Compiler of Statistics at the new General Register Office, and over the next half century, his annual reports, decennial supplements, and occasional studies gave vital statistics an importance in debates on public health which they have never lost. The foundations laid by Farr have been the basis of the work of many illustrious successors as Registrar-General in helping to educate both Parliament and the public as to the nature of endemic and epidemic diseases and the means necessary to combat them.[36]

In this century administrative developments have advanced from the domain of environmental hygiene to that of personal examination and treatment. The exposure of ill-health among recruits for the British Army during the Boer War helped prepare the way for the provision of school meals for necessitous children in 1906 and for the compulsory medical examination of school children the following year. In 1911 the National Insurance Act provided insurance against sickness or disablement for workers in certain precarious trades and for a 30-shilling maternity benefit for their wives. In the interwar years this act was extended to cover virtually all occupied workers. Its original provisions also covered treatment of insured workers who had contracted tuberculosis and the construction of sanatoria for them. Insurance commissioners were also empowered to support research into tuberculosis and other diseases, which work was carried on after 1920 under the aegis of the Medical Research Council. During the First World War the Local Government Board also helped establish a free service for the diagnosis and treatment of venereal disease and provided funds to local authorities committed to the establishment of infant and maternal welfare centres. In the latter context, acts regulating the education and registration of midwives were passed in 1902 and 1936 which helped improve the management of delivery.

The establishment of the Ministry of Health after the First World War and the emergence of the National Health Service out of the Emergency Medical Services of the Second World War helped unify these diverse strands of work relating to public health. By 1948 the state was finally in a position to plan the development of hospital provision, to extend health centres, and to provide domiciliary visits and help where required. What Aneurin Bevan unveiled during the third Labour government of 1945-51 was an impressive edifice of which any nation would be proud. Still, it is likely that health administration, like medical intervention, played by and large a permissive rather than a decisive role in the decline of mortality over the past century. For, whatever Simon, Farr or any of their distinguished successors were able to accomplish, death rates due to infectious disease would not have fallen had there not been a major improvement in nutrition over the last one hundred years.

III Nutrition and standards of living

Immunization, chemotherapy, and the treatment of deficiency diseases reduced levels of exposure to certain diseases and lowered case-fatality rates in others. The purification of water and food supplies, the provision of safe waste disposal, the paving of roads, and the removal of nuisances and derelict housing helped check the spread of other diseases endemic in the mid-nineteenth century. Medical inspection and treatment of select populations at state expense helped identify people who needed care and made it easier to isolate those who suffered from communicable diseases. All these developments contributed to the decline of mortality in Britain since 1870.

Changes in medical care and health administration, though, were necessary rather than sufficient causes of improvements in life expectation. The decisive variable was nutrition. Whatever the movement of the standard of living of the working population in the crucible years of the industrial revolution from 1780 and 1840, there is no doubt that in the second half of the nineteenth century there occurred a sustained and significant rise in real wages. Working-class children born in the 1850s and 1860s were the first unambiguously to receive some of the fruits of economic growth. As they grew into adolescence and early adulthood, their death rates began to decline and thereby initiated the overall trend. The same generation which married in the 1880s and 1890s were more likely by the turn of the century to give birth to infants with an improved chance of surviving the first year of life. By then fertility rates had fallen to an extent that made it possible to distribute more food to each member of smaller completed families. In this century, the secular improvement in standards of living and in nutritional levels has continued despite shortages imposed by two world wars and chronic unemployment in the interwar period.

Better nutrition meant increased resistance to viral and bacterial infection. Sanitary and medical intervention helped reduce exposure to infection, but of greater importance in the process of mortality decline was the enhancement of recovery rates from endemic diseases. Unfortunately we do not have relevant morbidity and case-fatality statistics and, therefore, cannot prove the argument beyond question. The overwhelming evidence in studies of the synergistic relationship between nutrition and infectious disease[37] leaves little doubt, though, that a sustained decline in mortality rates such as Britain experienced before the 1930s was impossible without major improvements in the quantity and quality of per capita food intake. Of crucial importance here was the opening up of the primary producing areas, together with greater efficiency in retailing which brought about a dramatic fall the price of food. And, after all it was on food that the working classes spent 60 per cent of their income.

These gains were particularly important in reducing the death rate due to airborne infections, which were responsible for more than 40 per cent of overall mortality decline. Overcrowding and other inadequacies of housing no doubt help spread tuberculosis, bronchitis, pneumonia, influenza, whooping cough and scarlet fever, but better nutrition made it possible for more people to recover from these endemic diseases of childhood and later years. The pattern of tuberculosis mortality shows the significance of nutritional change perhaps better than that of other diseases. In Denmark during the First World War, tuberculosis mortality rose until 1917 when the German Navy stopped exports of home-grown produce to Britain and the Allies. A domestic increase in consumption of agricultural goods led to an immediate sharp fall in the death rate due to tuberculosis.[38] In Britain, the death rate from respiratory tuberculosis increased during both world wars and probably reflected the inevitable dislocation of food supplies which followed the outbreak of hostilities. It is clear, though, that the increase in wartime mortality was due to the deaths of those who had already been afflicted with the disease in the pre-war period. These people were particularly vulnerable to relapses in their condition during unsettled times.[39] The fact that there were relatively few new active cases of the disease shows though, that after the administrative tangles of the first months of war were sorted out, pre-war nutritional levels were restored and for many of the poorest sections of society, actually improved substantially.[40] The trend in mortality due to other endemic infections, such as measles, further helps establish the centrality of improved nutrition even during wartime in the process of mortality decline.[41]

Evidence of improved nutrition may also be gathered indirectly from studies of the trend towards earlier physical maturation and towards the long-term increase in age-specific heights and weights of schoolchildren.[42] For example, over the first half of this century, the height of Glasgow five-year olds has increased by about two inches, that of nine-year-olds by three inches, and that of eleven-year-olds by four inches.[43] The cumulative effect of these gains meant that even the severe hardship caused by the world economic crisis of 1929-34 did not reverse the downward trend of mortality rates in the interwar period.[44] Just as the consequences of chronic malnutrition last throughout the lifespan of those who suffer it, so the shadow effect of improvements in nutrition extend well beyond their inception. In this respect our generation and our children's generation are the beneficiaries of cumulative advances in nutritional levels, which, together with sanitary improvements in the nineteenth-century and medical developments in the twentieth century, have reduced the suffering inflicted by disease and the mortality it brings in its wake.

Notes

All works are published in London unless otherwise noted.

[1] W. P. D. Logan, 'Mortality in England and Wales from 1848 to 1947', *Population Studies* (1950), p. 169.

[2] S. Preston, N. Keyfitz and R. Schoen, *Causes of Death* (New York, 1972), pp. 225, 261.

[3] G. Stolnitz, 'A century of international mortality trends: I, *Pop. Stud.* (1956), pp. 27-33. J.-C. Chasteland, 'Evolution générale de la mortalité en Europe occidentale de 1900 à 1950', *Population* (1964). S. Preston, *Mortality Patterns in National Populations* (New York, 1975), pp. 84-7.

[4] E. Lewis-Faning, 'A survey of the mortality in Dr Farr's 63 healthy districts of England and Wales during the period 1851-1925', *Journal of Hygiene* (1930), pp. 121-53.

[5] B. Benson, *Mortality Patterns in the North of England 1851-1900*, unpub. PhD., Johns Hopkins University, 1980. S. Johannsen, *The Demographic Transition in Cornwall, 1840-1910*, unpub. PhD., University of California at Berkeley, 1974.

[6] W. J. Martin, 'Vital statistics of the County of London in the years 1901 to 1951', *British Journal of Preventive and Social Medicine* (1955), p. 134.

[7] R. Ll. Gwilt, 'Mortality in the past hundred years', *Transactions of the Faculty of Actuaries* (1956), p. 77.

[8] G. Stolnitz, 'A century of international mortality trends: II', *Pop. Stud.* (1957), p. 31.

[9] J. M. Winter, 'Infant mortality, maternal mortality, and public health in Britain in the 1930s', *Journal of European Economic History* (1979), p. 458.

[10] Preston et al. *Causes of Death*, p. 227.

[11] J. M Winter, 'Some aspects of the demographic consequences of the First World War in Britain', *Pop. Stud.* (1976), pp. 539-52.

[12] P. Stocks, 'Fifty years of progress as shown by vital statistics', *British Medical Journal* (1950), i, p. 54.

[13] A. Davin, 'Imperialism and motherhood', *History Workshop* (1978), pp. 9-65.

[14] B. Woolf, 'Studies on infant mortality. Part II. Social aetiology of stillbirths and infant deaths in county boroughs of England and Wales', *Br. Jnl. Soc. Med.* (1974), pp. 119-24.

[15] C. Dyhouse, 'Working class mothers and infant mortality in Britain 1895-1914', unpublished paper.

[16] J. M. Winter, 'The impact of the First World War on civilian health in Britain', *Economic History Review* (1977), pp. 492-6. B. Woolf, 'Social conditions and infant mortality', *Mother and Child* (1944), p. 42.

[17] B. Woolf, 'Social conditions', p. 42.

[18] E. Buckatzsch, 'The Influence of social conditions on mortality rates', *Pop. Stud.* (1947), pp. 229-48.

[19] P. Stocks, 'The effects of occupation and its accompanying environment on mortality', *Journal of the Royal Statistical Society* (1938), pp. 670-707.

[20] R. Titmuss, *Birth, Poverty and Wealth* (1943), pp. 44-5.

[21] T. McKeown, *The Role of Medicine* (1976), chs 3-6.

[22] McKeown, *The Modern Rise of Population* (1976).

[23] 'Fifty years of medicine', *Br. Med. Jnl* (1950), i, p. 61.

[24] W. Leslie MacKenzie, *Scottish Mothers and Children* (Dunfermline, 1917). F. B. Smith, *The People's Health* (1979).

[25] McKeown comes close at times to advancing a monocausal view, on which see below.

[26] McKeown, *The Role of Medicine*, p. x.

[27] McKeown, *The Modern Rise of Population*.

[28] McKeown, *The Role of Medicine*, p. xiv.

[29] On the chequered history of nineteenth-century medical care, see Smith, *The People's Health*.

[30] C. Singer, 'Medical progress from 1850 to 1950', *Br. Med. Jnl* (1950), i, pp 57-60.

[31] H. Dale, 'Advances in medicinal therapeutics', *Br. Med. Jnl* (1950), i, p. 1. The following paragraphs are drawn from this useful summary.

[32] Dale, 'Advances', pp. 3-7.

[33] R. Lambert, *Sir John Simon 1816-1904* (1963), chs 11-14, 25.

[34] I. Buchanan, 'Infant feeding, sanitation, and diarrhoea in colliery communities, 1880-1911', in D. Oddy and D. Miller (eds), *The Making of the Modern British Diet*, vol. III, in press.

[35] M. Beaver, 'Population, infant mortality and milk', *Pop. Stud.* (1973), pp. 243-54.

[36] A. Newsholme, 'The measurement of progress in public health', *Economica* (1923), pp. 186-202.

[37] N. Scrimshaw, C. Taylor, and J. Gordon, 'Interactions of nutrition and infection', *American Journal of the Medical Sciences* (1959), pp. 363-403. P. Newberne and G. Williams, 'Nutritional influences on the course of infection', in H. Dunlop and H. Moon (eds), *Resistance to Infectious Disease* (Saskatoon, 1970). L. Mata and R. Wyatt, 'Host resistance to infection', *American Journal of Clinical Nutrition* (1971), pp. 976-86. W. Akroyd, 'Nutri-

tion and mortality in infancy', *Am Jnl. Clin. Nutr.* (1971), pp. 480-87. W. Page Faulk, L. Mata, and G. Edsall, 'Effects of malnutrition on the immune response in humans: a review', *Tropical Diseases Bulletin* (1975), pp. 89-103.

[38] R. and J. Dubos, *The White Plague. Tuberculosis, Man, and Society* (1953), p. 41.

[39] L. Cobbett, 'The Decline of tuberculosis and the increase in its mortality during the war', *Jnl. Hyg.* (1930),pp. 79-103.

[40] Winter, 'Civilian Health'.

[41] J. Brincker, 'Measles mortality', *Journal of the Royal Sanitary Institute* (1932-33), p. 118.

[42] J. Tanner, *Growth at Adolescence* (Oxford, 1962).

[43] J. Craig, 'The heights of Glasgow boys: secular and social influences', *Human Biology* (1963), p. 524.

[44] J. M. Winter, 'Infant mortality'.

Further reading

T. McKeown, *The Modern Rise of Population,* Edward Arnold, 1976. A controversial attack on the view that doctors contributed significantly to the conquest of infectious disease. The author establishes his case effectively, his argument for nutrition as the key element stands by elimination of all other variables. The book is an extreme statement, which must be treated with care.

B. Abel-Smith, *The Hospitals in England and Wales 1800-1948,* Heinemann 1964. The standard institutional history, well-documented and expressed. It provides the outline history of health administration of the period.

F. B. Smith, *The People's Health 1800-1910,* Croom Helm, 1977. A detailed account of popular medicine and some of the appalling consequences of it in the nineteenth century. The author relies heavily on medical journals, and only occasionally comments on demographic themes.

R. Titmuss, *Birth, Poverty, and Wealth,* Hamish Hamilton, 1943. A powerful argument that demographic inequality persisted in England and Wales despite aggregate gains in survival rates, over the period 1911-1931. The book was written before data for the 1930s were available, but it has influenced interpretations of the entire interwar period and after.

M. Beaver, 'Population, infant mortality and milk', *Population Studies* 1973, pp. 243-54. A sweeping survey of the impact of improvements in the purity and aggregate supply of milk on mortality trends since the eighteenth century. While convincing in reference to infant diarrhoea, this hypothesis is too monocausal to be completely persuasive.

R. J. and J. P. Dubos, *The White Plague. Tuberculosis, Man and Society* Gollancz, 1953. An elegant, but brief account of tuberculosis as a constant companion in pre-twentieth-century history.

J. C. Drummond and A. Wilbraham, *The Englishman's Food*, Cape, 1957. The standard account of nutrition. Mostly reliable, but needs to be read alongside more recent accounts of agriculture and public health since 1800.

W. P. D. Logan, 'Mortality in England and Wales from 1848 to 1947', *Population Studies* 1950, pp. 132-78. The best survey of the dimensions and components of mortality decline, but of less help on the causes of improvements in life expectation.

J. M. Winter, 'The Impact of the First World War on civilian health in Britain', *Economic History Review*, 1977, pp. 487-507. An interpretation of the effect of the Great War on mortality levels which emphasizes the unintentional but beneficial effects of the working of the war economy on working-class living standards and nutrition.

G. Stolnitz, 'A century of international mortality trends I-II', *Population Studies* 1955, pp. 24-55; 1956, pp. 17-42. A thorough and meticulous survey of the context within which mortality decline in Britain must be placed.

The health of the people

D.J. ODDY

Any study of the health of the population from late-Victorian times onwards, however brief or limited in scope, must first overcome a definitional and methodological problem regarding the use of the concept of health. With the lack of a consensus among contemporary medical authorities about the meaning of health, medical historians face a dilemma when seeking evidence for health in the past. This they solve by inverting normal scientific methods which assume that there will be an attempt to describe, measure, and define the phenomenon investigated. The nature of the available evidence is such that positive data on health and normal physical development are scarce, while evidence of mortality and morbidity can be found in abundance from a variety of sources. Studies of health tend to rationalize the use of what evidence is available: ill-health becomes the reciprocal of health, with the result that the emphasis is overwhelmingly on bodily disorders. Such studies become works of historical epidemiology rather than of human health and physical development. What is missing is a description of healthy late-Victorian *Homo sapiens*. The writings of the later Victorians reveal that they had some concept of such an animal but among the Social Darwinists it was commoner to describe deviation from the model than the model itself, particularly as they were concerned to provide evidence that a process of physical degeneration had set in with the expansion of urban industrial society in the nineteenth century. The theory of urban degeneration[1] meant that there was much concern with 'the condition of the rural population as a reservoir of national strength'.[2] Thus James Cantlie's *Degeneration amongst Londoners* (1885) provides a lurid description of the process of physical degeneration by the mid-1880s. His third-generation Londoner was height 5ft 1in.; aged 21, chest measurement 28in.; his head measured across from tip of ear to tip of ear 11in. (1½in. below the average). His aspect is pale, waxy: he is very narrow between the eyes and with a decided squint![3]

Similarly Freeman-Williams (1890) saw townsmen as 'neurotic, dyspeptic, pale and undersized in adult state'[4] requiring constant injections of 'fresh blood' from healthier rural populations. Sensationalism accelerated after the turn of the century into an outcry about 'National Deterioration' in 1904, and culminated in the formation of the Eugenics Society in 1907.

The concept of health as used in late-Victorian society will not be understood completely unless three essential ideas are grasped. First, with the evidence of poverty, ignorance and disease being fairly widespread, the concept of health to most observers could only mean the absence of ill-health. Indeed, the absence of ill-health remained unchanged as a residual definition of health until, in 1948, the World Health Organization introduced the new concept that health was not only the absence of disease or infirmity but also a state of physical, mental, and social well-being.[5] Second, the concept of degeneration came primarily from an association of ideas rather than any scientific theory. For an understanding of how health was discussed, one may leave aside the Mendelian theory of inheritance until some time after 1900, just as one may discount Darwin's theory of evolution. Most Victorian middle-class commentators, whether medically-qualified or not, associated towns with public health problems, overcrowded houses, deficient sanitation, casual work, low incomes, and epidemic disease. As population grew, so these problems were more evident, and as more people lived in towns, so by association it seemed likely that a greater proportion of the population was in ill-health and the pool of 'national strength' in the countryside was becoming smaller. Third, it was only towards the end of the nineteenth century that health began to be thought of as a 'normal' state. It might almost be said that in the 1880s and 1890s people began to discover 'good' health in the way that was to become more obvious with the growth of outdoor leisure activities in the twentieth century. Samuel Butler's *Erewhon* (1872) is probably the first evidence of reaction against the 'romantic glorification of suffering' which Victorian sentimentalism enjoyed.[6] Until then, *La Traviata* (or *La Dame aux Camelias*) and *La Boheme* glorified tubercular heroines; a number of Edgar Allan Poe's heroines were similarly infected; earlier in the nineteenth century, romantics such as Byron yearned for consumption; in O. Henry's *The Last Leaf*, the heroine dies of pneumonia. Sentimentalism continued almost until the end of the century, although Ibsen began a reaction against venereal disease

Table 1 Standardized mean stature of boys and girls, 1880-1921

1a: Boys by age

Date	5 (ins.)	10 (ins.)	13 (ins.)
1880	39.7	50.7	55.8
1905a	40.9	50.3	55.4
1905b	–	51.0	56.2
1908	41.1	–	57.1
1910	40.4	50.8	56.1
1921	40.9	49.9	54.7

1b: Boys by income group (at age 13)

Date	upper (ins.)	middle (ins.)	lower (ins.)
1880	57.4	55.8	53.2
1905a	56.8	56.1	54.7
1905b	57.8	56.5	55.2
1908	58.6	57.1	54.9
1910	–	–	–
1921	56.9	53.9	53.9

1c: Girls by age

Date	5 (ins.)	10 (ins.)	13 (ins.)
1880	39.8	49.0	56.2
1905a	40.8	49.9	56.1
1905b	–	50.7	57.3
1908	41.1	–	57.4
1910	40.2	50.9	56.7
1921	40.4	49.6	55.9

1d: Girls by income group (at age 13)

Date	upper (ins.)	middle (ins.)	lower (ins.)
1880	58.5	56.2	53.0
1905a	57.6	56.2	55.6
1905b	58.1	57.4	56.6
1908	–	57.4	55.9
1910	–	–	–
1921	57.8	54.7	55.2

Source: *British Medical Journal* (1953), 897-902. 1905a = Glasgow, 1905b = London

with *Ghosts* (1881): attention was focused on the 'social evil' by Eugene Brieux's *Damaged Goods* (1901). Thomas Mann's *Magic Mountain* (1926) became the 'swan song' (in Mann's own words) of sentimental attitudes to disease for the movement towards Butler's Utopia, where illness was a crime, was well under way by the turn of the century. After all, the glorification in a tragic end to life lost its appeal once fate had been replaced by the germ theory of disease.[7]

There is some evidence that Victorian society attempted to define the norms of physical development in a rather more scientific manner than the views of the Social Darwinists suggest. The British Association for the Advancement of Science carried out an anthropometric survey between 1878 and 1883, and there are a series of papers in the *Lancet* from the 1870s to 1914 which discuss the physical development of schoolchildren. Some evidence from the period was summarized by Dr E. M. B. Clements in the *British*

Table 2: United Kingdom food supplies and nutrient availability

2a: Food supply estimates expressed as weekly per capita food consumption.

Date	Bread (1b)	Potatoes (1b)	Sugar (oz)	Fats (oz)	Meat (1b)	Milk (pt)
1889-1903	6.7	3.2	22.9	21.6	2.2	3.3
1904-1913	6.9	3.6	23.8	22.6	2.2	4.1

2b: Daily nutrient content available per capita based on food supply estimates.

Date	Energy Value (kcal)	Protein (g)	Fat (g)	Carbo- hydrate (g)	Iron (mg)	Calcium (g)
1889-1903	2983	73	143	363	11.2	0.47
1904-1913	3171	77	154	381	11.8	0.54

Table 3:   Working-class dietary patterns 1887-1913

3a: Weekly food consumption of working-class families shown by dietary surveys

Date	Bread (lb)	Potatoes (lb)	Sugar (oz)	Fats (oz)	Meat (lb)	Milk (pt)
1887-1901	6.7	1.6	14.4	5.2	1.4	1.4
1902-1913	6.6	3.0	15.5	7.6	1.2	1.8

3b: Daily nutrient intake per capita of working-class families shown by dietary surveys.

Date	Energy value (kcal)	Protein (g)	Fat (g)	Carbo- hydrate (g)	Iron (mg)	Calcium (g)
1887-1901	2099	57	58	336	10.0	0.31
1902-1913	2398	71	65	375	12.1	0.46

Medical Journal.[8]The evidence in Table 1 demonstrates that Victorian children were smaller than children today and that there was a clearly marked social gradient of 2-4ins in height between 'upper' and 'lower' income groups. No attempt will be made to extend this comparison back over earlier periods of the nineteenth century, although in passing it might be added that what little data there are, whether between the 1830s and 1880s or from the 1880s to 1914, show no trend of a secular increase in heights or weights.[9]

There is nothing particularly surprising about this conclusion. The principal determinants of health are nutritional status and quality of environment. Evidence from the later part of the nineteenth century and the early years of the twentieth century suggests that it is difficult to translate the advance in real wages during the last quarter of the nineteenth century into improvements in nutrition or urban environment. Patterns of food consumption were fairly stable as food supplies kept pace with population growth as shown in Table 2, but there was little basis for the claim once made by H. L. Beales that increased amounts of animal products entered the diet during this period of rising real wages.[10] In fact working-class diets continued to be heavily dependent on starchy sources of energy and an analysis of family budgets between 1887 and 1913 suggests that increases in consumption of animal products were limited to very small amounts of dairy products — mainly fats and milk — as shown in Table 3. Even had H. L. Beales been right, there is enough evidence for the period before 1914 to show that limitations of nutrition and environment were still major determinants of health. Birth, infancy, early childhood, and maternity remained crises to be overcome. One example is the lack of any significant reduction in infant mortality in the late nineteenth century; another is the fact that deaths in early childhood (0-5 years) were still almost one-third of all deaths as late as 1908: both led to detailed public inquiries. Mortality figures also showed wide variations between regions, between town and country, and between social classes. As late as 1911, infant mortality rates in the upper and middle classes were 77 per 1000 compared with 113 per 1000 for skilled labour, and 152 per 1000 among unskilled occupations,[11] figures which were in part a reflection of the physical environment but which also raised questions in the minds of contemporaries about nutrition and family care. In consequence, between 1908 and 1914 much attention was given to the employment of married women and the effect that this had upon nutrition through the adequacy of meals, feeding practices, and the level of cleanliness and care in the home. However, since mortality rates in early childhood (0-5 years) for 1911-14 exceeded 200 per 1000 not only in a number of towns in the textile districts of the north-west where married women's employment was common, but also in areas such as the north-east, the midlands, and south Wales where married women's employment was low, there was no obvious correlation. Similarly, although married women's employment was blamed for a decline in breast feeding, the evidence for the decline was limited and a contrary view was offered in the

Second Report on Infant Mortality by figures which suggested that roughly two-thirds of the children in several English towns were still breast fed at the age of six months.[12] The great difficulty is to disentangle all the various influences at work on health. While most patent infant foods of the day provided poorly-balanced diets, the difficulty of obtaining adequate supplies of cow's milk free from bovine tuberculosis remained a major problem. The middle classes turned to the use of patent infant foods in these circumstances and yet the infant mortality in their families fell. 'Domestic discomfort' among the poorer classes, whether in terms of poor hygiene, overcrowding, lack of attention at confinements, or even excessive alcoholism (which showed a close correlation with high infant mortality areas), offset any retention of breast-feeding practices. Even more intangible in effects on health was the question of lack of care and parental concern which almost every investigation before 1914 discussed at length in terms of the 'feck-lessness' or 'ignorance' of working-class patterns of life. Although these discussions were obviously coloured by middle-class atti-tudes, there were areas where limited house room, lack of internal water supply, poor sanitation and cooking facilities, when coupled with the stoic acceptance of discomfort or hardship[13], were inimical to the healthy development of children.

It was only in the last few years before 1914 that the 1907 Education (Medical Inspections) Act[14] began to yield information about the health of children of board school age. Dr George Newman's first report as Chief Medical Officer, in 1910, produced a view of schoolchildren's state of health which R. H. Tawney saw as 'likely to be read in the future with the sensation aroused to-day by a study of the reports of the early Commissions on Child Labour in Factories and Mines':[15]

Speaking generally, it may be said that out of the six million children registered on the books of the Public Elementary Schools of England and Wales, about 10 per cent suffer from a serious defect in vision, from 3 to 5 per cent suffer from defective hearing, 1 to 3 per cent have suppurating ears, 6 to 8 per cent have adenoids or enlarged tonsils of sufficient degree to obstruct the nose or throat, and thus to require surgical treatment, about 40 per cent suffer from extensive and injurious decay of the teeth, about 30 to 40 per cent have unclean heads or bodies, about 1 per cent suffer from ringworm, 1 per cent from tuberculosis in readily recognizable form, from 1 to 2 per cent are afflicted with heart disease and a considerable percentage of children are suffering from a greater or lesser degree of malnutrition.

In the face of such obvious problems, Newman's lack of assessment of children's physical development is understandable, but a more direct discussion of growth was made by Arthur Greenwood (1913), who saw town children as both smaller and lighter than those of rural areas.[16] Such limitations on growth resulted principally from under-nutrition, a topic which had begun to attract comment from the 1880s onwards. In board schools, what began as a discussion of 'over-pressure' on pupils came to be recognized with greater accuracy as 'under-feeding' as early as 1884.[17] There was little disagreement by contemporaries with the Physical Deterioration Committee's conclusion in 1904 that 'a large number of children habitually attend school ill-fed'.[18] Provision of food in schools was not widespread and lay largely in the hands of voluntary bodies providing cocoa, breakfasts, and lunches. The Education (Provision of Meals) Act[19] did not extend this provision significantly, being intended to do no more than regularize this type of expenditure on the rates but, as rate expenditure was to be limited to school terms alone, it provided the opportunity for Dr Ralph Crowley to demonstrate the value of school meals by recording weight losses among children in Bradford during the holidays when school meals ceased.[20] Mr J. A. Pease, President of the Board of Education, admitted in the House of Commons in 1913 that 10 per cent of schoolchildren were suffering from defective nutrition; evidence from some English counties made this sound somewhat optimistic, a view which was confirmed by the first medical inspections in Scotland.[21] There seems little doubt that under these conditions physical development was slower, growth continuing perhaps until the mid-twenties before maturity was reached. Children who left school for manual employment were liable to have their physical development further restricted. In textile towns, where 'half-time' employment began at 12 years of age, there were distinct effects on children's physique, as explained by a factory inspector:

Employment of this character especially if carried on in high temperatures, rarely fosters growth or development; the stunted child elongates slightly in time, but remains very thin, loses colour, the muscles remain small, especially those of the upper limbs, the legs are inclined to become bowed, more particularly if heavy weights have to be habitually carried, the arch of the foot flatens (sic) and the teeth decay rapidly.[22]

An additional effect on girls was that 'at an age when girls brought up under wholesome conditions usually possess a luxuriant growth of hair, these factory girls have a scanty crop which, when tied back, is simply a wisp or "rat's tail" ', evidence which suggests a shortage of animal foods in the diet and possible deficiencies in both protein and vitamins. Other similar comments: 'dry, thin, and short or wispy'[23]; 'hard, dry, "staring" hair'[24]; and the 'harshness, roughness of the skin'[25] confirm the likelihood that deficient nutrition was affecting health and physical development.

These distortions of physical development were not so readily apparent in adulthood. Before 1914 there was no monitoring of adult health: the state, in A. J. P. Taylor's words, 'left the adult citizen alone'.[26] Concern about male physical development rested on defence needs and represented the fears of both Conservative and Liberal Imperialists that an urban society could not provide the type of manpower required to administer, police, and defend the enormous extent of the Empire. Army recruitment had been under discussion since 1897, but the increased demand for men during the South African War led Sir Frederick Maurice to give a somewhat sensational account of recruitment experiences which implied that 37.6 per cent of recruits had been found unfit for military service or subsequently invalided out. The Inspector-General of Army Recruiting's report for 1902 expressed this concern in Social Darwinist terms: 'The one subject which causes anxiety in the future as regards recruiting is the gradual deterioration of the physique of the working classes from whom the bulk of the recruits must always be drawn.' It was this hypothesis which the Physical Deterioration Committee began to discuss and from which the Army had to make a rapid tactical withdrawal, Sir William Taylor, the Director-General of the Army Medical Service, denying that any 'gradual deterioration' had been observed and rejecting the Inspector-General of Recruiting's conclusions as unjustified.[27] The Physical Deterioration Committee concluded, as was to be expected, that there was a lack of statistical evidence on which to base a proper study of health and physique, noting somewhat lamely that 'the impressions gathered from the great majority of the witnesses examined do not support the belief that there is any general progressive physical deterioration'.[28] In the years which followed, the physical condition of the population became the subject of a series of inquiries which assembled a mass of evidence. Besides the extensive study of infant mortality and the health of schoolchildren already referred to, there were other investigations into the diseases of tuberculosis and venereal disease and into the feeble-minded. Brought into juxtaposition, some aspects of these inquiries postulated enormous health problems: among the working classes, 10 per cent of men and 5 per cent of women were said to be suffering from venereal disease; 90 per cent of the population surviving beyond the age of 30 years were said to have been infected by tuberculosis at some time in their life.[29] However, none of these inquiries dealt with normal healthy development; not until the First World War was there need or attempt to describe normal physical development. To provide a standard for the National Service Medical Boards in 1917, Professor Arthur Keith took a sample of 1000 middle-class students at Cambridge as a norm. Of this group, 70 per cent were above 'full stature' (which, in terms of height, he set at 5ft 8ins.) and were placed in Grade I by Keith. His percentages allocated to lower grades were: Grade II, 20 per cent; Grade III, 7.5 per cent; Grade IV, 2.5 per cent. By contrast, in 1917-18 the Medical Boards experienced physical development significantly below Keith's standard in many areas. Even in the 18-year-old cohort born in 1900, 65 per cent of whom were placed in Grade I, the effects of restricted growth were to be found. The average height of nearly 16,000 young men examined in the West Midlands was only 5ft 5½ins. and their average weight was only 118lbs. A group of similar stature in Liverpool had an average chest measurement of under 3 lins. It should be remembered that the Medical Boards had no minimum standards below which men were rejected, hence the formation of 'bantam' battalions of men under 5ft in height, though men below 5ft 0ins. in height or less than 100lbs in weight or with a chest measurement smaller than 32ins were 'carefully scrutinized'.[30] The aggregate gradings by the Medical Boards are well known: only 36 per cent were placed in Grade I, which meant that 'only one in every three had attained the full normal standard of health and strength and was judged capable of enduring physical exertion suitable to his age.' More than 41 per cent of those examined were placed in Grades III and IV. The Medical Boards' gradings were summarized as follows:

medical examination showed that, of every nine men of military age in Great Britain, on the average three were perfectly fit and healthy; two were upon a definitely infirm plane of health and strength whether from some disability or some failure in development; three were incapable of undergoing more than a very moderate degree of physical exertion and could almost (in view of their age) be described with justice as physical wrecks; and the remaining man was a chronic invalid with a precarious hold upon life.[31]

In spite of this forthright view, there seems no reason to doubt the conclusion of the Medical Department of the Ministry of National Service that those examined were a fair representation of 'the manhood of military age of the country in the early twentieth century'.[32]

II

Despite the inadequacies of physique revealed among men conscripted in 1917-18, the civilian population experienced a period of full employment and rising money wages offset only partly by the wartime price inflation. J. M. Winter has suggested that the First World War should be seen as a period of advance in civilian health, but none of the figures offered by Clements indicate that this could be translated into gains in stature.[33] Within the period 1905-1920, Clements found no discernible increases in children's heights and, in general, that mean weights actually fell. The origins of the secular increase in growth which has been so evident in the twentieth century are to be found in the interwar years. Between *c*. 1920 and *c*. 1940, children of elementary school ages gained 2-3½ins in height and 5-13½lbs in weight,[34] despite the suggestion by Weir[35] that the periods of depression in the early 1920s and early 1930s were reflected in slower development of children. Contemporary observation of improvements in growth began to be made by School Medical Officers during the 1930s, despite the concern with malnutrition that developed in areas where long-term unemployment became marked. From the advantage of a later viewpoint Boyne, Aitken, and Leitch (1957) were able to discern some pattern in these changes.[36] Commenting on heights and weights of 12-year-olds, they noted a slight fall in the years before the First World War but that a gradual rise began in the 1920s. There was a 'suggestion of an arrest of progress' during the slump years, 1930-33, followed by a resumption of growth until the outbreak of war in 1939. Instead of the war arresting this trend, Weir claimed that the evacuation of many schoolchildren in 1940-41 resulted in an upsurge of growth which continued after the war when, between 1945 and 1953, heights continued to increase while weights 'rose steeply'.[5] This last burst of growth was widely noted: for the London County Council area boys' heights increased on average by 0.59ins between 1949 and 1954 and girls' heights 0.39ins, while weights increased by 3.3lbs and 2.2lbs respectively.[38] Even as early as 1949, sir Allen Daley, the Chief Medical Officer of the London County Council noted that 'by *pre-war* scales of growth, post-war children appear three months older than their true ages'.[39] These gains in stature were noted at each age during school life when children were medically examined, namely, five, eight, and 12 years of age. Looking back over its first half-century of operations, the School Medical Service's report in 1957 summarized the secular trend in growth. In urban areas, five-year-old children showed gains of 2-3ins in height and 4-6lbs in weight over the period 1907-57, while both eight- and 12 year olds had become 2-4ins taller and 7½-9½lbs heavier.[40]

Changing conditions during the Second World War had beneficial effects on children's growth which extended beyond the improvements in evacuees noted by Weir. Special investigations carried out by Dr E. R. Bransby for the Ministry of Health and the Board of Education began in 1940. By 1944, when 21 localities had

Table 4:   Nutritional assessment of school children in England and Wales in 1935

Area	Numbers examined (thousands)	Grading A and B (%)	C (%)	D (%)
London	189	94.25	5.67	0.08
West Riding	61	81.68	17.48	0.84
Birmingham	41	90.13	8.63	1.24
Durham County	40	77.40	19.80	2.70
Liverpool	37	88.50	10.10	1.40
Lancashire	36	89.30	10.10	0.50
Special Areas				
Newcastle	14.6	88.32	11.15	0.53
Jarrow	1.3	70.40	22.90	6.70
Sunderland	10	88.22	10.94	0.83
Glamorgan	14.8	82.00	16.57	1.39
Monmouth	9.7	84.60	15.10	0.17
Merthyr Tydfil	2.7	86.10	11.26	2.62
Pontypridd	1.9	75.70	19.45	4.76
Total	1687	88.70	10.60	0.70

Source: *The Health of the School Child 1935* (1936).

been surveyed, his results showed that in 17 areas boys heights had increased and in a further three areas they were the same as prewar standards. For girls, 14 areas showed an increase, while four remained the same. There were only limited examples of loss of height and/or weight compared with the pre-war period. Children between five and 14 years showed a general increase in height of the order of ¼-½in. and a gain in weight of 1½-2lbs.[41] There was general agreement that the reasons for the improving physical standards were largely nutritional, but that there was a substantial underlying economic factor. While the food policy imposed during the war had contributed to a fair distribution of available food supplies including, as the war progressed, some positive discrimination in favour of groups in the population with special needs such as workers engaged in heavy manual labour, and supplementary foods for children, full employment provided the economic basis from which many benefited. This was particularly true of the pre-war Special Areas. Dr T. H. Stephens, the School Medical Officer for Merthyr Tydfil, reported in 1944: 'The improved conditions are undoubtedly due to the present economic conditions existing in the County Borough, greater employment and to the fact that children were able to have a good midday meal and milk.'[42] It was in areas like Merthyr Tydfil that routine medical inspections had shown the extent of defective nutrition in schoolchildren before the Second World War. During the 1930s, when nearly 1.7m. medical inspections were made annually, between 10-11 per cent of children were given a nutritional assessment grade of 'C' or 'Slightly subnormal' and between 0.5-1 per cent were graded 'D' or 'bad'. Putting these grades together, means that between 11 and 12 per cent of schoolchildren medically examined in the 1930s were found to be under-nourished. The pronounced regional variation in these conditions which are shown in Table 4 reflected employment patterns closely.

Despite the conclusive nature of Dr H. Corry Mann's *The Diet of the Schoolchild* in demonstrating the value of foods such as milk for growth, findings which scientists pressed upon the Ministry of Health in the broader context of the debate on malnutrition in the 1930s, no government responsibility for food policy was admitted until the Luke Committee's Report was issued in 1937.[43] Supplementary feeding was therefore minimal in the inter-war years. In 1938, only 160,000, or just 4 per cent of elementary schoolchildren had school dinners, the bulk of which (110,000) were given free at 'feeding centres'. By that time, the school milk scheme had become well established since its first year of operation in 1935, and about 55 per cent of the school population, some 2.5m. pupils in all, drank milk at school in 1938. The initial effect of the war upon these schemes was disruptive: many feeding centres closed and there was a drop in milk consumption. Table 5 shows the extent of the deterioration until July 1940, when special financial provisions were introduced, followed by further measures in 1941 to increase the palatability of school meals by enlarging the allowances of meat and sugar. From that point, consumption expanded significantly and by the end of the war nearly 40 per cent of schoolchildren had school dinners and over 70 per cent had milk.[44] The uptake of milk and meals at school in Special Areas was a significant factor in the levelling-up of nutritional status among schoolchildren which occurred during the war. Table 6 shows the falling proportion of children graded 'C' or 'fair' (the prewar designation was 'slightly subnormal') together with the levels of school meals and milk consumption reached in the autumn of 1945. Grade 'D' (pre-war 'bad') also fell overall from 0.5 per cent in 1938 to 0.3 per cent in 1945. Even in bad areas, grade 'D' had been almost eliminated by 1945: in Jarrow, it fell from 4.84 per cent of children in 1938 to 0.25 per cent in 1945; in Pontypridd, from 2.03 to 0.52 per cent.[45]

The contribution made by these changes towards eradicating regional disparity in physical development was followed in the

Table 5: Numbers of children having school meals and milk in England and Wales during the Second World War

Date	Meals number (m)	percentage of school population	Milk number (m.)	percentage of school population
1938-39	0.150	4.4	2.500	55.0
July 1940	0.130	3.5	2.100	not known
Feb. 1941	0.279	6.5	2.479	57.6
Feb. 1942	0.607	14.0	3.386	77.9
Feb. 1943	1.048	23.5	3.371	76.8
Feb. 1944	1.495	32.8	3.428	76.3
Feb. 1945	1.650	36.3	3.265	73.0
Oct. 1945	1.840	39.7	3.322	71.7

Source: *The Health of the School Child 1939-45* (1947).

Table 6: Take-up of school meals and milk in areas showing nutritional improvement during the Second World War

Area	Proportion of school population (Oct. 1945) having meals and milk		Grade C nutritional assessment at routine medical examination	
	Meals (%)	Milk (%)	1938 (%)	1945 (%)
Counties				
Durham	30.1	73.7	23.4	17.26
Glamorgan	40.4	61.2	22.1	10.45
Monmouth	43.8	72.9	14.6	9.84
County Boroughs				
Gateshead	32.4	56.7	29.7	25.47
Merthyr Tydfil	63.7	76.1	26.6	7.40
England & Wales	39.7	71.7	10.8	8.90

Source: *The Health of the School Child 1939-45* (1947).

post-war years by a period in which improved medical treatment and more (and better) food contributed to a higher standard of living. By 1954, the School Medical Officer of the London County Council noted that within his school population differences in heights and weights by area had 'largely disappeared'.[46] But London, despite its poor districts, had never been noted for a high proportion of children with unsatisfactory nutrition: in 1953, less

Table 7:   Variation in heights and weights of five-year-old children in Sheffield (1956)

7a: Heights

Sex	Good district (ins)	Medium district (ins)	Poor district (ins)
Boys	43.77	43.37	42.71
Girls	43.30	42.67	42.32

7b: Weights

Sex	Good district (lb)	Medium district (lb)	Poor district (lb)
Boys	44.56	43.56	43.06
Girls	42.99	41.85	41.56

Source:*The Health of the School Child 1956-57* (1958).

than 6 per cent of its children were graded C or D (see Table 4). In the provinces and in Scotland, environmental differences still affected physical development. The effects of disparities in housing provision had been noted in Scotland earlier in the century: in the early 1930s, 13-year-old children living in accommodation of four or more rooms were 1in taller and around 4lbs heavier than those living in three rooms, and as much as 2.5ins taller and 8-9 lbs heavier than those living in one room.[47] Better growth by children in poorer areas in post-war years did not eliminate the social gradient in heights or weights. In Liverpool in 1949, children's weight differences at five years between 'good' schools and 'poor' schools was 2.3lbs; at eight years, 3lbs; and at 12 years, 4.6lbs.[48] By the mid-1950s, when routine medical inspections revealed less than 2 per cent of children as being in an unsatisfactory physical condition and obesity rather than under-nutrition had begun to catch the eye of medical observers, the social gradient could still be very marked. In Sheffield, as shown in Table 7, both heights and weights of five-year-olds showed that children from good districts were taller and heavier than those from less satisfactory areas. There was some feeling in the late-1950s that the social gradient was becoming less distinct,[49] but the 1947 birth cohort which formed the basis of the Newcastle Thousand Families study showed almost 5ins height difference between children of Social Class I and children of Social Class V at the age of 15 years, as in Table 8. It can also be noted from Table 8 that these variations in heights and weights developed despite close similarities of birth weights.[50]

Table 8: Growth according to social class in Newcastle-upon-Tyne in the 1950s

8a: Heights

Ages (years)	Social class				
	I (ins)	II (ins)	III (ins)	IV (ins)	V (ins)
3	37.4	37.2	36.7	36.5	36.0
5	45.3	44.3	43.5	43.4	43.0
9	52.0	51.8	50.8	50.3	50.1
13	60.4	60.2	59.3	58.8	58.6
15	65.5	64.6	62.5	63.7	62.7

8b Weights

Ages (years)	Social class				
	I (lb)	II (lb)	III (lb)	IV (lb)	V (lb)
Birth	7.54	7.56	7.35	7.37	7.37
3	33.5	32.7	32.3	31.5	31.5
5	46.2	44.9	42.7	42.1	42.0
9	66.7	62.5	60.1	58.1	58.7
13	102.3	97.6	94.5	90.2	92.0
15	126.2	120.4	116.0	114.0	112.9

Source: *The School Years in Newcastle-upon-Tyne 1952-62* (1974).

III

Children apart, evidence of positive advances in health and physique is more difficult to come by. A large cross-sectional survey of adult health was carried out between 1939 and 1945 in the course of medical inspections for military service. This was extended into the 1950s while conscription remained in force. Although the material relating to nearly 6m. medical inspections has been preserved in the Public Record Office, it has not yet been analysed, so that no comparison with the Report of the National Service Medical Boards for 1917-18 can be made. Similarly, little is known of the legacy of ill-health left by the First World War in the form of nearly 2m. applications for war pension, though this was but a temporary setback in the general improvement in adult health which began in the twentieth century.

The increasing longevity of the population was one sign of the improvement of health. Life expectancy at birth began to rise from the 1890s, when it was just over 43 years for males and just under 47 years for females. Even before the First World War, children born in England and Wales in 1911 had a life expectancy of 51.5 years for boys and 55.4 years for girls. This trend continued unabated as the century progressed, with life expectancy at birth for boys reaching 66.2 years in 1951, and 69 years in 1971. Girls' life expectancy made even greater progress, reaching 71.2 years by 1951, and 75.2 years by 1971.[51] The proportion of the elderly in the population also rose. The Census of England and Wales in 1911 showed that less than 7 per cent of the population were old people, but this had risen to 9.6 per cent by 1931. After the Second World War, the Registrar General's estimates for 1951 indicated that 13.6 per cent of the population were elderly, and by 1971 that over 16 per cent were of these age groups.[52]

At this point in the discussion, changing patterns of ill-health do begin to contribute to our knowledge of the health of the population. The increase in longevity during the first half of the century depended upon the continued decline in infectious diseases which, in the nineteenth century had brought death and stunted growth. The effect of these diseases was exacerbated during the Victorian age by low resistance to infective organisms among the poorer social classes which in turn reflected limitations in nutrition and environmental conditions. During the twentieth century, as people have survived longer, so degenerative diseases have become a major cause of mortality, a change notable because cardiovascular disease, cancer, and accidents, which are now among the principal causes of deaths, can be described as diseases of affluence which have grown in importance as the standard of living has risen. In another sense, too, they reflect changes in social conditions: in all these examples there is a factor which reflects personal consumption levels. Unfortunately, these causes of death tend to reflect levels of self-indulgence or, in other words, may be termed self-inflicted. However, the identification and eradication of infectious diseases by medical science, which has been the major achievement of the twentieth century, has not produced a more positive approach to health.

Rising standards of living have been coupled with a commitment to sustain a National Health Service since the Second World War. Expenditure on the National Health Service rose from £587m. in 1951 to £2,754m. in 1971; health and personal social services took 10.1 per cent of total public expenditure in 1951, rising to 11.4 per cent by 1971.[53] Of course, much of this expenditure has gone into high-technology areas of medicine. The hospitals, for example, have taken a growing proportion of expenditure, rising from 47.5 per cent in 1951-52 to 57.1 per cent in 1971-72,[54] while the proportion spent on dental, pharmaceutical, opthalmic, and general medical services have each declined over the same period. Up to and including the Second World War, poverty had been the principal factor involved in ill-health; after 1945 poverty had been largely eradicated, though income differentials and social class differences remained. During the 1960s and 1970s, with unemployment returning as a social problem from 1967 onwards, there has evolved a concern that inequalities in health have shown a remarkable persistence and, in some cases, may have been increasing.[55]

There seems little doubt that social attitudes to health have changed in post-war Britain; after all, self-diagnosis is a principal element in seeking medical advice. But the historian can gain little knowledge of the health of the population from medical sources. Bio-physics rather than epidemiology has come to dominate the health service; survey work has the lowest priority for nutritionists.[56] The DHSS Working Group Report *Inequalities in Health* has shown little more than the continued existence of a social gradient in disease patterns. Failure to maintain the anthropometric monitoring of schoolchildren was discernible in the reports of the School Health Service throughout the 1960s and up to the point of its transfer to the DHSS in 1973. Today it might almost be said that little more is known of the nation's physical development than when the British Association tried to collect the measurements of visitors to exhibitions in the 1880s. Residual definitions of health still predominate in social planning. It is ill-health which is discussed all too frequently rather than the health of the people.

Notes

[1] For the use of this concept, see G. Stedman Jones, *Outcast London* (Peregrine edition, 1976) ch. 6.

[2] *Report of the Inter-Departmental Committee on Physical Deterioration* Parliamentary Papers 1904 (Cd. 2175) XXXII, para. 189.

[3] J. Cantlie, *Degeneration amongst Londoners* (1885) Parkes Museum of Hygiene Lecture. Cited in Stedman Jones, op. cit. p. 127.

[4] J. P. Freeman-Williams, *The Effects of Town Life on the General Health* (1890) p. 5, cited in Stedman Jones, ibid.

[5] For a discussion of this concept, see R. Dubos, *Mirage of Health* (1960) ch. VII and S. Leff, *You . . . Your Health . . . Your Community* (1970) ch. 1.

[6] Dubos, ibid. Samuel Butler's concept of ill health as a crime is set out in *Erewhon* (1872) chs. X-XI. There is some slight basis for seeing this as a development in scientific thought: Butler had been influenced by Darwin's *Origin of Species* (1859) while in New Zealand and corresponded with him

on returning to England. See S. Butler, *Darwin on the Origin of Species* (1862, reprinted 1912).

[7] Robert Koch's isolation of the tubercle bacillus in 1882 had a much wider impact on theories of disease than the earlier discoveries of Louis Pasteur did. A brief history of scientific theories of the causation of disease is given in Dubos, op. cit. ch. IV.

[8] E. M. B. Clements, 'Changes in the mean stature and weight of British children over the past seventy years' *British Medical Journal*, 24 Oct. 1953, 897-902. Further examples are given in F. B. Smith, *The People's Health 1830-1910* (1979), pp. 175-178. There is also Dr A. A. Mumford's 'The physique of the modern boy' in *Transactions of the Manchester Statistical Society*, 1912-13, 127-168. Francis Galton's surveys and other late-nineteenth century anthropometric work are referred to in *I-D. Cttee. on Phys. Det.*, Vol III (Cd. 2186), Appendix IX.

[9] Clements, op. cit. A different view is expressed in J. M. Tanner, *Growth at Adolescence* (second edition, 1962) pp. 147-148, though the evidence offered for England before the twentieth century is inconclusive.

[10] H. L. Beales, 'The "Great Depression" in Industry and Trade', *Economic History Reivew* V (1934), 65-75, reprinted in E. M. Carus-Wilson, *Essays in Economic History* (1954), 406-416.

[11] Figures from the Registrar General for England and Wales cited in the *Second Report on Infant Mortality*, a supplement to the *42nd Annual Report of the Local Government Board*, P.P. 1913 (Cd. 6909) XXXII, 73.

[12] Ibid. p. 84. Additional evidence which suggested that the decline in breastfeeding was not as marked as the Committee on Physical Deterioration had assumed had already appeared in the first *Report on Infant Mortality*, a supplement to the *38th A. R. of the Local Government Board*, P. P. 1910 (Cd. 5263) XXXIX, 86.

[13] See *Report of the I-D. Cttee. on Phys. Det.* op. cit. paras. 110, 151, 264. Also the *Report* and *Second Report on Infant Mortality* op. cit. For the most obvious class attitudes, see *Report on Child Mortality*, a supplement to the *45th A. R. of the Local Government Board*, P. P. 1917-18 (Cd. 8496) XVI, 64. The stoic acceptance of hardship is well illustrated in F. Thompson. *Lark Rise to Candleford* (1954 edition) p. 40.

[14] 7 Edw. VII c. 43.

[15] Board of Education, *Annual Report for 1910 of the Chief Medical Officer*, P. P. 1911 (Cd. 5925) XVII, para. 314. See R. H. Tawney's introductory note to A. Greenwood, *The Health and Physique of School Children* (1913).

[16] Greenwood, ibid. pp. 25-6, 29-33.

[17] Mr Sydney Buxton spoke to a London School Board conference in these terms (*School Board Chronicle*, 13 December 1884, pp. 628-9) though it is difficult to pinpoint a particular year when this concern began to be translated into feeding programmes. Funds for the purposes of feeding schoolchildren were collected by newspapers from about 1880, notably the *Referee*, under G. R. Sims' editorship, and the *Globe*. Speaking before the

Physical Deterioration Committee, Mr A. Stirling claimed that the Destitute Children's Dinner Society went back to *c.* 1875; the Poor Children's Aid Society began work in 1886 and its feeding work was carried on by the London Schools Dinner Association (1889). Feeding schemes developed in many provincial towns in the 1890s.

[18] *Report of the I-D. Cttee. on Phys. Det.*, op. cit. para. 358.

[19] 6 Edw. VII c. 57.

[20] Dr Crowley's work and other observations which confirmed his findings are described in M. E. Bulkley, *The Feeding of School Children* (1914) ch. V.

[21] Hansard, 10 April 1913, vol. 51, 1381; Education (Scotland) Department, *First Report on the Medical Inspection of School Children in Scotland* (1913) ch. VI. Developmental retardation due to underfeeding was still considered to be operating after the First World War, as the following summary published in 1920 indicates: 'the experience of the Education Authorities during the last 14 years has demonstrated beyond all question, first, that there is a degree of physical defect and impairment among school children which prevents large numbers of them from receiving reasonable benefit from the education which the Authority provides . . . and secondly, that unless the Authority itself arranges for, or provides, means of treatment the great majority of ailing children will not in fact be treated, and a harvest of physical degeneration will result'. *Annual Report of the Chief Medical Officer of the Board of Education*, 1920, P. P. 1921 (Cmd. 1522) XL, p. 2.

[22] *Report of the I-D. Cttee. on Phys. Det.* op. cit. para.140.

[23] Ibid. para. 141; Vol. II (Cd. 2210) Q. 450.

[24] *First Report on Medical Inspection in Scotland*, op. cit. para.81.

[25] *Report of the I-D. Cttee on Phys. Det.* Vol. II, op. cit. Q. 450.

[26] A. J. P. Taylor, *English History 1914-45* (Penguin edition, 1970) p. 26.

[27] The campaign for physical efficiency was most clearly to be seen in Conservative journals. For a discussion of the diverse strands in the debate on national physique, see G. R. Searle, *The Quest for National Efficiency* (1971) pp. 60-67. Searle describes the review *Nineteenth Century* as 'the "official" mouthpiece of the "efficiency group" in the Boer War period' (pp. 148-9). The article by G. F. Smee, 'The deterioration in the national physique' in *Nineteenth Century* Vol. LIII (1903) 802, was the precursor of the 1904 Inter-Departmental Committee's inquiry. On the Boer War, see also *Contemporary Review*, Vol. LXXXI (1902), 78-86 'Where to get men'; Vol. LXXXIII (1903), 41-56 'National health: A soldier's study'. *Annual Report of the Inspector-General of Recruiting for the year 1902*, P. P. 1903 (Cd. 1417) XI, para. 150; *Report of the I-D. Cttee. on Phys. Det.* Vol. II, op. cit., evidence of Sir William Taylor, Q. 10.

[28] *Report of the I-D. Cttee. on Phys. Det.* op. cit., para. 68.

[29] There are extensive discussions of these aspects of health in the *Report of the Royal Commissioners on the Care and Control of the Feeble-Minded*, P. P. 1908 (Cd. 4202) XXXIX; *Report of the Royal Commission on Venereal Diseases*, P. P.

1916 (Cd. 8189) XVI; *Final Report of the Departmental Committee on Tuberculosis*, P. P. 1912-13 (Cd. 6654) XLVIII.

[30] *Report upon the Physical Examination of Men of Military Age by National Service Medical Boards*, P. P. 1919 (Cmd. 504) XXVI; *National Service Instruction (N. S. I. No. 3 of 1917)* P. P. 1917-18 (Cd. 8834) XXXVIII.

[31] *Report upon the Physical Examination*, op. cit. p. 22.

[32] Ibid. p. 5. In fact the Report did suggest an average level of physical development: 'there is already sufficient evidence to show that a combination of height 5ft 6ins, weight 130lbs, chest girth 34 ins, will be found to be approximately the average measurements of the Grade I men of military age' (p. 23).

[33] J. M. Winter, 'The impact of the First World War on civilian health in Britain', *Economic History Review*, 2nd. ser. Vol.XXX, 3 (1977) 487-507; Clements, op. cit. p. 901. In support of J. M. Winter's viewpoint, the *Annual Report of the Chief Medical Officer of the Board of Education*, 1918, P. P. 1919 (Cmd. 420) XXI, p. 13 noted 'the continuous decline in the percentage of children returned as poorly nourished'. Nevertheless, 2-3 per cent of children entering school showed a 'serious degree of rickets' (p. 45).

[34] Clements, op. cit. p. 901.

[35] J. B. de V. Weir, 'The assessment of the growth of schoolchildren with special reference to secular changes' *British Journal of Nutrition*, Vol. 6, 1 (1952) 19-33.

[36] A. W. Boyne, F. C. Aitken & I. Leitch, *Nutrition Abstracts and Reviews* Vol. 27 (1957) 1.

[37] Ibid.

[38] J. A. Scott, *Report on Heights and Weights of London School Children* London County Council (1954), cited in Ministry of Education, *The Health of the School Child 1954-55* (1956) p. 23.

[39] A. Daley, 'Heights and weights of London school children' *The Medical Officer*, 5 June 1948, cited in Ministry of Education, *The Health of the School Child 1948-49* (1952) p. 9.

[40] Ministry of Education, *The Health of the School Child 1956-57* (1958) p. 68.

[41] Ministry of Education, *The Health of the School Child 1939-45* (1947) pp. 20-21.

[42] Ibid. p. 19.

[43] Ministry of Health, *Advisory Committee on Nutrution: First Report* (1937); for H. Corry Mann's findings, see Medical Research Council, *Special Report Series No. 105* (1926).

[44] *Health of the School Child 1939-45*, op. cit. pp. 23-24.

[45] Ibid. p. 18.

[46] J. A. Scott, cited in *Health of the School Child 1954-55*, op. cit. p. 23.

[47] Scottish Health Services, *Report of the Committee on House Size* cited in Board of Education, *The Health of the School Child 1935* (1936) p. 28.

[48] *Health of the School Child 1948-49*, op. cit. p. 9.

[49] Ministry of Education, *The Health of the School Child 1958-59* (1960) p. 14.

[50] F. J. W. Miller, S. D. M. Court, E. G. Knox & S. Brandon, *The School Years in Newcastle-upon-Tyne 1952-62* (1974) p. 61.

[51] Central Statistical Office, *Annual Abstract of Statistics 1980* (1980) Table 2.33; *Statistical Abstracts of the United Kingdom*.

[52] Calculated from Table 2.34, *Annual Abstract of Statistics 1980*, op. cit., taking the retirement population of men over 65 years and women over 60 years as elderly; or see Central Statistical Office, *Social Trends*, No. 3 (1972) Table 1.

[53] *Social Trends* No. 3, op. cit., Table 148.

[54] Ibid., Table 150.

[55] Department of Health and Social Security, *Inequalities in Health* (1980).

[56] Agricultural Research Council/Medical Research Council, *Food and Nutrition Research* (1974) pp. 14-15.

Further reading

S. Leff, *The Health of the People*, Gollancz, 1950. An institutional study of the development of medical facilities from the early nineteenth century to 1948.

F. B. Smith, *The People s Health 1830-1910*, Croom Helm, 1979. Principally a discussion of disease and health disorders during the nineteenth century.

R. Dubos, *Mirage of Health*, George Allen and Unwin, 1960. A seminal work by an eminent scientist which views health as a dynamic process of biological and social adaptation to environmental stress.

J. B. Orr, *Food Health and Income*, Macmillan, 1936. A primary source for the interwar period relating low incomes with deficient diet and restricted physical growth.

Rowett Research Institute, *Food Diet and Health in Pre-War Britain*, Carnegie United Kingdom Trust, 1955. An insufficiently-known primary source on diet and growth for the interwar period, but which should be read in the context of criticism by A. H. J. Baines, D. F. Hollingsworth and I. Leitch, *Nutrition Abstracts and Reviews*, 33 (1963) 653-668.

J. M. Tanner, *Growth at Adolescence*, Blackwell, second edition, 1962. A standard work for the biology of growth. Historians may find his *Foetus into Man* (Open Books, 1978) more suitable for the 'biologically unsophisticated reader'.

T. McKeown, *The Role of Medicine*, Blackwell, 1979. Conceptually limited about health, though it claims to offer 'a new interpretation of human health history', this is a conventional text on social medicine.

I. Illich, *Medical Nemesis*, Calder and Boyars, 1975. Should be read as a purgative by those who find Leff or McKeown acceptable.

Working wives and their families

ELIZABETH ROBERTS

In the first two decades of this century fewer than 14 per cent of married and widowed women in England and Wales were employed in full time work;[1] by 1951 the percentage was 21.7 and by 1976 had risen to 49 per cent.[2] Historically, women, married and unmarried, were an integral part of the rural workforce and of domestic industry; with the coming of factories they found new employment in urban environments like the textile centres of Lancashire and Yorkshire. Married women in the working classes were constantly criticized by the better-off.[3] The intention of this chaper is to examine the lives of working wives and their families in three towns in north Lancashire during a comparatively short historical period, 1890-1940. The evidence will be drawn both from official records and from oral sources, the latter providing information about the familial, social and working lives of working-class women not otherwise readily available.[4]

The three towns are Barrow, Lancaster and Preston. Economically and socially they had certain similarities. Socially they all had large working-class populations which to a considerable extent shared a common culture and set of mores. Economically they had a substantial number of workers involved in the basic service industries of transport and building. There were, however, substantial economic and commercial differences between them. Barrow relied for its prosperity on three basic and interrelated heavy industries: the manufacture of iron and steel, engineering and shipbuilding. Its population rose from 51,712 in 1891 to a peak of 74,244 in 1921, falling back to 66,200 in 1931.[5] There were few married and widowed women in full-time employment: 5.8 per cent in 1901 and 6.9 per cent in 1911.[6] Lancaster was smaller than Barrow, 31,038 in 1891 rising to 43,383 in 1931,[7] but had a more complex and diversified economic structure. It retained many of the service functions of a former county town, such as an extensive retailing sector, an asylum, workhouse and prison. There was also employment for skilled men in its furniture and joinery works, but the typical Lancaster worker was likely to be employed in some aspect of the production of linoleum and oilcloth, including the manufacture of cotton for the backing of the oilcloth. In 1901, 10.2 per cent of married and widowed women were in full-time work, this figure rising to 11 per cent in 1911[8] (this was not far below the national average of 13.6 per cent). Preston was the largest of the three towns, the population rising from 107,573 in 1891 to 119,001 in 1931.[9] It was a textile town in the sense that its largest single occupational group was that of textile workers, 27,880 of them in 1891 and 18,383 in 1931. (This group never, however, formed an absolute majority of Preston workers; it was 47 per cent of the total work force in 1891 and 38 per cent in 1931.)[10] Besides producing cotton cloth, Preston had a heavy engineering works and, being the county town, a complex network of service occupations. Like other Lancashire towns with a large number of weaving sheds, Preston was characterized by a large percentage of married and widowed women in full-time work, 30.5 per cent in 1901 and 35 per cent in 1911.[11]

Because of the limitations of census data it is only possible to discover the occupations of these married women in the census returns of 1901 and 1911 and then only for Barrow and Preston. (The census returns of 1891, 1921 and 1931 provide details of total female employment but do not differentiate between the married and the unmarried.) In Barrow there is no clear pattern of employment. Until the 1890s there had been a flourishing jute works which employed a large number of women (1200 in 1891). It subsequently suffered a disastrous fire and never regained full production. It is likely, however, that its female employees were always predominantly unmarried girls: the 1901 census enumerated 444 unmarried jute workers but only 38 married ones. Indeed there was a total of only 646 married and widowed women in full-time work and of these the largest individual total was 119 food dealers. There were also boarding house keepers, domestic servants and dressmakers. The position was similar in 1911. In Preston patterns of employment were very different; 71 per cent of all married women in work in 1901 and 76 per cent in 1911 were engaged in textile production, usually as weavers but also as ring spinners, carders, winders and warpers. The remainder followed the same range of occupations as did the women in Barrow.[12]

This somewhat stark rehearsal of the census evidence is useful in determining the scale of married women's employment in the three

Table 1 Female Employment 1891-1931[14]

(Women employed expressed as a percentage
of the total number of women).

	Barrow	*Lancaster*	*Preston*
Women aged 10 & over 1891	32%	n/a	61%
Women aged 10 & over 1901	21%	30%	52%
Women aged 10 & over 1911	21%	29%	54%
Women aged 12 & over 1921	22%	30%	52%
Women aged 14 & over 1931	24%	33%	53%

towns in 1901 and 1911, but in the absence of comparable information for 1891, 1921 and 1931 it is rather difficult to be precise
about whether the percentage of employed married women was
rising, falling or constant. Scott and Tilly in *Women Work and Family*
argue that 'by the first decades of the twentieth century married
women in working-class families spent more time at home and less
time earning wages'.[13] It is probable that in this area of north
Lancashire the percentage of married women in work did decline
in the 1890s simply because the total percentage of all women in
work fell, as may be seen from Table 1. However, there seems little
evidence that this decline continued. As has been seen, there was a
small increase in the percentage of married women in work in all
three towns between 1901 and 1911 and as the total percentage of
women in work remained fairly constant after 1901 apart from the
war years which do not concern us here, there is no reason to
suppose that the percentage of employed married women declined.
There is certainly no oral evidence to suggest that this was the case.
One of the basic problems with census data is that it tells us
nothing about the majority of married women who are simply
dismissed as 'unoccupied'. Oral evidence is of very considerable
value in indicating the importance of part-time work for married
women in all three towns. In Barrow only one woman in the
sample had a full-time job after marriage (she became a cleaner in
Vickers after being widowed when her daughter was 17)[17] but
approximately 50 per cent had part-time work. In Lancaster 40
per cent of the sample and in Preston 42 per cent of the sample had
similar part-time occupations at some point in their married
lives.[16] We know that they covered only a small range of occupations, charring, washing, baby-minding, sewing, taking in
lodgers and trading, but it is impossible to quantify them further.
They were carried out for a varying number of hours in the week
and for very variable rates of pay. Indeed oral evidence reveals
some of the key characteristics of married women's employment in

the decades before the Second World War: it was casual, episodic and irregular. In Lancaster, for example, 23 per cent of women in the sample worked full-time at some point in their married life but only one woman (who had only one child) worked continually with only a short break for childbirth.[17] In Preston 46 per cent of the sample had a full-time job at some time after marriage but for the great majority this was broken up by periods at home and spells of part-time work.

There is no direct statistical data to indicate how many married women workers were mothers with dependent children. There is however some data which makes it possible to argue that many of them were. Firstly there is the oral evidence already mentioned. Secondly, beginning in the Census of 1921, it is possible to construct an age profile of women in full-time work.* Although this reveals a dramatic decline in the percentage of women employed in the age group 25-34 as compared with those aged 14-24, it still indicates that women were much more likely to be employed during the years of child-bearing (usually taken to be 15-44) than in subsequent years. In other words a married woman was more likely to be in full-time work when her children were young than she was likely to return to work after they had grown up. Michael Anderson[18] described this trend of a woman's employment *away* from factory work through her life-cycle as being already discernible in Preston in the mid-nineteenth century.[19]

Oral evidence certainly reinforces this picture of a mother working to support her children when dependent and then 'retiring' from full-time work as they started earning and contributing their wages to the family budget (see p. 146). It could be argued that out of the 35 per cent of married women in full-time work in 1911 in Preston a large percentage might have been childless. Again there is no direct evidence but it would seem improbable. The Royal Commission on Population, reporting in 1949, stated that in their survey of women married between 1900 and 1924 only 8.5 per cent had no children (whether voluntarily or involuntarily).[21]

There is therefore evidence to suggest that many of the married

*Ages of women in full-time employment, Preston 1921.[20]
Women in full-time work as a percentage of the total number of women in each age group

Ages							
14-19	20-24	25-34	35-44	45-54	55-59	60-64	65-70
86.7	84.9	61.0	43.8	32.9	28.7	24.4	20.3

women working in the period 1890-1940 had children; however we cannot say from official sources what percentage nor can we specify the size of their families.

Why did so many women work either full or part-time?[22] Conversely why did 50 per cent of the Barrow sample, 40 per cent of the Lancaster sample and 13 per cent of the Preston sample have no paid occupation? In 1901 Seebohm Rowntree published *Poverty, A Study of Town Life* and in it he argued that it was possible to draw a poverty line at 21s. 8d. for a family of four or five persons. Any family earning less than that was in primary poverty, which he defined as 'earning insufficient to obtain the minimum necessaries for the maintenance of mere physical efficiency'.[23] In the 1920s Bowley and Hogg, using a standard of bare physical efficiency, believed that expenditure of 37s. 6d. was necessary if this standard was to be achieved for a family of five.[24] The investigators in *The Social Survey of Merseyside*, begun in 1928, adopted the same standard[25] but Rowntree who conducted his second survey of York in the 1930s believed that an income of 53s. a week was then essential for a family of five to secure the necessities of a healthy life.[26] We need look no further than men's earnings during this period to find the explanation of why so many women had to go out to work. Before the First World War labourers in the three towns took home less, and often considerably less than Rowntree's basic minimum of 21s. 8d. The top rate appears to have been in Lancaster where Lord Ashton's labourers in the linoleum works earned £1-0-3d. In Barrow, Vickers' labourers earned 18s. as did railway labourers in all three towns.[27] Some labourers in Preston earned even less than this and, unlike their Barrow and Lancaster counterparts, they were paid on a casual basis whether on the docks, building sites or on farms. The father of one respondent was lucky to earn, as a casual labourer, a maximum of 2s. 6d. a day.[28] Weavers were not unskilled labourers but their wages would be very low. The records of the Preston Weavers, Winders and Warpers give many samples of low wages; in 1904 William Wilson of Astleyfield Mill, complaining against dismissal, gave his wages for the previous weeks, as 16s., 15s. 6d. and 15s.[29] In the inter-war period labourers in Barrow and Lancaster earned about £2 a week which put them above Bowley and Hogg's poverty line of the 1920s but below Rowntree's of the 1930s. These figures are, of course for those lucky ones with jobs. In this area the inter-war period was marked by high unemployment and short-time working. In Preston wages seem to have been significantly lower. Labouring wages as low as 30s. a week have been mentioned and textile wages were both erratic and low. A respondent whose husband was a weaver said he earned only 21s. in the week their first child was born in 1925.[30] A male weaver who claimed that his wages were £2-5s. in 1929 said that they had fallen to £1-19s. in 1939.[31] Weaving wages could and did vary from mill to mill, from week to week and from weaver to weaver, depending, among other things, on the width, type, thickness and the complexity of the weave of each 'cut' of cloth, the skill of the weaver, the mechanical reliability of the loom, the availability of the yarn and the aptitude and personality of the tackler or overlooker. We can be certain that, however these variables operated, weaving wages remained low. The Amalgamated Weavers Association in 1936 claimed that the average wage for weavers was £1-11s.-5d.[32]

It is clear from the oral evidence that when the husband's earnings were on or below the poverty line, then almost invariably the wife had to work. She worked to raise the family wage to a level above the poverty line, at which the family could be adequately clothed, fed and housed. She worked because she had to, a point made also by Cohen, Scott and Tilly about women in the whole of Britain.[33] There are few exceptions to this rule. In the Barrow sample there were only two families before the First World War where the father earned £1 or under and the wife did not have some wage earning job. In the first of these, income was made up by the sale of produce from an allotment and the wages of the children who started part-time work as young as nine (as delivery boys).[34] The father in the other family was a postman but earlier in his life he had had a tailor's shop which he gave up on health grounds; it is possible that savings from the business paid for the family's annual holiday and the purchase of their own home.[35] In Lancaster three labourers' families had mothers who did not earn wages. In two of them the allotment again was responsible for providing an important part of the family's diet; in the other one, father and children were skilled in 'living off the land', collecting a variety of foods both to eat and to sell.[36] (Other families also had these alternative strategies even when mother was a wage-earner.[37]) In Preston only one family had a total income below the poverty line, the mother being unable to work as she was an invalid, confined to bed. This family was extremely poor.

[What did your mother give you to eat?]

Bread and butter or some dry bread. I don't know Bread and margarine, we never had very much else. Baked potatoes, boiled potatoes and roast potatoes in front of the fire . . . Our Christmas dinner was rabbits.[38]

Scott and Tilly writing of the early decades of the twentieth century said, 'membership in a household still meant sharing in the economic support of the family unit as well as eating from one pot . . . As many family members worked as was necessary to earn a target income which would maintain a minimum standard of subsistence.'[39] It must be emphasized that in this area of north Lancashire the majority of the working-class continued to be concerned with the family wage, and families remained family wage economies until the Second World War. Married women worked not for reasons of personal satisfaction but to keep the family free from poor relief or charity.[40] The only exception was a small number of a group which in itself was exceptional, namely shopkeepers (see below pp 148-9). Some working-class women enjoyed their work. Some did not. But their reasons for working did not spring from individual needs or aspirations such as independence, the development of personality or the furtherance of a satisfying career. Whenever the mother worked for the family it was expected that, in time, the children would do so too; indeed in many families it was assumed that the mother would stop work only when the children's wages were sufficient to raise the family wage to an adequate level. As one respondent commented when asked whether his mother was still working at the time of her death:

Oh no. She would have given up a long while before then. My oldest brother was working, my sister and I was working, . . . She was pretty well off just at that time as we were growing up.[41]

Virtually all the respondents' mothers subscribed to the Victorian work ethic which, expressed somewhat simplistically, was a belief that salvation lay through work and damnation through idleness. They were part of a long historic process in which work had become rationalized through self-discipline, whereby the 'labourer must be turned into his own slave-driver.'[42] Most of their daughters also subscribed to this ideal but there were curious ambivalences in their attitudes. They were united in their condemnation of the woman with dirty house or children. They gloried in their own capacity for hard work, but the routine of women's work and the place where it was carried out were subjects about which different assumptions were made and on which different status values were bestowed according to the stratum of the working-class to which the women belonged. As has been seen, it was rare for a family where the father's wage was near the poverty line, not to have the mother and later the children in paid employment. Quite different assumptions were made about and within families where the father earned a 'target' income, usually presumed to be at the level of the wages of a skilled craftsman. If the father had this level of earnings, factors other than those of economic need affected the work pattern of the wife.

The burden of toil carried by women who cared for a home and family, and also did a wage-earning job was colossal,

It was bed and work all the time in those days, the good old days

remarked a Preston man ironically. Women who worked full-time were certainly *not* regarded as emancipated by their contemporaries, rather as drudges. Women whose husbands' earned sufficient money to clothe, feed and house the family preferred to have a reduced work load rather than the extra income. Among the daughters of the phenomenally hard working Victorian women it is possible to discern an increasingly complex attitude to work. They continue to work hard, they still condemn idleness; but the compulsive devotion to the work ethic of their parents is noticeably weaker. There is a greater appreciation of leisure, a noticeable regret on the part of those in wage-earning jobs at *having* to work so hard, and amongst the socially aspiring a desire to copy the life style of 'ladies' who were perceived as doing very little work. These two Preston women are representative of these attitudes. Mrs P. 1. P.'s mother worked after marriage, and so did her sister.

My sister was saying . . . 'Haven't we been awful'. Because I have gone out cleaning. She said 'Haven't we been daft what we have done'. I have had to do it. I've had to go out cleaning when my kids were young . . . My husband was only a labourer.[43]

Mrs B. 1. P.'s four daughters (born between 1925 and 1940) are now all professional women. She is proud of them but remarked, very revealingly,

I never thought I would bring up my children to work as hard as they do. They all go out to work and I brought them up as little ladies.[44]

There were also other considerations. It was a matter of pride for a man to be seen to be earning enough to save his wife from going out to work. There is no oral evidence indicating that working-class women questioned this widely held attitude. Indeed they reinforced their husbands' position by claiming that they would best fulfil their duty to their families by staying at home to devote all of their energies to the comfort and well-being of their husbands and children. Some wives of skilled men believed that they risked condemnation by their friends and neighbours if they went out to work. These quotations are typical of the attitudes of craftsmen and their wives. Mrs A. I. P.'s father was a pattern-maker in the heavy engineering works in Preston, having originally worked in Vickers in Barrow.

My mother was a winder in the cotton mills but she never worked after she was married because my father was one of those kind of men that didn't believe in women going to work. In fact he wouldn't have had fish and chips or pies for a meal, he had to have a proper cooked meal so, therefore, my mother had to be at home.

[Do you think your mother would have liked to have gone on working?]
No. She could have done but she didn't. I think she thought it was her duty to be at home and to look to us.[45]

Mrs S. 1. L.'s father was a tinsmith in Lancaster earning £2 a week before the First World War. Her friend Miss S. 2. L. whose father was a baker, reinforced her views.

My mother was a weaver at Storey's Mill.
['Did she work after she was married?']
I wouldn't think so . . . I was born in 1898 and my sister in 1901 so she'd have enough with two children wouldn't she?

Miss S. 2. L.: Then tradesmen were very proud of being able to keep their wives you see.

Mrs S. 1. L.: My father was nicely brought up and I think he wouldn't want her to go out to work.[40]

It is always tempting to project sets of perceptions and attitudes from one social class to another and from one period of time to another. Pre-war working-class married women in so far as they consciously thought about the question at all, perceived their emancipation as a movement away from outside paid employment and towards domesticity. Some modern sociologists and earlier middle-class feminists do not, and did not, see the question of married women's employment as did the women themselves. A. H. Halsey has written (erroneously): 'in the earlier decades the great majority of families depended entirely for their material support on male employment. The establishment of a new position for the mother independent of her link to the economy through her husband was therefore, a prominent theme of feminist reform'.[47] He quotes Eleanor Rathbone's attack on the campaign for a 'living wage' for men as 'a continuation of ancient male tyranny'.[48] Working-class economic realities and social perceptions were quite different.

Is it possible, then, to say that the wives of skilled workers never had paid employment? This was in fact the case in the samples in all three towns with two groups of interesting and important exceptions. Firstly, there was the small group of women whose husbands were unable or unwilling to provide for them for a variety of reasons: prolonged illness, unemployment, drunkenness, desertion and of course death. Secondly, there was a larger group of women, which overlapped the first, who worked in shops. Thirteen had their own shops, four being widows or deserted wives, the rest having husbands who followed their own job. Another 11 worked with their husbands in joint businesses. This group of shop-keeping women was a very interesting stratum of working-class life. Their husbands, with only one exception, were skilled men or shopkeepers. Within this occupational group it was not socially respectable for married women to 'go out to work', but it was quite acceptable for them to be involved in shop-keeping. Indeed these women were both seen to be, and perceived themselves to be, socially superior to those among whom they lived and from whom they derived their living. Shopkeepers were accepted as a 'bridge' group between the working and the middle-class, and shop-keeping was the most usual way of achieving upward social mobility for the aspiring members of the working-class. Some women shopkeepers did aim to become part of the middle-class but their social motivation was closely associated with economic considerations.

As a group, shop-keeping wives were moving in the 1890s towards the family consumer economy in which items hitherto regarded as luxuries by the working-class became necessities. Mrs M. 3. B., whose father was a shipwright, related how her mother opened a shop in her front parlour in the 1890s so that she could afford to send her five children to the Higher Grade School.[49] They all worked very hard to improve their standard of living by buying their own home, smart clothes, holidays and good, plentiful food. Consumerism was seen to bestow security and status. The standards set by the shopkeepers were slowly but increasingly aspired to by other working-class women, and former luxuries became necessities.

Movement towards the era of the family consumer economy should not, however, be overemphasized or predated. It was by no means completed by 1940 when many families still lived on or near the poverty line. What appears to have happened is that wives of men earning wages around the poverty line started work to raise their families' standard of living above that of mere subsistence. The degree to which that standard was raised depended on a complex series of variables: the number and spacing of the children (too many children too close together meant that even part-time work was difficult for some years, but on the other hand a large number of children contributed handsomely to the family wage at a later stage of the life cycle); the hours worked and wages received by the wife; the regularity of the husband's employment;

the pattern of family expenditure including the costs incurred as a result of the women's work and the wife's budgeting ability. As a consequence of the interaction of these variables some families, even with the mother earning, never succeeded in enjoying more than a poor standard of living. In other families, originally poor, there was an imperceptible shift from a woman's earnings being essential for adequate food, clothing and shelter towards a position where sufficient income was earned and enough savings made to enable the family to acquire goods and services hitherto unattainable.

Two illustrations, one from Barrow and one from Preston, illustrate this tendency. Mr P. 1. B's father was a labourer in the steelworks earning a basic 18s. a week. There were six children. Like other wives of unskilled men, Mrs P. felt a great need to earn money to help feed her family but like them she had no money to open a shop. She was also handicapped by her own illiteracy. Consequently she devised an ingenious and possibly unique way of making money.

She used to go to the saleroom and bid on things . . . anything she thought was going cheap she'd buy it, leave it there, go the following week and let it go again and she'd bid it and make a bob or two that way.

She managed eventually to make more than 'a bob or two' and was able to buy her own home and one for each of her children.[50] Miss T. 4. P.'s father was a 'scutcher' in the cotton mill earning only 18s. a week at the turn of the century rising to about £2 when he died in 1919. Even before his death Mrs T. had to work as a weaver. This she continued to do and was joined fairly rapidly by her three daughters. With two looms the girls earned only 13s. a week and so there was little chance of Mrs T. stopping work when they began. Gradually, however, savings were accumulated from the pooled family wage and by 1928 Mrs T. was able to buy a newly-built house, with a bathroom and garden.[51]

While the economic need of the family was the chief factor in determining married women's working patterns, of less importance was the apparent availability of work. Preston and to a smaller extent Lancaster, did undoubtedly give more opportunities for full-time paid employment for women than did Barrow, as is illustrated in the census returns. Part-time work (*which may or may not have been enumerated*)[52] seems to have been available as and when it was required in all three towns. Oral evidence, while recording many instances of men seeking, but failing, to find work, does not indicate women failing to find part-time work. The same cannot be said of women seeking full-time work. In the years of the depression women textile workers experienced difficulties in finding work as is evidenced in both oral and documentary sources.[53]

A more complex question is the relationship between the availability of women's full-time work and general wage levels. The generally lower levels of men's labouring wages in Preston as compared with those in Lancaster and Barrow does suggest that employers' calculations of wage levels were influenced by the expectation that married women and children, when they were old enough to do so, would work and contribute to the family wage. This was the view expressed in *Man Without Work*. The investigators wrote of Blackburn (only nine miles from Preston and economically similar): 'Wages have always been fixed in Blackburn on the assumption that several members of the family will be working' and 'the wages in most of the Lancashire cotton towns assume the double earnings of man and wife. The husband's wage alone would reduce many families into poverty and it was consequently necessary for the wife to earn all the time'.[54]

The existence of a large number of married women textile workers had another curious effect on Preston's family wages. Considerable expense was incurred by the full-time working mother, although as will be seen, these expenses, while reducing her own earnings, did spread her income to other families where the women did the washing, cooked or baby-minded for the cotton operative.

The phenomenon of the working mother cannot, however, be looked at solely in economic terms. There were social and familial consequences of her working.

A married woman's employment did affect her relationship with her husband and here there seem to be significant differences between Preston and the other two towns. In Barrow and Lancaster it was unusual for a man to do domestic work in his own home, except on occasions tasks which could be construed as 'Man's work', i.e. repairs to furniture and the fabric of the house and decorating. Sometimes this was the man's choice, sometimes the woman's but was typical of both labourers' and artisans' families.

Before that [i.e. when he retired] he wouldn't lift a pot, wash a pot, lift a hand at nothing.[55]

[Did he do anything in the house?]

My father! He wasn't allowed to.[56]

Oh give him a hammer and we wouldn't have had a house. I don't think he knew the end of a nail. If my mother wanted a shelf putting up, she put it up.[57]

Sometimes men like this Preston patternmaker rationalized their lack of involvement in domestic work.

'Every man to his trade' that was his motto . . . he said that if everybody did one another's jobs, they would all be out of work. He was a real Union man.[58]

Whether or not the wife worked part-time or not at all, there was a substantial degree of role separation within marriage. This was universally accepted and did not appear to create friction. The position in Preston was complicated. There were families like the one above where the role separation between husband and wife was complete but in families where there was a full-time working mother matters were very different.

He seemed to always do the Sunday dinner. He would clean up and wash up.[59]

Mrs W. 1. P. was a ring spinner,

I used to get them for the night after, if it was chops and onions I used to cook them and he would be home before me and he would warm them in the frying pan . . . I never wound a clock up in all my married life, I never made a fire and I never chopped wood and I never made a bed. He did all that whenever he had his tea and washed his hands . . . He was very good. I would be washing up at 1 o'clock in the morning and getting up at 5'clock to go to work. He would look to the boy and I would look to the girl.[60]

Husbands with full-time working wives helped in the home because without that help it is doubtful if their wives would have survived at all. Indeed when one looks again at the role relationships within marriage in non-textile families in all three towns, it is clear that there, also, husbands helped when it seemed vital to do so, usually in times of the wife's illness.

Elizabeth Bott in *Family and Social Network* investigated the subject of segregated conjugal roles.[61] Although her work was concerned with families in the 1950s, she postulated a theory which could have an earlier application. She argued that the degree of segregation of conjugal roles is related to the degree of connectedness in the total network of the family, those families which had a high degree of segregation in the role-relationship of husband and wife also having a close-knit network, many of their friends, neighbours and relatives knowing one another. Certainly this model could explain the segregated conjugal roles in Barrow and Lancaster where the great majority of families did have these close-knit networks. However, the study of Preston reveals the difficulty of applying sociological models to every occupational group. Husbands and wives in Preston textile families also had closely knit networks of neighbours and relatives, and yet there was noticeably less segregation in their conjugal roles. This does suggest that patterns of women's employment cannot be ignored in the study of role-relationships within marriage.

But despite the different roles displayed towards housework, there is no oral evidence to support the argument that full-time working wives and mothers exerted more power and influence within their marriage than did their contemporaries with part-time or no paid work. Diana Gittins argued that 'the power relationship would depend on the wife's working or not working.'[62] This was not the case; some of the most powerful women in all three towns, who were not so much their husbands' equals but rather the dominant partner in the marriage, worked either part-time or not at all.[63]

Whole-relationships within marriage are a complex subject and, like so many other aspects of this chapter, require much fuller treatment than is here possible; but they were affected by social and familial network patterns, the woman's employment, her control of the family's budget, the husband's drinking habits and the husband's occupation. (There were not many dominant patriarchs but those there were tended to be skilled craftsmen.)

It has long been accepted that textile workers limited their families. In 1832 Dr James Blundell informed a parliamentary committee that 'Where individuals are congregated in factories I conceive that means preventive of impregnation are more likely to be generally known and practised by young persons.'[64] Ethel M. Elderton reported in 1914: 'The most striking thing in the table seems to be the association between the presence of textile factories with consequent industrial employment of women and a rapid fall in the birth rate . . . It is probable that the woman who works in the factory meets more people and the knowledge gained by one woman reaches a far wider area than when her acquaintance is limited to people in the same street or village and thus in the textile districts knowledge as to the possibility of a limitation of the family is more widespread.'[65] The Fertility of Marriage Census of 1911, from which many subsequent historians drew their data,[66] not only argued that textile workers (be it men or women) had low fertility rates[67] but also that their patterns of fertility affected those of the area in which they lived. 'The low fertility of the textile industry is very largely shared by the general population of the area in which it was carried on.'[68]

These arguments present us with some problems, for there is no evidence that fertility rates in textile Preston were different from those in non-textile Barrow or from the national average as the following table shows.

Table 2 Legitimate Fertility Rates for Married Women aged 15-44 in 5 year averages[69]

	England & Wales	Preston	Barrow[70]
1891-5	259.2	275.6	259.8
1896-1900	243.6	256.5	237.8
1901-5	231.2	232.8	259.4
1906-10	213.5	211.6	223.1
1911-15	190.5	182.3	212.5
1916-20	158.1	144.1	210.7
1921-25	157.3	152.3	145.4
1926-30	130.9	125.0	123.6
1931-35	117.9	113.9	111.7
1936-40	116.7	111.6	128.5

The Fertility of Marriage Report, however, provides a possible explanation of Preston's apparently not unusual fertility rates. It admits to 'a source of fallacy'; 'the figures available show only fertility by husbands' and wives' occupations respectively, without reference in either case to that of the other spouse'.[71] Oral evidence indicates that women weavers with low fertility were frequently married to general labourers or members of other occupational groups appearing in the top 10 per cent of the most fertile men. One must presume that the fertility patterns of the husband's occupational group were more important than those of the wife. Oral evidence also indicates that women weavers were likely to have smaller families than women in general because they frequently (but not always) gave up weaving when their family began to grow, for it was expensive to have children minded (see pp. 157-9). In other words a woman's job was not so likely to affect her fertility rate as was her fertility rate likely to affect her employment. Women with growing families were likely to opt for part-time work. For the sake of her children and herself there was a point, usually before the birth of her fourth child, when it seemed more sensible to work part-time. In Preston only one woman with more than four children continued as a weaver.[72] In Lancaster there was also only one and she died when she was 32.[73] Conversely a woman's ability to carry out part-time work does not appear to have been affected by the number of children she had. In Preston 42 per cent of those in part-time work had more than six children, in Lancaster it was also 42 per cent and in Barrow 47 per cent.

What has *not* emerged from oral evidence are women weavers who were noticeably more informed on sexual matters than other women. Oral evidence is limited on the subject of sex and contraception, for traditional reticence on these matters still prevails;

but what evidence there is reveals that even in the 1920s and 1930s there was still widespread ignorance and that textile workers were as likely to be ignorant as other sections of the population. On the whole, the women who are willing to discuss this subject are anxious to point out that neither they nor their mothers deliberately limited their families. Conversely the women who are not anxious to discuss the matter are those with small families who might well have practised some form of contraception. These attitudes also suggest that birth control, although practised, was not regarded as a matter for pride or discussion. There is no evidence that women discussed sexual topics in the mill. The usual sources from which girls picked up the basic 'facts of life' are given as siblings and friends. Married women learned them from husbands and neighbours. Mrs B. 1. P. was a weaver before and after marriage.

[Did you want a big family, four is quite large isn't it?]

It is . . . I mean we never thought of it. They just came and that was that. I mean I was as green as grass when I got married and I don't think my husband were much . . . brighter. No, they just came . . . I would never like my children to be brought up in such ignorance . . . Well my first baby was born on a Tuesday and on the Saturday [before] I said to my husband "I'm bothered . . . how can a baby come out?" . . . I was terrified of this (i.e. her stomach) bursting. He said "But they don't come out there" so I said "where do they come out?" and he said "Where it goes in" and do you know, I nearly died![74]

Mrs P. 1. P. also worked as a weaver before and after marriage and had six children in the 1920s and 30s:

I went to the Infirmary again. There must have been tears in my eyes because I was thinking about keeping [i.e. feeding] them. He said "It's no good now it's too late". I felt like saying that it wasn't the woman's fault all the time. You are married and you have got to abide by these things you know . . . we would never take anything in those days. God has sent them and they had to be there. I'm not a religious person but that were my idea.[75]

Some respondents, of course, from all three towns had only one or two children. All that can be said about them with any certainty is that their incidence is not apparently connected with any particular occupation of either husband or wife.

Respondents who did not have, and were not themselves, full-time working mothers, assumed that children were better cared for if their mothers were at home for at least part of the day.[76] At the turn of the century there was a substantial body of official opinion which supported this view. Babies especially were considered to be at risk if their mothers worked. Preston's Medical Officer of Health reporting in 1902 on the causes of the high rates of infant mortality there noted: 'first among these causes is the employment of female labour in the mills . . . the return of a mother to her work within a short period after confinement, thus depriving the infant of a mother's care and of the sustenance which nature intended for it, constitutes even a still greater evil.'[77] In 1906 Sir George Newman published *Infant Mortality: a Social Problem* in which he drew attention to the apparently significant correlation between high rates of infant mortality and high percentages of married women in full-time work.[78] Newman's work has had a wide influence. Margaret Hewitt, generally sympathetic to the cause of the married cotton operatives, conceded that their employment endangered the lives of their babies.

This argument was originally supported by the present historian. Certainly the figures for Preston, Barrow and Lancaster would seem to confirm it.

Table 3 Infant mortality (deaths under 1 year per 1,000 live births) 1896-1901 and percentage married women in full-time work, 1901.[79]

	Barrow	*Lancaster*	*Preston*
Infant Mortality	162	172	236
Per cent married women in full-time work 1901	5.8%	10.2%	30.5%

Medical experts were united during the early decades of the century in condemning bottle and/or artificial feeding for babies, a principal cause of infant deaths from diarrhoea. In 1911 Preston Health Visitors investigated the homes of 111 babies who had died of this illness and found that 96 of them had been artificially fed.[80] Obviously mothers who worked in the cotton mill were much less likely to be able to breast-feed their babies than other women and oral evidence gives a frightening picture of bottles with long rubber tubes which were incapable of being adequately washed, still less sterilized.

Statistics from elsewhere, however, reveal the immense complexity of the whole subject of infant mortality. There is in fact no clear correlation between high rates of infant mortality and a high percentage of married women in full-time work. Manchester in 1901 had only 19 per cent of its married women in work and yet an average infant mortality rate of 211. Conversely Haslingden with 28.7 per cent of married women at work had a comparatively low average infant mortality rate of 163. The inconsistencies are numerous and it is clear that one cannot make a simplistic monocausal explanation for high rates of infant mortality, an argument developed very convincingly by Carol Dyhouse in *Working-class Mothers and Infant Mortality in England*.[81] Preston itself shows the difficulty of relating infant deaths to women's employment. In 1901, with 30.5 per cent of married women in work, the average infant mortality for the previous five years was 236. The comparable figures for 1911 and 1906-10 are 35 per cent and 161, i.e. more married women worked but fewer babies died. Does this mean that women working actually improved their babies' chances of survival by raising the family's standard of living? In 1908 a survey in Birmingham carried out by the Medical Officer of Health showed that the mortality rate among infants whose mothers worked was 190 while the rate for those whose mothers were at home was 207.[82]

The causes of infant death, the reasons for variations in mortality rates between areas, and explanations for the decline in these rates during the century continue to be debated by social and medical historians and by demographers. The whole question is complex and cannot be developed in this chapter; its complexity is best indicated by pointing out that the fall in Preston's infant mortality rate between 1901 and 1911 coincided with a rise in the percentage of married women employed, a completion of the replacement of earth privies with water closets, the appointment of the first Health Visitors and first qualified midwives and a drop in the zymotic disease rate.

Older children were also affected by their mother's work. Under school age children were brought up by child-minders, oral evidence indicating that the most usual minder was either a grandmother or aunt. Only a minority were cared for by non-relatives, these being usually neighbours. These patterns of child care persisted throughout the period but are strangly neglected in the Medical Officer of Health Reports. However, in 1930 the Health Visitors reported that of 35 children aged 0-2, not cared for by their mothers, 18 were left at home with relatives, 13 were cared for in the homes of relatives and only five were cared for by strangers.[83] The Health Visitors reported that the children were well-cared for and in good surroundings. There is little oral evidence either to suggest that these children were not well-cared for according to the standards of the time. Only one respondent expressed her unhappiness at having to leave her children and her anger when she discovered that the minder had not taken the child to the doctor as instructed. On another occasion she found the child wet and believed her nappy was not changed often enough.[84]

Being brought up by a familial and neighbourhood group was an experience shared by many working-class children regardless of their mother's occupation. Mr T. 3. P.'s sister chose to spend a large part of her time with her grandmother.

[Why did your sister live with your grandma?]

Well she wanted to go only for a short time and then she would come back home and then go back to her grandma. She stuck to her grandma until she got married.[85]

Mrs M. 3. P. worked as a charwoman three days a week in the 1920s and 30s but her mother and sister looked after the children even when she was at home because they enjoyed doing it.

Many a time she had them when I was at home . . . my two elder children never knew what sweets were only when grandma came . . . My sister helped bring the children up too . . . she used to take them out . . . She was proud of them. She's not married. They are as much her children as mine, in a sense.[86]

These close familial relationships required, of course, the extended family to live in close proximity and this was very common especially in Preston. Even in a town of migrants like Barrow, extended families both existed and lived near to each other, they migrated as a group and settled together, the bonds between them strengthened by their shared experiences.

When relatives could not care for a child, then a neighbour had to be asked, often an older woman no longer able to cope with the rigours of the mill. There is no evidence of unkindness or ill-treatment and only one woman already mentioned complained of neglect. (Her complaints are interesting, as is all her evidence, because it illustrates that even in the very poorest strata of society much more interest in matters of child health, hygiene and feeding was developing in the 1920s. Unfortunately again, changing patterns of child care is too large a topic to be dealt with here.) Many child-minders had an undoubted affection for their charges,

She loved children did my mother, she minded them for people while they went to work, did my mother.[87]

Apart from the safeguards this kind of affection could bring, working-class neighbourhoods exercised a powerful system of social control as this respondent realized. (Both he and his brothers and sister were minded by a neighbour after his grandmother's death.)

It had to be a reliable person . . . you often came to the point when it would be "Oh *not* her" and this was bush telegraph in the mill . . . our baby-minders, they were neighbours, they had to be good otherwise you were across the road and you got a bad name if you were a bad minder.[88]

There were few social fates worse than 'getting a bad name'.

Whilst standards of care were generally acceptable to the parents of the day, there was one effect of children being minded which should be mentioned. Mothers who worked full-time were always expected to pay their baby-minder, whether related or not, and however attached the minder was to the child.

She (i.e. his wife) would pay. You wouldn't get my mother to do anything like that unless you gave her something.[89]

Conversely there is no evidence of mothers who worked part-time ever paying their minders (they needed them much less of course). Child-minding costs further reduced the full-time working mother's disposable income.

When the wife and I worked, . . . her sister lived next door but one. We paid her for minding our oldest child David and he would be about two when Ella went out to work. We paid 10s a week for him being minded . . . I know it happened one week the wage was 18s and she had to pay her sister ten so she worked all week for 8s. She went to her mother's for her dinner and paid her and I went to my father's and paid there. So we were actually out of pocket sometimes.

[Can you remember how much you paid for your dinner?]

I think about 6d a day.[90]

Michael Anderson, writing of Preston in 1851 suggested that 'some children were interacting with their parents in a manner which can only be described as a short-run calculative instrumentality . . . Social relationships of any significance were only being maintained by a considerable section of the population when both parties were obtaining some fairly immediate advantage from them . . . In other words when exchanges were reciprocal and almost immediate.'[91] While there is no evidence of this calculative attitude to kin in Lancaster and Barrow, it can be said that in Preston, in textile families where there was a wage-earning woman in full-time work, then her relationship with her kin did have a financial dimension which is absent in the relationships of other women with their kin.[92]

The school children of working mothers were expected to work very hard in the house and to accept many responsibilities.[93] Many were expected to prepare the midday meal, others were in charge of getting their smaller brothers and sisters out of bed, giving them breakfast and taking them to the baby-minder. Then there was a busy time in the evening with more tasks.

You had to scrub the backyard and sometimes you'd help with the washing and washing was done at night after work.[94]

School children would be left for a long period after school, unsupervised.

Then after school we simply played in the street till mother came home. There were fairly rigid rules about it. For instance you were not allowed to let other children

into the house. On one occasion I did when it was raining . . . when mother came
home she was furious . . . I think it meant that mother didn't know what was going
on when she was away.[95]

This supervision 'from a distance' was obviously not as satisfactory as that extended by an adult on the spot. There was a clear
possibility of accidents, although none are recorded in the samples.
(Curiously, all the accidents mentioned were burns and scalds
which happened in the home when adults were present.) The
physical and social environment of children in the earlier decades
of this century were different from more recent days, as were
attitudes to child care. There was very little traffic on the street, for
instance, all children, whatever their mothers' occupation, 'played
out' for long periods, there being little room in small terraced
houses, and this outdoor play was not supervised directly by the
mother. This is not to say the children were uncontrolled: each
neighbourhood had a set of mores which prescribed acceptable
and unacceptable behaviour and were administered by sharp-
tongued neighbours and occasionally by the word or cuff or simply
the presence of the local policeman.

Some historians and respondents believe that working mothers
fed their families on a diet which was limited, expensive and
unnutritious. There does appear to have been a difference between
the diet of families where the mother worked full-time and where
she worked part-time or could afford not to work at all. In her book
Wives and Mothers in Victorian Industry, Margaret Hewitt examined
the effects of women working full-time in the Lancashire cotton
industry. She concluded that *in general* working-class standards of
housewifery were so low that women going out to work made very
little difference. 'The truth of the matter', she concludes 'was that
amongst the working-classes in general, the standards of domestic
accomplishment were deplorably low.'[94] Robert Roberts, writing
of Salford at the turn of the century explained why, in his opinion,
this was so. 'Many working women among our 3000 engaged as
they were all day in weaving, spinning and dyeing trades, had little
time to cook or indeed to learn how to, since their mothers before
them had often been similarly occupied in the mills. This, I think,
contributed to the low culinary standards which existed in the
Lancashire cotton towns before the First World War.'[97]

These comments require some elaboration in view of the oral
evidence from Barrow, Lancaster and Preston. Firstly, in Barrow
and Lancaster there is no evidence of low culinary standards in
working-class homes; indeed there is an abundance of evidence of
women able to feed their families on a very varied, inventive,
economical and nutritious diet. And virtually all the women re-

spondents speak of learning the skills of cooking from their mothers who, in turn, had learned them from their mothers.[98] The position in Preston was very much more complex. There were certainly women who were feeding their families in exactly the same way as their counterparts in Barrow and Lancaster. This is perhaps not surprising in view of the fact that the majority of working-class women were not working full-time in the cotton mills and that consequently they had time to cook and in due course had time to teach their daughters how to cook. There was also, however, what can be described as a textile diet, the one experienced by the families of women who worked most of their time in the mills.

When parents went out to work, cooking was a problem. Up and down town we had cook-houses. They went to work at 6 o'clock and then they came home at half past eight. They would come home and see if their children were all right, ready for school and had had their breakfast. The night before they would make a hotpot and they would cook potatoes, meat and onion. They would put it all in layers. Now they had bakehouses and when you were going to school at 9 o'clock, the oldest one would take this hotpot to the bakehouse and he would cook it for you while you were at school. Now at 12 o'clock when you were out, the first job that you did, you went to the cook-house and you got this hotpot. You took a towel with you and wrapped it round you and took that home. The mills closed at half past twelve till half past one. They came home and you had a hot dinner ready . . .

[What else would you have for your dinner?]

There was a tremendous lot of chip shops in Preston. They weren't cheap though. You could buy meat and potato pies . . . they were only 2d. Say you had a family of 5 or 6 and parents . . . if you bought pies, that would be sixteen old pence. You could make one of these hotpots for half as much as that.[99]

This extract indicates the often quoted elements of the textile diet — hotpots, pies, fish and chips (there was also tripe, which was another ready cooked food). It also shows the effort and organization needed to see that a hotpot was provided (though it should also be noted that by letting women come home, albeit briefly at 8.30 am, full-time work was adapted to the needs of married women). The extract also indicates the temptation there always was to choose instead the ready cooked meat and potato pie which appears to have had little of the former ingredient. These textile diets rarely included vegetables and puddings, except at weekends. They were monotonous, lacked vitamins, and, with their reliance on pastry and fried foods, probably contributed to the stomach disorders mentioned by some respondents. These foods were, of course, convenient; but, as the respondents point out, this facility, then as now, was expensive. The textile diet persisted up to the Second World War. Mr B. 9. P. was born in 1926, his mother was a weaver almost uninterruptedly until the family left Preston in 1937.

I never remember my mother cooking. I am sure she must have done but I don't remember it . . . food seems to have been potato based with a lot of bread . . . We had fish and chips occasionally and tripe and trotters and pies.[100]

When he finally got to the grammar school (in Yorkshire!), his teachers noted on his record that he was undernourished. Over time this diet persisted and increased in quantity. It also became a more important feature of diets in families where the mother did not work full-time. Trade directories indicate a dramatic increase in the provision of shops selling convenience foods. In 1892 there was one fish and chip shop in Preston to 1530 people; by 1936 there was one to 345. Similarly in 1892 there was one confectioner to 853 people; by 1936 there was one to 260.[101] Unfortunately there is no oral evidence about the 'textile diet' from before 1890 when there were no chip shops![102] One cannot say that families of textile workers ate well; one can argue that if the mothers had not worked their families might well have eaten a lot less.

Before the Second World War, when very few modern labour-saving devices were to be found in their homes, all working-class women had to work very hard. Those who had also to go out to work full-time often carried an almost unimaginable burden of endless toil. Women who undertook part-time jobs appear to have enjoyed the double satisfaction of contributing to the family income and of being able to devote energy and attention to the needs of their families. Rowntree worried about the 'deadening monotony' of working-class women's lives; but Scott and Tilly have warned that 'we ought not to apply middle-class standards of education and leisure to working-class women's activities'.[103] Respondents, too, are aware of changing perceptions and express ambivalent attitudes.

My mother, their life, well they had no life. It must have been a terrible life. It was all work. It was really drudgery. But they enjoyed it. It was their family and they lived for their families. It wasn't drudgery to them.[104]

Appendix

Respondents (in the order in which they appear in the chapter).
B. L. P. at the end of each respondent's initials indicate whether they came from Barrow, Lancaster or Preston.

Mrs P. 2. B. Born 1902. Father a boilermaker, one child. Mother a cook before marriage and a cleaner when widowed. Mrs P. 2. B. became a clerk. Two children. Married a fitter and turner.

Miss H. 4. L. born 1883. Father a colour mixer in Storeys Mill. One child. Mother before and after marriage a weaver. Miss H. 4. L. was a weaver all her life.

Mr T. 3. P. born 1886. Father an outdoor labourer, seven children born, four survived. Mother a warper before and for a brief time after marriage. As children grew up she was a part-time washerwoman and charwoman. Mr T. 3. P. became a shuttlemaker, then lost an arm, was unemployed for a long time and finally became an insurance agent. His wife (m. 1909) was a weaver before and after marriage. Three children, two survived.

Mrs B. 1. P. born 1900. Father was a moulder. Married three times. Mrs B. 1. P. had two half-sisters, three brothers and sisters of whom two survived and 13 step-brothers and sisters of whom ten survived. Mrs B. 1. P. was a weaver before marriage. She married a weaver who eventually became a tackler. She worked very episodically as a weaver but not after the birth of the second of her four children.

Mr G. 1. P. born 1903. Father was a slasher (wages 18s.). Eight children, six survived. Mother was a weaver before and after marriage until the children started work. She died aged 40 in 1920. Mr G. 1. P. became a weaver and later a warehouseman. His wife was a weaver before marriage and after until the birth of her second child. Five children, four survived.

Mr M. 1. B. born 1892. Father was a railway labourer, twelve children, ten survived. Mother a domestic servant before marriage, no job after. Mr M. 1. B. became a grocer's assistant in the Coop and later a Coop shop manager. His wife before and after marriage had a small shop which failed in the Depression. One child.

Mr F. 2. B. born 1900. Father a postman (formerly a tailor). Mother a domestic servant before marriage, no job after, three children. Mr F. 2. B. became a clerk on the railway, unmarried.

Mrs A. 1. L. born 1908. Father a labourer, two children. Mother a weaver before marriage, no job after. Mrs A. 1. L. became a weaver. No children.

Mrs A. 2. L. born 1907. Father a gardener, two children. Mother a weaver before marriage, no job after. Mrs A. 2. L. became a confectioner and married an electrician. One child.

Mr P. 2. L. born 1899. Father a labourer, nine children. Mother a confectioner before marriage, no job after. She died aged 40 in 1912. Mr P. 2. L. became a labourer. Two children.

Mrs S. 3. P. born 1892. Father was a carder, ten children, eight survived. Mother a mill-worker before marriage and for sometime after but in the respondent's memory was always an invalid with serious epilepsy. Mrs S. 3. P. became a ring spinner. She was only married for four days before her husband returned to France in the First World War and was killed. No children.

Mrs P. 1. P. born 1898. Father was a blacksmith. He deserted the family and died when the children were young. Five children, four survived. Mother was a hawker. Mrs P. 1. P. was a weaver before and after marriage (until after the birth of her second child). She later did part-time domestic work. Her husband was an outdoor labourer. Six children, four survived.

Mrs A. 1. P. born 1910. Father was a patternmaker, five children, four survived. Mother a winder before marriage, no work after. Mrs A. 1. P. became a weaver before and after marriage in 1940. Her husband was a printer. No children.

Mrs S.1. L. born 1898. Father a tinsmith, three children, two survived. Mother a weaver before marriage, no job after. Died in childbirth 1906. Mrs S. 1. L. became a shop assistant, (part-time after marriage). Husband a railway labourer. Three children.

Mrs M. 3. B. born 1886. Father a shipwright, ten children, five survived. Mother a cook before marriage, opened a shop in her own home after marriage. Mrs M. 3. B. became a pupil teacher and eventually (aged 32) married another teacher. No children.

Mr P. 1. B. born 1900. Father a labourer at the Steelworks, six children. Mother a labourer in the Jute Works before marriage, after marriage, dealing in the Auction Rooms. Mr P. 1. B. became a fitter and turner. Three children.

Miss T. 4. P. born 1912. Father was a scutcher, five children, four survived. Mother a weaver before and after marriage. Miss T. 4. P. became a weaver and remained one. Unmarried.

Mr M. 3. L. born 1906. Father a foreman joiner, three children, two survived. Mother a domestic servant before marriage, no job after. Mr M. 3. L. became a joiner and he married a girl who kept house for her father and brothers. Two children.

Mrs S. 2. B. born 1895. Father a labourer in the Steelworks, ten children. Mother went out nursing in homes and took in sewing. Mrs S. 2. B. was a tailoress. She married a labourer. Four children.

Mrs H. 2. B. born 1885. Father a carter for the railway, four children. Mother a domestic servant before marriage, after took in lodgers and sewing. Mrs H. 2. B. became a dressmaker and married a shop assistant. She had her own shop after marriage. No children.

Mrs W. 1. P. born 1899. Father a labourer in the Gasworks, nine children, eight survived. Mother died aged 32, no work, family brought up and partially supported by father's aunt. Mrs W. 1. P. became a ring spinner. Her husband was a commissionaire. Two children.

Mrs B. 1. L. born 1888. Father a labourer in a mill, five children. Mother a weaver before and after marriage. Died aged 32. Mrs B. 1.L. became a weaver, after marriage she took in lodgers and returned to weaving to send one of her daughters to grammar school. Her husband was a labourer. Four children.

Mrs M. 3. P. born 1898. Father a checker on the Docks, seven children, three survived. Mother a dressmaker before marriage, a part-time charwoman. Mrs M. 3. P. became a weaver and then worked in an electric lamp factory. After marriage she was a part-time charwoman. Her husband was a laboratory technician but was unemployed for long periods. Five children.

Mrs H. 3. L. born 1903. Father a weaver (at the Matting Mill), mother in domestic service before marriage and baby-minded and took in washing and sewing after marriage, ten children, seven survived. Mrs H. 3. L. became a weaver and worked periodically after marriage. Her husband had many jobs but spent most time as a stripper and grinder. Three children.

Mr T. 2. P. born 1903. Father a slasher's labourer, seven children, three survived. Mother a weaver before and after marriage. Mr T. 2. P. became a weaver, a munitions worker and finally worked on the railway. He married a worker from a biscuit factory. One child.

Mr B. 9. P. born 1927. Father a waiter, two children. Mother a weaver before and after marriage but also a washerwoman between weaving jobs. Mr B. 9. P. became a teacher, later a lecturer.

Mrs M. 1. P. born 1913. Father a fitter and turner, six children, five survived. Mother a weaver before marriage. After marriage, occasional baby-minding. Mrs M. 1. P. became a carder and later a shop assistant. Married an airman who was killed in 1945. Two children. Continued as a shop assistant.

Notes

[1] *Census of 1901*, Table 31, 13.2% of married and widowed women were in work. *Census of 1911*, Table 25, 13.6% of married and widowed women were in work.

[2] *Social Trends*, No. 8. 1977, HMSO, 1977, p.82. Table 5.3

[3] Margaret Hewitt, *Wives & Mothers in Victorian Industry* (1958), M. Hewitt presents a thorough review of the generally critical attitudes of the middle and upper classes to the working wife and mother in Victorian England.

[4] The evidence is taken from two SSRC-funded research projects, carried out under the aegis of the Centre for North West Regional Studies in the University of Lancaster. The first project, (which developed out of an initial pilot project assisted with a Nuffield Small Grant) took place in the years 1974-76 and was concerned with working-class social life in Barrow and Lancaster 1890-1930. The second project is a similar one in Preston but covers a longer period 1890-1940. In the Barrow and Lancaster project 200 interviews were carried out with 95 old people. In the Preston project 140 interviews have been carried out with 66 people. These interviews are transcribed, indexed and are available for consultation by researchers in the University of Lancaster library.

[5] *Census of 1891*, Vol. 1. Table 4.
Census of 1921, County of Lancaster, Table 1.
Census of 1931, County of Lancaster, Part 1, Table 3.

[6] *Census of 1901*, ibid, Table 35a.
Census of 1911, County of Lancaster, Table 25.

[7] *Census of 1891*, ibid, *Census of 1931*, ibid.

[8] *Census of 1901*, ibid, *Census of 1911*, ibid.

[9] *Census of 1891*, ibid, *Census of 1931*, ibid.

[10] *Census of 1891*, ibid, Table 7.
Census of 1931, ibid, Table 16.

[11] *Census of 1901*, ibid, *Census of 1911*, ibid.

[12] *Census of 1891*, ibid, Table 7.
Census of 1901, ibid, Table 35.
Census of 1911, ibid, Table 13.

[13] Louise Tilly & Joan Scott, *Women, Work & Family*, (1978), p.213

[14] *Census of 1901*, ibid, Table 35a
Census of 1911, ibid, Table 25
Census of 1921, ibid, Table 16
Census of 1931, ibid, Table 16

[15] Mrs P.2.B. Brief biographical details of respondents quoted in this chapter appear in Appendix 1, p.162.

[16] 48 respondents were interviewed in Barrow, 47 in Lancaster and 66 in Preston. The percentages of women given as having part-time work are percentages of the total number of married women having paid part-time occupations in the period 1890-1940. In some families both mothers and daughters are enumerated, in the cases of younger respondents married after 1940, only their mothers' employment is counted.

[17] Miss H.4.L.

[18] Michael Anderson, *Family Structure in Nineteenth Century Lancashire* (1971) p.71-72

[29] Osamu Saito, 'Who worked when? Lifetime profiles of labour force participation in Cardington and Corfe Castle in the late eighteenth and mid-nineteenth centuries'. *Local Population Studies No. 22* 1979. This article contains interesting age specific profiles of female participation in the labour force in these small communities.

[20] *Census of 1921* Table 18

[21] Royal Commission on Population Vol. I. (1949) [Cmd 7695] chap. VII.

[22] Those wishing to analyze theoretically the relationship of married women's work and economic systems will find useful, V.K. Oppenheimer; 'Structural sources of economic pressures for wives to work. An analytical framework'. *Journal of Family History* Vol. 4 No. 2, 1979, p.177. Dr Oppenheimer uses data from USA in the post-war period.

[23] B.S. Rowntree, *Poverty and Progress*, (1941), pp.28-9

[24] L.A. Bowley & M.H. Hogg, *Has Poverty Diminished?* (1925), p.37

[25] D. Caradog Jones, ed., *The Social Survey of Merseyside* (1934), Vol. 1. p.150

[26] B.S. Rowntree, *Poverty and Progress*, (1941), pp.28-9

[27] Elizabeth Roberts, 'Working-class standards of living in Barrow & Lancaster 1890-1914'; *Econ. Hist. Rev.* 2nd ser. Vol. XXX No. 2 1977. This article lists the documentary sources for these figures.

[28] Mr T.3.P.

[29] *The Preston Weavers, Winders & Warpers Association, Cases & Complaints Book*, 1904-09. Lancashire Record Office, BOX 1089.

[30] Mrs B.1.P.

[31] Mr G.1.P

[32] Census of weavers' wages taken by the Amalgamated Weavers Association in *Preston & District Power Loom Weavers Winders & Warpers Association Wages Calculations Book*, Lancashire Record Office. DOX 1089

[33] L. Tilly, J. Scott, M. Cohen, 'Women's work & European fertility patterns' *Journal of Interdisciplinary History*, V1. (1976) p.462

[34] Mr M.1.B.

[35] Mr F.2.B.

[36] Mrs A.1.L., Mrs A.2.L. and Mr P.2.L.

[37] Elizabeth Roberts, op.cit.

[38] Mrs S.3.P.

[39] L. Tilly and J. Scott, *Women Work & Family*, p.176

[40] L. Tilly, J. Scott, M. Cohen, 'Women's work & European fertility century Europe' *Comparative Studies in Society & History*, 17, (1975) Tilly and Scott made this point about nineteenth-century working-class and peasant women in Europe. The tradition remained powerful in Barrow, Lancaster and Preston well into the twentieth Century.

[41] Mr G.1.P., op.cit.

[42] E.P. Thompson, *The Making of the English Working Class*, (1968), p.392-3.

[43] Mrs P.1.P.

[44] Mrs B.1.P., op.cit.

[45] Mrs A.1.P.

[46] Mrs S.1.L.

[47] A.H. Halsey, *Changes in British Society*, (1978), p.101.

[48] Eleanor F. Rathbone, *The Disinherited Family*, (1924) p.ix.

[49] Mrs M.3.B.

[50] Mr P.1.B.

[51] Miss T.4.P.

[52] It is not possible to estimate the total number of women with part-time occupations. The census returns do not differentiate between full and part-time work although the occupation tables are usually presumed to refer to full-time work. The census enumerators, however, simply wrote down what each householder told them and whether a wife doing mornings a week charring was enumerated as a domestic servant must have depended on many individual factors. There is some evidence apart from a mass of oral evidence, to suggest that census returns did seriously under-

estimate women's part-time work. In an article on holiday resorts, John Walton and Paul McGloin demonstrate the underrecording of landladies in the census returns. In Keswick none are recorded for 1901 whereas local directories record 69. J. Walton and P. McGloin, 'Holiday resorts and their visitors, some sources for the local historian', *The Local Historian* Vol. 13 No. 6 (1979).

[53] The Preston unemployment returns for insured workers out of work in the interwar period differentiate between men and women but not between married and unmarried. Women constituted on average about one third of the total unemployed. Therefore at the height of the slump in 1930 over 5000 women were unemployed. *Preston Medical Officer of Health Reports* 1924-40.

[54] The Pilgrim Trust, *Men Without Work*, (1938), p.85 and p.235.

[55] Mr M.3.L.

[56] Mrs S. 2. B.

[57] Mr H. 2. B.

[58] Mrs A. 1. P., op. cit.

[59] Mr G. 1. P., op. cit.

[69] Mrs W. 1. P.

[61] Elizabeth Bott, *Family & Social Networks*, (1971).

[62] Diana Gittins, 'Women's work and family size between the wars . *Oral History*, Vol. 5. No. 2., p. 97.

[63] Elizabeth Roberts, 'Working-class women in the North West', *Oral History*, Vol. 5., No. 2.

[64] Quoted by Angus McLaren, 'Women's Work and Regulation of family size'. *History Workshop*, No. 4, 1977, p. 70.

[65] ibid, P. 78.

[66] J. W. Innes, *Class Fertility Trends in England & Wales 1876-1934*, (1938). Diana Gittins, op. cit., p. 87.

[67] *Census of England & Wales, 1911,* Vol. XIII *Fertility of Marriage, Part II*, p. cxiii and p. cxvii.

[68] *Census of 1911*, ibid, p. cxvii.

[69] Figures taken from Census, 1891, 1901, 1911, 1921 and 1931, Registrar General Annual Reports 1890-1940 and the annual reports of the Medical Officers of Health in Barrow and Preston.

[60] The fertility rates for the period 1911-20 in Barrow are undoubtedly too high. This period saw a huge influx of munition workers and their wives into the town, they arrived after the 1911 Census and left before that of 1921. Consequently their numbers cannot be estimated in the intercensal calculations. During the war, however, the Medical Officer of Health estimated the population to be over 90,500. The 1921 Census gave it as 74,244. It would seem safe, therefore, to suggest that there were in fact more married women than calculated on the basis of the census returns

and that therefore the fertility rates were considerably lower.

[71] *Fertility of Marriage*, ibid., p. cxiv.

[72] Mr G. 1. P. op. cit.

[73] Mrs B. 1. L.

[74] Mrs B. 1. P. op. cit.

[75] Mrs P. 1. P. op. cit.

[76] For typical examples of these attitudes, see pp. 147-8

[77] Medical Officer of Health, *Annual Medical Report for Preston, 1902*.

[78] George Newman, *Infant Mortality a Social Problem*, (1906), p. 103-10.

[79] Registrar General's Supplement to the Annual Report 1907, cmd. 2618. The average infant mortality figures are for 1896-1901. Employment figures from Census of 1901, Table 359.

[80] Medical Officer of Health, *Annual Report for Preston, 1911*.

[81] Carol Dyhouse, 'Working-class mothers and infant mortality in England, 1895-1914', *Journal of Social History*, Vol. 12., No. 2, 1978, p. 248-267.

[82] City of Birmingham Health Department, *Report on Industrial Employment of Married Women & Infant Mortality*, (1910) quoted in C. Dyhouse ibid.

[83] Medical Officer of Health, *Annual Report for Preston, 1930*.

[84] Mrs P. 1. P. op. cit.

[85] Mr T. 3. P. op. cit.

[86] Mrs M. 3. P.

[87] Mrs H. 3. L.

[88] Mr T. 2. P.

[89] Mr T. 3.P. op. cit.

[90] Mr G. 1. P. op. cit.

[91] Michael Anderson, *Family Structure in Nineteenth Century Lancashire*, (1971), p. 8.

[92] There is little documentary, as opposed to extensive oral evidence, on this 'financial aspect' in the relationships of full-time textile working women and their extended family. However in the brief report on child minding given by the Preston Health Visitors in the Preston Medical Officer of Health's Report from 1930, there are two revealing comments.

Thirteen children were left at the home of relatives at a small charge or without charge in return for some little service e.g. assistance with cleaning.

And later there is a reference to the charges for child minding, 10s.-12s. per week per child but 5s. and 6s. and 7s. as a charge to relations. (Oral evidence gives higher rates in families). There is no indication that this principle of charging relatives for baby minding was regarded as anything but a usual practice.

[93] These expectations of children's participations in family work patterns

were not confined to textile families. Elizabeth Roberts, 'Living and learning socialisation outside school', *Oral History*. Vol. 3 No. 2.

[94] Mr T. 2. P. op. cit.

[95] Mr B. 9. P.

[96] Margaret Hewitt, *Wives and Mothers in Victorian Industry*, (1958), p. 75.

[97] Robert Roberts, *The Classic Slum*, (1973), p. 107.

[98] Elizabeth Roberts, 'Working-class standards of living in Barrow & Lancaster', *Economic History Review*, Sec. Ser. Vol. XVX, No. 2, 1977. This article also discusses the reliability of oral evidence on such matters as diet.

[99] Mr G. 1. P. ibid.

[100] Mr B. 9. P. ibid.

[101] *Barretts Directory of Preston and the Fylde 1892*
Barretts' Directory of Preston and District 1936.

[102] Edwin Smith writing in the Journal of the Society of Arts in 1864 (Vol. 13) described the diet of the Lancashire cotton operatives as being one of bread, oatmeal, bacon, treacle, tea and coffee. Quoted in Margaret Hewitt op. cit.

[103] Scott and Tilly, *Women, Work and Family*, (1978), p. 212.

[104] Mrs M. 1. P.

Further reading

Louise Tilly and Joan Scott, *Women, Work and Family*, Holt, Rinehart and Winston, 1978. This substantive work examines the interrelationships of married women's work, their family budget and family relationships. It includes data from both England and France and from the pre-industrial as well as later periods. This work is essential reading for the student of married women's work.

Margaret Hewitt, *Wives and Mothers in Victorian Industry*, Rockliff, 1958. Margaret Hewitt presents a comprehensive review from official documents, journals and contemporary literature of the generally critical attitudes of the middle and upper classes to the working wife in Victorian England. There is particular reference to married working women in Staffordshire and Lancashire.

Elizabeth Roberts, 'Working-class standards of living in Barrow and Lancaster 1890-1912', *Econ. Hist. Rev.* 2nd ser. vol. xxx No. 2 1977. This article sets the value and importance of women's work in the wider context of working-class standards of living and the various strategies adopted by families to enable the women to balance their budgets.

Viola Klein, *Britain's Married Women Workers* Routledge and Kegan Paul, 1965. This is essential reading for those studying married women workers in the 1950s and 1960s. Based on official documents and interviews with 2030 people in 1957, it is a thorough and authoritative survey of the work done by women, their reasons for working and the effect of their work on their families.

Carol Dyhouse. 'Working-class mothers and infant mortality in England 1895-1914' *Journal of Social History* vol.12 No. 2 1978. This is a carefully argued and convincing case against the long held view that high infant mortality rates in this period were the result of working-class mothers' employment and/or their incompetence and ignorance.

Michael Anderson, *Family Structure in Nineteenth Century Lancashire*, Cambridge University Press, 1971. This seminal work includes an examination of married women's work although it is principally concerned with family structures and relationships. The study is concentrated mainly on Preston in the mid-nineteenth century. Much of the data is drawn from the census enumerators returns, the use of which was pioneered by Michael Anderson.

L. Tilly and J. Scott, 'Women's work and the family in nineteenth century Europe'. *Comparative Studies in Society and History* 17 1975. This is a very useful survey of patterns of both single and married women's paid employment in Europe in the nineteenth and early twentieth centuries. The reasons for women working are examined and there is evidence about the economic power wielded by women as the household manager and 'accountant'.

Pilgrim Trust. *Men Without Work*. Cambridge University Press, 1938. The Pilgrim Trust's investigation in the 1930s was into unemployment and its effects on the lives of the unemployed in Deptford, Leicester, Rhondda, Crook (Co. Durham), Liverpool and Blackburn. It includes a chapter on unemployed women (especially in Blackburn which has relevance to Preston).

Diana Gittins, 'Women's work and family size between the wars'. *Oral History* vol.5 No. 2. Although the data from Preston would tend to qualify some of Ms Gittins' arguments and conclusions, this is a stimulating article which examines the interrelationships of married women's work (or lack of it), the role of their family and their relationships with their husbands.

Angus McLaren, 'Women's work and regulation of family size', *History Workshop* No. 4 1977. This article examines the question of working-class women's use of abortion as a means of controlling family size in textile areas in the nineteenth century. Oral evidence from the later period while indicating that abortion was practised, does suggest that it was not at all a widespread practice.

The impact of immigration on British Society 1870-1980

COLIN HOLMES

I

As Kingsley Martin once observed, race like the theory of numbers drives mad those who study it.[1] When both are combined, the effects are likely to be even more fearsome. Nevertheless, they feature prominently in the following discussion which is concerned with the impact of immigration on British society over the past hundred years. Most of the evidence is drawn from episodes involving Jewish, Caribbean, Indian and Pakistani immigrants, since it is on these groups that information is most abundant.[2] Furthermore, the survey is limited to a number of specific themes. By way of introduction reference is made to the wide range of immigrants who have entered Britain since 1870 and this is followed by a discussion on the size, flow and concentration of immigrant communities. Against this background reactions towards immigration are then considered and particular attention is paid to the stress, almost ever-present in the debate, on the importance of numbers. This is followed by a discussion of government responses to the demands for immigration control and a consideration of the recent measures designed to improve race relations consequent upon the influx of a racially visible immigrant population. Finally, a step is taken outside the polemical minefield in which these issues are located, in order to assess the verifiable economic, social and cultural impact of immigration on the life of the receiving society. A final introductory emphasis. 'Immigrant' refers to newcomers, who have built a new life in Britain and sojourners and refugees whose stay has been temporary.

II

If we turn first of all to the immigrants who have entered Britain, it becomes clear that the influx of the Irish which had been a prominent feature of the 1840s was reduced to a dribble after 1870. Even so, some movement still continued.[3] So too did immigration from the European mainland, with the result that when George Sims compiled his survey on *Living London* he was able to write about French, German, Italian and Russian communities which formed part of the throbbing life in the capital.[4] Attention was diverted away from these newcomers, however, by the stream of Jewish immigrants fleeing from Tsarist persecution, who found refuge in Britain sometimes as transients en route to America but in other cases as permanent settlers.[5] But it was not Europe alone which provided the migrants: one also needs to take account of the small Chinese community in London and the seaports, as well as the occasional sighting of a West Indian or an African.[6] Such was the immigrant landscape in the years prior to the First World War.

With the outbreak of war in 1914 restrictions descended upon movement. But this did not mean that all immigration ceased. A number of Belgians, for instance, who were portrayed at first as victims in a David versus Goliath struggle against Germany, sought temporary refuge here.[7] The war also led to an increase in the size of the black population. Black workers were in a sellers' market as the armed forces took men out of the economy and although not all of them stayed and put down roots, some did, and through their presence effectively reconstituted a community which had first been in evidence in the sixteenth century but which had virtually disappeared by 1914. These newcomers were joined by other blacks who had fought in the war and were then demobilized in Britain.[8]

In the interwar years hostilities of a different kind brought in other newcomers. After the National Socialists came to power in Germany in 1933 all enemies of the state came under increasing pressure and after the *Anschluss* in 1938 similar conditions began to prevail in Austria. It was in such circumstances that individuals, many of them Jewish, began to leave Central Europe and make their home elsewhere,[9] in the course of which some came to Britain, to what Sigmund Freud called 'this strange country'.[10]

Although some movement took place between 1939 and 1945 it has been in the years following the Second World War that immigration has captured most attention. Shortly after the War, at a time of acute labour shortage, the Government not only allowed 10,000 members of the Polish forces to remain in Britain but actually recruited Baltic, Polish, Ukrainian, Italian, Austrian and German labour, arguing that foreign workers could make a useful contribution to the economy.[11] Following this, between 1951 and

1961, immigration from Ireland reached proportions which had not been seen since 1871-90, with movement being particularly high in the 1950s, and, a little later, with Britain's membership of the Common Market, immigration from countries within the European Economic Community was facilitated. But many immigrants have come from outside Europe. After the war recruitment 'widened dramatically to beyond the oceans'[13] to include newcomers from the West Indies and the Indian sub-continent. The first significant indication of this came in 1948 when about 400 West Indians arrived in search of work and became the pioneers of a West Indian movement which was to gather pace and reach its high point in the 1950s. These numbers were increased by immigrants departing mainly from the rural areas of India and Pakistan who, particularly since the 1960s, have injected an Asian dimension into British life.

In the late 1960s and early 1970s, in addition to arrivals from the Indian sub-continent, the number of Asians was further increased as Kenya, Uganda and Malawi, in pursuit of their Africanisation policies, extruded their Asian minorities, thousands of whom found a new home in Britain. More recently still, Asian immigration has also been stimulated by events in South East Asia, with the well publicised exit of the ethnic Chinese, and other clamouring fugitives, more than 10,000 of whom have so far arrived. At the same time as these developments were taking place it should not be overlooked that other immigrants, some temporary some permanent, were entering the country from areas such as the Old Commonwealth, from Hungary, following the abortive uprising in 1956, from South America, as fugitives from political persecution, and from the Middle East, either as temporary residents or in some cases as permanent settlers escaping from the rigours of a militant Islam.[14]

III

What has all this meant in terms of the ebb and flow of population? In considering this, and concentrating on the major developments, we can detect certain broad patterns.

From the beginning of the nineteenth century until the 1930s Britain witnessed a substantial net outward movement of population. All the constituent elements of what we now call the United Kingdom were in this position.[15] In the course of the world crisis and depression in the 1930s emigration was a less attractive prospect and this, together with a certain amount of returnee movement and the arrival of refugees from Europe, accounted for a

Table 1 Estimated population of New Commonwealth and Pakistani ethnic origin in Great Britain

Mid-year	NCWP (millions)	Percentage of GB Population
1971 (census year)	1.37	2.5
1972	1.45	2.7
1973	1.54	2.8
1974	1.61	3.0
1975	1.69	3.1
1976	1.77	3.3
1977	1.84	3.4
1978	1.92	3.5

Sources
OPCS *Population Trends* 9 (1977), pp.4-7
OPCS Monitor PP1/78/4, 29 August 1978
Personal information from OPCS

Note: It is important to consult the sources to understand how these figures have been estimated. As the text of the present paper indicates, the general area is full of difficulties.

reversal of the previous trend.[16]

In more recent years there has been generally a net outflow of population from Britain, although the early 1960s saw a significant lift in immigration from the Caribbean, India and Pakistan, particularly in the period immediately prior to the 1962 Commonwealth Immigrants Act, when a concerted attempt was made to arrive before this came into force.[17] From the mid-1960s the net outward flow of population has generally reasserted itself and primary immigration from the Caribbean, India and Pakistan, in other words excluding dependants, has been reduced substantially as a result of immigration controls.[18]

In terms of specific groups, the best estimate of Jewish immigration is that approximately 120,000 arrived between 1870 and 1914, particularly between 1882 and 1905. In recent years public attention has been concentrated mainly on the immigrants from the New Commonwealth, which is defined as all Commonwealth countries, except Australia, Canada and New Zealand. The latest figure we have at the time of writing for the number of New Commonwealth immigrants, along with those from Pakistan, is that of 1.1 million in mid-1978. The total population of NCWP ethnic origin at this time, including those born here and taking into account the children of mixed marriages, amounted to 1.9 million.[19]

Table 2

Alien immigrants estimated in the UK in the 1901 census	286 825
Alien immigrants resident in the County of London in the 1901 census	135 377
Russian and Polish aliens in the UK in the 1901 census	95 245
Russian and Polish aliens resident in the County of London in the 1901 census	53 537
Russian and Polish aliens enumerated in Stepney in the 1901 census	42 032

Source: Royal Commission on Alien Immigration, BPPIX (1903), p.14.

Once they were in Britain immigrants tended to congregate in certain areas, which have become loosely known as ghettos. The Irish, for example, packed themselves into areas of large towns and within such centres further subdivided into even smaller communities such as Aran Islanders or Kerrymen.[20] The Jewish immigrants who entered Britain from Russia followed a similar pattern and concentrated particularly in the East End of London. As a result, according to the 1901 census, four-fifths of the Russian-Poles (essentially Jews) in London lived in the borough of Stepney.[21]

This is not to suggest that the East End was the only major centre of Russian-Jewish settlement: a sizeable number also congregated in the Leylands district of Leeds.[22] It is hardly surprising that these areas attracted a good deal of interest at the time but this should not encourage us to overlook smaller immigrant concentrations. An Italian quarter was discernible in London around Saffron Hill and Hatton Garden[23] and Chinese communities could be observed in the dockland areas of Cardiff and Liverpool.[24]

A similar tendency towards concentration has been apparent among present-day immigrants. London has continued to be a magnet as it was in the nineteenth century and New Commonwealth and Pakistani immigrants have generally headed for the great conurbations. It is as a result of this trend that important settlements have developed in areas such as Handsworth in Birmingham and the St Paul's area of Bristol.[25]

But if broad patterns of movement and concentration can be identified, it should be emphasized that some government statistics on immigration are not particularly sound. A recent commentator, referring to the nineteenth century, remarked that the figures were 'unreliable for the early period'[26] and this can hardly be denied. Prior to the 1841 Census, no official statistics exist regarding the number of Irish-born residents in Britain, even though numbers increased steadily in the early years of the century. Indeed, the number of Irish immigrants permanently residing in Britain at any time has been difficult to determine owing to the presence of transients en route to other countries and temporary workers over in Britain for seasonal employment. Official figures do not identify these particular categories.[27]

As for the number of Jewish immigrants who entered Britain after 1870, the starting point for anyone interested in this is the 1836 Act which required the master of every ship arriving in England from abroad to submit a list of the aliens he was carrying. By the 1850s and '60s, however, this had fallen into almost total disuse outside London. It was revived in May 1890, although somewhat imperfectly, and the 1905 Aliens Act did little to remedy this state of affairs, since it did not distinguish between those who were coming to settle in Britain and those who passed through on the way to America, the '*goldene medina*'. When we add to this the fact that Jews were not specified as Jews in any official returns, it soon becomes clear that the annual increment of Jewish immigration is difficult to determine with total accuracy.[28]

Problems also exist regarding the recent arrival of immigrants from the New Commonwealth and Pakistan. Down to 1964 the data on entry was inadequate. Since then the situation has been partly remedied by the discontinuance of official migration figures based only on movement by long sea routes and their replacement by statistics derived from a sample of passengers arriving by principal sea and air routes, known as International Passenger Surveys.[29] This new procedure has resulted in a more accurate assessment of movement in and out of Britain but it also means that statistics from 1964 onwards cannot be married to those from 1963 and earlier.[30] It was on account of such confusion that the 1977-78 Report of the Select Committee on Race Relations and Immigration was so crushing in its comments on the collection of immigration statistics.[31]

IV

Against this background of constant ebb and flow,[32] a persistent stress has been apparent in all anti-immigration campaigns since 1870 on the number of immigrants who were allegedly entering the country or who might enter it. For example, at the turn of the century complaints concerning the immigration of cheap Asiatic labour were widely emphasized in Socialist circles and it was suggested that hordes of Chinese might be moved by cheap sea transport into the developed economies of the West.[33] Comment on the number of arrivals was also heard at the time of Jewish immigration and the recent influx of Caribbean, Indian and Pakistani migrants has resulted in a similar emphasis. Indeed, striking similarities in imagery have been present in the debates surrounding these two sets of newcomers.

At the time of the former, in 1891, the *Evening News* could complain about 'The Foreign Flood' or 'The Jewish Invasion'[34] and in 1902 the Bishop of Stepney alleged that 'The East End of London was being swamped by aliens who were coming in like an army of locusts eating up the native population or turning them out'. 'Christian churches', he remarked, were left like 'islands in the midst of an alien sea'.[35] Similar imagery was apparent elsewhere. William Walker, an undertaker, told the 1903 Royal Commission on Alien Immigration: 'There is no end to them in Whitechapel and Mile End. It is Jerusalem'; and William Rose, a carpenter, said in evidence to the same enquiry: 'It is like the waves of the sea — they simply keep spreading, but they do not retreat like the waves of the sea do'.[36] Moreover, if it were suggested that only parts of the country were affected, the reply came that in such areas it was the number of immigrants that gave the issue its significance. 'Ten grains of arsenic in a thousand loaves would be unnoticeable and perfectly harmless', it was remarked, 'but the same amount put into one loaf would kill the whole family that partook of it'.[37]

A comparison of such imagery with that manifested in the more recent debate is quite instructive. In 1954, it was asserted that immigrants were 'pouring in'[38] and in 1961 it was claimed that if the rate of increase continued, the New Commonwealth population would soon be in the majority.[39] Furthermore, Sir Cyril Osborne, who made that observation, solemnly contended that 400m. Indians might eventually settle in Britain.[40] And the overpowering, dark spectre, present in these early observations, has persisted. In 1971 *Spearhead* the organ of the National Front, blazoned the headline 'New Areas for Immigrant Flood'[41] and Enoch Powell, who has consistently claimed that 'the issue . . . of numbers and . . . the increase in numbers' rests at 'the very heart' of the immigration question,[42] has referred recently to 'a limitless and continuous inflow' of immigrants. In his view, Britain has been 'bailing out an ocean'.[43] And *The Times* has noticed 'the widespread popular belief' that there was 'no end to the flood of immigrants from the New Commonwealth and Pakistan'.[44] Apart from using similar imagery, recent critics, like their nineteenth-century counterparts, have also constantly and pointedly referred to the inadequacy of official statistics on immigration and the acknowledged deficiences in some of these have given them considerable room for manoeuvre.[45]

In addition, the question of numbers has extended itself recently into the area of immigrant birth rates. Early in 1979 it was alleged that these were at a terrifying level[46] and Enoch Powell raised the prospect that in the future London and other English cities would be 'one fifth, one quarter and one third New Commonwealth'.[47] This kind of fear, which has led some critics into the dark areas of immigrant sexual behaviour and genetic pollution, has never been far from the centre of the debate over the past few years.[48]

If we consider one strand among such claims, that official statistics on immigration and immigrant life have been unreliable, it has to be said that opponents of immigration have directed attention towards serious problems. We have already indicated as much[49] and there is other evidence, relating to recent immigration, which can be added to this. In 1968 *Colour and Citizenship* commented that the intelligent analysis of race relations in Britain was everywhere subject to difficulty and mis-construction because of the dearth of reliable information and a recent attempt by the Government to achieve an improvement in such matters by including ethnic questions in the census returns has been withdrawn after encountering strong opposition.[50] Such uncertainty has led to the exploitation and manipulation of data.[51]

The second major emphasis, that the number of immigrants entering the country has been excessive, has clearly assumed considerable importance in the debates over immigration during the last hundred years. Indeed, together with the third strand in the numbers argument, the claim that the birth rate among the New Commonwealth and Pakistani arrivals has been uncomfortably high, it has been used as a major justification of the restrictive legislation which has been passed since the 1960s.[52] It has to be recognized, however, that we need to understand more than these combined fears regarding numbers if we are to make sense of the public opposition which has been in evidence at any point during the last hundred years.

We need to start at the beginning and recognize that prior images have existed on all the major immigrant groups that have entered Britain since 1870. These stereotypes, sometimes refracted through the layered experiences, varying interests and resulting perceptions of many earlier generations and sometimes of more recent vintage, since they are in a process of constant creation, were seldom simple. They were often mixed or ambivalent, with impressions of superiority and inferiority, antipathy and sympathy, residing as co-habitants within one overall stereotype.[53]

We need therefore to take account of images which, once formed, possessed a remarkable durability and which could persist long after the social circumstances which had originally created them had died away. But how were such images related to the hostility which immigrants encountered? There are those who have stressed that if we wish to understand hostility towards minority groups we need to concentrate upon individual personalities;[54] that there are individuals who need to hate and who project a hatred derived from their own inadequacies upon minorities, including immigrant groups. It has been further suggested that among such individuals the hostile stereotypes present in society provide convenient images through which they can describe and explain their perceptions of the world.[55] We can discover people in this category over the past hundred years and even if their number accessible to historical investigation and identification has been small, they have nevertheless assumed an importance beyond their size.[56]

But it might be suggested that the maximum understanding of hostility towards immigrants would lead us away from the inner world of the personality towards a consideration of specific social contexts in which those with deep seated personality hatreds could make their greatest impact.[57] The basic social cause which has generated opposition has been a perceived threat to individual or group interests. This hostility, which has usually been specific rather than generalized, has arisen from a social context in which sections of the host and immigrant populations have had what they regard as conflicting interests to pursue and defend. Such conflict has been particularly acute at times of economic and social uncertainty or disequilibrium. Consequently, the years between 1880 and 1905, when the condition of England question was being vigorously debated, the years of adjustment immediately following the First World War, the uncertain atmosphere of the 1960s when it was realized that fundamental adjustments were needed to the British economy, and the insecure ambience of the mid- and late 1970s as this realization has hardened and intensified, have provided the broader stimulating canvas for this hostility. It has been in these circumstances that evolved stereotypes have been triggered into social significance. At such times they have helped to channel hostility towards certain groups and to justify attitudes and behaviour.[58]

If we now try to identify particular areas of conflict we might note first of all that since 1870 immigrants have been frequently accused of undercutting native labour. Whereas a supply of cheap workers could be welcomed by some employers, it could hardly be expected that sections of the existing labour force which felt threatened by such developments would respond in similar fashion. For example, in the 1880s clerks in the City of London, who were undergoing a status crisis at this time, protested against German competitors, viewed with a conditioned mixture of fear and admiration, who were anxious to gain experience with City firms.[59] Furthermore, at the time of the great Jewish immigration from Russia, while many Liberals vaunted the Smilesean qualities of the immigrants, asserting the traditional image of the Jew as 'the economic man', there was opposition from sections of the labour force which believed it faced competition from the immigrants, either directly or indirectly. In 1892, 1894 and 1895 such disconcerted cries received support at the Trade Union Congress, when Jewish immigrants were categorized as important agents in the sweating system who helped to depress the standard of living of British workers.[60] Later still, seamen claimed that Chinese hands in Liverpool and Cardiff undercut their British contemporaries and were correspondingly favoured by shipping lines. There was a tradition among British seamen that the Chinese were worthless as seamen; their only virtue was their cheapness and this strand of opposition, prevalent in the Seamen's Union, played a major part in the hostility expressed towards the Chinese in the early years of the present century.[61] A similar concern over employment was created in professional circles consequent upon the influx of Central European refugees in the 1930s; in a general sense there could be sympathy for the victims of Nazism, but this could be diminished if the refugees posed a threat to one's own career.[62] Although the later arrivals from the West Indies and India-Pakistan have not been perceived as an immediate threat to wages and employment, they have nevertheless been regarded in some quarters as a pool of cheap, mobile, undemanding labour — a view based on immediate surface impressions and received historical stereotypes — but for whose presence wages and conditions of work in some sectors of the economy would have been improved.[63] Finally, in discussing competitive pressures associated with immigrants, it is important to note that in the case of the two major immigrations from Russian Poland and the New Commonwealth and Pakistan, sharp local tensions have been generated through fears which related to the sale, allocation, and use of housing. Indeed, at the turn of the century, some of the keenest expressions of hostility in the East End arose out of this particular context.[64]

But we need to go beyond such considerations in locating the grounds of opposition towards immigrants. In the late nineteenth century some individuals directed hostility towards Jewish new-comers because, it was alleged, the Jews brought with them an historically conditioned approach to economic behaviour which would hold back the establishment of what these opposing voices regarded as a fair and just society.[65] In the East End itself such sophisticated emphases were not frequently heard but an earthy, persistent concern was expressed there about the habits and behaviour which the immigrants imported from the Russian Pale.[66] Around the same time although the so-called German Gypsies who travelled through Edwardian Britain did not pose an economic threat to any section of British society and as a mainly self-supporting group did not constitute much of a drain on public funds, their presence highlighted once again their traditional threat to the settled, sedentary life which had captured most of the population. Consequently, although the Gypsy Lore Society could delight in their presence and culture, others, particularly those among whom the Gypsies made their camps, identified with the voice of Sir Howard Vincent who asked: 'How are we to get rid of these wretched people?'[67] Other immigrant groups have encountered similar hostility. A few years later, while the police could view with tolerance the behaviour of the small Chinese community since it did not lead to breaches of the peace, others, stirred by the nature of their Christian consciences, became alarmed at the acknowledged gambling and drug-taking of the Oriental new-comers and proceeded to make wilder allegations about their sexual predilections.[68] Finally, in more recent times, the persistence of old cultural patterns among Asian immigrants has been attacked by those who have rejected the concept of integration and in the minds of others, almost certainly imbued with traditions of superiority derived from Britain's past, recent immigrants have become symbols of undesirable social and cultural change. 'Edgbaston Road used to be a lovely road', one Midlands voice proclaimed, 'you used to have nannies up that way, you know. Really good class people used to live there and it was a pleasure to walk in that area. Now they've taken over it's a slum. It's horrible'.[69] In short, immigration became associated with shocks to established, favoured, safe or known patterns of behaviour and this also raised hostility.

If at this point we draw together the essential drift of the preceding argument it might be summarized as follows. The threat of numbers has been given considerable prominence by opponents of immigration and hostility based upon this fear has been open to exploitation since not all the statistics on entry during the past hundred years have a clear, unchallenged quality to them. The volume of immigration has not always been recorded with total accuracy. Furthermore, fears have been powerfully fuelled by the concentration of immigrants in certain areas such as the East End of London, where immigration has at times contributed to the pressures on resources. Generalizations have then been drawn from such specific cases. But at all times we need to probe behind the emphasis on the size of immigration in order to locate the economic, social and cultural fears, based on an interaction of past and present influences, which have provided the bases of opposition to immigration, which have produced a context in which those with deep-seated personality hatreds could flourish, and which have underpinned the stress on numbers and given it its significance.

Before leaving this particular strand of the discussion a number of additional, parting emphases might be made. First of all, although it has to be recognized that there is a point beyond which immigration can create problems, this is not a constant and it cannot be predicted with accuracy, whether one is concerned with absolute numbers or the concentration in particular localities.[70] We would also do well to remind ourselves of the historical evidence that hostility and persecution have occurred against minorities of all types and sizes, 'native or new, growing or stationary'.[71] Furthermore, there is no conclusive evidence which would suggest that there is any one-to-one relationship between the proportions of an immigrant population or the rate of its increase and the development of public attitudes.[72]

Following on from this it can be said that no social group in Britain has shrunk from expressing hostility towards immigrants if it has perceived a threat to its livelihood, status or way of life. On some occasions such hostility has been translated into violence and at times immigrants have reciprocated in similar fashion, as the recent events in the St Paul's area of Bristol and in Brixton have illustrated.[73] Faced with hostility derived from perceptions of self interest[74] those immigrants that have fared best have been those whose interests coincided with the interests of strong sympathisers, those who could enlist support from influential quarters or those who could themselves exercise an influence over policy. Immigrants without similar support could be dangerously exposed.[75]

The foregoing analysis has attempted to explain hostility towards immigration but we have already noticed that quite differing reactions have been present in Britain, in the sense that at particular times some immigrants have been supported by certain sections of British society. Although such attitudes and behaviour are in opposition to those on which we have been concentrating, they can be understood through a similar kind of analytical process. In other words, in pursuit of their origins we should need once more to take into account the complex interaction of prior images and immediate perceptions, derived from the specific interests of individuals and groups in particular social contexts. An explanation of immigrants being accepted or tolerated on account of a transcendent moral tradition at the heart of British society leads us nowhere.[76]

V

How has Government responded to the pressures urging it to control immigration? We might now consider this with special reference to Jewish and New Commonwealth and Pakistani immigrants.

In 1870 there was no effective legislation which controlled the arrival of newcomers. The measures put through in emergency conditions during the French Revolution had lapsed and it was not until 1905 that an Aliens Act was passed by a Conservative government which hoped thereby to drive a wedge between Liberalism and Labour. The categories for exclusion were limited, however, and did nothing to prevent able bodied and persecuted refugees coming to Britain. Soon afterwards, in an atmosphere of war-like xenophobia, the Aliens Restriction Act was introduced in 1914 and was followed in 1919 by the Aliens Restriction (Amendment) Act, under which the admission and expulsion of aliens were controlled by powers exercised by Order in Council. This legislation, amended by Orders in Council, remained in force until 1971.[77]

Arrivals from the Empire, however, were not touched by any of these developments. This was consistent with the view that all its citizens were equal subjects of the Crown. And, as Empire faded into Commonwealth, this was given legislative reality in the 1948 British Nationality Act.[78] Soon, however, controls were introduced. The decisive years were the 1960s when a series of measures, the 1962 Commonwealth Immigrants Act, the 1965 White Paper *Immigration from the Commonwealth* and the 1968 Commonwealth Immigrants Act, regulated primary entry through a controlled voucher system. On the surface this legislation gave the impression of relating immigration to manpower needs but through its differential entry requirements the basic policy aim was to restrict the growth of a non-European population through the re-assertion of control in a metropolitan context over former dependent subjects. And it was in continuation of such thinking that in the 1971 Immigration Act — which has been effective since January 1973 — New Commonwealth immigrants had further restrictions placed upon their entry when Britain's membership of the EEC aided the entry of aliens from Common Market countries.[79]

This recent legislation was passed by successive governments which were anxious not to lose support through appearing defensive over what developed as a burning issue in the 1960s. Set on such a course, it has already been noticed in passing that restrictionist policy was often defended by reference to the number of immigrants entering Britain. Or, as one politician expressed it: 'Without integration limitation is inexcusable, without limitation integration is impossible'.[80] This justification might satisfy some, but it needs to be pointed out that a policy based on this premise is likely to produce its own problems. This is indicated by the fact that the legislation of the 1960s led to continual pressure for even greater control. In other words, once it is conceded, the drive for restriction is not easily restrained.[81] But the danger does not end there. It is only too easy for restrictive legislation to be regarded as an answer by itself to the problems associated with immigration. Yet, as we have been reminded recently, 'Control cannot build houses for the immigrants or the hosts; it cannot curb the unscrupulous landlord, break up the ghettoes or prohibit the formation of a sub-proletariat'.[82] And, to this, we must add that it cannot eradicate hostile, historically derived stereotypes; indeed, it is likely to reinforce such images and create new ones. By itself it cannot solve the problems raised or highlighted by immigration.[83] It stands a better prospect of making them worse by hiding behind a smokescreen of control and avoiding alternative and possibly awkward policies.[84]

At the same time as legislation to control immigration was being passed in the 1960s and 1970s, events were set in train for the first time in British history to promote inter-racial relations and prohibit acts of racial discrimination.[85]

In 1962 a non-statutory body, the Commonwealth Immigrants Advisory Council (CIAC) was established to advise the Home Secretary, when requested, on matters affecting the welfare of Commonwealth immigrants in Britain. Then, in 1964, on the recommendation of the CIAC, the first National Committee for Commonwealth Immigrants (NCCI) was founded and given the task of co-ordinating and invigorating the work of statutory and voluntary bodies engaged in immigrant welfare. A year later, a larger NCCI took over the role of the CIAC and the old NCCI. But these bodies never enlisted the support of major immigrant organizations and had no way of involving them in their work. When the NCCI broke up in confusion following the Home Secretary's decision to restrict the immigration of British citizens from East Africa, it was replaced in the 1968 Race Relations Act by the Community Relations Commission (CRC) which was entrusted with the task of securing harmonious community relations. But this new organization was no better equipped to deal with political questions or problems of discrimination[86] in the sense that it had very restricted powers which limited its effectiveness. Indeed, all the bodies so far mentioned suffered from this as well as from the fact that they were formed under the shadow of legislation to restrict immigration. Against this background, they could be viewed as paternalistic buffer institutions which mopped up immigrants with ability, tamed them, and changed little in the process.[87]

In parallel with such developments official attempts were made to combat discrimination. It had become evident by the 1960s that New Commonwealth immigrants were subjected to considerable discrimination when they applied for employment, in the conditions under which they sometimes worked, in their efforts to obtain accommodation and, more generally, in the treatment they received when they tried to obtain certain essential services. Faced with this, the 1965 Race Relations Act was passed to prevent discrimination in public places. The Act also called for the use of conciliation measures to deal with offences relating to race relations and set up a Race Relations Board to supervise conciliation procedures.[88] But all this was tokenism. The Act did not enable the Board to intervene in key areas such as employment and housing. Furthermore, the Board had no legal teeth. It could do no more than conciliate contending parties. As evidence persisted that substantial discrimination was taking place the 1968 Race Relations Act extended the scope of legislation to cover areas such as employment, housing, credit and banking and insurance facilities. The same measure also increased the size and the powers of the Race Relations Board.[89]

Then, in 1976, yet another Race Relations Act was passed which abolished the Community Relations Commission and the Race Relations Board and established in their place the Commission for Racial Equality (CRE) which was entrusted both with the promotion of interracial relations and the prohibition of discrimination. All the signs are, however, that this merger has created its own problems. Those interested in the Commission's judicial role have doubts about its being performed by an organization concerned primarily with good community relations and social work. And, like its earlier counterparts, the Commission lacks any representa-

tive base and has only slender links with major immigrant organizations.[90] As a result it has achieved very little and, at the time
of writing, it has just undergone a membership crisis. In view of its
origins and history it is difficult to summon up a belief in its future.

VI

So far we have been concerned with opinions from interested
parties engaged in the immigration debate during the past hundred years and government responses which have emerged against
this background. Can we now cut through the plethora of claims
and counter claims and ascertain the main economic, social and
cultural consequences of immigration on the life of the
receiving society?

  If we take the first of these themes, there are four areas on which
we might focus attention: the impact of immigration on employment and wages, its effects on economic growth or production,
and, in the case of recent West Indian, Indian and Pakistani
immigration, its consequences for the balance of payments and
inflation, two of the chronic economic problems that Britain has
faced over the past few years. But while there is no difficulty in
isolating the major areas which call for discussion, beyond that
point difficulties begin to arise. We cannot say very much about
most groups because our information is deficient and we are
restricted essentially to a consideration of Jewish, West Indian and
Indo-Pakistani immigration. But even here there are problems: on
certain themes data is far from plentiful and, in addition, economists have rarely spoken with one voice. Almost every opinion
finds its opposite and this needs to be kept constantly in mind in
the following discussion.[91]

  The Royal Commission on Alien Immigration noted in 1903
that there was 'great conflict of testimony' regarding the impact of
Jewish newcomers on employment and wages. Their immigration
coincided with a new system of sub-division of labour in boot-
making, ready made clothing and cabinet making, which resulted
in the production of a different and cheaper article, and such
developments made it difficult to isolate the impact of immigration
upon workers in those trades. But, as regards employment, as far
as the Commission could ascertain, there was no evidence to
suggest that skilled labour was displaced or adversely affected.
However, the newcomers did help to produce gluts in the unskilled
labour market, particularly in the East End, and it was also
remarked that very severe competition had resulted among the
lower grades of alien immigrant labour. Furthermore, the Com-

mission found it impossible to say how much, if any, of the work done by alien labour would have been performed by native female or other labour if there had been no alien immigration.[92]

As for the impact of Jewish immigration on wages, an assessment of the situation in the clothing trades has suggested that Jewish immigrant workers were sweated in their working conditions and hours of work but not in their hourly earnings. In other words in this sector of the economy they did not undercut wages.[93] And an even more recent survey has claimed that any general impact on wages was slight.[94] Any lowering of wages, of course, would imply that some displacement of labour occurred but, against this, it has to be noted that over the medium and longer term Jewish immigrant enterprise won new markets and stimulated local employment and wage rates. However, the extent of these developments cannot be determined with accuracy.[95]

In the case of West Indian and Asian immigration, the major movement into Britain took place in the 1950s and early 1960s. At this time certain types of labour were in short supply and immigration tended to correlate with unfilled vacancies.[96] And, over the last few years, the impact on employment has been limited because of other developments. It has been apparent that trade unions have been prepared to discriminate against immigrants.[97] Furthermore, some control over immigrant economic activity has also been attempted by immigrant organizations which have acted to prevent undercutting.[98] If, in addition to this, one also takes into account the active, unremitting discrimination by sections of the receiving society, the result has been that in a variety of ways employment competition from Caribbean, Indian and Pakistani migrants has been tightly controlled. Furthermore, these newcomers have been made to bear the brunt of recessions in the economy. This is clearly shown by the fact that they have suffered disproportionately from deflationary unemployment. Faced with these conditions many of them have concentrated in those occupations where it has been difficult to recruit workers or have been confined to their own form of separate economy, as in the clothing industry in the East End.[99]

As for the impact of West Indian and Asian immigration on wages, there is conflicting testimony. In the 1960s there were economists who suggested that such labour reduced cost pressures. Although the immigrants did not generally compete directly for employment and 'split' the labour market, it was argued that their presence prevented wages in certain sectors from rising as they might otherwise have done.[100] In conjunction with this it was further argued that it was this cheap labour that kept the cost of the social services in check.[101] It was further contended, on the basis of this, that a general influence might be exerted over wage levels which would reduce cost-push inflationary forces, assist in the process of price restraint and lead ultimately to an increase in real wages.[102] In contrast to this, however, more recent opinion has suggested that the immigration into Britain at this time from the New Commonwealth did not exercise a significant effect on the general or relative level of wages. But it should be emphasized that this is an issue which is far from decided. Little empirical enquiry has been conducted into the question and the data is sparse.[103]

If we now direct our attention to the impact of immigration on the production of wealth, at the time of Jewish immigration pro-immigrant circles emphasized the creative economic role of the immigrants and the 1903 Royal Commission was sympathetic to this. It was suggested that the three main industries in which immigrants were heavily involved had expanded the demand for their goods in Britain, had increased their manufacture and had raised the demand for raw materials in these industries, the cumulative effect of which had been to give employment indirectly to the indigenous labour force.[104] Such conclusions, however, were impressions and could hardly be dignified by any grander term. Furthermore, we are only a little better informed about the longer term economic activity of the immigrants and their children.[105]

When we turn to immigration from the Caribbean, India and Pakistan, a consideration of its impact has to be set within the context of the discussion which has taken place since the Second World War on the dynamics of economic growth. There are those who have argued that immigration has unclear or even negative consequences on growth rates.[106] Set against this, however, are the views of those to whom the supply of labour to the manufacturing sector has been of crucial significance in the recent growth of West European economies and who have claimed that any country which has not recruited large supplies of immigrant labour or been blessed with a 'reserve army' in agriculture has been seriously disadvantaged.[107] In line with this it has been suggested that the long hours worked particularly by Asian immigrants, their greater mobility and their preparedness to put up with inferior working conditions, have provided employers with an economic flexibility they might not otherwise have enjoyed.[108] If we accept this line of argument, these benefits have not been confined to indigenous employers: immigrant capitalists in the clothing trades and the restaurant business have also gained. In contrast to this, however, it has been suggested that even in the years when there has been a net addition to population through immigration it has not been of a size to make a significant effect upon the economy.[109] And there are some commentators who have queried whether, in view of other pressing problems, a supply of cheap labour could have greatly accelerated the rate of economic growth.[110] As with the question of employment and wages, there is also a great deal we do not know. How important, for example, have immigrant labour and capital been in sustaining an economic life in the decaying inner-city areas? And, more specifically, what has been the economic impact of the Kenyan Asians, widely heralded as the 'Jews of Africa', whose entepreneurial skills it was proclaimed on entry would add a vital economic ingredient to British life?

These discussions which have taken place on the relationship between recent immigration and economic growth have frequently led to a consideration of its impact on the course of inflation and the balance of payments. In considering the first of these, some commentators have argued that immigration is inflationary in the short term[111] whereas others have contended that its inflationary effects are noticeable only on a longer perspective.[112] In contrast to both, there are some who have suggested that immigration tends to be disinflationary.[113] In short, there has been little theoretical agreement among the specialists, and very little empirical research has been undertaken. As for the other issue, the balance of payments, whereas some commentators have expressed concern at the level of remittances by immigrants to relatives abroad others have claimed that they have not been of sufficient size to affect the current balances.[114] In addition, whereas there have been those who have emphasized the propensity of immigrants to import, others have pointed out that this source accounted for only a small percentage of Britain's total import bill between 1961 and 1966. Expert opinion, it is clear, has once again been divided. It can only be concluded that we still remain very much in the dark on such matters.[115]

At this juncture we might turn to consider the social impact of immigration, bearing in mind that its economic and social aspects cannot be easily disentangled. For instance, the type of houses and the particular areas in which immigrants have lived cannot be separated absolutely from the kind of work they have done and the money they have earned. In fact, there has been a tendency for newcomers to concentrate initially in certain well-defined areas, partly to establish close links with fellow immigrants in a new and strange environment but also because of the discrimination which many immigrants have encountered in relation to both jobs and housing.

In the case of the Jewish immigrants from the Russian Pale, we have noticed that they settled initially in Stepney.[116] Immigrants crowded into certain properties and some entrepreneurs within their community, as well as other landlords, exploited this situation to their own advantage. However, there is no substantial evidence to clinch the argument that Jewish immigrants *created* the social problems of the East End, such as the displacement of a settled community, overcrowding, preferential letting arrangements and key money rackets, which remained prominent issues from 1890 until 1904-5. Like the Irish who preceded them, their presence complicated a situation which had more intricate social origins.[117] As for New Commonwealth and Pakistani immigrants, who have been particularly affected by discrimination in employment and housing markets, it has been apparent that many of them have congregated initially as a replacement population in the decaying areas of major cities and formed part of the lowest rung of the so-called 'housing classes'. In these areas they have concentrated in particular properties and like earlier arrivals have been accused of creating housing problems and causing the deterioration of the district, whereas in fact it would be more accurate once again to say that immigrants have brought into sharper focus more deep-seated problems already present in the major areas of settlement which they have then had to endure.[118]

Over the course of time many Jewish immigrants dispersed from the East End towards more 'gilded ghettos' in North London. Consequently, their major impact on the East End, and the same is true for other major areas of settlement, was essentially short term. Similarly, many recent immigrants, from Poland and Cyprus, who concentrated at first in certain areas have gradually become dispersed and the same is true for many Chinese. This is less evident among NCWP immigrants. There is a powerful body of evidence which suggests, significantly, that concentration and segregation among the Asian minority might be on the increase. Social discrimination has a key role in this.[119]

In this consideration of the social impact of immigration we need to do more than notice its effects on housing and related issues. Through their presence all the major arrivals of the past hundred years have raised important questions involving the role of the state, such as: to what extent should it provide the basic elements of social support for its citizens? What role should it adopt in remedying the disadvantages which immigrants have faced in, say, education? Does it have a role to play in trying to ensure that groups from a variety of backgrounds live together in tolerable harmony? This is another way of saying that immigration has generated a debate on the scope and ethos of social policy, that it has tested the problem solving capacities of the state and that in some cases, by encouraging state intervention, it has exposed social policy as a focus for host-immigrant resentment.[120] We need to be aware of this wider picture.

The concentration of immigrants in particular areas has implications for our final theme, in the sense that it is in the major areas of immigrant settlement that some of the most distinct signs of the cultural impact of immigration have been displayed. This was clearly apparent in the emergence of a Jewish East End in the late nineteenth century and in the parallel transformation of the Leylands area of Leeds.[121] The early concentration of Negroes and Chinese also led to cultural changes in certain seaport towns[122] and today parts of Southall have assumed a strong Asian ambience.[123] In all such areas patterns from the immigrants' past have been recreated; shops, foodstores, restaurants, clubs, credit organizations, *stiebels* and mosques catering for various immigrant needs have all been established. In some instances the process has been graphically illustrated, as in the East End, where a Huguenot church which later became a synagogue has been converted recently into a mosque for the Bengali community.[124] It is of course in areas such as Handsworth, the St Paul's district of Bristol, and parts of Southall and the East End where these changes have primarily taken place that the social problems associated with immigration have been most often in the news.[125]

However, we need to do more than identify elements from the immigrants' past life which have been introduced into Britain. With some groups such as the Maltese, there has been an erosion of national consciousness[126] and this has also been apparent in sections of the Polish community.[127] Elsewhere, however, the story is different. The Chinese, for example, have shown no inclination to shed what they regard as their own superior culture.[128] And we have been told that second generation Punjabi Sikhs have almost universally rejected the idea of 'becoming English'; they have modified and reformed their parents' values rather than abandoned them completely. This process, symbolized by the re-adoption of the turban, has been described as their own 'overt expression of a separate ethnicity'.[129] In similar vein many young Jamaicans have not carried on old cultural patterns; nor have they become English. Rather, they have adapted to their situation by a new process of creolization.[130] This is another way of saying that in some instances immigration into Britain has resulted not only in the retention of old cultural patterns in a new environment but has also resulted in the emergence of new ones. Such consciousness has owed a great deal to the rejection, hostility and discrimination which immigrants have perceived and encountered in their new environment. In other words it has emerged as a quest for survival in a strange land and in some cases these expressions of cultural difference have contained or developed a political dimension, which has led to defensive confrontations with white society, when struggles in Britain against disadvantages in unemployment, housing and education have become linked with the battles of blacks elsewhere and have led to the corresponding worship of the same political saints.[131]

But the cultural impact has not ended there. Some immigrants, from a variety of backgrounds, have expanded and developed levels of perception which have had a relevance beyond the interests of their own racial or ethnic group. Through their life experiences they have succeeded in providing fresh and vibrant perspectives on a much wider area of British society. Furthermore, some of those who have been regarded as outsiders have seemingly derived a creative impulse from the tension of their situation which has resulted in their making a contribution to more than merely national understanding.[132] This should not cause us to forget, however, that for others the life of an immigrant, with its special strains and problems, has proved a burden which has enabled them to do little more than survive, supported by bitter-sweet memories of an increasingly remote earlier known land.

If, at this point, we pause for a moment and take stock, it ought to be clear by now that the economic, social and cultural impact of immigration on Britain has assumed considerable complexity and directly attributable influences are difficult to isolate. In such circumstances it has often happened that simple connections have been made and easy explanations have been sought. This has been the picture in the past; there is little reason to anticipate a different future.

VII

On that pessimistic note we end this survey of immigration into Britain. But before doing so, we might remind ourselves that it is not only over the last hundred years that an immigrant population has been added to British society. 'Wherever homo sapiens made his first and on the whole regrettable appearance', it has been written, 'it was not in Britain; all our ancestors came from somewhere else'.[133] We have concentrated here upon only a fragment; a frame in a revolving reel. In this respect, if we switch metaphors and borrow from the imagery of the debate we have just been considering, those who have engaged our attention should be regarded as only some of the main tributaries derived from the stream of immigrants entering Britain over the past hundred years, in the course of which they have all written new chapters in their own lives as well as in ours. Indeed, it is a history which is still being written.

Notes

[1] In *Harold Laski* (1953), p. 9.

[2] Pakistan left the Commonwealth in 1972. Pakistanis ceased to be regarded as New Commonwealth immigrants in the summer of 1973.

[3] J. A. Jackson. *The Irish in Britain* (1963), p. XIV. For a recent important study of the Irish in London, mainly in the 1850s and 1860s, see L. H. Lees, *Exiles of Erin, Irish Migrants in Victorian London* (Manchester, 1979).

[4] G. Sims, *Living London* (3 vols. 1901-3), in scattered chapters.

[5] L. P. Gartner. *The Jewish Immigrant in England 1870-1914* (First published, 1960, second edition 1973), remains the best study.

[6] Ng Kwee Choo, *The Chinese in London* (1968), chapter 1; J. Walvin, *Black and White: The Negro in English Society, 1555-1945* (1973), pp. 198-9, 202-5; J. P. May, 'The Chinese in Britain 1860-1914', in C. Holmes (ed.), *Immigrants and Minorities in British Society* (1978), chapter 5.

[7] There is no existing study of this episode.

[8] Walvin, op. cit., p. 205.

[9] A. J. Sherman, *Island Refuge. Britain and Refugees from the Third Reich 1933-39* (1973).

[10] E. L. Freud (ed.), *The Letters of Sigmund Freud and Arnold Zweig* (1970), p. 164.

[11] J. A. Tannahill, *European Volunteer Workers in Britain* (Manchester, 1958).

[12] G. P. Freeman, *Immigrant Labor and Racial Conflict in Industrial Societies. The French and British Experience 1945-1975* (Princeton, 1979), p. 65.

[13] V. G. Kiernan, 'Britons old and new', in Holmes, op. cit., p. 54.

[14] J. Rex and S. Tomlinson, *Colonial Immigrants in a British City* (1979) has a useful chronological table which sets out many of the developments referred to here.

[15] R. K. Kelsall, *Population* (4 edn., 1979), p. 29.

[16] Ibid.

[17] Freeman. op. cit., p. 24.

[18] See *New Society*, 22 November 1979, for recent discussion of this.

[19] Gartner, op. cit., p. 29; OPCS Monitor pp. 1 79/9, 22 November 1979 and other OPCS information.

[20] Jackson, op. cit., p. 18.

[21] *Royal Commission on Alien Immigration*, BPP IX (1903), p.14 (henceforth *RC* 1903).

[22] J. Buckman, 'The economic and social history of alien immigration to Leeds', PhD, Strathclyde, 1968, is the best study.

[23] R. Palmer, 'The Italians: patterns of migration to London', in J. L. Watson (ed.), *Between Two Cultures* (Oxford, 1977), p. 245. See also the classic work, R. F. Foerster, *The Italian Emigration of Our Times* (New York, 1968. First published 1919), pp. 203-5.

[24] Choo, op. cit., chapter 1.

[25] Rex and Tomlinson, op. cit., is concerned with Handsworth. A. H. Richmond, *Migration and Race Relations in an English City. A Study in Bristol* (1973), discusses the St Paul's area, as does K. Pryce, *Endless Pressure* (Harmondsworth, 1979).

[26] Kelsall, op. cit., p. 29.

[27] Jackson, op. cit., p. 11.

[28] L. P. Gartner, 'Notes on the statistics of Jewish immigration to England 1870-1914', *Jewish Social Studies*, vol. XXII (1960), pp. 97-102. See also J. A. Garrard, *The English and Immigration 1880-1910* (1971), pp. 213-6.

[29] In order to be classified as an immigrant it is necessary to have been out of the country for at least 12 months and to have expressed the intention to reside in the country for at least 12 months after entry. Movement between Eire and the United Kingdom is not available in this statistical series.

[30] See Kelsall, op. cit., p. 32.

[31] *Select Committee on Race Relations and Immigration*, vol. 1, Report, 1977-78 (London, 1978), pp. XV-XXV.

[32] See above pp. 174-5

[33] J. P. May, 'The British working class and the Chinese 1870-1911', MA, Warwick, 1973.

[34] Quoted in B. Gainer, *The Alien Invasion* (1972), pp. 12, 169.

[35] Garrard, op. cit., p. 51.

[36] *RC* 1903, pp. 298, 302.

[37] Garrard, op. cit., p. 52.

[38] P. Foot, *Immigration and Race in British Politics* (Harmondsworth, 1965), p. 165.

[39] Ibid., p. 129.

[40] Ibid., p. 246.

[41] *Spearhead*, no. 46, September 1971 (front cover).

[42] B. Smithies and P. Fiddick, *Enoch Powell on Immigration* (1969), p. 68.

[43] *Parliamentary Debates* (Commons), vol. 912 (1975-6), col. 49. See ibid., col. 48 for a striking reference to the 'steady, large, inexorably continuing flow' of immigrants.

[44] *The Times*, 25 May 1976.

[45] See above pp. 176-7

[46] *Spearhead*, no. 127, March 1979, p. 4.

[47] Reported in the *Daily Telegraph*, 16 August 1979. For Powell's latest speech on this theme, to the Monday Club in Dorking, see ibid., 14 July 1980.

[48] *Spearhead*, no. 112, December 1977, p. 5 and ibid., no. 116, August 1978, p.6

[49] See above, pp. 176-7.

[50] E. J. B. Rose (ed.), *Colour and Citizenship* (1969), p. 91. On the ethnic census issue see J. Gould, 'Ethnicity and the 1981 British Census', *Patterns of Prejudice*, vol. 14 (January 1980), pp. 24-31. The decision not to include a reference to ethnic origins was given in *Parliamentary Debates* (Commons), vol. 983 (1979-80), cols. 1301-9. For later comment on ethnicity and census returns, see *New Community*, vol. 8 (1980), pp.3-26.

[51] See the correspondence in *The Guardian*, 25 August 1979.

[52] Freeman, op. cit., pp. 138-9. For official comment see *Parliamentary Debates* (Commons), vol. 649 (1961), cols. 694-5 and ibid., vol. 969 (1979), col. 1121.

[53] For comment on the importance of pre-existing images related to Jewish and New Commonwealth and Pakistani immigrants see Garrard, op. cit., pp. 86-7 and Rex and Tomlinson, op. cit., pp. 285-93, respectively. See J. Higham, 'Anti-semitism in the gilded age', *Mississippi Valley Historical Review*, vol. LXIII (1956-7), pp. 562-5 for reference to the mixed nature of stereotypes. See Rex and Tomlinson, op. cit., pp. 37 for additional comment on mixed images.

[54] See the general discussion in G. E. Simpson and J. M. Yinger, *Racial and Cultural Minorities* (4 edn, New York, 1972), chapter 3.

[55] See the comment in Richmond, op. cit., p. 4.

[56] C. Holmes, *Anti-Semitism in British Society 1876-1939* (1979), pp. 230-1.

[57] Rose, op. cit., p. 533; Holmes, *Anti-Semitism*, pp. 173, 231; J. Rex and R. Moore, *Race, Community and Conflict* (1967), pp. 3, 12.

[58] Rex and Tomlinson, op. cit., p. 14 for a recognition of the fact that relations between newcomers and the host society can vary along several axes. See also Simpson and Yinger, op. cit., p. 163 for the significance of cultural stereotypes.

[59] G. Anderson, 'German clerks in England, 1870-1914; another aspect of the great depression debate', in K. J. Lunn (ed.) *Hosts, Immigrants and Newcomers. Historical Responses to Newcomers in British Society 1870-1914* (Folkestone and New York, 1980), pp. 201-21.

[60] Garrard, op. cit., pp. 31-3.

[61] The chief concern of May in Holmes, *Immigrants and Minorities*.

[62] Holmes, *Anti-Semitism*, p. 206.

[63] C. Jones, *Immigration and Social Policy in Britain* (1977), p. 141.

[64] J. J. Bennett, 'East end newspaper opinion and Jewish immigration 1885-1905', M. Phil., Sheffield, 1979. See also below, p. 190-1

[65] C. Holmes, 'J. A. Hobson and the Jews' in Holmes, *Immigrants and Minorities*, pp. 130, 147.

[66] Garrard, op. cit., pp. 48-51.

[67] See Holmes, 'The German gypsy question in Britain 1904-1906', in Lunn, op. cit., pp. 134-59.

[68] See May in Holmes, *Immigrants and Minorities*, pp. 113-4. For additional comment on Chinese immigrants and drugs, see V. Berridge, 'East end opium dens and narcotic use in Britain', *The London Journal*, vol. 4 (1978), pp. 3-28.

[69] Quoted, among other places, in Jones, op. cit., p. 137.

[70] R. I. Woods, 'Population turnover, tipping points and markov chains', *Transactions of the Institute of British Geographers*, new series, vol. 2 (1977), pp. 473-89, carries a useful summary of recent thought on such matters.

[71] See the letter of Ruth Glass in *The Times*, 16 February 1968. See also S. Allen, *New Minorities. Old Conflicts* (New York, 1971), pp. 59-60.

[72] Freeman, op. cit., p. 278.

[73] See May, MA thesis; Holmes, *Anti-Semitism*, chapter 6; G. Alderman. 'The anti-jewish riots of august 1911 in South Wales', *Welsh History Review*, vol. VI (1972), pp. 190-200; R. May and R. Cohen, 'The interaction between race and colonialism: a case study of the Liverpool race riots of 1919', *Race*, vol. XVI (1974), pp. 11-26; Bethnal Green and Stepney Trades Council, *Blood on the Streets* (1978); N. Evans, 'The South Wales race riots of 1919', *Llafur*, vol. 3 (Spring 1980), pp. 5-29, provide a range of information on violence against immigrants. The violence in Bristol has just been the subject of an official, local enquiry. For some speculation on future levels of racial violence in Britain see J. Rex, 'Black power or just another brick in the wall', *The Times Higher Education Supplement*, 20 June 1980.

[74] Kiernan in Holmes, *Immigrants and Minorities*, p. 50 brings this out very clearly.

[75] Holmes in Lunn, op. cit., pp. 149-50; G. Dench, *The Maltese in London* (1975); see also C. Holmes, 'Anti-semitism and the BUF', in K. Lunn and R. C. Thurlow (eds.), *British Fascism* (1980), pp. 129-30.

[76] See the related discussion by Holmes in Lunn and Thurlow, op. cit., p. 129. See also Allen, op. cit., p. 3.

[77] S. C. on Race Relations and Immigration, pp. IX-XI.

[78] N. Deakin, 'The British Nationality Act of 1948: a brief study of the mythology of race relations', *Race,* vol. II (1969), pp. 77-83.

[79] See Freeman, op. cit., pp. 46, 58-9, 133.

[80] Quoted by Rex and Tomlinson, op. cit., p. 53. See also note 52 above.

[81] Freeman, op. cit., p. 60.

[82] Foot, op. cit., p. 248.

[83] *The Times*, 1 February 1978.

[84] Jones, op. cit., p. 162 noted that none of the problems associated with immigration had been tackled with the same vigour as that given to the control of immigration.

[85] For a recent discussion of the legislation of the 1960s on race and immigration see J. Lea, 'The contradictions of the sixties race relations legislation', in National Deviancy Conference, *Permissiveness and Control* (1980), pp. 122-48.

[86] Jones, op. cit., p. 158. See also J. Rex, 'Black militancy and class conflict', in R. Miles and A. Phizacklea, *Racism and Political Action* (1979), p. 88.

[87] I. Katznelson, *Black Men, White Cities. Race, Politics and Migration in the United States and Britain 1948-68* (1973), chapter II, partic. pp. 177-80.

[88] Freeman, op. cit., p. 54.

[89] Jones, op. cit., p. 159.

[90] Rex in Miles and Phizacklea, op. cit., p. 88.

[91] Freeman, op. cit., p. 173. See also Runnymede Trust, 'Trade Unions and immigrant workers', *New Community*, vol. IV. (1974-6). p. 22.

[92] *RC* 1903, pp. 19-20.

[93] S. Lerner, 'The impact of the Jewish immigration of 1880-1914 on the London clothing industry and the Trade Unions', *Bulletin of the Society for the Study of Labour History*, vol. XII (Spring 1966), p. 13.

[94] E. H. Hunt, *Regional Wage Variations in Britain 1850-1914* (Oxford, 1973), p. 319.

[95] Ibid., p. 321.

[96] C. Peach, *West Indian Migration to Britain: A Social Geography* (1965), chapters IV and V; D. Brooks, *Race and Labour in London Transport* (1975), p. 257.

[97] *The Times*, 12 December 1979, provides recent evidence of discrimination by Trade Unions. On more general but related matters, Runnymede Trust, in *New Community*, vol. IV (1974-6), pp. 27-9 notes an improvement over time in union attitudes towards immigrants but acknowledges the persistence of a gap between good intentions and practice and Rex in Miles and Phizacklea, op. cit., pp. 77-8 draws attention to the fact that at times the interests of immigrant trade unionists have been sacrificed by the trade union movement.

[98] See the comments of Paul Harrison on the Indian Workers' Association in 'The patience of Southall', *New Society*, 4 April 1974.

[99] On discrimination see, for example, D. J. Smith, *The Facts of Racial Disadvantage* (Harmondsworth, 1976), pp. 56-63, 68, 112-4 and, for a specific group, M. Anwar, *The Myth of Return. Pakistanis in Britain* (1979),

p. 285. Additional comment is carried by Rex and Tomlinson, op.cit., p. 278. For unemployment among New Commonwealth and Pakistani immigrants see Rose, op. cit., p.180; Rex and Tomlinson, op.cit., pp.110, 116-7; K. Jones and A. D. Smith, *The Economic Impact of Commonwealth Immigration* (1970), pp. 44-5; S. Castles and G. Kosack, *Immigrant Workers and Class Structure in Western Europe* (1973), pp. 90-3; see also *The Times*, 18 July 1980 and 11 August 1980.

[100] R. G. Opie, 'Britain's immigrants: Do they help the economy?', *New Statesman*, 15 March 1968, p. 324.

[101] Rose, op. cit., p. 648: see also K. Jones, 'Immigrants and the social services', *National Institute Economic Review*, No. 41 (August 1967), pp. 28-40.

[102] Opie, loc. cit., p. 324.

[103] Castles and Kosack, op. cit., pp. 376-82. Enquiries to the Transport and General Workers Union, the National Union of Public Employees and the Commission for Racial Equality drew a blank.

[104] *RC* 1903, pp. 19-20.

[105] B. Kosmin, 'Exclusion and opportunity. Traditions of work among British Jews', in S. Wallman (ed.), *Ethnicity at Work* (1979), pp. 37-68, is the most recent analysis of Jewish occupations.

[106] E. J. Mishan's 'Does immigration confer economic benefits on the host country?', in Institute of Economic Affairs, *Economic Issues in Immigration* (1970), pp. 91-122, is a well-known statement of this position.

[107] A point of view associated particularly with C. P. Kindleberger, *Europe's Post-War Growth. The Role of Labor Supply* (Cambridge, Mass., 1961).

[108] Anwar, op. cit., p. 215, Freeman, op. cit., p. 188; B. Cohen and P. Jenner, 'The Employment of Immigrants: A Case Study within the Wool Industry', *Race*, vol. X (1969), p. 54; P. Harrison in *New Society*, 4 April 1974.

[109] Castles and Kosack, op. cit., p. 424.

[110] J. Cornwall, *Modern Capitalism* (1977), pp. 70, 92.

[111] E. J. Mishan and L. J. Needleman, 'Immigration: some economic effects', *Lloyds Bank Review*, no. 81 (July, 1966), p. 35.

[112] Castles and Kosack, op. cit., pp. 388-9.

[113] Kindleberger op. cit., p. 3.

[114] Castles and Kosack, op. cit., p. 394.

[115] Ibid., pp. 394-5 covers this ground.

[116] See above p. 176.

[117] See Jackson, op. cit., p. 62 and Gainer, op. cit., pp. 36-44.

[118] The impact of New Commonwealth and Pakistani immigration on housing has generated a vast literature. Among early studies reference might be made to Rex and Moore, *Race, Community and Conflict* and Rose,

op. cit., chapters 12 and 17. See also *Report of the Committee on Housing in Greater London*, 1965, Cmnd. 2605, p. 203; K. Leech, 'Housing and immigration crisis in London', *Race*, vol. VIII (1967), pp.329-44 and Richmond, op. cit., chapter 6 for additional early comment. Rex and Tomlinson, op. cit., pp. 127-57 provide material of later vintage on Handsworth. The whole situation has been monitored over many years in reports by Political and Economic Planning.

[119] M. Freedman (ed.), *A Minority in Britain* (1955), pp.140-1 notes the dispersal of Jews living in London. S. Patterson, 'The Poles: an exile community in Britain', in Watson, op. cit., p. 221 comments on the Polish experience and P. Constantinides, 'The Greek Cypriots: factors in the maintenance of an ethnic identity', in ibid., pp. 278-9 refers to Greek Cypriot mobility; J. L. Watson, 'The Chinese: Hong Kong villagers in the British catering trade', in ibid., p. 181 comments on the dispersal of the Chinese. For evidence of continuing concentration among immigrants see R. I. Woods. 'Ethnic segregation in Birmingham in the 1960s and 1970s', *Ethnic and Racial Studies*, vol. 2 (1979), pp. 455-76.

[120] Jones, op. cit.

[121] On the Leeds ghetto see E. E. Burgess, 'The soul of the Leeds ghetto', cuttings from the *Yorkshire Evening News*, 1925 (Leeds Public Library).

[122] M. Banton, *The Coloured Quarter* (1955), is a classic study.

[123] P. Harrison in *New Society*, 4 April 1974, pp. 7-11; see also *The Times*, 9 June 1976.

[124] N. Deakin, 'The vitality of a tradition', in Holmes, *Immigrants and Minorities*, pp. 159-60.

[125] See Pryce, op. cit., on St Paul's and Rex and Tomlinson, op. cit., on Handsworth.

[126] Dench, op. cit., chapters 3, 4, 5.

[127] Patterson in Watson, op. cit., p. 240.

[128] Watson, ibid., p. 205.

[129] R. Ballard and C. Ballard, 'The Sikhs: the development of south Asian settlements in Britain', ibid., p. 47.

[130] N. Foner, 'The Jamaicans; cultural and social change among migrants in Britain', ibid., pp. 120, 145-6. Rex and Tomlinson, op. cit., p. 235 refer to Rastafari as 'the most important single fact about West Indian society and culture in Britain'.

[131] See Rex in Miles and Phizacklea, op. cit., pp. 83-92. for recent comment.

[132] Kiernan in Holmes, *Immigrants and Minorities* raises this at a number of points. See also K. Newton, *The Sociology of British Communism* (1969), chapter 7 and P. Anderson, 'Components of the national cult', in A. Cockburn and R. Blackburn (eds.), *Student Power* (Harmondsworth, 1969), pp. 229-77.

[133] Kiernan in Holmes, *Immigrants and Minorities*, p. 23.

* This paper was finally revised and submitted in mid-September 1981. I am indebted to the Nuffield Foundation which is financing the work on which the discussion is based.

Further reading

Michael Banton, *The Coloured Quarter*, Cape, 1955. A detailed study of the Black population in Stepney in the late 1940s and the early 1950s. The investigation was concerned with the extent to which the immigrants were being assimilated to the settled population. It remains a major example of the 'assimilationist approach' which dominated ethnic studies in Britain until the late 1960s.

Paul Foot, *Immigration and Race in British Politics*, Penguin, 1966. A passionate essay, written at the height of the controversy over New Commonwealth and Pakistani immigration in the 1960s. It provides a vivid account of extreme reactions to immigration between the 1880s and 1960s. Written from a socialist viewpoint.

L. P. Gartner, *The Jewish Immigrant in England 1870-1914*, Allen and Unwin, 1960. A pioneer study of the great Jewish immigration from Tsarist Russia. It concentrates chiefly on London, at the expense of other communities, and says little about the anti-semitism which the newcomers had to face, but it is a superb study of Jewish immigrant life and draws upon an unrivalled range of sources.

Colin Holmes (ed.), *Immigrants and Minorities in British Society*, Allen and Unwin, 1978. An attempt to create a general interest in the history of immigration into Britain. It contains chapters which discuss Irish, Chinese, German and Jewish minorities. It also carries a general survey of immigration into Britain from the Roman times to the present day. There is a useful bibliography.

J. A. Jackson, *The Irish in Britain*, Routledge and Kegan Paul, 1963. Written at a time when there was no published account of Irish settlement in England, Wales or Britain as a whole, it is still the major general survey of Irish immigration and forms a useful starting point and essential quarrying ground for other more detailed studies. It covers the period from the late eighteenth century to 1960.

Kenneth Lunn, *Hosts, Immigrants and Minorities. Historical Responses to Newcomers in British Society 1870-1914*, Dawson, 1980. A collection of essays dealing essentially with host responses to a wide range of newcomers in British society. It is particularly strong on the reactions of organized labour and the working class between 1870 and 1914. A work which calls for and deserves close attention.

E. J. B. Rose (ed.), *Colour and Citizenship*, Oxford University Press, 1969. A survey which was intended by its compilers as an unofficial Royal Commission on New Commonwealth immigration. In parts, as in its discussion of the incidence of prejudice, it is methodologically suspect. It survives essentially as an important monument to the concept of integration which replaced the old assimilationist approach to race relations in Britain.

John Rex and Sally Tomlinson, *Colonial Immigrants in a British City: a Class Analysis*, Routledge and Kegan Paul 1979. The most recent work from Rex which continues his interest in race relations in an urban context. It is a detailed, local study of Handsworth in the late 1970s, but set against a wider context of racialism and colonialism. There is a particularly useful chronological table outlining the major developments in the history of New Commonwealth and Pakistani immigration.

J. A. Tannahill, *European Volunteer Workers in Britain*, Manchester University Press, 1958. An analysis of the little known, government-encouraged immigration of displaced workers from Europe which began in 1947. An 'insider's account', written by a civil servant, and stronger on the administrative aspects of the episode than it is on the lives of the immigrants or reactions to their arrival. It remains, however, a generally useful, interesting and underrated study.

James L. Watson, *Between Two Cultures*, Blackwell, 1977. A survey of a number of immigrant groups that have recently arrived in Britain. Although lacking somewhat in historical perspective, it possesses the particular virtue that its contributors write knowledgeably about the sending societies of the immigrants and the importance of the past in shaping the present and future lives of Britain's newcomers.

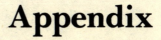

Appendix

Appendix: population statistics

Table 1 United Kingdom Population 1851-2001 ('000s)

Year	England & Wales	Scotland	N. Ireland	Total
1851	17,928	2,889	1,443	22,260
1901	32,528	4,472	1,237	38,237
1951	43,758	5,096	1,371	50,225
1981	49,219	5,168	1,536	55,923
1991	50,240	5,181	1,578	56,999
2001	51,270	5,158	1,620	58,048

Sources
For years 1851, 1901 and 1951, Mitchell, B.R. and Jones, H.G. (1971) *Second Abstract of British Historical Statistics*.

For 1981, 1991, 2001 midyear estimates, Central Statistical Office (1980) *Annual Abstract of Statistics 1980* p.8.

Table 2 Geographical distribution of the population of the United Kingdom 1851-1978 ('000s)

	1851%	1911%	1951%	1978%
England				
S. East	5,103(22.9)	11,744(27.9)	15,127(30.1)	16,832(30.2)
S.West	2,223(10.0)	2,687(6.3)	3,229(6.4)	4,296(7.7)
E.Anglia	1,022(4.6)	1,192(2.8)	1,382(2.8)	1,843(3.3)
E.Midlands	1,429(6.4)	2,263(5.4)	2,893(5.8)	3,750(6.7)
W.Midlands	1,714(7.7)	3,277(7.8)	4,423(8.8)	5,154(9.2)
Yorks & Humberside	1,789(8.0)	3,877(9.2)	4,522(9.0)	4,878(8.7)
N.West	2,987(11.2)	5,796(13.8)	6,447(12.8)	6,498(11.6)
North	969(4.4)	2,815(6.7)	3,137(6.2)	3,099(5.6)
Wales	1,189(5.3)	2,421(5.8)	2,599(5.2)	2,768(5.0)
Scotland	2,889(13.0)	4,761(11.3)	5,096(10.1)	5,168(9.3)
N.Ireland	1,443(6.5)	1,251(3.0)	1,371(2.7)	1,536(2.8)
United Kingdom	22,257	42,084	50,226	55,822

Sources For 1851 estimates for Standard Regions based on census data. Central Statistical Office (1980) op. cit. Table 2A census totals for 1911 and 1951; mid-year estimates for 1978.

Table 3a Age structure of the population of England and Wales 1851-2001 ('000s)

Age	1851	%	1901	%	1951	%	1981	%	2001	%
0-4	2,348		3,717		3,718		2,980		3,542	
5-9	2,092	35.4	3,487	32.4	3,162	22.2	3,226	20.4	3,819	21.8
10-14	1,913		3,342		2,812		3,858		3,823	
15-64	10,743	60.0	20,465	62.9	29,241	66.8	31,742	64.5	32,799	64.0
65+	830	4.6	1,518	4.7	4,825	11.0	7,413	15.1	7,287	14.2
Total	17,926	100	32,529	100	43,758	100	49,219	100	51,270	100

Sources:
Mitchell, B.R. and Deane, P. (1962) *Abstract of British Historical Statistics* pp 12-13 for census totals in 1851, 1901 and 1951. Central Statistical Office (1980) op. cit. pp 22-3 for mid year estimates projected from a 1978 base for 1981 and 2001.

Table 3b Age structure of the population of Scotland 1851-2001 ('000s)

Age Group	1851	%	1901	%	1951	%	1981	%	2001	%
0-4	372		533		471		325		357	
5-9	340	35.6	493	33.4	398	24.6	352	21.4	395	22.5
10-14	318		469		387		430		409	
15-64	1,723	59.6	2,761	61.7	3,334	65.4	3,335	64.5	3,294	63.9
65+	138	4.8	216	4.8	506	9.9	726	14.1	703	13.6
Total	2,891	100	4,472	99.9	5,096	99.9	5,168	100	5,158	100

Sources See Table 3a

Table 4a Marital condition of the population of England and Wales and Scotland 1861-1971
(per 1,000 population in each age group)

Males Age Groups		1861 E.W	Scot	1901 E.W	Scot	1951 E.W	Scot	1971 E.W	Scot
All ages	S	612	658	608	655	438	500	438	476
	M	351	309	357	312	523	458	526	488
	W	37	33	35	33	35	40	28	31
	D	–	–	–	–	4	2	8	5
15-19	S	995	996	997	997	995	995	979	977
	M	5	4	3	3	5	5	21	23
	W	–	–	–	–	–	–	–	–
	D	–	–	–	–	–	–	–	–
20-24	S	775	833	826	874	762	800	632	617
	M	223	165	173	125	237	199	366	381
	W	2	2	1	1	1	1	–	–
	D	–	–	–	–	–	–	2	2
25-34	S	318	386	359	452	272	335	201	198
	M	667	600	631	536	720	658	786	792
	W	15	14	10	12	3	4	1	1
	D	–	–	–	–	5	3	12	9
35-44	S	142	182	158	211	120	158	109	117
	M	821	782	812	755	862	823	870	867
	W	37	36	30	34	9	13	5	5
	D	–	–	–	–	9	6	16	11
45-54	S	105	135	110	146	92	130	94	114
	M	821	792	819	780	877	833	875	856
	W	74	73	71	74	24	32	15	20
	D	–	–	–	–	7	5	7	10
55-64	S	90	126	89	121	78	118	81	110
	M	761	739	764	733	850	792	862	824
	W	149	135	147	146	68	87	45	58
	D	–	–	–	–	4	3	13	8
65-74	S	84	112	78	107	84	130	74	112
	M	627	640	630	621	733	648	793	731
	W	289	248	292	272	181	220	125	151
	D	–	–	–	–	2	1	8	6
75-84	S	74	93	66	101	78*	113*	64*	103*
	M	438	491	444	452	507	436	581	503
	W	488	416	490	447	413	448	352	392
	D	–	–	–	–	2	2	3	3
85 and over	S	74	81	62	95	–	–	–	–
	M	272	338	263	280	–	–	–	–
	W	654	581	675	625	–	–	–	–
	D	–	–	–	–	–	–	–	–

*75 and over

S = Single; M = Married; W = Widowed; D = Divorced

Sources

Mitchell, B.R. and Deane, P. (1962) op. cit. pp 15, 17, for 1851 and 1901.
Central Statistical Office (1981) *Annual Abstract of Statistics 1981* pp 18-19 for 1951 and 1971.

Table 4b Marital condition of the population of England and Wales and Scotland 1861-1971
(per 1,000 population in each age group)

Females Age Groups		1861		1901		1951		1971	
		E.W	Scot	E.W	Scot	E.W	Scot	E.W.	Scot
All ages	S	587	426	586	428	405	475	380	425
	M	339	444	340	456	488	428	498	457
	W	74	130	74	116	102	94	111	109
	D	–	–	–	–	6	4	11	9
15-19	S	970	973	985	979	956	956	913	921
	M	30	27	15	21	44	35	87	79
	W	–	–	–	–	–	–	–	–
	D	–	–	–	–	–	–	–	–
20-24	S	664	741	726	764	518	603	397	420
	M	331	255	272	234	480	395	597	574
	W	5	4	2	2	1	1	1	1
	D	–	–	–	–	1	1	5	5
25-34	S	305	392	340	404	182	242	107	119
	M	667	577	643	579	797	740	869	859
	W	28	31	17	17	10	11	4	5
	D	–	–	–	–	11	7	20	17
35-44	S	159	237	185	239	137	179	72	95
	M	762	668	751	696	821	779	888	866
	W	79	95	64	65	29	34	17	21
	D	–	–	–	–	13	8	23	18
45-54	S	119	201	136	192	151	203	81	116
	M	720	610	705	645	759	697	836	790
	W	161	189	159	163	80	94	61	76
	D	–	–	–	–	10	6	22	17
55-64	S	109	205	117	181	155	209	105	149
	M	589	461	569	500	624	558	699	631
	W	302	334	314	319	215	229	178	208
	D	–	–	–	–	6	4	18	12
65-74	S	105	211	111	190	155	216	135	198
	M	400	295	368	310	429	376	463	386
	W	495	494	521	500	413	405	391	409
	D	–	–	–	–	3	2	11	7
75-84	S	102	210	111	202	165*	222*	154*	225*
	M	202	148	176	140	201	166	188	150
	W	696	642	713	658	632	611	654	622
	D	–	–	–	–	1	1	4	3
85 and over	S	91	186	119	207	–	–	–	–
	M	77	53	59	40	–	–	–	–
	W	832	761	822	752	–	–	–	–
	D	–	–	–	–	–	–	–	–

*75 and over

Sources
Mitchell, B.R. and Deane, P. (1962) op. cit. pp 15, 17, for 1851 and 1901.
Central Statistical Office (1981) *Annual Abstract of Statistics 1981* pp 18-19 for 1951 and 1971.

Table 5 Births, deaths and marriages per 1000 mean population in England and Wales and Scotland 1851-1975

Period	Births		Deaths		Marriages	
	E-W	S	E-W	S	E-W	S
1851-55	34.0	–	23.5	–	17.2	–
1871-75	35.5	35.0	23.3	23.6	17.1	15.0
1900-05	28.2	29.2	16.0	17.0	15.6	14.0
1931-35	15.0	18.2	12.0	13.2	16.1	14.3
1951-55	15.3	17.9	11.7	12.1	15.9	16.3
1971-75	14.0	14.5	11.9	12.3	16.3	15.9

Sources
Mitchell, B.R. and Deane, P (1962) op. cit. pp 29-46 for 1851-55 and 1871-75: Halsey, A.H. (Ed) (1972) *Trends in British Society since 1900* p. 31 for birth and death rates 1901-05, 1931-35 and 1951-55: Central Statistical Office (1981) *Annual Abstract of Statistics 1981* pp 35-6; for birth and marriage rates 1971-75: Mitchell, B.R. and Jones, H.G. (1971) p.30 for marriage rates 1951-55; United Nations (1976) *Demographic Year Book 1975*, p.313 for death rates 1971-75.

Table 6 Expectation of life at selected ages: England and Wales 1838-1976

Period	At Birth		At Age 15		At Age 65	
	Males	Females	Males	Females	Males	Females
1838-54	39.9	41.8	43.2	43.9	10.8	11.5
1891-1900	44.1	47.8	45.2	47.6	10.3	11.3
1950-52	66.5	71.5	54.4	58.9	11.7	14.3
1974-76	69.6	75.8	56.2	62.1	12.4	16.4

Source
Office of Population Censuses and Surveys (1978) *Demographic Review 1977* Table 2.5 p 19.

Index

Index

THE PHILOSOPHY
OF MIND

Edited by
JONATHAN GLOVER

OXFORD UNIVERSITY PRESS
1976

Oxford University Press, Walton Street, Oxford OX2 6DP

OXFORD   LONDON   GLASGOW   NEW YORK
TORONTO   MELBOURNE   WELLINGTON   CAPE TOWN
IBADAN   NAIROBI   DAR ES SALAAM   LUSAKA   ADDIS ABABA
KUALA LUMPUR   SINGAPORE   JAKARTA   HONG KONG   TOKYO
DELHI   BOMBAY   CALCUTTA   MADRAS   KARACHI

ISBN 0 19 875038 2

Printed in Great Britain by
Butler & Tanner Ltd, Frome and London

CONTENTS

INTRODUCTION

THE problems about the mind that are called philosophical concern the general framework of our thinking about particular mental phenomena. These problems arise when we think, in the context of everyday relationships, about the thoughts, feelings, and actions of other people. They also arise, in a scientific context, when we think about the relationship between states of consciousness and the psychological or neurophysiological models advanced as explanations of behaviour.

Any attempt to classify philosophical questions about the mind under a few simple headings is bound to have some degree of arbitrariness, if only because of the extent to which these questions are interrelated. But one reasonably plausible way of dividing up the problems is under these headings:

1. Interpretations: problems of justifying the interpretations we place upon the conduct and mental states of other people, and of ourselves.

2. Problems of the description and classification of the phenomena of mental states and behaviour.

3. Models: problems raised by models of the mind, or of particular kinds of mental activity, whether proposed by psychologists, or unreflectively presupposed by ordinary people in their thinking about the mind.

4. The mind–body problem: the question of the relationship between conscious experiences and either behaviour or states of the brain.

5. Problems of personal identity: the question of what, if anything, justifies the view that, despite physical and mental changes, I remain the same person over a period of time; the related question of what kind of alterations in someone would make it no longer reasonable to regard him as the same person; the question of what the unity of a mind at any one time consists in.

1. INTERPRETATIONS

In thinking about why other people behave as they do, we form some impression of how they see the world, of the general pattern of their desires, of various emotional states to which they are prone, and of different character traits that they have. These interpretations are often far from self-evident, as conversations about mutual friends show, and as discussion of an interpretation with the person in question can show even more. Are X's political views the result of a reaction against his family background, or are they the result of sustained thought about the possible forms of social organization? Is Y in a state of self-deception when he says, and apparently believes, that he accepted a knighthood simply to please his wife? Does Z feel discomfort more intensely than other people, or does he just make more fuss?

Similar problems arise in interpreting our own mental states and behaviour. How can I be sure that my own motives are what they seem? Did I fail in a task because I lacked the ability, or because I did not try hard enough? Do I remember something that happened when I was three, or do I simply imagine it? (Or remember remembering it?) Do I still intend to write a letter decided on last year, but not yet written?

These interpretations are sometimes a matter of taking someone's utterances or behaviour in some context as giving a basis for ascribing a particular motive, attitude, or experience to him. Sometimes they are a matter of finding an explanation of a mental state whose existence is not in question, as when a person's friend or psycho-analyst tries to find the cause of his state of depression. In the case of interpretations of ourselves, the same questions arise, but there is the additional evidence of our own experiences, together with the increased bias that often operates in our judgements about ourselves.

The central philosophical questions here are about the standards of evidence that justify either ascribing an inner state to someone, or propounding an explanatory psychological hypothesis. One extreme view is the sceptical position about 'other minds', which suggests that we have no way of justifying any inferences from observable behaviour to mental states, and so I have no grounds for ascribing any such states to anyone other than myself. The intuitive implausibility of this view is such that it lacks supporters, although, as with Berkeley's paradoxical views about matter, there is a disturbing lack of agreement as to the nature of its refutation.

But among those of us who have no serious doubts that other people have mental states there is great variation in the confidence or caution with which interpretations are proposed. You may be confident that some politician's motive for taking up a particular issue is ambition, while I may be undecided between this interpretation and some more charitable one. Where I am more cautious about interpreting the evidence than you are, those who agree with you will say that I lack insight, while those who agree with me will think of you as making unjustifiable speculations.

Are there any general criteria which an interpretation must satisfy in order to be reasonably deserving of belief? This is the question posed by Farrell in the special context of a psycho-analytic interpretation. Farrell looks at several different kinds of claim an analyst might make in support of the truth of his explanatory hypothesis about a patient. Finding these all in different ways unsatisfactory, he makes the pessimistic suggestion that a psycho-analytic interpretation may not be a genuine hypothesis which is either true or false, but may be a statement whose main point is instrumental, proposed in order to change the patient rather than to explain his state.

There are various questions raised by this account of psycho-analytic interpretation. How much does it matter that it does not seem to be the way analysts themselves see their suggestions? Does the fact that a proposed explanation has an instrumental function rule out the possibility that it is true or false? It seems open to us to think that psycho-analytic interpretations are often either false or at least inadequately supported by evidence, whether or not they have beneficial effects on the patient.

But the issues raised by Farrell have a wider application than merely within psycho-analysis. The pictures we have of people, of their present ways of seeing the world, and of how they arrived at them, normally go some way beyond what a severely sceptical examination of the evidence would warrant. On what basis should we accept or reject them? It seems quite implausible that these everyday interpretations of people are neither true nor false, but have some merely instrumental function. Here there is a great deal of philosophical work yet to be done.

2. PROBLEMS OF DESCRIPTION AND CLASSIFICATION

When we try to describe our thoughts and other mental states with any precision, we often run into difficulties. What exactly is going on when I have someone's name on the tip of my tongue? Perhaps this experience is usually followed by my being able to give the name. But what is the special quality of the experience by which I recognize it? Or, to take a possibly related problem, how much of our thinking is in words, or is conscious at all? When I remember which day of the week it is, are the words that pass through my mind 'it is Wednesday today' or 'today is Wednesday'? If this question has no answer because the thought has no particular embodiment in words, there is a further question: what, if anything, does it consist in? Is there perhaps some image or sequence of images? If so, how do we know that these are correctly translatable by the words 'today is Wednesday'?

Other problems are of classification. Is a particular emotional state one of shame or embarrassment? Is pain a kind of sensation, or something else? Is pleasure at the opposite end of the same dimension as pain, or have pleasure and pain not much to do with each other? How should we define 'memory' or 'imagination'? Are motives to be included among the causes of actions?

At this point someone may ask whether the increasingly accurate and refined description and classification of mental phenomena serve any purpose. Admittedly, people do not all find the same questions interesting, and the philosophy of mind no doubt has its share of articles drawing footling and scholastic distinctions. But some of the work of description and classification can be defended as of interest in its own right, whether or not any further purpose is served. To read Ryle, Austin, or Hart on voluntary action can give the intellectual pleasure of replacing blurred ideas by sharp ones. It is also arguable that an adequate science of psychology is unlikely to make do with the fuzzy concepts of mental processes that most people, including psychologists, now have. This is not to make the exaggerated claim that the philosopher of mind is a sort of Linnaeus to a future psychological Darwin. But psychological theories dealing with thinking, motivation, imagination, and other of the more complex mental processes often have a certain crudity. This is unlikely to be dispelled without attention to the detailed sorting-out of distinguishable mental phenomena that has characterized recent work in the philosophy of mind. It should also be said that among the most important mental phenomena to be located on the conceptual map are those discovered in experimental psychology: the note of fastidious disdain for the empirical that has been a feature of some philosophical writings is especially inappropriate to this field.

If detailed conceptual analysis can give finer powers of discrimination between mental phenomena, it may also help to remove the air of paradox that our concepts give to some mental states. Gardiner's sensitive discussion of self-deception is an attempt to rid that concept of its air of self-contradiction, without destroying it in the process. His discussion, using examples from real life and from novels, concentrates on the ways in which self-deception is and is not similar to deceiving someone else, and leaves us less tempted by an all-or-nothing acceptance or rejection of the mental model implicit in our vocabulary.

3. MODELS OF THE MIND

There is always a tendency to think of mental phenomena by analogy with familiar physical phenomena. This is not only true of psychologists with their models of the mind based on computers or holograms. Other people have their more homely models, in which, perhaps almost unconsciously, they think of their memory in terms of a filing cabinet, their emotional states in terms of the weather, or their sense of time in terms of an inner clock. Popper has suggested that the traditional empiricist view of the acquisition of knowledge presupposes a view of the mind as a bucket into which information drops, and has suggested that a searchlight model would be more apt. The power of a model often lies in the vividness with which it dramatizes some aspects of the phenomena, and its distorting effect often lies in its power to blind us to other aspects. Part of the growth of our understanding of the mind consists in cruder models being replaced by more sophisticated ones, as the result of either conceptual or empirical criticism.

One of the most powerful models in current sociology and social psychology is that of role-playing. It is obvious that, in many social situations, people's conduct is greatly influenced by the conventional expectations of others. We know what is expected of us as husbands, wives, fathers, mothers, or children, as firemen, guests, patients, students, or the bereaved. And, on the whole, we conform. The similarities to an actor playing a part are clear. These aspects of social life have been illustrated in telling detail by writers such as Goffman. But the role-playing model can itself be taken too seriously, to the neglect of other aspects of the mind. Goffman himself at times seems to suggest that the self is simply reducible to a series of roles, as though we could never relax and come off stage except by means of 'role distance', a phenomenon no less structured by social expectations.

One result of a very literal following of this theoretical model could be the view that our behaviour is very narrowly restricted by social roles, and that it would in general be pointless to ask someone to stand back from his role as a soldier or whatever and to appraise his own conduct simply as a person. It is this result that Cohen's paper argues is mistaken. Cohen claims that beliefs cannot be justified by appealing to social roles, and thus that it is always possible to stand back from our social roles and appraise our beliefs and actions independently of them. He presents this separation of beliefs from roles as a form of freedom, and suggests that 'a man is free only if he enjoys a certain unity of mind, only if he can express his thoughts not as appertaining to a role, but as belonging to him as a unit'. Among the problems left by Cohen's paper is that of giving a clear account of the kind of unity of the mind that such freedom is said to presuppose. This problem is taken up again in the later articles by Nagel, Williams, and Parfit.

Deutsch's discussion of models used in psychological explanation is a defence of the possibility of a distinctive task for psychological theory. Presumably the mechanisms at work when we see things, think about things, imagine things, and so forth are neurophysiological and neurochemical. This has often led psychologists to assume that mechanistic explanation of mental phenomena must involve understanding of the neurophysiological processes involved. Since at the moment we understand fairly little about these processes, this assumption has tended in practice to lead psychologists to

produce 'theories' consisting either of unfounded neurophysiological speculation, or else to seek mere correlations between stimulus and response without
postulating any kind of explanatory internal mechanism. Deutsch gives an
admirably clear account of the middle way between these extremes. A postulated explanatory mechanism can be specified in terms of its structural properties without discussing its neurophysiological embodiment. Like a flow
diagram of a computer, such an abstractly described mechanism will generate predictions which will be testable in behavioural studies, and will be subject to appropriate modification where the predictions prove false. In this
way progress can be made in psychological explanation in the absence of
new physiological information.

4. THE MIND–BODY PROBLEM

The most general features of the conceptual framework a person uses when
thinking about the mind concern the status of our experiences. What is the
relationship between states of consciousness and observable behaviour?
What is the relationship between states of consciousness and states of the
brain?

The history of this problem since the seventeenth century has largely been
one of reactions against dualism, which was most uncompromisingly stated
by Descartes. According to dualism, mental states have an existence that
is entirely non-physical. My feelings of exasperation are located in time but
not in space. They may be correlated with opening advertising material telling me I have already won a prize, with my response of vigorously tearing
it up, or with changes in the electrical and chemical activity in some region
of my brain. But, on the dualist view, my feelings are different in kind from
anything that could be observed, either by passers-by or by neurophysiologists.

The difficulties of dualism are notorious. If mental states are in principle
not publicly observable, how can we know that we are justified in ascribing
them to other people at all? Even if you have mental states, how can I know
that the correlations between them and behaviour or states of the brain are
the same in you as in me? May not your cheerful smile be correlated with
a state feeling like my depression? And how are we to describe the links
between mental states and other states? If they are causal, how does the
causal process operate? Do mental processes interfere with the normal
chemical processes at synapses, as Eccles has suggested? If the links are not
causal, states of consciousness become mere epiphenomena, so that my
thoughts, moods, and decisions are powerless to influence my actions. These
implausibilities and problems, together with the difficulty on the dualist view

of explaining how different mental states are assigned to the same mind, have led to an energetic search for alternative views.

One obvious way of trying to escape from dualism is to eliminate supposedly non-physical mental states by 'reducing' them to actual or potential behaviour. 'Behaviourism' is a term with many meanings. Within psychology, varieties of behaviourism stretch from J. B. Watson's crude identification of thinking with sub-vocal movements of the larynx, through B. F. Skinner's attempts to construct theories in terms of stimulus and response without any intervening mechanism, to the methodological platitude that, provided 'behaviour' is interpreted broadly enough to include speech, the scientific study of the minds of others draws all its non-physiological evidence from the study of behaviour. Of greater importance to the mind–body problem is the doctrine, developed by Ryle and others, of logical behaviourism. On this view, we do not need to postulate any non-physical states of the kind believed in by the dualist: talk of mental states is a way of referring to actual or potential patterns of behaviour.

For the logical behaviourist, when someone is angry this does not consist in some private state, without physical location, of which he alone can be aware. Rather, to be angry is to behave in an angry way: to be flushed, trembling, banging the table, or abusive. Or, to take account of an obvious objection, if the person is not behaving in any of the appropriate ways, it must be true that he would be doing so but for the fact, say, that he is talking to his boss. On this view, anger consists in angry behaviour, either actualized, or else inhibited by certain specifiable conditions.

Logical behaviourism runs into a number of difficulties. In the first place, it is hard to see how it can account for the way we use mental states to explain behaviour. To say that someone is trembling because he is angry would not explain anything if being angry simply consisted in the behaviour to be explained. There is also the problem of accounting for my knowledge of my own mental states. I do seem, at least in some ways, to know more about my mental states than other people do, and also to know about them in a different way. It is not clear what a behaviourist can say about this. Further difficulties concern the hypothetical statements the behaviourist must make in order to explain what it is to be angry but not at the moment displaying anger in behaviour. The logical analysis of hypothetical statements in itself presents great problems, and the behaviourist has the additional problem of constructing a hypothetical statement saying under exactly which conditions the appropriate behaviour would appear. These problems seem likely to be serious ones even for a behaviourist account of a state like anger, but arise still more acutely for mental images or dreams.

There are various doctrines at one remove from behaviourism, according to which mental states are not reducible to actual or potential behaviour, but are still far less detachable from behaviour than traditional dualists have supposed. Behaviourism in its most uncompromising form asserts that certain statements about behaviour and certain statements about mental states entail each other. These other doctrines, in the very different forms in which they are proposed by Wittgenstein and by Strawson, reject this claim. There are still logical links between statements about mental states and statements about bodily states or behaviour, but they are far more subtle, some would say more elusive, than entailment. Neither in the view of Wittgenstein nor in that of Strawson can mental states be analysed without remainder into behaviour. These theories are of exceptional interest, but they too leave us with problems. No completely clear account of the precise logical links between mental states and their outward manifestations on this kind of view has yet appeared. And, in so far as mental states are not completely analysable in terms of behaviour, the old question, if it is a genuine one, of what exactly mental states *are* seems still to arise.

Another influential view of mental states is the mind–brain identity theory, or central state materialism, often known simply as 'materialism'. On this theory, mental states are identical with states of the brain. For a long time people have known in a general way the importance of the brain for states of consciousness, but as neurophysiologists begin to fill in some of the detail, the relation between conscious states and brain states seems to pose more urgent questions than that between conscious states and behaviour. Penfield's work stimulating the brain and asking people to report on their experiences, the work of Luria and others on the effects of brain lesions on experience, and the work of Hubel and Wiesel on the part played by cortical cells in visual perception have all dramatized the detailed dependence of conscious states on brain functioning.

This empirical work, combined with philosophical dissatisfaction with all forms of dualism and behaviourism, has led to the increasing popularity and development of the materialist view, in the writings of Feigl, Place, Smart, Armstrong, and others. The attractions of the view are obvious. It leaves no problem of explaining how mind and brain interact, and there is no problem about mental states as causal explanations of behaviour. For a materialist, there is nothing about someone else's mind that cannot in principle be observed and be made the subject of scientific investigation. And many people's intuitive sense of what is plausible differs from that expressed by Sherrington's remark: 'That our being should consist of two separate elements, offers, I suppose, no greater inherent improbability than that it should rest on one only.'

But materialism too has its problems. There are difficulties in giving a satisfactory account of the identity relation that is supposed to hold between mental states and brain states. There is the suggestion that, even if these states are identical, they must have two different kinds of property, those accessible to introspection and those observed by neurosurgeons. And there are doubts, such as those raised in Davidson's paper, about the possibility of obtaining the detailed psycho-physical laws that most materialists have thought a precondition of the adequacy of their theory. As with dualism and behaviourism, there is still disagreement over the extent to which the difficulties in the materialist view can be overcome. It has been suggested by Feyerabend that, even if these difficulties are serious, we should not be in a hurry to dismiss materialism on their account. Even fruitful new theories can show defects at birth, and when these are later eliminated we are often glad we did not opt for infanticide.

The lack of any generally accepted solution to the mind–body problem suggests a rather sceptical line of thought. Suppose future work on the brain were to give materialists all the psycho-physical laws they hope for. Every mental state would be correlated with some physical or chemical state of the brain. The materialist would then claim that the mental states *were* the states of the brain, while the dualist would see no reason to shift from his own interpretation, that neurophysiologists had shown correlations between two quite different kinds of state. At this point it is clear that nothing empirical is at stake between the two theories. And disputes about what kinds of things exist, or how many kinds of things exist, start to seem empty when they no longer have empirical content. The old dispute about whether, as well as particular red objects existing, there also exists an abstract entity called 'redness', does not make most of us wait trembling for its solution, since nothing much hangs on it. A linguistic decision, combined with tolerance of other people's ways of talking, is all that seems called for. Those who think it important which conceptual framework we use for thinking about mind and body have some arguing to do. Is it that all the frameworks but one are logically incoherent? Or is it that one way of thinking about the mind is more likely to help us in scientific investigation, or more likely to help us to think clearly about such questions as the animal boundaries of consciousness? Unless some case of this sort can be made out, it seems likely that future theorists will think of our present discussions as primitive in their obsession with a metaphysical search for the true ontology.

The papers in this selection that bear on the mind–body problem do so from rather different angles. Hampshire's paper on the relation between mental states and their expression in behaviour is written from a standpoint that is neither behaviourist nor dualist. On the traditional dualist view, we identify our mental states by their introspectible properties, and then discover that they happen to be correlated with certain patterns of behaviour. Hampshire claims that, on the contrary, there are logical links between feelings and their associated behaviour. This, he suggests, is because the way we distinguish between different feelings, such as fear or anger, is by the different patterns of behaviour towards which they are the controlled inclinations. This attractive idea itself illustrates the complex relationship between conceptual theses about the mind and empirical work in psychology or anthropology. For, while Hampshire's claim is that feelings *cannot* be identified except via their links with behaviour, his argument also has links with Darwin's attempt to answer the empirical question of how we come to have emotional states at all.

Putnam considers machines programmed to act, like the rational man of economic theory, as maximizers of expected utility, and which thus have states in some ways analogous to our preferences and beliefs. He argues that the possibility of any given programme being physically instantiated in various different ways tells against a 'materialist' interpretation by which we *identify* these preferences and beliefs with the physical events in any particular set of wires. Putnam suggests that a parallel argument applies to human beings. His own view, briefly sketched out at the end of his paper, is that, for people as for his machines, to know about their mental states is to know about their 'functional organization'. This view, which harmonizes well with Deutsch's programme for psychology, differs from the traditional theories about mind and body, but is hard to evaluate without fuller elaboration. In particular some account is needed of how my awareness of my own mental states can be thought of as my being aware of my own 'functional organization'.

Davidson's paper outlines a position he has developed more fully in other papers. Arguing for a position he calls 'anomalous monism', he claims that there can be no precise laws linking mental states such as beliefs and preferences with physical states. But, since psychological events do have causal relationships with physical events, both must be subsumable under some system of causal laws. If there are no precise psycho-physical laws, the causal laws must be purely physical. From this argument Davidson concludes that psychological events must be describable in physical terms, and so must *be* physical events.

Davidson's position is interesting in that it combines a materialist view of mental events with an insistence that descriptions of them in psychological terms will never show a perfect fit when matched with physical descriptions. The most ingenious (and perhaps most contentious) part of his view is the argument against precise psycho-physical laws. For this he appeals to the 'holistic character of the cognitive field'. He says that we can only attribute beliefs and preferences to people in the context of assuming that their whole pattern of beliefs and preferences form a roughly coherent system. In interpreting someone's behaviour, assessing it as evidence for beliefs and preferences, we must always have a bias towards ascribing consistent attitudes to him. This bias will mean that our ascriptions of attitudes will always be tentative, revisable in the light of new evidence about other parts of the system. The suggestion is that no such pressures are at work on our ascriptions of physical states, and so we cannot hope for detailed rigid links between mental and physical descriptions.

What seems to need further argument here is the claim that these considerations about the holistic character of the cognitive field prove the impossibility of precise psycho-physical laws. A more traditional materialist might claim that we could develop psycho-physical laws in relatively unproblematic cases. We could then, in cases where we are uncertain which attitudes to ascribe to someone, use his physical state as part of the evidence. Our ascriptions of beliefs and preferences would then have to satisfy both requirements of coherence *and* requirements of not flouting well-based psycho-physical laws. There then seem to be two possibilities. We could either succeed in developing a detailed system of psycho-physical laws, or else these two requirements would prove too much, and tear our system apart. What reason have we *now* for assuming the second outcome rather than the first?

5. PROBLEMS OF PERSONAL IDENTITY

Problems of personal identity can arise when someone thinks about the social roles he plays. 'Of course, now I am a sergeant-major, I have to go through the motions of being quite ferocious, but really I am gentle and retiring.' The doubts about statements of this sort are about the extent to which it is possible to detach a person's self from his public behaviour in social contexts. If 'that is not the real me', what is?

Similar questions arise when we think about our existence over a long period. Should a young man starting a job be interested in the pension scheme? Someone might argue that the man of twenty has nothing much in common with the man of sixty-five of the distant future. 'Yes, but it will still be *me*, won't it?' One problem is seeing what this reply means, and deciding how much force it has.

When pressed about what it is that makes someone the same person over time, people usually give one of two answers, or some combination of them. The first answer cites various kinds of mental continuity: the man of sixty-five remembers a fair amount of his past, including events before he was twenty, and some of his beliefs, attitudes, and preferences have stayed constant over time. The second answer cites various kinds of physical continuity:

the man at the later stage is recognizably an older version of the man at the earlier stage. More fundamentally, his body has traced out a single and continuous path through space and time.

There has been much philosophical debate about the relative importance of physical and mental factors for personal identity. Real cases that have presented difficulties include people who, after a car crash, have suffered total amnesia and radical changes of personality. Do we, relying on observable physical criteria, say that we still have the same person, or do we, using the mental criteria, say that we now have a different person in the same body? The decision here is relevant to how we assess the plight of the man in Kafka's *Metamorphosis* who could be controversially described as waking up one morning in the body of an insect. It is also relevant to traditional views about personal survival of bodily death (relevant not directly to their truth, but to the prior question of whether such views are even intelligible).

Problems are also raised by cases where a single body seems to be 'inhabited' by several different personalities. How many people or minds are we dealing with, one or several? The same question arises in interpreting the fascinating work of Sperry and others on animals and people where the connections between the two cerebral hemispheres have been cut. Nagel's paper gives a lucid and economical description of this work, and shows that the phenomena resist easy classification into some clear-cut number of minds being present. The split-brain patient functions in some respects as though controlled by a single centre of consciousness, but in a number of laboratory tests there are striking signs of two independent centres of consciousness. And Nagel produces impressive objections to the view that the patient sometimes has one mind and sometimes two. It is hard not to see such cases as casting doubt on our usual assumption that minds are countable and have clear-cut boundaries. The idea of something between the presence of one mind and the presence of two requires some revision of our unreflective conceptual scheme.

The paper by Williams makes controlled use of science-fiction techniques to cast further doubt on our normal ways of thinking about personal identity. The device he uses is to present us with situations in which a person's brain is cleared of the information it contains and re-programmed with other information. You and I enter a machine. Two people emerge, one with my body and your memories, intentions, and character, the other with your body and my memories, intentions, and character. Which, if either, will be me? With great ingenuity, Williams constructs an example which makes us inclined to opt for one answer, and an example which makes us equally inclined to opt for the diametrically opposed answer. He then uses arguments designed to make us feel dissatisfied with the ways of escape that consist in saying that the question is undecidable, or, that it is one to be settled by arbitrary convention.

Parfit's paper aims to remove our disquiet over problem cases such as those discussed by Williams. On the view that he puts forward, personal identity just consists in bodily and psychological continuity. Once we know the various facts about these continuities, the 'problem cases' cannot present a problem—for there is nothing left to know. We are puzzled by such cases because we hold a different view about the nature of our own identity. 'Would it be me?' seems to us a question which must always have an answer. For this to be so, personal identity would have to be a further fact, independent of the facts about the continuities. Parfit denies that there is any such further fact. And he points out that, while this 'further fact' seems to us all-or-nothing, psychological continuity is in part a matter of degree. The question 'Will the man of sixty still be me?' should, he thinks, be compared with the question 'Will Britain still be the same nation in a hundred years' time?'

When students are wondering whether they would enjoy doing philosophy, I often give them the papers by Williams and Parfit to read, on the grounds that anyone not excited by them is likely to be, as far as philosophy is concerned, intellectually dead. But their merits are not merely as intellectual stimulus: they also weaken the grip of conventional ideas about ourselves. If Parfit's ideas turn out to be correct, they provide a kind of solution to the problems posed by Williams. But Parfit's solution is scarcely more comforting than Williams's unanswered questions. For the correctness of this solution may help to undermine some of our other beliefs about rationality, death, justice, and personal commitments. Those who like a quiet intellectual life must hope the Parfit theory is wrong.

6. CONCLUDING NOTE

Anyone compiling an anthology of this kind must be aware of the many aspects of the field that go unrepresented. In this one, perhaps the most glaring omission is its failure to reflect the stimulus given to the subject by Chomsky's work in linguistics. Other matters not discussed include perception and the theory of action. The last two topics are covered in separate volumes in the series, and Chomsky's work is discussed in Searle's volume on *Philosophy of Language*.

Some of the readings chosen here are more closely related to psychology than is usual in the philosophy of mind. I doubt if it is useful to try to draw a sharp boundary between psychology and the philosophy of mind. And I am sure it is the opposite of useful for those in the two fields to treat each other with the distance of neighbours who have quarrelled. It seems likely that if two lists were drawn up of the best dozen books ever written in the philosophy of mind and in psychology, William James's *Principles of Psychology* would appear in both. The great gap in the present scene is the absence of any treatment of conscious experience in the spirit of William James.

I

THE CRITERIA FOR A
PSYCHO-ANALYTIC INTERPRETATION[1]

B. A. FARRELL

I

LET us consider the following case.[2] An adolescent boy, whom I shall call
John, was approaching seventeen years of age when he was sent to a clinical
psychologist for vocational guidance. The difficulty was that he was quite
uncertain what career to take up. His school reports stated that his work
was uneven—sometimes he did good work and expressed himself well, on
other occasions his spelling and expression were poor; and the reports stated
repeatedly that he was disappointing in examinations. He was due to take
eight 'O' level subjects at the end of the academic year; but his showing
at school suggested that entry to university would be difficult or late. He
was the youngest child of a family of three, the others being sisters aged
thirty and twenty-seven. These had university careers, and the father was
a successful company executive. When the boy John was nine years old, the
father was given an appointment abroad and the boy went to live as a
boarder in a public school. It became apparent, both from the boy himself
and from his elder sister, that he had found adjustment in his school very
difficult in the first two terms and had missed his parents considerably. However, the parents thought that John had subsequently developed well at
school. He was good at sport, and took part in the social life of the school.
But he made less progress educationally, was late in attempting G.C.E., was
in the second stream form, and the headmaster had doubts about his capacity

From *Proceedings of the Aristotelian Society*, Supp. Vol. (1962). Reprinted by permission of the
Editor of the Aristotelian Society.

[1] The symposiasts and the Aristotelian Society are grateful to the patient and his father for permission to reproduce extracts from the case notes contained in this symposium.

[2] I wish at the outset to thank Dr. P. M. Turquet, Psychiatric Consultant at the Tavistock Clinic,
London, for his great kindness and generosity in allowing, and arranging for, us to make use
of this case material—thereby giving us a unique opportunity to get to closer quarters with psycho-
analytic discourse and practice, and the problems they generate. I also wish to thank Mr. H.
Phillipson, Senior Clinical Psychologist at the Tavistock Clinic, London, for his help in providing
me with relevant material.

for sixth-form work. On psychological examination it was found that intellectually John had quite outstanding abilities—well up to good 'A' level
and university work—but that he was making use of them poorly and ineffi-
ciently, especially in any test requiring self-expression. The way he attempted
the tests revealed a great fear of making mistakes and of things getting out
of control. In short, the immediate problem John presented was one of intellectual under-functioning. In the light of the total picture he revealed, it
was thought that he might benefit from analytic treatment. This was begun,
when he was sixteen years ten months old, with three sessions a week. There
were various interruptions, owing to illness and school holidays. By July
1961 he had had eighty sessions, of which seventy-seven are available in typescript records.

Now let us look at a tiny extract from these records. In session 16 John
began by saying that he was quite looking forward to the holidays, for one
thing because his father had arranged for him to have some car driving lessons. Session 18 (the first one after the holidays a few weeks later) opened
and ran as follows for almost half of its length.

J 1. I found those driving lessons which I had were quite a—were quite a
test really. H'm, I must say when I first started, I was extremely nervous
and then after a couple of lessons I managed to settle down a bit and gradually I got more confident and now I am feeling quite O.K. about it, but right
at the beginning—I was pretty nervous, really, I found, you know, I was
sweating on the line all the time.

T 1. Any idea what about?

J 2. I don't know really. Just, I suppose, it was general nervousness, but it
was—I found it a big jump from just cycling my bicycle around and then
to start driving a car. I found really that—well—on a bicycle you can get
into small places, but in a car, you know, you have to be far more careful
about it and really, it was just being out on the roads with, well, loads of
other people in cars and things, and I was a bit—a bit nervous about—well,
just *being* there, the fact that I was unaccustomed to driving a car and being
on a main road and just having to keep your end up and not making mistakes. The instructor was quite helpful, quite a nice chap, but it was the first
few lessons, going through all the traffic, I found a bit hectic, but now I just
find it a matter of course. I find it a lot easier and doing things without
thinking about it. Before I had to think about everything before I actually
did it and now it all comes quite naturally. (Pause)

T 2. Like coming here.

J 3. Well—(pause)

T3. But it seems to me too that, when you start on something, some presumption comes up in your mind, makes you sweat along the line. I wonder what that presumption is.

J 4. Well, I have often been told, and it has been hinted at, and I thought about it that you start on something and you don't think that you are going to succeed in it and you haven't got confidence in yourself to—to do it and to finish the job.

T 4. To take it successfully to a conclusion.

J 5. Yes (pause). I think that could be applied to quite a number of things.

T 5. And in that sense also applied to coming here. Let me be more accurate, also coming here you are not sure that you can successfully take treatment through to a successful conclusion—something won't go wrong on the way.

J6. I was afraid of that in the beginning and even now I am not absolutely positive.

T 6. This came out a moment ago when I suggested to you that reality was connected with coming here, and you were very doubtful. You said: Well, I am not really quite sure about 'here' at the moment. You said: Well. You were not going to commit yourself.

J 7. Well, that is the sort of thing, where at that moment I'd rather—kind of—sit on the fence.

T 7. M'm, and you are not certain that you'll take this through. What's going to happen?

J 8. Well, it is determination that has got to see it through, but whether it will work or not—

T 8. Yes, I wonder what you picture is going to happen, because it seems that you feel that something will go wrong. In what way will it go wrong? How will it go wrong? What is going to come up, (*J*: Well) what's going to come up and prevent it from going right?

J 9. I don't know. I just got that feeling, it is just sort of there, you know. I suppose I am like that in quite lots of things. I don't believe it until it has been proved, until I have seen it—with quite a number of things and—it happens a lot at school—in a match, for instance. Somebody says: Oh, we will beat this team; and I say: Well, O.K., I believe it when we have done it, when it is over. Perhaps I never like to commit myself. (Pause)

T 9. You are having some anxiety about committing yourself afresh, as it were, to a term's work here.

J 10. Well, it's not really the same. I have been here before, so really it is a bit different and when, and when I was driving the car, I have never been driving a car before in my life, you see, but I have been here before, and I know what it is like.

T10. And it is the thing father does, driving a car.

J11. Yes he does. He—well—about before last Christmas, I think it was, he sort of tried to get me interested, but I wasn't really, and he said: All right, now, I'll show you how to work the gears; and he showed me, but I didn't take it in because I didn't bother. Partly because I just could not be fagged. Well, I just, well, I felt quite happy as I was with my bike at that time, and I think, was a bit scared to go on the roads by car. Well then, I think, he thought: right, well you have got to learn to drive some time or other, I might as well learn now and so my mother booked up the lessons at the school. Well, at first I wasn't—desperately keen. I only did it because, well, it had to be done some time and that was as good a time as any.

T11. Yes, but I think our problem is to understand here a little bit more why you weren't keen, why you weren't interested when father showed you the gears, why you are still so unhappy on your luck. I think it is because you always feel frightened to do directly something that father does. It comes too near the sort of wishes to be like father, and yet dare you be father. I think you feel it is very frightening to be father (*J*: Yes) and in this sense it is easier for you then, I think, to be, I think, the little boy, and you yourself stressed the jump from riding a bike to driving a car. Whilst in one sense it is quite a big change, nevertheless you feel it is an enormous change, as if it was some sort of change from boyhood to adulthood.

J12. There is that in it. There was also the fact that it was my bicycle, it didn't cost an awful lot of money compared with the car and the car was my father's. Well, if anything happened to the car, well, father would be pretty annoyed, I know. If I smashed my bike up, well, that is my look out, and I know if my father rode my bike and smashed it up, I would be pretty fed up about it and goodness knows what he would be about the car costing so much more. That was one side of it.

T12. And father gets angry when you use his things?

J13. No, he is not particularly worried. He—well, I have been out in his car and he sort of lets me know when he is not terribly pleased with something, and that was the only sort of thing that I was really scared about. I mean I use all his tools he has got, all that kind of thing and well—quite a lot of his bits and pieces that he has got around.

T13. So that it is not quite true that in reality outside he gets very angry, but that your picture is that inside, the picture that you have of him inside you, is of his being very likely to turn into an angry person (*J*: Yes). And that this is a picture very much mirrored on how angry *you* get, it is *you* who will get very fed up, it is you who gets very angry, if something of yours is used and broken. Again, it is noticeable in this connection how much you keep this anger within you, because when your bicycle was used by one of the people at school and there was a difficulty in coming here, because the tyre was flat, your anger here was really very controlled, your anger was very muted. Yes, you said you were pretty fed up and what a nuisance it was, but this was not said I think, with the full force of the anger. [Here a few words are inaudible] you keep a great deal of this anger inside you, very bottled up, controlling it very hard, and are, I think, in a way, I think, rather frightened to show it, and I think at any moment you confuse your anger, which you have to control in this sort of way with this large, expensive object, a car, which you then picture as being angry at yourself, getting out of hand; and it is your own anger that you are afraid of, that you are afraid will get out of hand, and you have to, I think, quite carefully control it. You used the word 'fed up' rather than saying: I am angry. I am fed up, you said, as if you had to mute it, as if you had to diminish it, diminishing your feeling of anger, I think, because you were afraid of it getting out of control. (Pause)

J 14. I don't really know what to say to that. I can't really remember myself getting really angry with somebody, not really getting right out of hand, you know, completely losing yourself. (Pause)

I shall select an, or one, interpretative remark, or interpretation, by the analyst for examination. Consider the remark in T 11: 'I think it is because you always feel frightened to do directly something that father does.' Let me number it 'T 11,2' for convenience of reference, the '2' standing for the second complete sentence in T 11. I shall pose the following question about this remark. By reference to what criteria or considerations can we determine, with a reasonable degree of assurance, whether it be true or false?

Let us note some preliminary difficulties that we meet when we try to answer this question.

(i) Just because an analytic session has been tape recorded and put into typescript, we must not assume that the typescript record is then automatically a complete and perfect record of what was said in the session. It may be. When I carefully compared the first typescript draft of the part of session 18 quoted above with the tape record, I detected about seventy-five errors in it, some of which may not have been unimportant. I still doubt whether the record as I quote it above is free from error.

(ii) I have boldly picked out sentence T 11,2 as being 'an or one interpretative remark or interpretation'. But am I being fair or a bit arbitrary in doing this? For where does the interpretation the analyst is offering John at this point really end? Does it end with the sentence I picked out—T 11,2? This feels wrong because T 11,2 has very intimate links with what follows, whatever these links may be. But if we do include the following sentence (T 11,3) as part of this 'one interpretation', where are we going to stop? It looks as if we might then be forced to include most, or even the whole, of T 11 as 'one' interpretation. But this would make our example of 'an interpretation' too unwieldy for us to investigate, and probably misrepresent the way analysts normally use the expression 'an interpretation'. This uncertainty simply draws our attention to the point that the criteria of an (or one) interpretation are far from clear. (What is the number of the interpretations offered in T 13, for instance?) I suggest that, having noted this difficulty, we keep it in mind and pass on.

(iii) It is characteristic of a number of interpretations in this whole record that they are far from clear. For example, just what is meant exactly by the remark in T 11,4: 'I think you feel it very frightening to be father'? This point is important because uncertainty about the meaning of p may hold us up in our hunt for its truth criteria. Fortunately for us, however, interpretation T 11,2 *is* pretty clear (the word 'directly' in it is perhaps the chief worry). So we can avoid getting bogged down at the outset by the need to clarify the remark we are proposing to examine. Should we feel irritated at what may seem to us the woolly obscurity that recurs in the analyst's remarks, we have to bear in mind that these remarks were made extempore for the benefit of a patient, not after reflection for a concentration of philosophers.

II

With these preliminaries out of the way, let us consider T 11,2. What are its truth criteria?

Consider the criterion of acceptance, or personal avowal. It may be suggested that it is necessary for John to accept T 11,2 before we can be reasonably sure that it is true.

Suppose we try to apply this criterion. Did John accept T 11,2 or not? What are we to say here? John did not do anything like explicitly avow in the course of this session that the remark T 11,2 is true. Nor have I been able to find that he did so in any of the other seventy-seven sessions that have been put into type. What is more, John could hardly be expected to accept T 11,2 or to react to it verbally in any way at all *at the time*, because to do so would be to interrupt the analyst in full flood; and this is something that a well-mannered adolescent like John does not often do. Likewise, only more so, for the stream of interpretative remarks making up T 13. John can hardly be expected to accept or reject at once, or even at any later time, every one of the interpretative remarks in T 13. One is apt to sympathize with him reacting to T 13 with the remark (J 14): 'I don't really know what to say to that'! So it looks as if the criterion of acceptance does not apply to T 11,2.

But this may only be the case if we adopt the narrow use of the expressions 'an (one) interpretation' which we mentioned above, and according to which the remark T 11,2 would constitute an (or one) interpretation. Suppose we widen the use of these expressions in some way or other that will allow us to take T 11,2 along with the next sentence and a half, with which it seems closely related, and to regard this whole sequence of remarks as an (or one) interpretation. (That is to say, the interpretation will now extend from the beginning of T 11,2 to the middle of T 11,4 ('... very frightening to be father').) Did John accept *this* interpretation? The answer depends, in part, I suppose on what we make of the word 'Yes' from John that follows this interpretation, and appears in the middle of T 11,4. Is this 'Yes' a 'Yes' of acceptance? Or is it a 'Yes' with a query in it, a 'Yes' of 'Well-it's-possible-I'll-consider-that-but-let-me-hear-more-first'? Or what? This question seems to face one when one listens to the tape record, and compares the character of this 'Yes' with the different and more clear-cut 'Yes' in T 13. It appears, therefore, that we can only say John accepted the interpretation (T 11,2—middle 4) if we are prepared to *hear* his 'Yes' in T 11 *as* the 'Yes' of acceptance. Accordingly, when I take this 'Yes' to be one of acceptance, I am making a judgement about this utterance of John's that is rather like the judgement I make about an ambiguous figure, or a picture in a Thematic Apperception Test. In other words, it would seem that I am reacting to the boy's utterance here rather in the way that I do to the material of a projective test, and am making something like a projective judgement about it. The same is true of the analyst. Should he, relying on this utterance alone, take it to be the 'Yes' of acceptance, he would also seem to be making a projective judgement about it, or something akin to one. The upshot, then, appears to be as follows. We can only apply the criterion of acceptance in this instance by the aid of a projective judgement, or something like it. This means that we cannot use the criterion here as an 'objective' standard to test, or help to determine, whether this interpretation is true or not. If it is necessary to obtain John's personal avowal, or acceptance, before we can be reasonably sure that this interpretation is true, then it is uncertain whether we have obtained an avowal here or not. In this instance the criterion seems to be inapplicable and hence unhelpful.

But surely the criterion of acceptance does not characteristically apply to single utterances in the yea or nay fashion I have suggested? No, it does not characteristically work in this fashion. An analyst will normally require more than a simple 'Yes' from a patient before he is satisfied that the patient has come to see that the interpretation is true, and, therefore, has genuinely and insightfully accepted it. This is particularly so, perhaps, with a polite adolescent 'yes-sirring' patient like John. But precisely *what* more is normally required? And does the full record of the boy John supply it? These questions may or may not be fair ones to put to an analyst. But they serve to indicate that we are no longer concerned with a simple matter of avowal or non-avowal. We now seem to be concerned with a much more complex question, and one which the analyst answers by the aid of his clinical judgement. Such a judgement is not self-guaranteeing. On the contrary, it could be argued that it is partly projective in character and hence infected with uncertainty. If this is so, then it is again far from a straightforward, objective matter to determine whether any given interpretation is really accepted or not. Thus, with T 11,2, I find it difficult to discover anything in the record that suggests that John did accept it at the time, or later on in the analysis. About T 11,2–4, I can find material that suggests that John accepted it, or a view like it or containing it, at a later stage in the analysis.[3] But observe that I use the word 'suggests'. For if I am challenged to defend myself here on either count, I can only do so by saying: 'Well, it looks to me as if . . .', or 'It seems to me that here John is saying . . .', and so on. I am inclined to believe that analysts would speak in the same sort of way as I do about this material. But this way of speaking is not the characteristic locution of, say, the experimental psychologist. It is more like the locution characteristic of the clinical worker—forever putting an interpretation on his material in his constant striving to see significance in it.

I asked the question: Precisely what more than a mere yea or nay is normally required by an analyst before he will be satisfied that a patient has accepted an interpretation? This question may be an unfair or an unreasonable one to put. But it will obviously help us to obtain a better idea of what the analyst requires if we can find some negative examples. Can we find instances where an offered interpretation has been withdrawn in the light of non-acceptance by the patient? Well, I have not been able to find any in this record of the boy John. But before we start moving from this to any further conclusions, let us note that it is probably a complete mistake to suppose that the typescript record should necessarily reveal any such mistaken interpretations. For it is contrary to standard analytic practice for the analyst to say anything such as: 'Ah! I see I am wrong about that interpretation—I withdraw it!' At best, perhaps, one might find in the record that the analyst had given up pressing one line of interpretation, and suspect that he had done so in view of the negative responses from the patient. How-

---

[3] In sessions 32 and 33.

ever, one could only tell whether it was these negative responses from the patient that had made him withdraw by inspecting, or otherwise discovering, what does not appear in the session records at all—namely, the analyst's views or opinions about the patient as the analysis continues. If these were recorded in sufficient detail at suitable intervals, one might be able to compare the session records with the analyst's opinion records about the patient, and note: (a) where the latter's negative responses were connected with the analyst's then withdrawing (or changing) some view of his about the patient; and (b) where he subsequently ceased offering an interpretation, or interpretations, related to this view. If we could find such examples we would have the negative instances we require, or something close to them. But analysts do not normally record their sessions, and, I gather, most of them do not keep full opinion records either.

In the case of John, I have only seen *one* such opinion record, and, to my knowledge, this is the only one that exists. It was composed very kindly at my request at about sessions 25 to 28. It was meant for my guidance and not for publication, and it was put together at great speed. Admittedly, therefore, it may not give an adequate view of the analyst's opinions at the time. However, I am forced to say that this opinion record does not appear to me to contain any example at all of an interpretation, or interpretative line, that was withdrawn in the light of John's own conduct in the sessions. The record does contain a description of John's attitude to his father, but this is not sufficiently detailed for us to be able to use it to find an example of an interpretation which concerned his attitudes to his father, and which was withdrawn.

I have been concerned with two interpretative remarks alone, T 11,2 and T 11,2–4; and I have exhibited some of the difficulties that arise when we try to apply the criterion of acceptance or avowal to them. How far do these or similar difficulties arise about *other* interpretative remarks made in the course of this analysis of John? The answer to this depends on a careful, objective study of the records to discover how far T 11,2 and T 11,2–4 are *representative* remarks in the relevant respects. Such a study has not been made. All I can do in its absence is to offer my impression—for the very little that this is worth. My impression is that T 11,2 and T 11,2–4 are *not* as *un*representative as we may be inclined to suppose at the outset. The reader can form his own impression by looking again at the extract from session 18 quoted above. This session is, I think, a good example of the analysis in its early phase.

The conclusion about the criterion of acceptance seems to be this. It is difficult to apply the criterion to T 11,2 and T 11,2–4. When one does so, it is difficult to be reasonably sure that one has applied it correctly. So one is left uncertain whether these two remarks (T 11,2 and T 11,2–4) satisfy or fail to satisfy this truth condition that is alleged to be necessary. In so far as T 11,2 and T 11,2–4 are representative, the difficulty is a general one.

But, of course, this whole discussion leaves various questions untouched. For instance, the point could be made that what really shows whether an interpretation is true or false is not anything crude, such as whether John says 'Yes' or 'No'. Such remarks may not mean much anyway in view of resistance difficulties and other defences he may be using. What matters is whether the interpretation elicits from the patient responses that can reasonably be explained as being associated with, and hence the outcome of, the offered interpretation. If an interpretation does have such a result—if it is, in this sense, 'enactive'—then we have good grounds for supposing that the interpretation is on or near the mark, that it is true or getting near to the truth.

This is an important suggestion. But it runs into the usual snags. Is T 11,2 enactive or not? It seems doubtful whether it elicited anything from John. But this is not enough to oblige the analyst to withdraw T 11,2. Obviously not. So enactivity is not a necessary condition for the truth of T 11,2. What about T 11,2–4? Is this enactive? We may be able to point to certain supporting material in the record. But the criterion is so vague that if—on the strength of this material—we go on to judge that the interpretation is enactive, we will produce a judgement that is probably clinical in character. Moreover, it is doubtful whether the criterion is open to much improvement. If we try to tighten it in a way sufficient to give us an agreed answer in every case, we will make it clinically useless. If it is to have clinical value, it will have to remain fairly loose. This means that if, and when, analysts do actually check an interpretation by reference to its enactivity, they are doing something very different, and far removed, from the ordinary attempts of a scientific worker to test an hypothesis.[4]

III

Let us consider a criterion of quite a different sort. Suppose we challenged an analyst to defend T 11,2. He might argue as follows. 'Given the sort of person John is, and given the sort of material he produces here (in session 18) and in previous sessions, it is very likely that his fear of driving the car is a manifestation of his fear of doing what his father does. For this is what analytic experience with similar material would lead one to expect.' We could now use this defence to say that, for us to be reasonably sure that T 11,2 is true, T 11,2 must be in accord with past analytic experience in the way

[4] But cf. J. O. Wisdom (1957), 'Psycho-analytic Technology', *Brit. J. for the Phil. of Science*, 7, 13–28.

just mentioned. I shall call this 'the criterion of analogy'. Will this criterion do?

Let us recognize at once that it has an air of artificiality about it. Part of the reason for this, I think, is that analysts do not make much *explicit* use of this criterion. For they do not find it easy or natural to exhibit their relevant past experience by, for example, running out a series of past cases which are similar to John in the relevant respects. They are somewhat inhibited from doing this, because they also look at any given case as being importantly different from every other. In this respect the practice of analysts is apt to differ from that of the main body of psychiatrists, for whom reference to series of similar cases is a standard form of argument.[5] Yet, if challenged to support T 11,2 an analyst might say, for example: 'Well, it looked to me like a father-fear at work here.' If we challenged him by pointing to material in John's record that he had apparently not noticed and which suggested, for example, that the car represented the breast and that the boy was afraid both of smashing it and of his wish to do so—if we took this line, the analyst might react in more than one way. For instance, he might agree that both interpretations may be correct about John, and that this is just a case of over-determination. Or he might accept that T 11,2 was perhaps not at work here, or not as important as he had originally supposed. But for the analyst to make either of these moves is to reveal that he makes *implicit* use of past material, and hence of the criterion of analogy.

However, let us waive the difficulty that this suggested criterion may be somewhat artificial. Let us suppose that John's fear is indeed analogous to previous cases, or past analytic experience, on which the analyst is relying here. The next question we have to ask is this. What reason have we to believe that the previous cases, in which fears resembling John's have been manifested, are cases in which these symptoms are manifestations of father-fears? If the answer consists in appealing to examples of analytic treatment of the sort we are examining with John, then the answer is not much help. For such an appeal assumes that psycho-analytic method is valid—that by means of it one can really arrive at, for example, the real character of people's fears and what they are manifestations of. But the offering and use of interpretations is an essential part of psycho-analytic method. To ask, therefore, for the criteria of a psycho-analytic interpretation, as we are doing, is in effect to question the validity of the method. It is to ask, *inter alia*, how we know that by means of this method we arrive at the truth about a patient. Hence, to defend T 11,2 by an appeal to past analytic experience is to beg the question. It is to assume the validity of the very technique whose validity we

[5] Cf. *passim:* Mayer-Gross, Slater, and Roth (1954), *Clinical Psychiatry* (London); D. Russell Davis (1957), *An Introduction to Psychopathology* (London).

are investigating. Suppose, however, that the answer does not consist of pointing to cases of a similar sort, but to evidence of quite a different type. What would this evidence be like? Clearly, as analytic experience is not self-supporting here, we require evidence from outside—external to and independent of the analytic session. But where is this evidence? We all know that appeals to 'cures' or 'improvement' are of little help. Appeals to the work of the experimental and objective psychologist are much more promising. But as yet, in spite of a large and growing body of knowledge coming from this work, what has been achieved in this quarter is still far removed from interpretations such as T 11,2 and not yet sufficient to underpin them securely.

The upshot, then, is this. It may be necessary that T 11,2 should satisfy the criterion of analogy for us to be reasonably assured that it is true. But the criterion seems too weak to give us the reasonable assurance we want.

IV

An analyst could also defend T 11,2 in the following way. 'Part of my business is to try all the time to understand what is going on. Why does the patient offer this material now? What does it mean to him? And so on. When the patient John brought up the material about the car lessons, I offered T 11,2 in order, *inter alia*, to help him to face his fear of doing what father does. And I believe T 11,2 to be true because it helps to make John's fears about car driving intelligible—it makes sense out of them, it tells us what the car driving means to him. Moreover, T 11,2 does not stand alone. The analysis brought up a whole mass of material about John's attitudes towards his father—how he views him as a successful figure, whom he feels he must emulate but with whom he also feels he won't be able to compete. And so on. (The extract quoted above only gives us a small glimpse of all this further father-material.) Part, also, of my business is to try to make the whole mass of father-material intelligible. But I obviously cannot do this in isolation, by itself alone. I must consider it in relation to the material as a whole, and I must try to form an intelligible view of the whole personality of the boy and his difficulties. Now my supposition in T 11,2 does not stand alone, but forms part of a comprehensive account, or narrative, that I could give about the boy as a whole, including his attitudes to his father. It is this fact that gives T 11,2 strong additional support, and really makes it worthy of serious consideration. For by means of this narrative we are able to explain the boy's response to his car driving lessons by showing how it is a manifestation of his general attitudes to his father and of his personality as a whole. T 11,2 enables us to fit an item in the material (namely, his fear about the car driving) into the jigsaw about his personality as a whole; and this is what really gives T 11,2 its strength.'

Let us say that, in offering this defence of T 11,2, the analyst is appealing to 'the criterion of intelligibility'. It is very evident that this criterion, as stated, is extremely vague, and is far too large a topic to pursue adequately here. Accordingly, I shall only raise two difficulties about it.

(A) Let us agree to say that T 11,2 satisfies this criterion—that it makes sense out of the boy's fears, that it makes them intelligible. This fact would only give us reasonable assurance that T 11,2 was true if T 11,2 were the *only* interpretation that could be offered which satisfied this criterion, or which satisfied it anything like as well. We cannot be reasonably sure, therefore, that T 11,2 is true until we are reasonably sure that there is no alternative interpretation available of equal, or near equal, strength to explain the boy's fears, and so make them intelligible. But as soon as we try to satisfy ourselves on this question, we plunge at once into the endless sea of current, very technical dispute and discussion about the genesis of phobias and the conceptual schemes we ought to employ in dealing with personality. Thus, for example, it has been argued—with some clinical and experimental backing[6]—that the main contributory cause of a phobic response *can* be a single frightening occurrence. Consequently, it could also be argued that John's fears about car driving *may* have their main source in the acute fright that he might have given himself once, when, for example, as a small boy he released the brakes of the family car and made it run downhill. Of course, John's fear of driving may also be connected with his father. But if the *main* source springs from a traumatic incident of the sort indicated, then T 11,2 is at worst false, and at best only a small part of the truth. Consequently, we cannot be reasonably confident that T 11,2 is true of John unless we have good reason to think that there is no equally plausible alternative available to explain the boy's fears. I doubt whether the data and the analytic record about John enable us to decide this particular question about him. This difficulty about T 11,2 is likely to be a recurrent one—the present state of psychopathology and personality theory being what it is. So I doubt whether we can often apply the criterion of intelligibility with much confidence.

But what of the claim that T 11,2 gains great strength from the fact that it forms part of a comprehensive narrative about the boy's attitudes to his father and about his personality as a whole? Is this correct?

[6] Cf. J. Woodward (1959), 'Emotional disturbances of burned children', *Brit. Med. J.*, **1**, 1009–13; R. R. Grinker and J. P. Spiegel (1945), *Men under Stress*, Ch. 5, Case 13 (Philadelphia); J. H. Masserman (1943), *Behaviour and Neurosis* (Chicago). For general discussions, see, for example: D. Russell Davis, op. cit., and H. Gwynne Jones (1960) in H. J. Eysenck (ed.), *Handbook of Abnormal Psychology*, Ch. 13.

Let us answer this question by taking an interpretation which is not near to common sense, such as T 11,2, and which may seem quite crazy. In session 66 John discussed waste and his attitude to money. The analyst ended the session with a long sequence of remarks in which he said that John seemed to have the very strong feeling that an object he might want might not always be there, that, for example, having spent some pocket money, he was then without it and this was to him 'a very dreaded state'. The analyst continued: 'Somehow I think this must be linked very much to your relationship with mother ... and essentially her breast'; and he then proceeded to develop this. Let us consider this last interpretation. We need not stay to ask what there was in the record to suggest and back it. Let us ask instead: how could this interpretation fit into and form part of a comprehensive narrative about John's difficulties and personality as a whole?

Suppose that I am an analyst and that the sort of narrative I use about personality and its development is a Kleino-Freudian one. Suppose I am confronted with the boy John and his poor examination results, and general difficulties of intellectual under-functioning. I could then use the Kleino-Freudian scheme to produce a specific and comprehensive narrative about John to make these facts intelligible; and the gist of part of my explanation might be baldly expressed in the following form.

(i) When children suffer from loss of parental objects, they are liable to mislay objects in general.

John suffered in this way (e.g. on being left at boarding school at nine).

We have reason, therefore, to believe that he, too, is liable to mislay objects in general.

(ii) When a person is liable to mislay objects in general, he will find it difficult to do well in examinations (i.e. to lay his hands on the objects of his learning and to show, or express, the results of his search).

John is liable to mislay objects.

We have reason, therefore, to believe that John finds it difficult to learn and to show the results.

When I am now confronted, in session 66, with John's concern about being without money, etc., it is natural for me to offer the interpretation that this is connected with his mother and the breast that he has lost. It is natural for me to offer this 'crazy' interpretation because it is the obvious way to apply a Kleino-Freudian scheme to this particular material in 66; and by so doing I can bring John's attitudes to money within the scope of a more comprehensive narrative about his learning difficulties and personality as a whole. So it is clear that this interpretation about the breast does not stand alone, but forms part of, or can be accommodated within, a more comprehensive narrative designed to give an intelligible picture of John and his problems.

But does this fact give the 'breast' interpretation much added weight, and sufficient to entitle us to be reasonably assured of its truth? Hardly. For the weight that accrues in this way to an accommodated interpretation obviously depends on the strength of the comprehensive narrative which accommodates it. Now the specific narrative I have used about John has a strained and far-fetched appearance; and it is very likely that there will be other competing narratives in the field, which seem, prima facie, just as, or even more, plausible and reasonable than my Kleino-Freudian story about John. So the fact that I can fit John's concern about waste and money into a comprehensive narrative about him by means of the 'breast' interpretation does not, by itself, give this interpretation much support. Further discussion at this point is likely to shift, and indeed should shift, away from the interpretation itself and concentrate on the *sort* of comprehensive narrative we ought to use. If, therefore, we try to defend the 'breast' interpretation in this way, we shall fail to obtain consensus and the reasonable assurance we want.

The same considerations apply, *mutatis mutandis,* to the 'uncrazy' interpretation T 11,2. If T 11,2 can be fitted into a story about John's attitudes to his father, which in turn can be fitted into a comprehensive narrative about the boy as a whole, then this fact only gives T 11,2 great weight, or support, if we have reasonable assurance that this specific comprehensive narrative about John is itself true. In the absence of such assurance, T 11,2 will be left a bit in the air.

(B) The second difficulty about the criterion of intelligibility is quite a different one. It could be said that it is very doubtful whether the criterion functions typically in the way we have presented it, and that our way of presenting it just misrepresents what happens in psycho-analysis.

Suppose that I am an analyst working within the Kleino-Freudian tradition. It could be argued that, when a patient presents me with material, what I actually do is this. I try to make the material intelligible by fitting a specific Kleino-Freudian narrative to it; or, if you like, by bringing it within the scope of a narrative of this basic Kleino-Freudian sort or type. I do this quite naturally, because this basic type of narrative is the one that enables me to make what seems sense out of the data that come up in analysis. When, therefore, I offer an interpretation, I do not do so in a wholly *ad hoc,* or empirical way. On the contrary, I offer it in an attempt to fit the basic type of narrative I use in my work to the data. The interpretation represents such an attempted fit. If a certain interpretation does in fact help me to fit this basic Kleino-Freudian story to the data, then it will go to form part of a specific, comprehensive narrative of this type; and I retain the interpretation.

If, on the other hand, an offered interpretation does not help me to form a specific narrative of this type about a patient, if I find it getting in the way, then I drop the idea it contains and explore some other way of making sense out of the certain item in the data that the offered interpretation was meant to deal with. Such an interpretation, offered but then not pressed, represents an unsuccessful attempt to fit the basic type of narrative to the material. From this it is evident that I do allow the material, or data, presented by a patient to count for and against a particular *application* of the basic type of narrative. But I do not allow, or use, the material to count against the *basic type of narrative itself* that I employ.[7]

Now if this is a correct account of what I actually do, it follows that I cannot use the criterion of intelligibility to defend an interpretation in the way originally depicted. I cannot use it to show that we have reasonable assurance that an interpretation is true. At most I can use it to show that we have reasonable assurance that a certain interpretation represents the correct application of the basic type of Kleino-Freudian narrative I use to deal with psycho-analytic material. It could be argued, no doubt, that it is a necessary condition of the truth of an interpretation that it can be accommodated within a comprehensive narrative about a patient. If a particular interpretation, say, T 11,2, can be so accommodated, then this would count in favour of its truth. But the mere fact that an analyst can, and does, fit an interpretation into such a comprehensive narrative, whether of the Kleino-Freudian type or any other, does not in itself give us reasonable assurance that the interpretation is true. The way in which I — as a supposed analyst — actually use the Kleino-Freudian discourse may or may not be typical of analysts in this or any other tradition. But if my behaviour is typical, it follows that the criterion of intelligibility will fail generally to provide the reasonable guarantee that we want.

V

I end this paper by mentioning two further topics that suggest themselves at this point.

I. Let us assume that the criticisms I have brought against the suggested criteria either do not hold, or can be satisfactorily countered. Let us assume, that is to say, that the criteria we have discussed are all good necessary criteria. Let us assume, further, that they are satisfied by some interpretation, such as T 11,2 or T 13,1, and satisfied in a way that is as convincing as we could hope for. Is this fact *sufficient* to give us reasonable assurance that the interpretation is true?

[7] On the general point raised here, cf. K. R. Popper (1957), 'Philosophy of Science: a Personal Report', in C. A. Mace (ed.), *British Philosophy in the Mid-Century* (London).

It seems doubtful. The doubt stems from the relation between analyst and patient. This is admittedly a very special relation, and one which is markedly different from the normal relation between two conversationalists in ordinary life. Now it has been maintained that this special relation lays the patient open to suggestion from the analyst, and, more important, renders him highly suggestible. Accordingly, if an analyst starts fitting a certain basic type of narrative to the patient, the latter is liable to come to accept the interpretations that are offered him as being true of himself. Hence, the fact that an interpretation of, say, a Kleino-Freudian type convincingly satisfies the criteria we have discussed is not sufficient to show that this interpretation is really true of the patient. The most this fact does show is that the analyst is being very successful in transforming the patient into a 'Kleino-Freudian type' of person—one whom a Kleino-Freudian narrative obviously fits, and hence of whom the interpretations appear to be true both to patient and analyst.[8]

The strength of this objection depends largely on the hypothesis that the special relation in analysis opens wide the door to suggestion and suggestibility in the way indicated. This is clearly a matter which requires scientific investigation. To the best of my knowledge, no adequate investigation of this hypothesis and its related problems has yet been made. It is not much, if any, use for analysts to repudiate the hypothesis on the strength of convictions derived from their own experience as analysts. For the validity of psycho-analytic method, and hence of their own experience as analysts, is precisely what is in question here. Nor is the mere impression of the outsider of much, if any, use either. Thus, it is very tempting to point to the fact that in session 18 the analyst seems to be doing as much talking as the boy John, and seems very obviously to be exerting enormous pressure on this tight, polite, and withdrawn adolescent. But something much more, or other, than the mere quantity of speech and a sense of pressure is required to substantiate the hypothesis that psycho-analytic method works in the way alleged. However, though we cannot appeal to a definitive scientific answer, we are confronted by the fact that quite a good case can be made out in support of this hypothesis. The case rests on general considerations of a technical character, considerations which draw attention to the similarity between psycho-analytic method and other techniques of human transformation, such as religious conversion and brain-washing. As long as we are confronted by this reasonable objection to psycho-analytic method, it is doubtful whether the criteria we have considered are sufficient to give us reasonable assurance that an interpretation is true.

II. Why is our search for criteria so difficult and frustrating? Is there, per-

[8] Cf. Popper's reference to the 'Oedipus effect', loc. cit.

haps, any general reason that helps us to account for this? I am inclined to think there may be.

When I set out, near the beginning of this paper, in search of the truth criteria for an interpretation, I took over the general, if not universal, assumption about interpretations. This is the assumption that when an analyst offers an interpretation, he is uttering a statement that is primarily declaratory in character, and which. therefore, serves primarily to express an hypothesis about the patient. If this assumption were true, then it would be quite in order and natural to search for truth criteria; and one might expect, perhaps, that it would be a relatively straightforward matter to discover them. But it is doubtful whether this general assumption is true. Thus, when a statement such as T 11,2 is offered to the patient, its primary function does not seem to be declaratory and hypothesis-stating at all. Its chief point seems to be an instrumental one. For the analyst is primarily interested: (a) in disturbing, goading, and impelling John into recognizing and talking about his own feelings, attitudes, etc., at the time, quite ignoring whether and to what extent John's feelings, etc., are an artefact of the analysis itself; and (b) in changing John from a tight, withdrawn adolescent, who is intellectually under-functioning, into a more relaxed outgoing individual, who is no longer so anxiety-bound that he is unable to show his examiners what he can do. T 11,2 is uttered as part of a long, persistent, and many-sided attempt to change the boy in this way. Moreover, as we have already noted, the utterance of T 11,2 may indeed be artefact producing, and thereby help to change the patient so as to make the interpretation seem to be true of him. It could be argued, therefore, that T 11,2 is primarily a transforming statement, and in this respect is characteristic of interpretations offered by analysts.

What follows from this contention? One possible consequence is that it is illegitimate, and therefore absurd, to suppose that an interpretative utterance can be true or false at all. From this it follows that an interpretation has no truth criteria. It is quite understandable, therefore, that our search for such criteria has been difficult and frustrating; for there are none to be found. Another possible but weaker consequence is this. Though an interpretation is primarily a transforming statement, it nevertheless retains hypothesis-stating, and hence declaratory, features. But these are apt to be overlaid by, and lost in, the complicated instrumental context in which this sort of statement functions. Consequently, even though such a statement has declaratory features, it may be difficult on many occasions to discover from its context just what its truth criteria are. Indeed, it may be so difficult as to make the search for truth criteria hardly worth while. For even when one tries to state and use the obvious candidates, one is likely to find that actually they cannot be applied at all, or applied to much effect. This is just what we discovered with T 11,2; and it is the natural outcome of the fact that T 11,2 is primarily a transforming statement. However, on either view, the stronger or the weaker, we can still ask certain very important questions about T 11,2. These are questions about its appropriateness—the point and value of offering it when and how the analyst did.[9]

But this conclusion—in either its stronger or its weaker form—seems to be rather small and uninteresting beer. For all it seems to amount to is that it is logically impossible or practically difficult to find the truth criteria of an interpretation when this is uttered *within* the context of the analytic session. This conclusion does not say that an interpretation has no truth criteria when uttered *outside* this context. Moreover, it is clear that, even if we accept the conclusion in its stronger form (in which an interpretation-in-session is not an hypothesis at all and hence uncheckable and unfalsifiable), we cannot go on to say that the *generalizations* of psycho-analytic theory are uncheckable and unfalsifiable. The inference does not follow at all.[10] However, this conclusion is not quite as small and trivial as it may seem. It has important implications for psycho-analytic theory and method. For one thing, it would appear to loosen the connection traditionally supposed to exist between psycho-analytic theory and the clinical data. We may now have to rethink the evidential relation between the theory and the interpretations used in applying it therapeutically. For another, the conclusion may serve to alter the character of analytic practice. At present interpretations are offered in the guise of hypotheses. But it may not be helpful to offer them in this form to a patient who happens to have read this paper and accepted the conclusion we have just discussed! Freud once wrote as follows:

It is true that during the analysis Hans had to be told many things that he could not say himself, that he had to be presented with thoughts which he had so far shown no sign of possessing, and that his attention had to be turned in the direction from which his father was expecting something to come. This detracts from the evidental value of the analysis; but the procedure is the same in every case. For a psycho-analysis is not an impartial scientific investigation, but a therapeutic measure. Its essence is not to prove anything, but merely to alter something. In a psycho-analysis the physician always gives his patient (sometimes to a greater and sometimes to a less extent) the conscious anticipatory image by the help of which he is put in a position to recognise and to grasp the unconscious material.[11]

---

[9] Cf. P. Alexander and A. MacIntyre (1955), 'Cause and Cure in Psychotherapy', *Arist. Soc.*, Supp. Vol., **29** (London).

    It is interesting to record that a very good case can be made for the view that John did change in the desired direction during the period of the analysis. His improvement is shown in his examination results, in his performance when retested psychologically, and it is suggested by his way of talking in later sessions, as a tape recording can reveal. Of course, such evidence by itself does not show what contribution, if any, the analysis made to this happy transformation.

[10] Cf. B. A. Farrell (1961), 'Can Psychoanalysis be refuted?', *Inquiry*, vol. i, 16–36.

[11] S. Freud, 'Analysis of a Phobia in a five-year-old boy' (1909), *Coll. Papers*, vol. iii.

It is a pity that Freud does not appear to have followed up the insights contained in this passage, and, in particular, to have asked how far the acceptance of psycho-analytic method as a therapeutic and transforming procedure is compatible with the claim that the method enables the patient 'to recognise and to grasp the unconscious material', and thus to discover the truth about himself. However, I confess that I am unclear about the implications of all this for psycho-analysis. I have not yet been able to carry my personal analysis beyond this point.

II

ERROR, FAITH, AND SELF-DECEPTION

PATRICK GARDINER

I

WHEN, in the eighteenth century, Bishop Butler discussed what he called 'self-deceit'[1] it was in a predominantly moral context; he was concerned, that is to say, with cases in which an individual might be said not to recognize, or not to acknowledge fully to himself, such things as his own faults and failings. Men, Butler claimed, have a striking 'partiality to themselves', a partiality apt to make them 'think and reason and judge quite differently upon any matter relating to themselves, from what they do in cases of others where they are not interested'. In consequence, they are often to be discovered assessing their own conduct in a manner curiously at odds with that in which they are accustomed to assess the behaviour of their fellows; moreover, it is not uncommon to find them talking and acting as if they were 'perfect strangers' to their own characters and as if they were ignorant of many of their deepest purposings and preoccupations. For it is precisely regarding such matters that our judgement is liable to be most distorted and unreliable:

Though a man hath the best eyes in the world, he cannot see any way but that which he turns them. Thus these persons, without passing over the least, the most minute thing, which can possibly be urged in favour of themselves, shall overlook entirely the plainest and most obvious things on the other side ...; and their deliberation concerning an action to be done, or reflection upon it afterwards, is not to see whether it be right, but to find reasons to justify or palliate it; palliate it, not to others, but themselves.[2]

It is in the operations of this tendency, whereby partiality and a concern for our own interests not only influences the 'temper and passions' but also 'reaches to the understanding', that Butler discerns the essence of the peculiar 'internal hypocrisy' he has in mind. In extreme instances it helps to explain

From *Proceedings of the Aristotelian Society* (1969–70). Reprinted by permission of the Editor of the Aristotelian Society.

[1] *Works*, vol. 2, pp. 118–32.
[2] Ibid., p. 122.

how a man, previously of respected character and strongly held principles, may on a particular occasion undertake some manifestly evil design or plan with surprising coolness, subsequently looking back on what he has done with a no less astonishing lack of compunction or remorse. More typically, however, it displays itself in situations in which the moral issues are more shadowy and ill-defined, and where it is hard to draw a sharp line indicating the point at which right ends and wrong begins. Yet even in the most favourable type of case there may be in the man's mind, if not 'proper knowledge', at least a residual 'suspicion' that all is not quite as it should be. In this respect the self-deceiver may be compared with one whose momentary glimpse of a scene is sufficient to intimate to him that it is of a disagreeable complexion and who then shuts his eyes to avoid a clear apprehension of the unsavoury details; for 'it is as easy to close the eyes of the mind as those of the body: and the former is more frequently done with wilfulness, and yet not attended to, than the latter'.[3] Butler concludes that self-deception, being a species of dishonesty and 'falseness of heart', augments rather than extenuates guilt, and that if people are going to indulge in wrongdoing at all it will be better for it to spring 'from the common vicious passions without such refinements, than from this deep and calm source of delusion'.

From a contemporary standpoint Butler's account may seem, psychologically speaking, to have a rather out-dated air. It is perhaps only during the last hundred years or so that the phenomenon with which he was dealing has come to acquire the central position it now occupies in our thinking, a general recognition of its significance, and of the subtly ramifying roles it plays in influencing human experience and behaviour, constituting a crucial point of difference between our present picture of man and the models of earlier times. Conceptions of the mind such as those suggested by nineteenth-century romantic thought, theories of false consciousness of the kind purveyed by Hegel and Marx, the perceptive portrayals of human character and motivation undertaken by novelists like Flaubert, Proust, and James—all these have combined to enlarge and deepen our sensitivity to the possibilities of self-deception, while also introducing modifications and extensions to the concept itself. It is therefore not surprising if Butler's discussion should impress us as being a little thin and two-dimensional. But even when taken within its own terms of reference it may strike us as unduly narrow, especially in its concentration (which we noted at the outset) upon the moral implications of self-deception. Possibly because of his clerical preoccupations, Butler treats the subject almost entirely from the point of view of wrongful action and the application of double standards, tending to identify the circumstances in which self-deception characteristically manifests itself as ones

[3] *Works*, vol. 2, p. 128.

involving some sort of conflict, open or suppressed, between the forces of selfish desire and those of conscientious scruple. It may be objected, however, that even at the simplest level occasions for self-deception arise which are quite unrelated to moral considerations. A man may, for instance, be thought of as deceiving himself concerning his prospects or his abilities in a manner that does not presuppose the existence of anything *morally* untoward from which he is trying to hide or which he is unwilling to face. Moreover, as such examples also show, it is far from clear that the primary or most frequent objects of self-deception are such things as a man's own character traits or his motives and intentions. Misapprehensions concerning how things stand in the world confronting him are equally plausible candidates, and very common. Thus a general's misappreciation of the military state of affairs in which he is placed may be described in these terms; and a politician, engaged upon a project on which he has staked the reputation of himself or his country, may be spoken of as sinking deeper and deeper into self-deception regarding the objective chances of a successful outcome. Retrospectively, too, a man whose plans have turned out badly may be said to have 'convinced himself' that he had no real choice in the matter, the situation as he now represents it to himself having been one that permitted of no other feasible line of action.

Yet, despite such deficiencies and when all allowance has been made for the various accretions and modifications to which the concept has been subject since he wrote, Butler's account remains of value in pointing up certain features that still seem central to the notion and to underlie its normal use and functioning in everyday contexts. The idea that men may be, in some sense, their own dupes, that they may hold beliefs or opinions which are not only erroneous or poorly supported but which also appear to be tailor-made to suit their wishes or convenience and to involve an evasion of, or blindness to, facts of whose existence it is hard to imagine them wholly ignorant or unaware—this, it can be argued, continues to be found engrained in the conception of self-deception as we at present possess and understand it. But thus interpreted, it may be felt to harbour difficulties about which Butler, in so far as he recognized them, had not a great deal to say. For the question round which they revolve is not, How does self-deception, as a familiar psychological phenomenon, occur? Rather it is the question, How, given that a certain view of what constitutes self-deception is correct, *could* it occur?

The kind of problem sometimes said to arise here can be brought out by comparing what is supposed to happen when somebody is self-deceived with standard cases of deception proper, or 'other-deception'. If a man sets out to deceive another, he tries to make him believe something which he himself knows, or believes, not to be so; such an attempt commonly takes the form of lying, although it need not—there are other methods, such as behaving (or arranging things) in certain ways that may be, depending upon the circumstances, appropriate. In so far as he is successful, the other will have been caused to accept something incompatible with what he, the deceiver, holds to be the case. It has been claimed, however, that when this is used as a model whereby to explicate the notion of self-deception, unwelcome paradoxes ensue. For it is surely odd to suggest that somebody could try to make, and succeed in making, himself believe something which he, *ex hypothesi*, at the same time believes not to be true. In so far as lying, e.g., is a deliberate attempt to misinform, or conceal the truth from, the person lied to, it is essential that the liar should know and accept what it is that he is trying to hide from his victim; it is also a presupposition of this type of undertaking that the intended victim should not be aware of the deceiver's aims. But the transposition of these conditions to cases where the roles of deceiver and deceived are allegedly occupied by one and the same individual might lead one to conclude that self-deception is a contradictory or incoherent enterprise, incapable of fulfilment. Sartre, in his chapter on *mauvaise foi* in *L'Être et le Néant*, expresses graphically but not unperceptively the dilemma involved. After claiming that, in instances of ordinary deception, 'consciousness . . . utilises for its own profit the ontological duality of myself and myself in the eyes of the Other', Sartre goes on to contrast the situation in 'bad faith', where this is regarded as a kind of lying to oneself: 'the duality of the deceiver and the deceived does not exist here'.[4] But that means that I must 'know in my capacity as deceiver the truth which is hidden from me in my capacity as the one deceived . . . and this not at two different moments, which at a pinch would allow us to re-establish a semblance of duality—but in the unitary structure of a single project'. To this consideration, according to which bad faith involves the contradictory supposition that a man can know and be ignorant of the same thing at the same time, Sartre adds a 'further difficulty' that stems from the 'translucency of consciousness'. If I lie, then I must be aware of doing so—'I must be in good faith, at least to the extent that I am conscious of my bad faith'. This, however, is an admission that is ruinous to the whole undertaking. For it is a condition of my being deceived that I should not be aware that deception is being attempted or practised; consequently in the case being considered the lie 'falls back and collapses beneath my look'. On the other hand, since for Sartre it can hardly be denied that *mauvaise foi* in some form is a pervasive aspect of the lives of 'a very great number of people', a somewhat uncomfort-

---

[4] This and the immediately following quotations are from *Being and Nothingness*, trans. H. Barnes, pp. 49 f.

able *impasse* seems to have been reached: 'our embarrassment then appears extreme since we can neither reject nor comprehend bad faith'.

One way out, which Sartre himself considers at some length and which he attributes to psycho-analysis, consists, in effect, in arguing that self-deception is really after all a form of other-deception, so that the above difficulties—resting as they do upon the assumed identity of the deceiver and the deceived—do not arise. This amounts to the claim that there is an actual split, or 'duality', within the mind of the 'self-deceived' individual. In Freudian terms, this may amount to postulating a 'censor' standing between the conscious 'ego' (the true 'I') and those elements in the psyche which are referred to the 'id' and which are unconscious. On such an hypothesis, I am prevented (I do not prevent myself) from recognizing certain things about myself—for example, the presence of deep-lying wishes or fears—in a manner parallel to that in which, in interpersonal contexts, I may be intentionally prevented by another from learning of matters he does not wish me to know. Sartre's chief objection to this theory is that the difficulty it might be thought to remove merely re-emerges at a different level. How, for instance, is the status of the censor itself to be conceived? If it is to perform the functions assigned to it—selecting the drives to be repressed or concealed, interpreting and resisting the analyst's probings, and so forth—it must presumably be aware of the material in question and aware of its own activity in seeking to stop this material from rising to explicit consciousness. But this implies that the censor in its turn is 'in bad faith'; it both knows and at the same time seeks to conceal from itself what it knows, and the original paradox recurs. It might, of course, be argued that all the theory requires is that the censor should hide the truth from the ego (and perhaps the analyst), not that it should do so from itself as well. But to this Sartre could—and, I think, would—reply that the addition of a further 'autonomous consciousness' to the existing ego amounts to no more than a verbal subterfuge which once again leaves everything as it was. For what does talk of such a dual consciousness subsisting within one and the same individual really come down to, if not to saying (as before) that the man is both aware and unaware of the truth, both lying and yet (mysteriously) deceived by his lies? What has been presented is a restatement, rather than a solution, of the problem, and psycho-analysis has not, therefore, 'gained anything for us'.

It is not my intention to consider Sartre's specific criticisms of psycho-analysis here: such a discussion would raise technical issues in psycho-analytical theory, as well as others relating to more general aspects of Sartre's polemic against the Freudian doctrine of the unconscious, which lie well beyond the scope of the present paper. In any case, the precise relevance of the explanatory constructs of psycho-analysis to the topic in hand is far from clear; whether these have illuminated or (as Sartre holds) obscured the operations of self-deception in certain domains, the fact remains that we are dealing with a concept that is non-technical in character and that seems to have been in common currency—at least in essentials—long before the advent of psycho-analysis itself. So let us return to the element of paradox alleged to lie at the heart of this notion, which has been seen as constituting a threat to its status as an intelligible idea.

II

A tempting line of approach, recently adopted by philosophers who have been impressed by difficulties of the sort Sartre raised, consists in simply denying the propriety of interpreting self-deception in terms that construe it as a reflexive analogue of deception proper. Once its unfortunate associations with the misleading model of other-deception have been severed, they argue, no further reason exists for refusing it the title of full logical respectability.

Thus Canfield and Gustafson, in their succinct contribution to the theme,[5] suggest that the notion of self-deception can be fruitfully and non-paradoxically treated by interpreting it as a species of self-command. They claim that, if self-command is understood on the model of commanding others and conceived of as a matter of obeying orders addressed to oneself, 'odd-sounding results' follow. But these can be avoided. Assimilating the notion of self-command to that of a man's making himself do something, they contend that all that is required for a statement of the form 'X makes himself do Y' to be true is that X should do Y under 'adverse circumstances'; such circumstances would involve obstacles or difficulties of a kind likely to disincline an agent from doing whatever it is that is in question. Since self-deception may be understood as being essentially a matter of a person's making himself believe something, it is argued that a similar analysis is applicable here. Thus to say that a man deceives himself about a given proposition is to say that he believes it in 'belief-adverse circumstances'—in other words, circumstances in which the evidence is heavily weighted against the truth of the proposition believed. It is claimed that this interpretation avoids the obvious problems raised by more conventional accounts: thus it has the advantage that we no longer have to attribute to the self-deceiver incompatible beliefs and, in particular, need not conclude from standard examples that a man, aware of something's being the case, can somehow 'fool himself' into supposing that it is not. The interpretation offered is also said to be 'neutral'

[5] 'Self-Deception', by J. V. Canfield and D. F. Gustafson, *Analysis* (1962).

with regard to the 'psychological mechanisms', whatever they may be, which lead a man to believe something in the face of strong evidence to the contrary.

Despite its attractive economy, the proposed analysis does not seem to me acceptable. Not only does it leave one with the uncomfortable suspicion that the baby has disappeared with the bath-water: there is also a prima facie oddity about the suggestion that self-deception can be treated as a form of something so apparently disparate as self-command; nor, again, is it intuitively evident that the former can be so shortly equated with 'making oneself believe something'. But however this may be, a closer inspection of the argument reveals difficulties more immediately germane to the kind of problem it was designed to obviate.

As has been seen, Canfield and Gustafson compare doing something under certain 'adverse' conditions with believing something under certain 'adverse' conditions. In making such a comparison, they might be supposed to mean that, just as a man may perform an action though strongly disinclined to do so because of factors like the hardship or inconvenience involved, so a man may believe a proposition though strongly disinclined to do so because of the weight of the evidence against it. Now there undoubtedly are relatively unproblematic cases in which a person may be described as believing something to be true in spite of a strongly felt disinclination to do so—he may, for instance, recognize its unwelcome implications for the success of some project in which he is engaged and yet none the less give his reluctant assent to it. But this is hardly the sense of 'being disinclined to believe' that is relevant here. A man's disinclination to believe a given proposition because he realizes that, if it is true, his interests will be affected in certain ways is one thing; his disinclination to believe it on the basis of the evidence before him is another. In the case of the former he has reasons for not *wishing* to believe it, whereas in the case of the latter he has reasons for not *believing* it, *simpliciter*. And while settling the question of whether somebody is disinclined to believe a proposition in the first way is not, as such, to settle the question of whether he actually disbelieves it, it is not at all clear that the same holds when he is said to be disinclined in the second way. For what—in the absence of anything further—can this really mean if not that he does not believe it, or at the least that he is very dubious as to its truth?

If what has just been maintained is correct, it does (I think) raise a serious doubt concerning the suggestion that, when self-deception is treated as 'belief under adverse circumstances' in the recommended manner, the usual difficulties associated with the concept automatically disappear. For how is the phrase 'under adverse circumstances' to be understood? If it refers to conditions in which the believer would prefer that the proposition he believes were false, no obvious paradox is involved; moreover, such an interpretation would lend some force to the analogy drawn between 'making oneself do something and 'making oneself believe something'. For, if 'making oneself do something' is thought of as covering cases in which one does things that are found, for some reason, unattractive, 'making oneself believe something' may be construed—in one conceivable use of this expression—as covering cases in which one believes things which one is disinclined to believe because of their unpalatable or disagreeable implications. Thus a man may remind himself that it is useless burying his head in the sands and that he must accept the truth about his situation, however bitter. It is evident, though, that this is not so much self-deception as its direct opposite—the man refuses to allow himself to be deluded by false hopes. And it is not, of course, in this sense that Canfield and Gustafson do wish to interpret 'making oneself believe something'. When they speak of 'belief under adverse circumstances' they have in view (as we saw) conditions in which holding the belief in question is evidentially unjustified or unwarranted; thus making oneself believe something, in the sense relevant to self-deception, will be a matter of believing it against one's reason rather than against one's will. But now the position no longer looks so straightforward. For (to revert to the point made earlier) if a man is said to be disinclined by strongly unfavourable evidence to believe a certain proposition, this seems tantamount to attributing to him disbelief in the proposition concerned. How, than, can he be held at the same time to believe it? Has not the kind of paradox the proposed analysis was designed to remove returned once more?

There are complications here to which we shall have to recur at a later stage. It could be, however, that the above argument in any case misrepresents the original thesis. For it has been assumed that the self-deceiver is supposed to recognize the strength of the contrary evidence, and yet to believe notwithstanding. Perhaps, though, what was meant is that, while *objectively* speaking the evidence points to the falsity of the belief, the self-deceiver does not or need not realize this, either because he is unaware of the existence of the evidence or else because, though aware of it, he does not appreciate its significance. But this alternative account presents difficulties of its own. In the first place, a man could hardly be said to be making himself *do* something unless certain aspects of his undertaking appeared to him in an unfavourable light; if, therefore, the close relation alleged to subsist between self-command and self-deception is to hold, it would seem that there must be a corresponding recognition of unfavourable circumstances in the case of the latter as well. Secondly, and more crucially, if the element of recognition is omitted, it is no longer clear on the account given what differentiates self-deception from various common forms of error or confusion: a man who believes something when the evidence points the other way is not necessarily described as self-deceived—he may, for instance, be deemed ignorant or just foolish. Thus this version of the thesis apparently only avoids the initial paradox at the cost of obliterating certain familiar and essential distinctions. The heroic course might, of course, be taken of simply denying that such distinctions can validly be drawn, and a degree of support for this approach could indeed be extracted from a consideration of some varieties of idiomatic usage. Thus, as has been correctly observed,[6] it is possible to cite instances where saying of a person that he has deceived himself about a particular matter seems to come down to asserting no more than that his judgement was mistaken and that he should have known better. But, while this may be admitted, such uses appear to be peripheral and not to reflect the cardinal features of the concept as normally understood. So long as a question like 'Was he just making a plain and needless error or was he, on the other hand, the victim of some kind of self-deception?' can naturally arise and be taken to embody genuine alternatives, any assimilation, on the lines proposed, of self-deception to mere belief in the face of strong contrary evidence will continue to strike us as being (at best) insufficient. We seem, in other words, to have arrived at the following unsatisfactory position: either we must accept a watered-down version of the concept that fails adequately to capture its primary function in thought and language, or else we must simply acquiesce in the existence of paradoxes viewed by many philosophers as falling well below the threshold of what is logically tolerable.

III

Can this dilemma be overcome? Rather than seek to remove those features of self-deception declared to be paradoxical by producing an analysis in which they no longer appear at all, it may be argued that we should try instead to show that, though ineliminable, they are in fact susceptible to an innocuous interpretation. This, if I understand him rightly, is the line favoured by Penelhum.[7]

Penelhum considers that some indication that the self-deceiver holds conflicting beliefs is requisite if his case is to be distinguished from that of an individual who is, say, merely ignorant of the contrary evidence or who has, through sheer carelessness or stupidity, failed to appreciate its bearing and implications. Thus, in order to forestall the sort of objection to which Canfield and Gustafson (on one version of their thesis) were found to be exposed, it is necessary to insist that the self-deceiver 'must not only know the strong evidence, but see what it points to'. But then the conclusion seems inescap-

---

[6] See F. A. Siegler, 'Demos on Lying to Oneself', *Journal of Philosophy* (1962).

[7] Penelhum, 'Pleasure and Falsity', *American Philosophical Quarterly* (1964): a suggestive article to which I am indebted.

able that he in some manner accepts the proposition which he also, *qua* subject of deception, rejects. Is this an impossible situation? Penelhum's answer is that, properly characterized, it is not: what we have here is a 'conflict state' in which there is 'partial satisfaction of the opposed criteria for belief and for disbelief'; in this way we can settle for 'consistent description of inconsistent behaviour'. The suggestion, in short, appears to be that, since self-deception does not require that the conditions for full belief and for full disbelief should be jointly and simultaneously fulfilled in the case of a single individual, no insuperable difficulties arise; the fact that they have been thought to do so has perhaps been due to taking too literally the analogy with other-deception.

Such an approach seems, in a general way, to have much to recommend it. All the same, there are puzzling lacunae in Penelhum's own account as it stands. The conditions he finally sets out as being together 'sufficient' to establish self-deception are belief in the face of strong evidence, coupled with the subject's knowledge of the evidence and his recognition of its import; these are affirmed to hold over matters other than 'one's own inner states', the latter presumably being exempted on the grounds that they are not ascertained by the subject on the basis of evidence. The qualification is clearly important in view of the frequency of self-deception concerning such things as intentions and emotions:[8] yet, even in cases where the conditions appear to be more or less straightforwardly applicable, there are problems.

One might ask, for instance, how the conditions mentioned are themselves to be interpreted. Penelhum, apart from referring to the 'partial satisfaction' of criteria for belief and disbelief, also speaks of the 'behavioural ambivalence characteristic of self-deception'; but the question of how exactly these expressions are to be understood is left rather obscure. Thus suppose we ask what the ascription of a counter-evidential belief to the self-deceiver amounts to. It is scarcely enough to be told that he will 'tend to declare his disbelief in that to which he sees the evidence points', or even that he has a tendency to act in certain ways consonant with such a declaration. For he might be quite insincere, merely lying or pretending, and (as Penelhum himself stresses) there must be 'some reason' to say that the self-deceiver believes what he asserts. Various considerations could be adduced here; demeanour, perhaps, or apparent absence of motive for deceiving others, or again the fact that the sort of behaviour manifested does not seem to be switched on or off according to whether the man has grounds for thinking himself observed. But be these as they may, a more fundamental difficulty arises concerning the other two conditions cited as 'severally necessary' for self-

---

[8] Cf. Penelhum's own discussion (op. cit., Section III) of the possibility of self-deception regarding pleasure and its objects.

deception—knowledge of the unfavourable evidence and recognition of its implications. In what manner, for example, is such knowledge supposed to express itself? By the man's openly stating or otherwise indicating that he is clearly aware in his own mind of the existence and significance of the evidence in question? If this is what is meant, we might possibly speak of conflict. But what form would it take, and would it be describable as 'self-deception'?

In fact, a number of possibilities suggest themselves. One might, for instance, consider the phenomenon of what has been called 'half-belief'.[9] This, it is emphasized, does not consist in a person's believing something in a guarded or qualified fashion; rather, it is a matter of his giving strong signs of believing a given proposition in certain contexts and of disbelieving it in others. An example that is sometimes offered is that of superstitious belief, and generally speaking this seems to accord pretty well with Penelhum's conception of a 'conflict state'. Thus there may be 'behavioural ambivalence' inasmuch as a person may exhibit superstitious responses in some situations, while in others not. Moreover, responses of the first type may occur, and 'symptoms' of belief be manifested, despite an apparent recognition on the part of the subject that they lack any kind of rational or evidential justification—he may even speak of himself as experiencing 'unreasonable qualms' which beset him in certain circumstances and which continue nevertheless to influence his behaviour.[10]

Again, there is the case of so-called 'hunches', attributed to people thought of as having some sort of intuitive 'feel' for a situation or outcome. This is certainly distinguishable from superstitious belief of the ordinary kind: amongst other things, what is involved may be viewed as not being necessarily or wholly irrational and as embodying an unformulated (perhaps—as in some personal relations—unformulable) grasp of subtle intimations and nuances. In so far, however, as it is characterized in such terms, it tends to be contrasted with standard cases of belief upon evidence, and may indeed strike its possessor as implying something directly contrary to that which, on strictly evidential grounds, he is entitled to accept. Yet he may all the same follow it, and without being under any misapprehension as to what he is doing. But should we wish to speak of full conviction here? There may be deliberation in his mode of subscription to it which suggests resistance; he has (say) uncomfortable moments, nagging doubts. And how, it might

[9] See, e.g., H. H. Price, 'Half-Belief', *Proc. Arist. Soc.*, Supp. Vol. (1964).
[10] This may be disputed on the grounds that nothing could be counted as a genuine 'belief' which the subject himself recognized to be foolish or misguided: cf. Stuart Hampshire, *Freedom of the Individual*, p. 76 et seq. It is not, however, altogether clear whether Hampshire wishes to base his claim upon actual usage or whether he intends it to be understood as a piece of salutary legislation.

be inquired, could he not? For it is understood that he sees where the evidence available to him points, and what could this mean in the absence of some degree of assent to the conclusion it indicates? Once more, there is conflict, emerging perhaps in hesitations, or in 'contradictory' moves that he makes.

A third and more striking type of case is the following. We can image a man—for example, a political or military leader—who is under no illusions concerning the unfavourable bearing of the evidence for the success of his plans but who nevertheless continues to believe that he will ultimately succeed because (let us suppose) of some deeply rooted faith, either in his own destiny or in that of the country or cause he represents. Such an individual may discount the empirical factors which weigh so heavily against his prospects, not because he fails to realize their significance, but because he does not regard them as constituting something which, in the last analysis, he need or should treat as a reason for despair—he might even think of it as yielding to temptation to do so: furthermore, his attitude may be wholly continuous with patterns of thought and behaviour he has exhibited on other occasions and cannot therefore be represented as a temporary lapse into irrationality. Thus the former Nazi minister, Speer, describes Hitler in his memoirs in these terms:

This phenomenon of confidence in victory at a time of continuous defeat is not explicable, however, by his energy alone … The more events drove him into a corner, the more stubbornly did he cling to his faith in his destiny. *Of course he appreciated the military facts realistically … he was capable, too, of perceiving the hopelessness of some situation*, but was not to be shaken in his belief that at the last moment fate would have some turn of fortune in store for him. Of all Hitler's abnormalities, this unshakeable belief in his lucky star was the most abnormal [my italics].

This somewhat unpleasing example is interesting in that, among other things, it gives grounds for wondering whether the assumption previously referred to, namely, that if a man grasps the implications of what he himself allows to be strong evidence there must be a sense in which he unavoidably believes what it points to, should be so easily granted. For in certain exceptional circumstances may there not be overriding considerations which can be cited in rebuttal of such a presumption? Thus in a case like the one described above, it is not obvious that there need even have been a 'conflict-state' of the kind to which Penelhum alludes: one might be driven to the conclusion that the Nazi ruler just did believe, fully believe, in his ultimate success, and that his condition was therefore significantly different from the one Speer ascribes to himself when speaking of the 'odd mental cleavage' he experienced as a result, on the one hand, of the fanatical confidence with which Hitler infected him and, on the other, of his own considered appreciation of the situation as spelling inevitable disaster.

No doubt there is a complex network of problems concerning the relations between rational and non-rational belief underlying each of the three types of case I have outlined. My chief purpose in presenting these, however, has been to inquire whether, with the criteria proposed by Penelhum in mind, they can be said to constitute plausible illustrations of self-deception as they stand. And it is not, I think, clear that they can. What is common to the cases portrayed is a more or less explicit preparedness to confront and take into account facts and inferences of the sort that an impartial critic of some of the subject's beliefs and attitudes might bring to bear; the subject, moreover, feels the force of these objections and responds, either by admitting (to himself or to others) that his condition is one of ambivalence or 'two-mindedness' or else by a conscious refusal to be disconcerted by them in the light of some independent consideration to which he is generally committed and which seems to him unquestionable (as, e.g., an 'article of faith'). What typically happens in self-deception, however, appears to be crucially different from this.

IV

As Butler himself was at pains to stress, it is characteristic of the self-deceiver, not merely that his beliefs and opinions concerning certain matters should seem to be at variance with what the available facts would lead an objective observer to conclude, but that he should also and at the same time seem to be surprisingly and conspicuously unaware of this. In other words, the normal conditions for ascribing knowledge of such things as the evidence and its import are not satisfied in his case, or not wholly satisfied, we tend to find that his conception of the facts contains curious errors and omissions and that his manner of interpreting them is in various respects eccentric or askew. In this sense, the beliefs expressed by such a man are not extraneous to, or detachable from, his manifest view of the circumstances and of what the evidence obliges him to accept, but are, so to speak, all of a piece with this—there is no sharp or discriminable dividing-line between the two. Likewise, if he is questioned or challenged, he may be expected to answer in terms that suggest, not that what he affirms is in some way quixotic, off-beat, or in need of special justification or excuse, but rather that he anticipates his interlocutor will find it—as he himself seems to—perfectly reasonable and acceptable according to ordinary criteria. And up to a point, indeed, his interlocutor may so find it; part of the pattern has been picked out correctly, forming within its limits a plausible and intelligible picture. But only up to a point: odd pieces appear to be unaccountably missing, while others give the impression of having been fitted on in a forced or suspiciously contrived fashion.

Thus a man deserted by his mistress may be discovered continually treating scraps of information, which strike a detached spectator as trifling or even as providing additional confirmation that his feeling is no longer returned, as clues that show that he is after all still loved. When these fragments are taken by themselves and in isolation, the significance so accorded them may not seem altogether to lack warrant; but assembled in a wider context and set beside other factors which, though palpable enough, appear mysteriously to have eluded consideration, they assume a quite different complexion, making the interpretation put upon them look baseless and unreal. For a description of such states of mind and the distortions they involve one can, as always, turn to novels: for instance, to Proust's portrayal of his narrator's reactions after the disappearance of Albertine. Or one might consider the attitude which James attributes to the central character of *The Ambassadors*, Strether. This haunted figure, who as a middle-aged visitor in Paris becomes fascinated by a mode of living that seems to embody all that he himself has missed, consistently omits from his reflections and calculations a true conception of the relationship between the two people who chiefly preoccupy him; it is implied, furthermore, that their liaison, if admitted, would confuse his purposes and also flaw the ideal picture he has constructed for himself. It is not so much that he does not explicitly draw the right inferences from what he sees and hears as that the very idea of doing so seems not to occur to him at all. As he expresses it later, when something happens that finally forces him to acknowledge the truth:

He almost blushed, in the dark, for the way he had dressed the possibility in vagueness, as a little girl might have dressed her doll ... 'What on earth—that's what I want to know now—had you then supposed?' He recognised at last that he had really been trying all along to suppose nothing.[11]

What light do such examples as these throw upon the problem before us? They suggest, at the least, that if the analysis of self-deception as involving some kind of 'conflict state' is to be retained, this must not be understood in a way that implies that the self-deceiver may himself be clearly or in general aware of it. Although there is room (notoriously) for gradations and variations here, it remains a mark of the man to whom this condition is attributed that he characteristically and with apparent sincerity presents his position as a unitary and coherent one, consonant with the facts as he sees them or depicts them to himself; if moments of doubt and self-questioning

[11] Henry James, *The Ambassadors*, vol. 2, p. 238.

arise, these will tend to be quickly displaced by others in which considerations favouring the belief ostensibly subscribed to reassert themselves, the factors that occasioned disquiet either slipping out of sight or else being in some manner explained away. Hence, if it is maintained that, despite everything, the self-deceiver 'really knows' the true nature and bearing of the contrary evidence, such a claim cannot be made with a view to those criteria whose satisfaction is standardly thought requisite for knowledge of the relevant type to be ascribed. Instead we must presumably appeal to others of an 'indirect' or inferential character, involving references to such items as the circumstances in which he is placed, various verbal or behavioural 'give aways' of whose significance he himself is not taken to be fully aware, and possibly the reactions he exhibits under certain specific conditions, like shock or intoxication.

Interpreted along these lines, Penelhum's attempt to provide a 'consistent description of inconsistent behaviour' that avoids the usual paradoxes has a fair measure of plausibility: in particular, it permits a distinction to be drawn between self-deception and plain ignorance or stupidity, while at the same time no longer being seemingly open to the objection that it unwarrantably conflates the former with separate attitudes of mind, amongst which might be numbered certain kinds of faith.[12] Yet it may be felt, even so, not to be finally satisfactory, if only because it fails to do justice to a factor which, in their different ways, both Butler and Sartre emphasize and which also obtrudes itself, quite unmistakably, at the end of the passage quoted from James's novel. For the element of intention, implicit in the use of the verb 'deceive' in ordinary interpersonal contexts, appears to be carried over when it is reflexively employed; if the self-deceiver's avowed beliefs do not correspond to or accurately reflect the facts, if indeed they are at variance with those which he himself—in some sense—may be said to hold, this is not to be understood as something merely fortuitous. As a recent critic of Penelhum's position has argued,[13] self-deception may be considered essentially to imply some kind of purposive refusal to face the truth or interpret the evidence realistically; the misjudgements and apprehensions in question are, so to speak, 'self-induced'. But such an admission might appear to return us yet again to the quagmire of paradox. It may be possible, without

---

[12] Penelhum himself appears to make the distinction between faith and self-deception turn on the question of the truth of the proposition or propositions believed: thus he writes that 'if the subject turns out to have been right after all he is not of course said to have been deceiving himself but to have had faith'. But this, as I have given reasons for thinking, is surely to locate the difference in the wrong place. In any case the notion of faith, unlike that of knowledge, seems to carry no special implications with regard to truth (which is not, of course, to suggest that it necessarily involves some kind of uncertainty—see, e.g., Bradley, *Ethical Studies*, p. 326).

[13] H. Fingarette, *Self-Deception* (1969), pp. 28–9.

absurdity, to characterize a man's condition as involving the partial satisfaction of criteria for both belief and disbelief; but matters are surely otherwise when this condition is alleged to have been brought about and maintained by his intentionally concealing from himself what he at the same time knows or believes to be the case. How could a project of this nature be even intelligibly entertained, let alone implemented? Are we not, in fact, back with Sartre's lie that 'collapses beneath my look'?

Certainly the notion that a man could tell himself a string of lies with the explicit intention and expectation of making himself believe them seems, on the face of it, to invite Sartre's strictures. But does the above claim concerning the purposive aspect of self-deception really require us to suppose that this, or something like it, represents a genuine possibility? There is much that could be said here: I have space, however, only to make two brief observations.

In the first place, there exists a tendency, perhaps endemic amongst philosophers of a certain temperament and persuasion, to treat human attitudes and behaviour as if they were more reflective and deliberate, more subject to the direction and control of the conscious will, than experience suggests to be the case. The influence of such assumptions is often marked in existentialist approaches, with their insistence upon freedom and responsibility, and may help to explain some of Sartre's oscillations when discussing the origins and nature of *mauvaise foi*.[14] But, while these approaches have proved illuminating in many ways, there seems no reason to think that the purposiveness ascribable to self-deception need be interpreted in a manner that implies the sort of full-fledged conscious deliberateness that causes trouble. It is here, of course, that Freudian accounts come into their own; but it may be pointed out that we are in any case familiar in a general fashion with instances of behaviour that impress us as being informed by a distinctive purpose, for all that the subject himself gives no indication of being aware of it. Thus, in the specific instance of self-deception, what occurs may bear significant points of resemblance with ordinary cases of interpersonal lying or pretence, despite there being here no apparent realization on the subject's part, or at best only an intermittent one, that he is falsifying things or making them look other than they are: from this point of view, Strether's retrospective acknowledgement of what he had 'really' been trying to do all along may be seen more as an interpretation of his reactions to the situation that faced him than as a phenomenological description of his state of mind at the time.

---

[14] Fingarette (op. cit., pp. 94–5) is justly critical of these. Yet, despite his own careful and interesting distinctions (both here and elsewhere), his treatment of self-deception as involving 'self-covering' policies not to 'spell out' certain things appears in some respects to exemplify the tendency to which I have referred, and to raise problems similar to those it is designed to solve.

Such an impression or interpretation would seem, moreover, to be insepar- ably dependent upon our thinking the man in question to have some compel- ling interest in the truth of what he appears to believe or (alternatively) in the falsity of what he seems not to have taken into consideration. And this brings me to my second point. The role of motives in self-deception has been to some extent ignored or played down in recent discussions of the topic, yet it is surely crucial.[15] It is, for example, not clear what could be meant by, or what justification there could be for, speaking of somebody as deceiv- ing himself if it were at the same time contended that what he was said to be deceiving himself about was a matter of total indifference to him, in no way related to his wants, fears, hopes, and so forth: could we, e.g., intelligibly talk about 'disinterested' or 'gratuitous' self-deception? It might even be argued, with this in mind, that self-deception really comes down to no more than being mistaken with a motive: a self-deceiver is simply a man who wrongly believes something to be true which he would not have believed to be true in the absence of the particular interest in the matter concerned that he has. There is thus no need to postulate some species of 'conflict state' to account for the difference between *plain* ignorance or error and self-decep- tion, for that is taken care of. This proposal is, for obvious reasons, not with- out attractions; it would seem, too, to accord with some (though not all) of the things that Butler, for example, has to say on the subject. Yet, generally speaking, I think that it offers too short a way with the problem. What, for instance, becomes of the distinction—seemingly recognizable, if not clear- cut—between self-deception and mere wishful thinking?

In conclusion, I should like to say this. When discussing the present topic it seems important that we should be neither hamstrung nor panicked by the terminology and metaphors that come spontaneously to us. For these are liable to hypnotize us into adopting an 'all or nothing' approach, accord- ing to which the available alternatives reduce themselves to two: rigid adherence to the other-deception model in every particular, or else its more or less complete abandonment. In the light of the difficulties entailed by the first alternative, it is not surprising that some philosophers have opted for the second. But there is a third way open. This consists in examining in- stances in which men are said to be self-deceived and, without prejudging the issue in deference to the existing vocabulary, try to see what actually happens. If this is done, we shall (I suspect) find analogies and similarities with cases of deception proper that are sufficient to make the reflexive exten- sion of the concept appear, within limits, reasonably appropriate. But the instances themselves will form a variegated spectrum, and the analogies can

---

[15] Penelhum admits that motives are 'usual' and are often relevant in practice: he does not, how- ever, allow them to be more than this.

in any event never be more than partial ones. Which we select, which we find it most natural to press, will no doubt be partly determined by our particular moral viewpoint or conception of human nature.

III

BELIEFS AND ROLES

GERALD A. COHEN

Then the political economist replies to me: You do not transgress my laws: but see what Cousin Ethics and Cousin Religion have to say about it. My political economic ethics and religion have nothing to reproach you with—But whom am I now to believe, political economy or ethics? ... It stems from the very nature of alienation that each sphere applies to me a different and opposite yardstick—ethics one and political economy another; for each is a specific alienation of man and focuses attention on a particular round of alienated essential activity, and each stands in an alienated relation to the other.

Karl Marx, 1844

(A comment on some applications of the idea of a language-game.)

1. INTRODUCTION

This paper argues within a limited but important context for a claim akin to one argued more generally by Stuart Hampshire in *Thought and Action* and absolutely generally by Jean-Paul Sartre in *Being and Nothingness*. Hampshire discusses conjunctures in which a man, on attaining self-knowledge, 'steps back' from his character and situation, assesses them afresh, and attempts a new posture in the world. Sartre is more radical, since he holds that 'stepping back' (*se reculer*) is possible and indeed unavoidable at every moment in a man's life, and that self-renovation may always be achieved. Each regards the capacity to 'withdraw' as a manifestation of human freedom, though for Hampshire freedom is something to be acquired and augmented, while for Sartre man *is* freedom (in the way a physical object *is* matter). Neither doctrine commands unqualified assent, but I believe that the metaphor of 'withdrawal' aptly describes what they treat, and that withdrawal is indeed a form of freedom. In this paper I characterize one kind of withdrawal, evidenced in the way a man's beliefs must, as long as he is sane, transcend the positions he occupies in society.

For Sartre, a man deceives himself in framing a picture of himself unless he admits that it depicts no more than a past from which he is disengaged,

From *Proceedings of the Aristotelian Society* (1966–7) Reprinted by permission of the Editor of the Aristotelian Society.

and which, therefore, can have no influence on his present thoughts, feelings, and decisions. He applies this principle in his remarks on homosexuality[1] when he forbids an obvious homosexual to say either 'I am a homosexual' or 'I am not a homosexual'. He rejects the first because the normal apparatus of reference and prediction cannot function in discourse about human beings, unless what is predicated is an act of disengagement, or what is referred to is not really a man but only a fragment of the history which a man projects into the world. He rejects the second because in his past choices the man was a homosexual, as much one as any person ever is anything.

I find this extreme conclusion and the reasoning which leads to it extravagant. But there is a dimension, explored in this paper, in which the homosexual can and must withdraw from his homosexuality: he need not, and, if he is sane, he cannot think and believe *as* a homosexual. He can think and believe *only* as a man. He believes what he does under any description which applies to him, and therefore under no description in particular. This yields a sense in which in thought and assertion we are free of our natures and circumstances, and hence a sense in which consciousness gives us freedom, and a region within which we must always step back. A man must take responsibility for the beliefs which he expresses; he cannot shift it on to some aspect of himself, like his role. Here is a freedom he cannot escape, because he cannot but escape from himself and his situation.

To be a homosexual is not, except peripherally, to occupy a social role. But the claims of the last paragraph will be brought into sharper focus if we restrict ourselves to roles, partly because those claims seem disconfirmed by things people say about and do with the roles they play. So while my thesis and arguments relate to roles, they are to be received as belonging to a larger case which is only intimated here.

My thesis is that to cite one's role is never to give a good reason for a belief one holds, and that his occupancy of a certain role can never function as a belief-grounding reason in the thinking of a sane man.

2. THE AMERICAN PROFESSOR AND THE JAPANESE MAN-OF-ALL-ROLES

We need never take account of our social roles in forming and defending our beliefs, but the freedom which this gives us is not one we always acknowledge. I begin with two cases in which people behave as though they lacked this freedom.

An American professor had a son who was enrolled in the university where he taught. The boy was intellectually able, and eager to take up an academic career. Accident had prevented him from preparing for an important ex-

[1] *Being and Nothingness*, trans. Hazel E. Barnes (Methuen, 1957), pp. 63–4.

amination, but he knew how to cheat effectively in the examination chamber. He was in a dilemma, for he thought that cheating was wrong, but he felt his talents and aspirations might justify it in this instance. He consulted his father, who said, 'As your father, I must consider your welfare paramount, and I think you ought to cheat; but as a member of the Discipline Committee, I think you should obey the rules.'

The professor thought he had given a complete and proper answer to his son, and he objected when it was insisted that he had to commit himself not as a father or as a professor, but as a man. This insistence is what I want to defend.

The second example is drawn from *The Mikado*, by W. S. Gilbert.[2] Ko-Ko, the Lord High Executioner, asks his lieutenant, Pooh-Bah, how much public money he ought to spend on his approaching marriage. Pooh-Bah replies: 'Speaking as your Private Secretary, I should say that, as the city will have to pay for it, don't stint yourself, do it well.' Ko-Ko accepts the advice. But Pooh-Bah now robes himself as Chancellor of the Exchequer, and warns that due economy must be observed. He then invokes another status he enjoys, and again changes his recommendation. And so on, until he agrees to act at the bidding not of conviction but of a bribe, which Ko-Ko offers him, and which he accepts, as a man.

The audience finds this scene very funny. Whatever explains their laughter would serve to justify a philosophically critical reaction to the professor. For Pooh-Bah's conduct is an extreme version of the professor's, and an object of philosophical critique is frequently an attenuated version of something which, fuller blown, is laughable, and this seems to apply to the examples at hand. Why, then, does Pooh-Bah provoke laughter?

One stimulus to laughter is the ridiculous, which can be found in at least two interesting domains: (a) common experience, and (b) transgressions of binding rules. Correspondingly, we may laugh (a) when we are made to confront an absurd aspect of life which we do not attend to while living, often because of an interest we have in concealing it or suppressing our response to it;[3] or (b) when we recognize a principle violated by the behaviour or events the joke relates.

Pooh-Bah is amusing on both counts. (a) His tactics are a dramatic exaggeration of familiar ones, whereby people (b) contrive to avoid an implication of such speech-acts as advising. We laugh, and in the case of the professor we are disturbed, because we recognize that, contrary to a common pretence, a man cannot attach *his* advice to the role he plays.

The implication forbidding this is from advice to belief. It will be agreed

[2] *Original Plays* (London, 1906), pp. 182–3.
[3] This is part of Freud's theory in *Wit and its Relation to the Unconscious*.

that a man who asserts that *p* presents himself as believing that *p*. Now a man who advises *A* to φ similarly presents himself as believing that φ-ing is the best thing for *A* to do. The paradoxicality of '*P*, but I do not believe that *p*' is matched by 'I advise you to φ, but I do not believe it is the best thing for you to do.' In highly institutionalized contexts those words could be unparadoxical, for a role occupant might dissociate himself from the advice it is his office to transmit (note, however, that Pooh-Bah does not do so: that would spoil the joke). But the same holds for the first string of words, which are intelligible on the lips of a messenger. That messenger would not be asserting that *p*, but relaying the assertion of another, so that his utterance is properly reported not as above but as follows: '"*P*", but I do not believe that *p*.' But no more is the official just considered giving *his* advice: he is letting the institution speak through him.

You can pass on the official advice and dissociate yourself from it, and you can, of course, give it and agree with it. What you cannot do is to give it as *your* advice just because you are that official: your reason for agreeing with it cannot be that it is your role to give it. For while it may be your duty to advise φ-ing, it cannot be your duty to believe that φ-ing is the best thing to do. To claim that it can is to assert the tie between beliefs and roles denied in this paper, and refuted in section 4.

3. THE NOTION OF A SOCIAL ROLE

It is necessary to distinguish those descriptions which apply to a man in virtue of his occupancy of a social role or position from those which, like the following, do not: 'gifted story-teller', 'mild-mannered man', 'neurotic', 'leper', 'freethinker', 'sufferer from hay fever', 'beautiful woman', 'wise man'. I suggest the following rough definition:

A description of a person allocates him to a social role or position *in the measure that* the attribution to him of some rights and/or duties is insepar-able from the application of the description, unless that a man falls under the description follows from the mere fact that he is a man.

The italicized words are entered to reflect the fact that there is a *continuum* between what are unquestionably social roles and what are unquestionably not such. Some theisms and some political theories hold that there are rights and/or duties which appertain to men as men. In the absence of a refutation of these doctrines, the excluding condition is necessary to prevent humanity being counted as a social role.

The definition offers clarification of what is ordinarily understood by 'occupying a role' rather than 'playing (or performing) a role'. Hence my use of the phrase 'social role or *position*': one may occupy but one does not play a position in society; and it is possible to occupy a role without playing it, because of refusal or inability to perform.

The definition reflects the fact that terms like 'barrister' and 'Chancellor of the Exchequer' indisputably apply to occupants of social roles, since rights and duties are so intimately tied to these descriptions that the following statements are self-contradictory:

(i) John is a barrister, but he does not have the right to plead in court, or to advise authoritatively on legal questions, and he never has the duty to defend clients when suitably called upon to do so.

(ii) Sir William is Chancellor of the Exchequer, but he does not have the duty or right to propose taxes of any kind or to prepare a budget.

'A man who has promised to ...' would not naturally be thought to allocate a person to a social role, but it may seem to do so on the proposed conditions. Promises, however, create not duties but obligations.[4] Roughly, the former are more general than, and are among what give rise to, the latter. The distinction is rough because a social role can itself be interpreted as a nexus of undertakings, given and received. (Even membership in society has been understood in this way, by social contract theorists.)

The proposed conditions do need to be supplemented in order to exclude roles which are not social roles (i.e. roles in society), but which can be occupied, like the role of 'the man who will defend the third hill' (a role in a battle) or of 'a dealer in cards' (a role in a game), to be contrasted with 'the dealer at the Piccadilly Casino' (a role in society). The supplementary condition would be a complex requirement on how the role is established. I shall not provide it here, since all my claims about social roles can be maintained for non-social roles, by means of similar arguments.

The notion of a social role having been clarified,[5] it is now possible to argue for the thesis presented at the end of section 1.

4. DEFENDING THE THESIS

I wish to claim that a man cannot cite his role to show either that it is acceptable or that it is necessary for him to hold a certain belief. I am disallowing moves like 'It is permissible for me to believe this, I'm a ...' and moves like 'I must believe this, I'm a ...', where in each case the blank is filled by a description allocating the speaker to a role. The difference between

---

[4] See E. J. Lemmon, 'Moral Dilemmas', *Philosophical Review* (1962), 139–43.
[5] For further discussion, including an attempt to distinguish and relate social roles, dramatic roles, and roles in the sense of functions, see my 'Being, Consciousness and Roles', in Abramsky (ed.), *Essays in Honour of E. H. Carr* (Macmillan, 1974), esp. pp. 93–5.

the two prohibitions will be ignored in the sequel, since any argument for or against one will, suitably redeployed, operate for or against the other.

The argument of this section has seven stages: (A) Reasons why roles cannot be grounds for beliefs. (B) An objection, exploiting beliefs of a special sort. (C) Reply to the objection. (D) Two attempts to refute C. (E) Reply to D-1. (F) Reply to D-2. (G) Final attempt to weld beliefs to roles.

(A) I begin by showing that knowledge cannot attach to a role, and I move from this to the demonstration that belief cannot either.

A person cannot know something which he (logically) cannot transmit to another. In this sense, knowledge can never be anyone's special property: to give it to another is never to alienate it. It follows that nothing can make it one's private property, and so one's occupancy of a role cannot do so. Of course there can be a special connection between possessing knowledge and occupying a role, where knowledge is necessary to playing the role well, or sometimes even at all, so that a man lacking it could not play the role he occupies. But there is no role such that one (logically) cannot occupy it without having the knowledge necessary to playing it well; and one can leave any role while retaining the knowledge associated with it. An ambitious ignoramus can manage to secure employment as a physicist, and an informed physicist does not automatically forget what he knows when he retires.

The publicity of knowledge applies to the grounds a man has for his beliefs, and it applies, through the grounds, to the beliefs themselves. This is as true of moral beliefs as of any other kind. If the professor had meant, 'From my perspective as a father, I can see that your welfare matters; from my perspective as a university official, I can see that the ban on cheating matters,' there would not be the same objection to his behaviour, since the visions he would have been claiming are conveyable to others. A man's occupancy of a role may give him access to a range of evidence, or to a relevant point of view, but these can be shared, and with them the beliefs they support. A man can use his role to defend his beliefs only if he can enable another to use it as well.

The obstacle to accepting a man's role as justifying a belief he has is that, in the normal case, what a man presents as justifying his belief, he also presents as justifying the proposition he believes. This is what the publicity of grounds amounts to. Saying 'I believe that p, because I have seen (or read, or been told) that q' commits one to saying 'Because q, p is likely (or certain).' Yet though men say things like 'As a stockbroker (since I am a stockbroker), I believe that capitalism is a good thing,' they do not, unless bereft of sense, say 'Since I am a stockbroker, capitalism is a good thing.' They cite their roles to justify a belief where they would not do so to justify the proposition believed. *A* can say that *B* is justified in believing that *p*, yet deny that *p* is justified, if, for example, *A* has evidence *B* lacks, and, lacking it, can rationally believe that *p*. But *A* cannot say that *A* is justified in believing that *p*, without being willing to add that *p* is justified, and this foils the stockbroker in the example above. He is not prepared to *treat* as a ground what he *gives* as a ground.

(B) But an opponent might say that this shows only that a role must be a very special sort of ground, and he might claim that it can be. He might defend this by directing attention to cases where beliefs characteristically, and, as he might say, properly, lack the normal sort of grounds, or at least demand a leap beyond them. He might invite us to consider men who occupy roles which can be cited in support of beliefs which are not standardly grounded:

Clergymen of some Christian confessions are untrue to their callings unless they believe[6] that God's will is in everything. They must hold that the whole course of the universe is completely subject to Providence. Consider such a clergyman who also occupies the role of coach on the local football team. When he is involved in a game he believes that the will and effort of the players alone determine the outcome. In *that* context he does not need to experience God's will to perform his role: it might even hinder his effectiveness if he did. So some beliefs are appropriate for him as a clergyman, in vicarage and pulpit, while others attach to him as a coach, on the playing field and in the locker room.

(C) To counter this argument, let us assume that the team plays away from home in a town whose field lies adjacent to a large and imposing cathedral. We can imagine that the goals are recorded in neon on the bell-tower of the cathedral, so that the clergyman-coach cannot avoid looking at it. Now the circumstances which led him to—supposedly justified—inconsistent beliefs, coalesce in one situation. He becomes aware of the conflict and therefore (logically) cannot retain both beliefs. It follows that his beliefs are not attached to his roles, for while he must give up at least one belief, he need give up neither role. (Though it may be that he ought to.)

(D) But the opponent might try to invalidate this response by arguing that, if it were correct, then, by parity of reasoning, we could (1) detach rights and duties from roles and (2) detach beliefs from evidence.

(1) A man might occupy two roles, each of which gives him rights and, in particular situations,[7] imposes obligations on him. Circumstances are

---

[6] I suppose here that what distinguishes a Christian from a non-Christian is not knowledge but belief. Some Christians—and some non-Christians—would disagree.

[7] The explanation of this qualification is on p. 57.

conceivable in which he could not exercise a right deriving from one role because of an obligation deriving from the other, and in which he could not fulfil all his role-obligations, because they conflicted. But he would not therefore cease to occupy either role. So on the principle of argument (C) roles would have to be separated from rights and duties, and this is impossible, by definition.

(2) Whenever a conflict of beliefs comes to light, one must be dropped, and not only when what inclines a man to each belief is uncitable in its support. A man who believes p and believes not-p on separate occasions on good but not conclusive evidence will have to give up at least one belief when he confronts both ranges of evidence at one time. But evidence remains citable in defence of a belief, so argument (C) must be fallacious.

(E) There are two fatal weaknesses in argument (D-1). (i) The fact that a man cannot fulfil conflicting obligations does not show that he ceases to have them,[8] nor does he fail to have a right which he sometimes cannot exercise. Occasional impossibility of fulfilment or exercise removes neither an obligation nor a right, but one noticed inconsistency is enough to destroy a belief. (D-1) requires as a premise the negation of these truths about rights and obligations. (ii) If the conflicts discussed in (D-1) were sufficiently regular and frequent, it would be wrong to conclude, as that argument does, that there would be no repercussions on the man's occupancy of the conflict-generating roles. Duties which occasionally engender conflicts can reasonably be imposed on a man,[9] but if the conflicts become frequent, it becomes impossible to attribute the duties; and if a man is very often unable to exercise a right because of a duty which he has, he could not be said to be in unqualified possession of it, or to be a full occupant of the role which grants it. By sharp contrast, a man can constantly encounter situations in which a conflict in his beliefs becomes manifest to him without (logically) having to give up any of the roles playing which causes the conflict.

(F) Argument (D-2) does show that argument (C) is insufficient as it stands, but it can be amended by taking into account the considerations which follow, and the amended version will frustrate the objection.

That evidence can be used to justify beliefs is plain from the conflict situation itself, for the man described in (D-2) is not totally at a loss what to believe when he faces the disturbing collocation of evidence. He now weighs the conflicting evidence together, and reaches a new conclusion,

---

[8] This is convincingly argued by Bernard Williams in 'Ethical Consistency'. *PAS*. Supp. Vol. (1965).
[9] Williams makes a similar point about rules in 'Consistency and Realism', *PAS*, Supp. Vol. (1966), 15–16.

which he is entitled to consider better justified than what he believed before.

But the attempt to use roles as justifications breaks down utterly in the conflict situation. The man's beliefs do not progress because of the conflict. There is no way for him to revise them by weighing the claims of his roles against one another; to do so would involve an impossible manipulation of belief on the part of the will (see 5(B) below). The fact that evidence justifies belief comes out very clearly in the conflict situation, and that roles do not justify it comes out just as clearly. And this vitiates the parallel drawn in (D-2).

(G) But now my opponent suggests a way in which beliefs, if not, as things are, attached to roles, might be made to do so. He notes that, as a matter of fact, there is no social position such that a man fails to occupy it if he lacks relevantly special beliefs. A clergyman, indeed the Pope himself (in Roman Catholic law and usage), retains his post even when he loses his faith. But might it not have been otherwise? Could it not have been laid down that if and when a Pope ceases to believe, he ceases to be Pope, his apparently papal actions becoming null and void, so that, if his lapse were discovered, bishops he had appointed in his unbelieving state would lose title to their bishoprics? Merely utilitarian factors, the argument continues, explain why there are no such roles: it is difficult to tell whether a man has lost a belief; it would be intolerable to disappoint people who had received benefits from the faithless 'Pope'; etc.

The opponent has described a coherent possibility, but it is not the possibility that belief in God be part of the papal role. Instead, what we would have is a strict belief requirement for entry into and tenure of the papacy. Belief in God would be a qualification needed to occupy the role, but not part of it. If policemen have to be six feet tall, it is yet no part of a policeman's role to be six feet tall, and no legislation could make it part of his role to be so. The same applies, *mutatis mutandis*, to the Pope's belief in God in the situation the opponent envisages.

Finally, even if in some sense which has escaped me a belief could be made part of a role, it would not follow that its occupant could cite the role in justifying his adherence to the belief which would partly constitute it, and that is the point at issue.

If I am right, a person's role is never a reason for him to believe anything. Yet how are we to understand such remarks as 'As Chancellor, you should believe in balancing the budget', addressed to a lax finance minister by a cabinet colleague? That is, indeed, a conceptually faultless reprimand, but it asks not that the man should honour an undertaking to have a belief, but that he should not hold the office unless he has it.

5. TWO OBJECTIONS

I hope to clarify my position by considering two objections.

(A) A crucial premiss in argument (C) of the last section was that a man who becomes aware of a conflict in his beliefs (logically) cannot retain them intact. This would entail that no behaviour could show him knowingly believing that p and believing that not-p. But an opponent might hope to construct a case of such behaviour, and thereby block my argument:

A woman owns precious pearls which she wishes to keep in the safest place in her house. She sits at her dressing table, rolling them into a semi-circular chute. Because of a tilt, each pearl comes to rest in the middle of the chute, but she then anxiously removes it, only to roll it in again as before. Conversation with her might force us to say that she believes both that the chute is the safest place for the pearls and that it is not. It might be quite wrong to judge that she is in doubt whether p, where p = 'the chute is the safest place for the pearls'. She firmly believes p and she firmly believes not-p: she exhibits not wavering behaviour but full engagement in tasks whose aims are contradictory, and whose executions are too close in time to permit a denial that she is aware of the conflict.

I need not reject this characterization of the woman's state of mind, for it could not be used to construct a counter-example to my thesis about roles, since the woman's condition is schizoid, and I allowed that beliefs could attach to roles in the absence of sanity. I also presented the separation of beliefs from roles as a form of freedom, and the fact that schizoid behaviour is reckoned unfree supports this. If it be claimed that the woman is so deranged that beliefs cannot be ascribed to her at all, then the way is open for me to argue that beliefs *simpliciter*, not merely those of a sane man, involve freedom.

Reflection on schizoid states suggests that a man is free only if he enjoys a certain unity of mind, and thus can express his thoughts not as appertaining to a role but as belonging to him integrally. It appears that Bradley was right to judge that a Humean view of the self, in removing its unity, destroys its freedom.[10] The account of the human self as a collection of roles, which we meet in the next section, is a sociological counterpart of Hume, and would also cancel our freedom. The freedom we have but pretend we lack when hiding within our roles is lost when the mind's unity is lost.

[10] See *Ethical Studies*, Essay I.

(B) There is a claim made by Kant to which there are counter-examples which might seem to affect my thesis as well:

> We cannot possibly conceive a reason consciously receiving a bias from any other quarter with respect to its judgments, for then the subject would ascribe the determination of its judgment not to its own reason, but to an impulse. It must regard itself as the author of its principles independent on foreign influences.[11]

It might appear that this is what I am affirming with respect to one 'quarter', a person's social position. But I do not agree with Kant, and must distinguish my contention from his.

As I understand Kant's claim, cases like the following show it is false. Consider a racially bigoted headmaster to whom a West Indian teacher of obvious talent has applied for a job. Suppose his bias inclines him to underestimate the capacity of the applicant. In the course of interviewing him, he becomes aware of his bias and that it threatens to cloud his judgement. Why can he not allow his bias to prevail? It is not that, through an act of will, he believes otherwise than as the evidence dictates, but he wilfully allows his belief to be determined by his racialist sentiment.[12]

A man can know that his thinking is subject to bias, can experience the bias and acquiesce in it, and one source of bias can be his social position. It is satisfying for a stockbroker to believe in capitalism (see p. 58 above), and he may allow his assessment of that economic system to be guided by his desire for that satisfaction. Yet whatever produces his belief, it is *his* belief, rather than his only *qua* stockbroker, so that, e.g., *qua* citizen, it is open to him to believe otherwise. Stockbrokerhood may bias his judgement, but the judgement biased is just a man's judgement, not that of a man in his role of stockbroker, and he cannot appeal to his being a stockbroker in an attempt to defend it. I am indeed the 'author of my principles', though not 'independent on foreign influences'. I am committed to the beliefs I have and cannot, while sane, escape this responsibility by retreating into the role or roles I occupy.

What is true—but this is less than what Kant maintained—is that a man cannot in full and clear consciousness direct his beliefs against reason, or, what is closely connected, announce that he is doing so and expect his declaration to be accepted. As Sartre has it, 'the decision to be in bad faith does not dare speak its name'.[13] It is not in full and clear consciousness

---

[11] *Fundamental Principles of the Metaphysics of Ethics*, trans. T. K. Abbott (Longmans, 1955), p. 81.

[12] The distinction drawn in the above sentence is, I believe, the basis of a solution to the well-known philosophical problem of self-deception.

[13] *Being and Nothingness*, p. 68.

that the bigoted headmaster believes the West Indian deficient: his decision not to control his bias is a decision *not* to be clear in his thinking.

6. CONNECTIONS TO POLITICAL PHILOSOPHY*

As the quotation at the beginning of this paper shows, part of Karl Marx's doctrine of alienation is concerned with circumstances in which implications of the kind discussed on pp. 55–6 are violated, with the result that human relations become either mechanical or oppressive. When J. O. Urmson points out[14] that a soldier, occupying the role of messenger, can announce, 'Your son, I am sorry to say, is dead,' without being understood to express a personal regret, he is revealing that mechanization of human life sometimes occurs. And the explanation of it is not only 'the steady flow of human pretence' which 'has shaped the language',[15] but also the background of material urgency and scarcity, against which, as Marx perceived, men are forced to invent their language-games and play their roles. If Pooh-Bah did not enjoy occupying discrepant roles, we should perhaps laugh not at him but at the institutional framework in which he functions.

I said that where the implication fails to obtain, human relations become either mechanical or oppressive. The difference can be exhibited by reference to the relation between advice on the one hand, and belief and preference on the other. If I advise someone to ϕ without believing it is best for him to ϕ, and/or without wanting him to, then *either* (a) I have no view on whether it is best for him to ϕ (and/or I do not care whether he does or not); *or* (b) I think it is best for him not to ϕ (and/or I want him not to).

In the first case I behave mechanically: I am a person functioning as though I were a thing; I am the vehicle of my role, not it of me, and I run smoothly. This is what Pooh-Bah pretends to be. He represents each piece of advice he gives as not only consistent with the position he invokes to support it, but as the sole advice he can give from that position. If this were true, it would be strange to ask for his opinions: they could be deduced from the offices he fills. His roles work so mechanically that it is hard to see why anyone has to occupy them: Ko-Ko could have consulted a handbook listing the official beliefs of Private Secretaries, Chancellors of the Exchequer, etc.

In case (b), the alienation is oppressive, because my behaviour will weigh

---

* Editor's note: Mr. Cohen had intended to omit or truncate this section in his revised version of the paper, but was persuaded not to do so by me. Anyone inclined to think worse of the paper as the result of the inclusion of this section should think worse of my judgement rather than Mr. Cohen's.

[14] 'Parenthetical Verbs', in Charles Caton (ed.), *Philosophy and Ordinary Language* (University of Illinois, 1963), pp. 225 ff.

[15] Bernard Williams, Inaugural Lecture on *Morality and the Emotions*, p. 12.

heavily on my heart: what transpires in my mind runs counter to what I do.

This distinction may give some order to the many situations and attitudes which are thought to be expressive of alienation. When the worker mutely accommodates himself to the dehumanization imposed by the factory, he is mechanically alienated; when he suffers from that treatment he is not, he is oppressed. Social critics differ in the sort of alienation they emphasize. When Mills speaks of the 'cheerful robot'[16] and Marcuse of *One-Dimensional Man*, the topic is mechanical alienation. Oppressive alienation is Freud's concern in *Civilisation and its Discontents*.

In oppressive alienation *psyche* and society are at odds with one another. In mechanical alienation, the *psyche* is absorbed into society. It would be misleading to say that Marx looked to a future harmony of *psyche* and society, for he sometimes hoped to abolish society altogether, in a certain sense, to eliminate all roles. 'Human emancipation will only be complete when the real, individual man has absorbed into himself the abstract citizen,'[17] when men reappropriate the energy which has issued from them and has petrified in a social superstructure, which must tumble to the ground. Then they will be able to confront one another, and themselves, without the mediation of institutions.[18]

Hegel's political philosophy gives the impression that he was intent on engulfing the individual within his social role, so that in all his thinking and feeling he would respond *as* a father or *as* a farmer or *as* a civil servant. But if we locate his social theory within his more comprehensive doctrine of human powers, his total Philosophy of Spirit, we find that Absolute Spirit, the dimension of thought and knowledge, transcends Objective Spirit with its social rights and duties. (Marx would have abolished Objective and Absolute Spirit as independent domains, and integrated them into Subjective Spirit—the life of each individual man.) For Hegel reflection is superior to social action, for it is in thought that men most fully enjoy their essential nature: freedom.[19] It is the claims of a freedom similar to this which I have advanced in this paper.

Today there are sociologists who appear Hegelian, who would promote the doctrine, 'Where Subjective Spirit was, Objective Spirit shall be.' Erving Goffman explicitly maintains that the self is nothing more than the sum of

---

[16] *The Sociological Imagination* (Oxford University Press, New York, 1959), p. 171.

[17] 'On the Jewish Question', in T. B. Bottomore, *Karl Marx: Early Writings*, p. 31.

[18] For more in this vein, see my 'Marx's Dialectic of Labour', *Philosophy and Public Affairs* (Spring, 1974), 258–9.

[19] Thus Bradley, following Hegel, urges the demands of the morality of duty and station, but finds it necessary to gesture far beyond it in seeking man's self-realization.

the roles it plays.[20] But he is not Hegelian because he does not provide for the activity of Absolute Spirit, which releases men from the narrowness and particularity of their social positions.

An acceptance of Goffman's picture of the self leads to two equal and opposite distortions of our attitudes to man and society. When the individual is thought of as a set of roles, he may receive the callous treatment appropriate to a thing: he may be shifted from role to role, without regard to the impact change of station has on him. If the other direction of the assimilation is stressed, and sets of roles are conceived as persons, the social *status quo* is then protected: when roles constitute selfhood, to change society is to mangle human beings.

7. CONCLUSION

There are theories which would engulf personality in role-playing; there are people who present themselves as so engulfed; there are institutions which foster engulfment. The propensity to engulfment should be resisted in theory and in practice, for it poses a threat to the exercise of our freedom, and, ultimately, some threat to freedom itself.

---

[20] See, e.g., *Asylums* (Doubleday, 1961), p. 168; *The Presentation of Self in Everyday Life* (Doubleday, 1959), p. 253; *Encounters* (Bobbs-Merrill, 1961), pp. 114–15. In the last work Goffman voices a desire to 'combat the touching tendency to keep part of the world safe from sociology' (p. 152). The present inquiry promotes that tendency. (Goffman respects the difference between roles and selves when he describes particular cases, but I am criticizing the general theory which he wrongly thinks sustains or grows out of his empirical work.)

IV

THE STRUCTURAL BASIS OF BEHAVIOUR

J. A. DEUTSCH

It is perhaps because psychological explanations have been logically so mongrel that attention has been focused on the logical status of the constituents or entities composing them. The present writer believes that this is a mistake and that much of the speculation regarding these entities has obscured the essential problem of distinguishing between various types of explanation.

The two stages of a structural explanation.—An animal's behaviour is produced by certain structures of which the organism is composed. An explanation of its behaviour may be sought by specifying those structures or systems which produce its behaviour. Ideally, if we knew an animal's physiology and anatomy in great detail and also knew the way the environment acted on detailed structures, we should be able to explain in a satisfying manner why, given certain conditions, the animal behaved in the way it did.

This is 'explanation' in a sense which differs radically from the previous type, that of subsumption under a certain generalization about behaviour. The former is an explanation in terms of other behaviour of a like nature, the latter explanation in terms of observations or hypotheses about the underlying structure.

This second kind would seem more fruitful in psychology, as in science generally. We are observing the operations of a mechanism. If we knew what this mechanism was, the 'generalization' type of explanation would be rather secondary and derivable from the structural type of explanation. This means that it would be possible to deduce logically the behaviour of a mechanism whose structure we knew. On the other hand it would not be possible to deduce the structure of a mechanism by knowing its behaviour. We could merely infer it. There are always many mechanisms consistent with a certain specific behaviour. The statement about the mechanism plays the role of a hypothesis. The hypothesis entails the conclusions which it is called upon to explain; the conclusions do not entail the hypothesis. That is why the

From *The Structural Basis of Behaviour* (Cambridge University Press, 1962), pp. 10–16. Reprinted by permission of the author and the publishers.

physiologist is in theory able to deduce certain overt behaviour by studying the mechanism and why the psychologist cannot do the reverse. This may sound rather pessimistic. It looks as if the student of behaviour can never provide an explanation of his own observation. This, however, is too hasty a conclusion from the argument. Merely because he cannot deduce the mechanism does not mean that he cannot form hypotheses about it. He may still be able to infer, although he cannot deduce. The hypotheses about the mechanism which are thus put forward will tend to entail statements about the behaviour of an animal which have not been tested. If these predictions turn out to be correct this strengthens the hypothesis. If they are false, the theory tends to be refuted. Though psychologists as students of behaviour cannot put forward hypotheses of absolute certainty, they can make suggestions whose plausibility may be enhanced or lessened by experiment.

To this type of procedure the objection can be made that it involves the creation of physiological mythology; for to suggest physiological mechanisms without direct observational warrant for their existence is fanciful. There is a great deal of substance in this objection but it cannot be treated as an objection to all kinds of attempts to arrive at a structural explanation. It applies only to a particular type of speculation—that which cannot in principle be checked by observations undertaken on the behaviour of the animal as a whole or, in other words, the type of observations normally made by psychologists. These speculations concern the embodiment of the system employed. For instance, to attempt to guess at the particular change which occurs in the central nervous system during learning in the framework of a theory purporting to explain behaviour is not only unnecessary but also purely speculative. That some type of change occurs may be inferred from the behaviour of an animal. What this type of change is cannot be arrived at, nor is it very important for the psychologist to know. This can be shown by taking the example of an insightful learning machine. To be told that the semipermanent change in the machine which occurs when it learns is due to a uniselector arm coming to rest does not help us to understand the behavioural properties of the machine. Nor can it be checked by performing experiments on the behaviour of the machine. For the change could equally well be due to a self-holding relay, a dekatron selector, or any type of gadget known to technology capable of being turned from one steady state into another. In the same way to speculate about terminal end boutons in the way that Hebb does or about changes of synaptic resistance seems to be trying to answer a question irrelevant, strictly speaking, to the psychological theorist. What behaviour would one of these assumptions explain which the others would not?

This would seem a good argument against speculating about the mechanism underlying behaviour, but not against attempting to infer the type of mechanism or the system producing behaviour. Clearly, the question about what the actual physical change is which occurs during learning in the machine is the wrong type of question to ask and to attempt to answer. For, whatever the answer, we still do not understand how the machine learns. Nor if we hazard a guess about it can we verify it, if we are restricted to observing the machine's behaviour. Information about the physical identity of the parts of the machine sheds an extraordinarily feeble light on the explanation of the machine's capacities. It is about as useful as a map of the disposition of its parts in space, the pursuit of the knowledge of which in the animal is the preoccupation of much of physiological psychology. Now there is a tendency to argue that, since it is not profitable to speculate about the physical properties of the parts of a machine and, since a machine is made up of physical parts, it is not profitable to speculate about the machine at all. Hence, it is advocated that we should seek only to construct general statements about behaviour and leave what produces it to the physiologist.

Thus it appears that theoretical psychology must either do too much or too little. According to one school of thought we must only redescribe in a more economical manner. According to the other school we must either wait for physiology and anatomy or dream up our own. However, there appears to be a third possibility. It may be brought out if we again consider the example of the insightful learning machine. It was stated above that the change which occurs in learning in the machine could be engineered in many different ways. Any component which could be made to assume either of two steady states could be used. Similarly, the rest of the 'central nervous system' could be constructed of completely different types of components without affecting the behavioural capacities of the machine. The precise properties of the parts do not matter; it is only their general relationships to each other which give the machine as a whole its behavioural properties. These general relationships can be described in a highly abstract way, for instance, by the use of Boolean algebra. This highly abstract system thus derived can be embodied in a theoretically infinite variety of physical counterparts. Nevertheless, the machines thus made will have the same behavioural properties, given the same sensory and motor side. Therefore, if we wish to explain the behaviour of one of these machines, the relevant and enlightening information is about this abstract system and not about its particular embodiment. Further, given the system or abstract structure alone of the machine, we can deduce its properties and predict its behaviour. On the other hand, the knowledge that the machine operates mechanically, electromechanically, or electronically does not help us very much at all.

An example based on this principle may be taken from an application of Boolean algebra to switching circuits by Shannon. In order to work out problems concerning switching systems, he uses a calculus exactly analogous to the calculus of propositions in symbolic logic. Each switching element is regarded as being either 'open' or 'closed', just as propositions in logic are either 'false' or 'true'. From the symbolic interrelations of the elements can be deduced the properties of the network acting as a whole. Such expressions as $0·0 = 0$ (a closed circuit in parallel with a closed circuit is a closed circuit) or $1 + 0 = 1$ (an open circuit in series with a closed circuit is an open circuit) clearly make no reference as to how any circuit is closed or opened or what the physical counterpart is of being in series or in parallel. Yet it is from manipulating expressions such as these that the properties of complex switching systems may be deduced. We do not need to know the physical identity of the elements of the calculus in order to be able to design systems to perform a set of operations or to display a certain type of behaviour. We do not need to know the empirical content of a set of propositions in order to decide whether a given argument is valid. All we need to know is the truth or falsity of each proposition and the way the propositions are connected.

Now this argument is not directed against physiological knowledge; for direct observational evidence about the workings of a system whose properties we must normally infer is valuable. From observations on accessible parts we may glean valuable hints or corroborating evidence about the type of organization which it would be plausible to infer. An example of this may be found in the relation of Burns's work on cortical propagation to the type of system postulated for form recognition. On the other hand, it is an argument against the necessity for a certain type of physiological speculation in which many psychological theorists have felt themselves obliged to indulge. There has been no clear distinction between that part of an explanation of behaviour which can be expressed as an abstract system and the identification of the elements of this system in terms of actual physical counterparts. The foregoing analysis has tried to make it clear that it is possible to separate these two steps. Once the distinction is clear it becomes fairly obvious that a psychologist need only speculate about the system and not its embodiment. It is not incumbent upon a theorist to suggest what is the embodiment of his hypothesis; a complete specification of its embodiment would add very little to the explanatory power of his system.

These two stages of explanation should be recognized as being separate. The purely intellectual aspect of the confusion of a system with its embodiment is lamentable enough, but the practical consequences are even worse. The theorist infects his critics with the confusion, and explanations tend to be rejected because their author made a faulty guess about the embodiment of the system he put forward. This threatens to be the fate of Köhler and Wallach's theory of figural after-effects. Here the system has been put by Köhler into a certain electrophysiological fancy dress and his critics have concentrated on tearing this to pieces under the impression that they were disposing of the explanation.

Another consequence of the failure to keep these two stages of explanation separate is a loss of rigour in the systems which really do the main job of explaining. An air of precision is lent to the author's system by detailed physiological identification of its elements, an endeavour inspired by the mistaken belief that we cannot understand how a mechanism works unless we know the identity of its parts. Meanwhile, the system which is the crux of the explanation is never clearly stated, disguised as it is in its identification, and would not do the job with which it was credited, however we chose to interpret it physically.

The fact that a system can be interpreted in various ways has some interesting consequences. First, it is possible to express a theory in terms of a model by giving it an identification which is already familiar and thus easier to think about than a completely abstract system. The identification is here a mere psychological aid and does not add or detract from the explanatory value of the system itself. This is often not understood. For instance, Lehrman in a recent article attacks the Tinbergen–Lorenz theory, which uses hydraulics to clothe its system on the grounds that no hydraulic arrangements have been found in the central nervous system.

Second, machine models of a system can actually be made by choosing appropriate physical counterparts. These will then display the behaviour which the system was designed to explain. If the original system was complicated enough the physical model will 'compute' the predictions to be made from it. The endeavour to make a model may also reveal inadequacies in the theory. It is impossible to make a machine work by wishful thinking. It is, however, only too easy to gloss over theoretical inadequacies on paper. Further, the construction of a machine gives some measure of the simplicity and economy of a system.

But perhaps the greatest benefit to be derived from the construction of actual machine models is a practical one. The fabrication of a concrete model gives a far more vivid insight into the relation between structure and behaviour. It provides an experience of inestimable intellectual value for the psychologist, especially as it is one which cannot be satisfactorily conveyed verbally.

CONCLUDING CONSIDERATIONS

What implications have these points for the construction of psychological theory? Most psychologists would agree that the behaviour of an animal is produced by some underlying physiological structure. Now even though it has been agreed that it is impossible to infer the complete details of this mechanism, the possibility remains that we can attempt to construct theories about the type of machine operating. That is, it might still be feasible to formulate a more general hypothesis but one which would reconstruct the more important, albeit more abstract, design of the mechanism whose external behaviour we observe. There would thus be a middle road between the absurdities of the pseudo-physiologist and the sterility of positivism run wild.

The argument which is put against this type of hypothesis construction is that we can never know that we are right and, therefore, by implication, any attempt to make such theories is worthless. Here again, in this objection there is no appreciation of the limited objectives of scientific procedure. Merely because we cannot have absolute certainty—and this is true of any scientific belief—it does not mean that we must renounce any beliefs whatsoever. We can be content with adopting the ones which on the evidence appear to be the most plausible. In any case, it is unlikely that any hypothesis in psychology can at present be of more than a provisional nature. It should be sufficient that a theory leads to further predictions concerning the outcome of experiments which have not yet been performed. In this way it will be possible to establish precisely in what way the present theories do not fit the facts and to use experiments to narrow the range of theoretical possibility. It is difficult to envisage an ordered scientific advance in any other way. The number of possible experiments that can be performed is infinite. Without some sort of policy which leads to a narrowing of theoretical possibilities, experiments proliferate chaotically. Of facts there is already too much in psychology, of evidence too little.

V

FEELING AND EXPRESSION

STUART HAMPSHIRE

I SHALL argue that, in the particular case of feeling, the inner life of the mind is to be understood as a development from something more primitive in every man's behaviour, of which it is the residue and the shadow. Secondly, that the primitive faculty of imitation, and of imitative play and fiction, are a necessary background to the communication of feeling.

The first problem is: how do we identify a mere something that we feel as anger or as amusement? There is at least one necessary connection that is clear in the normal use of language. If I am amused, I am inclined, or disposed, or have a tendency, to laugh or to smile. If I am angry, I am inclined, or disposed, or have a tendency, to attack or to behave aggressively. Wherever there is this necessary connection between an identifiable feeling or emotion, and the inclination to behave in an identifiable way, the pattern of behaviour may be called the natural expression of the feeling. A certain pattern of behaviour is a natural expression of a certain feeling, if, in distinguishing this feeling from other feelings with which it might be confused, we would specify an inclination towards this particular pattern of behaviour, together with some standard circumstances, actually existing or believed to exist, which provoke the inclination. So in explaining what anger is, as opposed to some other emotion, I would refer to a disposition to attack when the subject has been, or believes that he has been, in some way harmed or hurt.

Human beings are from the beginning recognized as potential language-users, and as potential observers of social conventions which they will later learn to formulate. The conditions of application of the vocabulary of feelings to human beings are determined by the fact that two capacities—the capacity to control their inclinations, and the capacity to identify their inclinations, and their circumstances, in words—are gradually developed together. I know that I am angry, and I am able authoritatively to disclose

From *Feeling and Expression*, Inaugural Lecture for University College, London (H. K. Lewis and Co., Ltd., London, 1960); reprinted in *Freedom of Mind* (Clarendon Press, 1972). Reprinted by permission of the author.

that I am, because I know what I am inclined to do, which is to attack; and I can identify the external situation that is associated in my mind with this inclination. If I do not try to attack, I must have inhibited the natural expression of my anger, which remains as a merely felt inclination. If I have deliberately cut off the natural expression of the anger, then I will certainly know what the residual feeling is, in at least one sense of this deceiving phrase. The subject's own identification of the inner perturbation as a case of anger rather than of some other emotion, such as fear, would not be intelligible, if it were not for the inclination that remains as the shadow of the natural behaviour. About the contained excitement that he feels, the angry man may ask 'What is this feeling that I have?' He identifies it as a feeling or sentiment of a certain kind in virtue of his inclination to act in a certain way, taken together with those features of the situation with which he associates his action or inclination. The vocabulary of feeling and sentiment with which we communicate, each sometimes subjects, sometimes observers, could never be established if this primary identification of an inclination to behave in a certain way could not be made prior to the classification of inner and contained feeling.

The contrast between that which a man feels inclined to do, and that which he is by social convention required to do, runs all through his experience. He therefore easily learns to abstract his inner perturbations, and the controlled inclinations associated with them, from the behaviour that was their original context, and to attend to these perturbations, and the associated inclinations, as separate subjects of interest. If he restrains himself from doing something that he is inclined to do, he must at least know, through the exercise of this restraint, what it is that he is inclined to do. He can identify his own state of mind from his own incipient behaviour, taken together with the external situation. He is at the same time learning to read these signs in the incipient behaviour of others.

At this point we come to the central distinction between natural and conventional signs of feeling. If one could state this distinction exactly, many problems both of the philosophy of mind, and also of aesthetics, would lie open to clarification. At least it is evident that any surviving residue of the distinctive behaviour of an angry man is by itself to be counted as a natural sign of anger. In order to recognize some residual behaviour as a sign of anger, it is not necessary that one should have learnt a general rule of significance, as the rule of use of a conventional sign has to be independently learnt. The residue is taken as a sign, because it is immediately recognizable as a part subtracted from a whole. For this reason no general rule of correlation needs to be learnt between sign and thing signified. Suppose that I see half the surface of a familiar kind of physical object: no learnt general rule of correlation is required to explain the sense in which I immediately take this visible half-surface as the sign of the presence of the whole.

The medium of behaviour is the body. Bodily expression may take many distinguishable and subtle forms. The more obvious sub-headings are posture, gesture, facial expression. Posture, gesture, facial expression are often immediately legible by others, as signs of an inclination to behave in a specific way, when they are the last vanishing vestige of a familiar and classifiable pattern of behaviour. So the man who looks daggers at his neighbour has cut off the action of aggression, and the vestige of it remains in his glance, voluntarily or involuntarily directed. The man who cowers or shrinks, only sketching the action of flight, makes a gesture, or assumes a posture, that is the suggestion of the action, with the effective remainder of it removed. The inclination has shown itself, and, because it is less than quarter realized, the truncated action is legible as a sign of the contained, and therefore felt and inner, inclination.

But we cannot continue any further along this path, following the notion of expression, without noticing that we have from the beginning left out of account one of the most fundamental of the facts of human nature. Fundamental as it is, it is none the less a fact omitted from many contemporary philosophies of mind, which are in consequence misshapen. There is a primitive activity, or rather, a set of primitive activities, which involve the use of natural signs, in childhood and throughout life: that set of activities which can be very roughly grouped together under the heading of imitation. From the beginning of their development, men not only learn not to behave as they feel inclined to behave, and learn to cut off the natural expression of their feelings. They also concurrently have the instinct to mimic, and the institution of mimicking, the forms of behaviour which they observe in others. In imitative play they go through the motions of doing things without believing that the conditions for effectively doing them are present and therefore without the intention of actually doing them.

Imitation is one primitive and natural way of learning routines and customs and the use of language itself, and it is the child's first way of entry into social life. That it must be counted as an original disposition of men seems certain. The overt behaviour, and the visible expression, of a man who is angry or amused are in imitation adopted gratuitously, in the absence both of the type of external occasion, actual or believed to be actual, and of the ensuing inclinations, that are essential to real anger or real amusement. We have here the converse of an inclination to behave in a certain way, of which the manifestation is inhibited; there is the behaviour alone, without the original inclination to effective action behind it. The power to conceal a present inclination, and the power to simulate a non-existent one, come into existence together. It is difficult, and perhaps impossible, to suppose creatures, capable of full communication in a language, who possessed the one power without also possessing the other. No one who has been angry has, in addition, to learn the rules for expressing anger, as he has to learn how to *say* that he is angry in the course of learning a language. He does not normally need to look in a mirror to see that his physiognomy is correct, and that his posture and facial expression are the right signs to convey that which he wants them to convey. When he sees in another the facial expression and posture of an angry man, and sees them as such, he would know what to imitate, if he was imitating the expression *as* an expression of anger. This is part of his ability to place himself in the position of another, where this involves reconstructing in himself the disposition of another man through their natural expression. So the operation of sympathy, which was mysterious in Hume's immaterialist philosophy, may pass through this primitive tendency to imitate an expression, which may bring into existence the whole of which it is naturally a part. But if a man was imitating the face and posture of another, as he sees them in front of him, without any thought of them as natural signs, he would so far have no ground to distinguish the relevant and expressive, from the irrelevant and inexpressive, features of the physical object which he sees before him. He would then be aiming at a photographic likeness, or at a copy, of the face; and for this he might indeed need a mirror.

Imitative play takes many forms. It is commonly a form of fiction. That kind of fiction which is imitative play may begin at an age when the idea of a true statement, and of the use of conventional signs to convey information, has not yet occurred to a child as a distinct possibility. The child may merely imitate for the original pleasure of creating a likeness, and under these conditions we would normally speak of his imitation as mere play. Imitation and play are the two related concepts that in general aesthetics have to be explored in great detail; imitative play enters into the present inquiry only as a form of human communication that has to be considered alongside the use of conventional signs, and alongside the use of language. When a child has learnt to use conventional signs according to rules, and then learnt how to convey information and to make statements, and thereby to distinguish truth from fiction, playing at doing things, and imitating others for the sake of imitation, become for him autonomous activities, distinguishable from all others, and requiring their own particular skill. Then he may engage in imitative play, deliberately and at will, and knowing what he is doing. He assumes the expression and posture of an angry father, or of a frightened child, distinguishing this fiction from fact. The success of the imitation, as imitation, carries its own satisfaction with it, as truth-telling carries its own satisfaction with it. They are both cases of making or doing something which matches, and which is in its own medium an equivalent of, an independent reality. The making, or discovery for oneself, of such an equivalence is at once the source and the evidence of an adequate grasp of the reality. The making of an equivalence may be taken as a kind of mastery of the independent reality, a reduction of it to our own terms, and its independence may no longer be felt as threatening. The ancient problem is to find the points at which imitation, as the making of a match that is a likeness, supplements, or replaces, the kind of matching that, as an arrangement of conventional signs according to learnt general rules, can for this reason constitute knowledge. We do not here have simple and unmixed opposites, but rather a continuous scale from natural to conventional sign, from likeness to statement, and complicated intertwinings of the two. We are more ready to speak of *knowledge* of reality in proportion as the medium, in which the match or equivalence is found, consists of conventional signs arranged in accordance with a system of rules, which are learnt as general rules of interpretation and of syntax. A good map of the countryside by itself conveys knowledge of the countryside, but is scarcely a likeness. A good free sketch of the countryside may constitute a kind of likeness; in virtue of its comparative freedom, where freedom is opposed to rule, it is less readily considered as by itself conveying knowledge of the countryside.

The sense in which we may come to discriminate more exactly the various emotions and sentiments through an imitation of their natural expression may be approached through an analogy. Suppose that I am asked what a particular person is like: it might be difficult to find the exactly fitting words to describe that which is peculiar to this man. I might then turn to parody, and in imitation of him reproduce some of the idioms, turns of phrase, tones of voice, that are typical of him, isolating them from their more commonplace accompaniments. If it is admitted that I have in fact succeeded in my imitation in isolating that which is peculiar to him, it will be admitted that I have in a sense answered the inquiry. But the answer was in sensory terms and not in a conceptual or discursive form. Suppose similarly I am asked, not about an individual, or group of individuals, but rather about a general and abstract thing—'What is it like to be jealous?' or, a rather different question, 'What is it for a man to be jealous (e.g. rather than envious)?'—I might similarly convey that which is peculiar to this emotion by isolating in an imitation the typical features of its natural expression. In the literature of aesthetics one will meet the portentous phrase—'Seeing the universal in a concrete and sensory embodiment.' One can, I think, forget this phrase with its pseudo-logical air and try to be a little more precise.

There is a rough general law of revealing imitation that is most clearly illustrated in the fundamental arts of mimicry and parody. He who mimics the speech and expression of another communicates more effectively the personal peculiarities of his victim in so far as the likeness in speech and expression shows through an unlikeness, with the imitation superimposed on an alien and contrasting personality. The essential qualities of the thing imitated are then filtered through the resisting medium. A totally faithful reproduction of the voice by a reproducing machine would not serve the same cognitive purposes as a revealing imitation. There would not be that primary abstraction that is involved in any contrivance of a likeness in a naturally resisting medium. In the representative arts the medium, and the conventions governing the use of the medium, produce this tension between likeness and unlikeness in the imitation, which makes the imitation revealing. The solidity of material objects is most strongly felt, as a visual experience enjoyed for its own sake, when a likeness is contrived on a flat surface. The recessions of space can also be vividly revealed and enjoyed through a contrived equivalence in this resisting medium. So also the making of an equivalence of the natural expression of an emotion in a resisting medium seems to give some insight into the general nature of the emotion itself. Because we are faced with an imitation, we respond to it, not with an immediate inclination to action, as with any direct expression of emotion in an individual suffering man, but rather in a contemplative way. Any too complete copying and reproduction of a natural expression of feeling tends to excite in us a disposition towards appropriate action. This will destroy a purely contemplative and inquiring attitude. For this reason the representation of feeling in any of the arts must always be in some way distanced and filtered by the artificialities of the art: for instance, by the mere existence of a stage in a theatre, which still may be not enough to prevent a too immediate, or a confused, response in the audience. A representation is felt to be obscene, when there is a felt conflict in the audience between the contemplative and inquiring attitude, the attitude of the perceiver, and the controlled disposition to act. Then the conditions of a revealing fiction have been destroyed, as they are destroyed by a successful *trompe l'œil* painting, which is designed to excite a disposition to respond as we would respond to the material thing represented.

In any representation of persons in any medium, and particularly of a face, we naturally look for physiognomic features within the representation. We try inquiringly to read through the conventions of representation some expression in the face. In direct dealings with men, and outside the context of fiction, we perceive, and react to, the physiognomy of persons almost as immediately as to the full behaviour of which the facial expression is the residue. The expression, considered by itself, is as much a sign, or even a part, of incipient behaviour as it is a sign of inner feeling. Expression can therefore be considered as the connecting arch between a person's disposition to behave in a certain way, which, if it is inhibited, may remain as an invisible affect, and his perceptible behaviour.

Because of the connecting arch of expression, we cannot truthfully say, as many philosophers have implied, that we perceive only the behaviour of others, if behaviour is interpreted as that which is described in terms of effective actions performed and in socially recognized routines. We perceive also that kind of residual, shadow behaviour which constitutes an expression. And we can show that we have perceived it by adopting the same expression in imitation, without trying to reproduce, item by item, the physical features of the face or posture of another. The criterion of identity, which here justifies the phrase 'same expression', is to be found partly in the common behaviour of which the expression, in each case, is taken to be the residue, and in part also in certain common physical changes. The phrase 'same expression', in virtue of its connecting role, cannot derive its sense exclusively from one side or the other. If therefore I am to imitate successfully your angry expression, it seems that I must pass an exacting double test. I must make, within the medium of my own face, an equivalent of the deviations from the peaceful norm in your face; and at the same time the whole, or gestalt, must be convincing as a sketch of aggressive behaviour by me.

Consider now the link between feelings as dispositions to behave in certain ways and the full corresponding behaviour. I have suggested successive stages of the interiorization of feeling. First, there is the angry man who, being provoked, immediately attacks. If, in answer to the question 'Why did he attack?' we were to answer merely 'Because he was angry,' the explanation would be, on its own level, complete. Compare with this 'Why did he laugh?'—'Because he was amused.' There is no unexplained gap between the disposition attributed to him and the behaviour to be explained. To ask the further question 'Why does his amusement lead to laughter?' would be like questioning a tautology. The question would suggest that the questioner did not know what is meant by 'amusement' or by 'laughter'. If we have said that he was angry, we have already said that, considering himself to have been provoked, he was inclined to attack. The connecting 'because', in giving the reasons for action, has here its minimum force; it makes no allusion to any implied general proposition correlating his behaviour with any independently identifiable event, or with any ulterior calculation. The inquiry into the reasons for his behaviour could only be pressed further by asking why he was angry. This line of inquiry will only terminate when it leads to those fundamental dispositions that constitute a standard of normal response. At the second stage, there is the angry man who, being angry, is inclined to behave aggressively, but for some reason controls his inclination.

Suppose that we identify the contortion of his face as a scowl: we imply that he is behaving as an angry man behaves in at least one respect. 'Scowl' is a physiognomic predicate, as opposed to a physical state description. A scowl, or an angry glance, are allowed to survive, when the rest of the behaviour is inhibited, partly because they are largely ineffective as action. Generally speaking, we effectively do things, and make changes in the world, in the primary sense of these words, that is, in the sense that is associated with physical change, with our hands and with other limbs rather than with our face. This is a contingent matter of fact, a fact of natural history. When a disposition to behave in a certain way is controlled, the last vestige of the behaviour is apt to survive in facial expression, and particularly in the eyes, as being the ineffective part of the behaviour, the most subtle and insubstantial, and therefore the most immediately expressive of the inner movement of the mind. If the angry man had shaken his clenched fists at his adversary, he would have gone through motions that show only too coarsely his inclination to attack. This gesture is the full action that flows from the inclination without its proper climax, and rendered ineffective; and therefore it is an unmistakable natural sign. If a movement is seen effectively to serve some evident and familiar human need or purpose, its significance as gesture is lost. The behaviour generally needs to be uneconomic and useless, as action, in order to be taken as a sign. Again the imitation is effective as imitation, just because it is in this respect also strikingly unlike that which is imitated.

If a feeling or sentiment necessarily includes a disposition to a certain pattern of behaviour, and if every feeling therefore has its appropriate physiognomy, it follows that every feeling can be portrayed in some perceptible imitation, and that its occurrence on any occasion can be communicated by some perceptible natural sign. As it is of the nature of feelings or sentiments that they can be expressed by natural signs, so it is of the nature of a thought, and of a process of thought, that any perceptible expression of it is a conventional sign, the significance of which is determined by learnt rules of use and of syntax. My facial expression and gestures may express my expectancy and excitement. But I cannot (logically cannot) express my thought that my prodigal son will return without converting my gestures into separate signals which require rules of interpretation and of syntax. When Wittgenstein suggested that the words 'I am in pain' can be said to replace a cry of pain, he concentrated an immense transition, a whole natural history, into this single word 'replace'.

It will be evident that, in dwelling on the notion of expression, I am hoping to correct a particular philosophical view of the relation of feeling to behaviour, and therefore of the relation of mind to body: namely, that prevailing, semi-Cartesian view which leaves us with the difficult problem: Can the existence of a feeling or sentiment, independently identified, ever be validly inferred from the behaviour with which it happens to be correlated? And if this cannot be a valid inductive inference, can there be any test that guarantees that the terms of our common psychological vocabulary are applied with a common significance? If not, how is rational communication about our inner feelings ever possible at all?

The picture from which this problem arises is of feelings and states of mind, which are *first* distinguished and identified by the subject as feelings of certain kinds, and which are then *independently* found to have typical manifestations in behaviour. The manifestations in behaviour are conceived as something altogether independent which is added to the states of mind. We move, as it were, outwards from the identification of a specific feeling to the recognition that certain patterns of behaviour are contingently connected with it. I have been suggesting an order of dependence in classification that is the very reverse: that we must first have distinguished certain patterns of behaviour in certain standard circumstances, actual or notional; and then, on the basis of this kind of classification, we can distinguish the various inner sentiments as controlled inclinations to behave in these ways in these standard circumstances. We arrive at the distinctions between the different feelings and sentiments by abstracting from the manifesting behaviour. In our classifications we move, as it were, inwards from expressive behaviour to inner feeling.

Between these two philosophies of mind there are two principal dividing lines. The first raises one of the most general of all philosophical issues, and one that has been at the centre of recent discussion. What conditions are necessary for the establishment of a common vocabulary? Must the common vocabulary, including the vocabulary of states of mind, be established on a common basis of reference to publicly observable things? Must any classification of a state of mind be in principle testable by reference to something other than the felt quality of the experience? Or can I identify my feeling immediately as a feeling of a certain kind, irrespective of anything else, as it seems that I may recognize and name a shade of colour that appears in my visual field? This problem of the conditions of classification leads to the second issue between the philosophies. Does the order in which every man learns to apply mental concepts of certain types in common language determine the conditions of application attached to these concepts? I believe that the answer to this second question must be 'Yes', and that this answer already settles the issue of classification, as it applies to the more refined distinctions within the vocabulary of sentiment and emotion. Entry into a certain 'form of life' is a necessary background to using and attaching a sense to these concepts: namely, entry into that adult human form of life which includes, among other things, the habit of deliberately controlling the natural expression of inclination, and includes also a growing knowledge of restraining conventions of speech and of behaviour. It is characteristic of the more refined concepts, which we use to distinguish between one sentiment and another, that the subject's own avowals are a necessary part of the conditions of their application. A person gradually acquires the power to apply these distinctions, both to himself and to others, in conjunction with his power to dissociate his inclinations from their immediate natural expression. When I speak of *deriving* the concept of feeling and sentiment from the concept of inhibited behaviour, the order implied is both the order in which a person learns the use of two classes of expression, and also the order in which he himself acquires the faculties of mind to which these expressions refer. Whenever these two orders coincide, the method of derivation will be appropriate to fixing the sense of the concepts in question; and they will coincide, whenever the subject's own avowals play a necessary part in the application of the concept.

Consider a concept of a contrasting kind: that of intelligence, which is a power or capacity, and therefore not a disposition, in the sense in which an inclination is a disposition. A person's avowal that he is intelligent has no special authority in determining whether in fact he is. We have no difficulty in determining that a child is in fact an intelligent child, when he is still too young to be a judge of intelligence either in himself or in others. There is therefore no reason to demand that the conditions of application of this concept should be explained genetically, that is, by reference to the order of a human being's development. Similarly, of a creature, infant or animal, which is incapable of confessing to anger or fear, we can evidently say that it is angry or frightened. The standard behaviour in standard circumstances, notional or actual, is sufficient to give this kind of application of these elementary concepts a definite sense. But as soon as more finely marked distinctions between dispositions and sentiments are drawn—for example, between anger and indignation, between fear and embarrassment—and as soon as we begin to apply a full vocabulary of intentional states, the testimony of the subject, and therefore his developed capacity to make these distinctions for himself, are indispensable in giving the distinctions a sense. Manifestations in behaviour become in these cases correspondingly less decisive in determining whether the concepts have been correctly applied in any particular case.

The derivation of the concept of inner feeling and sentiment from that of inhibited dispositions still leaves a final problem, and one that has been abundantly discussed among philosophers in recent years: What is a disposition? When we say of a man that he is disposed, or inclines, or wants, to do something, which he is not actually doing, what kind of potential behaviour is this? Until we have answered this question, we have still said little that is definite and clear about the relation of the inner life of feeling to perceptible behaviour. I have time only to say something negative in order to prevent misunderstanding: that to attribute a disposition to someone, in the sense of 'disposition' that enters into the analysis of the concepts of feeling and sentiment, is not to make a hypothetical statement about him, to the effect that he would behave in certain ways if certain conditions were satisfied. The word 'disposition' has sometimes been used in such a way that a capacity or power, such as intelligence, is to be counted as a disposition. It is at least plausible to interpret statements about capacities and powers as implicit hypothetical statements about possible performances. The kind of disposition that is an inclination to behave in a certain way is something that may occur at a certain moment, and may then immediately disappear, although it may also continue over a certain period of time. Both the statement that it occurred at a certain moment, and the statement that it lasted for a certain period, are irreducibly categorical statements about that person at that time or during that period. As statements, they are no less categorical than the statement that a man had at a certain time a certain facial expression.

The analysis of inclinations to action in terms of hypotheticals might be defended, on the ground that a statement that someone was inclined to do something entails the statement that he would have done it, or tried to do it, if he had not restrained himself, or, alternatively, if another inclination had not supervened. But I think that it could be shown that the hypothetical statement allegedly entailed here is vacuous (cf. 'If nothing occurs to prevent it, it will rain tomorrow.') The conditions specified in the words 'If another inclination had not supervened' and 'If he had not restrained himself' are too utterly unrestricted and general to allow the hypothetical statement a sufficiently definite sense. There would be no acceptable method of establishing the truth or falsity of the hypothetical statement except by a reference to the original inclination. The alleged analysis would therefore be circular.

I make this point, briefly and dogmatically, in order to dissociate myself from that philosophy which might be called logical behaviourism: the philosophy that claims that statements about the inner world of feeling and of sentiment are all in principle reducible to complicated statements about overt behaviour. My motive in dwelling on the concepts of expression and imitation, and on the derivation of inner feeling from inhibited behaviour, is precisely to point to a possible middle way, which is neither a Cartesian dualism on the one hand, nor on the other hand a reduction of that which is distinctively mental to its overt behavioural expression.

VI

THE MENTAL LIFE OF SOME MACHINES

HILARY PUTNAM

(The following paper makes use of a notion of a 'Turing Machine', the conception of the English mathematician and logician, A. M. Turing. A Turing Machine is essentially an effective computational *procedure* for problem-solving. However, since a Turing Machine is, in principle, physically realizable, it is commonly spoken of as if it were an unspecified computer, described by a set of rules in its *machine table*, and operating in a finite number of internal configurations or *states* while scanning, erasing, and printing a fixed number of symbols on an infinite tape. For details see Putnam's essay 'Minds and Machines', cited in footnote 1).

1

I N this paper I want to discuss the nature of various 'mentalistic' notions in terms of a machine analogue. In an earlier paper,[1] I tried to show that the conceptual issues surrounding the traditional mind–body problem have nothing to do with the supposedly special character of human subjective experience, but arise for any computing system of a certain kind of richness and complexity, in particular for any computing system able to construct theories concerning its own nature. In that paper I was primarily interested in the issues having to do with mind–body identity. In the present paper the focus will be rather in trying to shed light on the character of such notions as preferring, believing, feeling. I hope to show by considering the use of these words in connection with a machine analogue that the traditional alternatives—materialism, dualism, logical behaviourism—are incorrect, even in the case of these machines. My objectives are not merely destructive ones; I hope by indicating what the character of these words is in the case of the machine analogue to suggest to some extent what their character is in application to human beings.

One question which I shall not discuss, except for these remarks at the outset, is the question to what extent the application of such terms as 'preference' to Turing Machines represents a change or extension of meaning.

From H. N. Castaneda (ed.), *Intentionality, Minds and Perception* (Wayne State University Press, 1967), © 1967 by Wayne State University Press. Reprinted by permission of the author and the publishers.
[1] 'Minds and Machines', in New York University Institute of Philosophy, *Dimensions of Mind* (ed. Sidney Hook) (New York, New York University Press, 1960), pp. 148–79.

I shall not discuss this question because, as will become clear, it is not too relevant to my undertaking. Even if the sense in which the Turing Machines I shall describe may be said to 'prefer' one thing to another is *very* different in *many* ways from the sense in which a human being is said to prefer one thing to another, this does not run contrary to anything that I claim. What I claim is that seeing why it is that the analogues of materialism, dualism, and logical behaviourism are false in the case of these Turing Machines will enable us to see why the theories are incorrect in the case of human beings, and seeing what these terms might mean in the case of Turing Machines will at least suggest to us important logical features of these terms which have previously been overlooked by philosophers.

In this paper, then, I am going to consider a hypothetical 'community' made up of 'agents', each of whom is in fact a Turing Machine, or, more precisely, a finite automaton. (Of the many equivalent definitions of 'finite automaton', the most useful for present purposes is the one that results if the definition of a Turing Machine is modified by specifying that the tape should be *finite*.) The Turing Machines I want to consider will differ from the abstract Turing Machines considered in logical theory in that we will consider them to be equipped with sense organs by means of which they can scan their environment, and with suitable motor organs which they are capable of controlling. We may think of the sense organs as causing certain 'reports' to be printed on the tape of the machine at certain times, and we may think of the machine as being constructed so that when certain 'operant' symbols are printed by the machine on its tape, its motor organs execute appropriate actions. This is the natural generalization of a Turing Machine to allow for interaction with an environment.

The fundamental concept we want to discuss will be the concept of *preference*. In order to give this concept formal content with respect to the behaviour of these 'agents', we will suppose that each of these agents is described by a rational preference function, in the sense of economic theory.[2] We will suppose that our Turing Machines are sufficiently complex so as to be able to make reasonably good estimates of the probability of various states of affairs. Given the inductive estimates made by a machine, the behaviour of the machine will then be completely determined by the fact that the machine is to obey the rule: act so as to maximize the estimated utility.

The reader should note that the term 'utility' is completely eliminable here.

---

[2] John von Neumann and Oskar Morgenstern. *Theory of Games and Economic Behavior.* 3rd edn. (Princeton, N.J., Princeton University Press, 1953), pp. 26 f., 83 *et passim.* Von Neumann and Morgenstern think of such a function as an assignment of co-ordinates (in an *n*-dimensional space) to objects, the sum of the co-ordinates being the 'value' of the object. Here it will be convenient to think of it as a function assigning a 'utility' to 'possible worlds' (or 'state descriptions' in the sense of Carnap).

What we are saying is that there is associated with each machine a certain mathematical function, called a utility function, such that that function together with another function, the machine's 'degree of confirmation' function, completely determines the machine's behaviour in accordance with a certain rule and certain theorems of the probability calculus.[3] In short, our machines are *rational agents* in the sense in which that term is used in inductive logic and economic theory. If the rational preference functions of these machines resemble the rational preference functions of idealized human beings, and the computing skills of the machines are approximately equal to the computing skills of human beings, then the behaviour of these machines will closely resemble the behaviour of (idealized) human beings. We can complicate this model by introducing into the behaviour of these machines certain irrationalities which resemble the irrationalities in the behaviour of actual human beings (e.g., failure of the transitivity of preference), but this will not be attempted here.

What then does 'prefer' mean as applied to one of these machines? As a start it simply means that the function which controls the behaviour of the machine (more precisely, the function which together with the machine's inductive logic controls the behaviour of the machine) assigns a higher weight to the first alternative than to the second. Even at the outset we can see that the relation of preferring to behaviour is going to be quite complicated for these machines. For example, if one of these machines prefers A to B, it does not necessarily follow that in any concrete situation it will choose A rather than B. In deciding whether to choose A rather than B, the machine will have to consider what the consequences of its choice are likely to be in the concrete situation, and this may well bring in 'values' of the machine other than the preference that the machine assigns to A over B. We might say that if the machine prefers A to B then that means that *ceteris paribus* the machine will choose A over B, and we might despair of ever spelling out in any precise way the *ceteris paribus* clause. In an analogous way, Miss Anscombe[4] has suggested that if someone intends not to have an accident then that means that, *ceteris paribus*, he will choose methods of driving from one place to another that are likely to minimize the chance of having an accident. She has suggested that in this kind of case the *ceteris paribus* clause could not *in principle* be spelled out in detail. On this basis she has gone on to suggest a fundamental difference between what she calls practical

---

[3] Cf. Rudolf Carnap, *Logical Foundations of Probability* (Chicago, University of Chicago Press, 1950), esp. pp. 253–79.
[4] G. E. M. Anscombe, *Intention* (Ithaca, N.Y., Cornell University Press, 1957), esp. pp. 59–61. I wish to emphasize that the view I am criticizing occurs in only three pages of what I regard as an excellent book.

reason and scientific reason. This conclusion should be viewed with some suspicion, however. The fact is that she has shown that certain proposed methods of spelling out the *ceteris paribus* clause in question would not work; but these methods would not work in the case of our machines either. It hardly follows that our machines exhibit in their ordinary 'behaviour' a form of reasoning fundamentally different from scientific reasoning. On the contrary, given a rational preference function, always acting so as to maximize the estimated utility is exhibiting scientific reasoning of a very high order.

Miss Anscombe might reply that actual human beings do not have rational preference functions. However, von Neumann and Morgenstern have shown, and this is the fundamental result in the area, that any agent whose preferences are consistent always does behave in a way which can be interpreted in terms of at least one rational preference function. Miss Anscombe might reply that actual human beings do not have consistent preferences; but this would be to say that the difference between practical reason and scientific reason is that practical reason is often in fact more or less irrational—that everyone's practical reasoning is irrational in some areas. This is like saying that deductive logic is different in principle from the logic contained in any textbook because everyone's deductive reasoning is bad in some areas. The fact is that Miss Anscombe's remarks on intentions are supposed to apply not only to the intentional behaviour of more or less irrational human beings but just as much to the intentional behaviour of an ideally rational human being with a rich and complex system of values. I think this is quite clear from reading her whole book. But for such an agent one of her major conclusions is just false: the practical reasoning of such an agent would be, as we have seen, not at all unlike scientific reasoning.[5]

---

[5] Some of the differences between practical and theoretical reasoning pointed out by Miss Anscombe do hold. For instance, that the main premiss must mention something wanted, and that the conclusion must be an action (although 'there is no objection to inventing a form of words by which he *accompanies* this action, which we may call the conclusion in a verbalized form', ibid., p. 60). What I challenge is the claim that the conclusion (in 'verbalized form') does not follow *deductively* from the premisses (at least in many cases—cf. here n. 1 on p. 58) and cannot be made to follow, unless the major premiss is an 'insane' one which no one would accept. This leads Miss Anscombe to the view that Aristotle was really engaged in 'describing an order which is there whenever actions are done with intentions' (p. 79). This comes perilously close to suggesting that engaging in practical reasoning is merely performing actions with intentions. Mary Mothersill, in 'Anscombe's Account of the Practical Syllogism', *Philosophical Review*, lxxi (1962), 448–61, criticizes Miss Anscombe on this same point but seems to miss the force of her argument. To say, as Mothersill does, that 'do everything conducive to not having a car crash' has a '*noninsane*' interpretation is surely true but no help, since *on the noninsane interpretation*, 'Do *this*' does not follow deductively from the major premiss together with *this* is conducive to not having a car crash—*this* may not be an *appropriate* action, and 'do everything' means (on the 'noninsane' interpretation) 'do everything appropriate' ibid., p. 455). Mothersill seems to assume that 'assuming appropriate conditions' could be spelled out, but this is just what Anscombe is denying.

The point in a nutshell is that practical reasoning *is* fundamentally different from scientific reasoning if we think of scientific reasoning as consisting of syllogisms, the premisses of which can in principle be spelled out exactly, and we think of practical reasoning as consisting of so-called 'practical syllogisms' whose premisses must in all interesting cases contain ineliminable *ceteris paribus* clauses. However, actual scientific reasoning involves modes of connecting premisses and conclusions much more complex than the syllogism, and decision-making, either actual or idealized, involves modes of reasoning which are depicted much too inexactly by being forced into the traditional mould of the 'practical syllogism'. The complex weighing of multitudinous conflicting alternatives and values does admit of deductive schematization; but not the type of deductive schematization considered by Miss Anscombe (and Aristotle).

Before going on, I should like to make one comment which may perhaps prevent some misunderstandings. A Turing Machine is simply a system having a discrete set of states which are related in certain ways. Usually we think of a Turing Machine as having a memory in the form of a paper tape upon which it prints symbols; however, this can be regarded as mere metaphor. Instead, in the case of a finite automaton, i.e. a Turing Machine whose tape is finite instead of potentially infinite, the tape may be thought of as physically realized in the form of any finite system of memory storage. What we mean by a 'symbol' is simply any sort of *trace* which can be placed in this memory storage and later 'scanned' by some mechanism or other. We can generalize further by allowing the 'machine' to 'print' more than one symbol at a time and to scan more than one symbol at a time. Turing has shown that these generalizations leave the class of Turing Machines essentially unchanged. Note then that a Turing Machine need not even be a *machine*. A Turing Machine might very well be a biological organism. The question whether an actual human being is a Turing Machine (or rather, a finite automaton), or whether the brain of a human being is a Turing Machine, is an empirical question. Today we know nothing strictly incompatible with the hypothesis that you and I are one and all Turing Machines, although we know some things that make this unlikely. Strictly speaking, a Turing Machine need not even be a physical system: anything capable of going through a succession of states in time can be a Turing Machine. Thus, to the Cartesian dualist, who likes to think of the human mind as a self-contained system in some sort of causal interaction with the body, one can say that from the point of view of pure logic it is entirely possible that the human mind is a Turing Machine (assuming that the human mind is capable of some large but finite set of states, which seems certainly ture). To the person who believes that human beings have souls and that personality and memory reside in the soul and survive bodily death, one may say again that from the standpoint of pure logic it is entirely possible that the human soul is a Turing Machine, or rather a finite automaton.

Although it is likely that human brain states form a discrete set and that human mental states form a discrete set, no matter what meaning may be given to the somewhat ambiguous notion of a mental state, it is somewhat unlikely that either the mind or the brain is a Turing Machine. Reasoning *a priori* one would think it more likely that the interconnections among the various brain states and mental states of a human being are probabilistic rather than deterministic and that time-delays play an important role. However, empirical evidence is scarce. The reason is that an automaton whose states are connected by probabilistic laws and whose behaviour involves time-delays can be arbitrarily well simulated by the behaviour of a Turing Machine. Thus, in the nature of the case, mere empirical data cannot decide between the hypothesis that the human brain (respectively, *mind*) is a Turing Machine and the hypothesis that it is a more complex kind of automaton with probabilistic relations and time-delays.

There is another respect in which our model is certainly oversimplified, however, even if the human brain and mind *are* Turing Machines. As has already been remarked, the necessary and sufficient condition that someone's behaviour at a given time should be consistent with the assignment of some rational preference function is that his choices be consistent—e.g. if he prefers A to B and he prefers B to C, then he prefers A to C. But even this very weak axiom of transitivity is violated by the preferences of very many, perhaps all, actual people. Thus, it is doubtful that any actual human being's pattern of choices is consistent with the assignment of a rational preference function. Moreover, even if someone's pattern of preferences is consistent with the assignment of a rational preference function, it is doubtful that people consistently obey the rule: maximize the estimated utility.

And, finally, our model is not dynamical. That is to say, it does not allow for the change of the rational preference function with time—although this last feature can be modified. Thus our model is an overly simple and overly rationalistic one in a number of respects. However, it would be easy, in principle, although perhaps impossible in practice, to complicate our model in all these respects—to make the model dynamical, to allow for irrationalities in preference, to allow for irrationalities in the inductive logic of the machine, to allow for deviations from the rule: maximize the estimated utility. But I do not believe that any of these complications would affect the philosophical conclusions reached in this paper. In other words, I do not believe that the philosophical conclusions of this paper would be changed if we replaced the notion of a Turing Machine by the notion of a K-machine, where the notion of a K-machine were made sufficiently rich and complex so that human brains and minds were, literally, K-machines.

Besides saying that they are Turing Machines and that they have rational preference functions, I shall say nothing about my hypothetical 'agents'. They could be artefacts, they could be biological organisms, they could even be human beings. In particular then, I shall nowhere specify in this paper that the 'agents' in my 'community' are alive or not alive, conscious or not conscious. There is, however, a sense in which we may say of these agents, regardless of their physical realization, that they are *conscious of* certain things and *not conscious of* others. Moreover, if they have periods of what answers to sleep, then there is one use of 'conscious' and 'unconscious' in which we may say that they are 'conscious' at certain times and 'unconscious' at others.

2. MATERIALISM

It does not, I think, have to be shown that Cartesian dualism is untenable as a description of the 'inner life' of these machines and of the relation of that inner life to their behaviour. The 'agents' are simply certain systems of states in certain causal interrelations; *all* of their states are causally interrelated. There are not two separate 'worlds', a 'world' of 'inner' states and a 'world' of 'outer' states in some peculiar kind of correlation or connection. They are not ghosts in Turing Machines, they *are* Turing Machines.

But what of materialism? If materialism as a philosophical doctrine is correct as an account of the mental life of *any* organism, then it should *certainly* be correct as an account of what corresponds to the 'mental life' of *these* agents—at least if we imagine the agents to be realized as automata built out of flip-flops, relays, vacuum tubes, and so forth. But even in this last case I shall argue that traditional materialism is incorrect.

Traditional materialism (which is pretty much of a philosopher's straw man by now) holds that mental conduct words are definable in terms of concepts referring to physical-chemical composition. If this is right, then the predicate 'T prefers A to B' should be definable in terms of the physical-chemical composition of our Turing Machines. But in fact there is no logically valid inference from the premiss that one of our Turing Machines has a certain physical-chemical composition to the conclusion that it prefers A to B, in the sense explained above, nor from the premiss that it prefers A to B to the conclusion that it has a certain physical-chemical composition. These are logically independent statements about our Turing Machines even if they are *just* machines.

Let us quickly verify this. Suppose we are given as a premiss that T_1 prefers A to B. We can then infer that T_1 must have been programmed in a certain way. In particular, its programme must involve a rational preference function which assigns a higher value to A than to B. Suppose that we are given not just this information, but are given the specific machine table of the machine T_1. We can still draw no inference whatsoever to the physical-chemical composition of T_1, for the reason that the *same* Turing Machine (from the standpoint of the machine table) may be physically realized in a potential infinity of ways. Even if in fact a machine belonging to our community prefers A to B when and only when flip-flop 57 is on, this is a purely contingent fact. Our machine might have been exactly the same in all 'psychological' respects without consisting of flip-flops at all.

What of inferences in the reverse direction? Suppose that we are given the information that machine T_1 has a certain physical-chemical composition, can we infer that it has a certain rational preference function? This reduces to the question: can we infer the machine table of the machine from its physical-chemical composition? As an empirical matter, there is no doubt that we *can*, at least in simple cases. But we are concerned here with the question of logically valid inferences, not empirically successful ones. In order to know that a machine has a certain machine table, we must know how many significantly different states the machine is capable of and how these are causally related. This cannot be inferred from the physical-chemical composition of the machine unless, in addition to knowing the physical-chemical composition, we also know the *laws of nature*. We don't have to know all the laws of nature, we only have to know some relevant finite set; but there is no way of specifying in advance just what finite set of the laws of nature will have to be given in addition to the physical-chemical composition of the machine before we are able to show that the machine in question has a certain machine table. From the single fact that a machine has a certain physical-chemical composition it does not follow either that it has or that it does not have any particular rational preference function and hence that it does or does not prefer A to B.

Given a description of the physical-chemical composition of a machine *and* a statement of all the laws of nature (for simplicity we will assume these to be finite), can we infer that the machine prefers A to B? Suppose, for the sake of definiteness, the laws of nature are of the classical atomistic kind; that is, they describe how individual elementary particles behave, and there is a composition function which enables us to tell how any isolated complex of elementary particles will behave. Finally, the physical-chemical composition of the machine is described by describing a certain complex of elementary particles. Even in this case, we cannot as a matter of *pure logic* deduce from the statements given that the machine has a particular machine table, or a particular rational preference function, unless in addition to being given the physical-chemical composition of the machine and the laws of nature, we are given the additional premiss (which from the formal point of view is a logically independent statement) that we have been given a description of *all* of the machine. Suppose, for the sake of an example, that there exist in addition to elementary particles, entities unknown to physical theory— 'bundles of ectoplasm'—and that the whole machine consists of elementary particles and some 'bundles of ectoplasm' in some complex kind of causal interrelationship. Then when we give the physical-chemical composition of the machine, in the usual sense, we are only describing a *substructure* of the total machine. From this description of the substructure plus the laws of nature in the ordinary sense (the laws governing the behaviour of *isolated systems* of elementary particles) we can deduce how this substructure will behave *as long as there are no interactions with the remainder of the structure* (the 'bundles of ectoplasm'). Since it is not a fact of pure logic that the physical-chemical description of the machine is a description of all of the machine, one cannot by pure logic deduce that the machine has any particular machine table or any particular rational preference function from a description of the physical-chemical composition of the machine and the laws of nature.

Logically, the situation just discussed is analogous to the situation which arises when certain philosophers attempt to treat universal generalizations as (possibly infinite) conjunctions, i.e. the proposal has been made to analyse 'all crows are black' as '(a_1 is a crow $\supset a_1$ is black) & (a_2 is a crow $\supset a_2$ is black) & (a_3 is a crow $\supset a_3$ is black)...' where a_1, a_2...is a possibly infinite list of individual constants designating all crows. The mistake here is that although this conjunction does indeed follow from the statement that all crows are black, the statement that all crows are black does not follow from the conjunction without the additional universal premiss: 'a_1, a_2, ... are all the crows there are'. It might be contended that the possibility that there exist causal agents unknown to modern physics and not consisting of elementary particles is so remote that it should be neglected. But this is to leave the context of logical analysis altogether. Moreover, we have only to reflect for a moment to remember that today we know of a host of causal agencies which would have been left out in any inventory of the 'furniture of the world' taken by a nineteenth-century physicist. Atoms and their solar system-like components, electrons and nucleons, might possibly have been guessed at by the nineteenth-century physicist; but what of mesons, and what of the quanta of the gravitational field, if these turn out to exist? No, the hypothesis that any inventory includes a list of all ultimate 'building blocks' of causal processes that there are is a synthetic one and cannot be regarded as true by pure logic.

Materialism, as I admitted before, is today a philosopher's straw man. Modern materialists (or 'identity theorists', as they prefer to be called) do not maintain that the *intensions* of such terms as 'preference' can be given in physical-chemical terms but only that there is a physical referent. Their formulation would be, roughly, that preferring A to B is *synthetically identical with* possessing certain more or less stable features of the physical-chemical composition (e.g. 'preferring A to B is a fairly lasting state of the human cerebral cortex'). This runs into the difficulty that *preference* is a universal, not a particular—preferring A to B is a *relation* between an organism and two alternatives—and the 'is' appropriate to *universals* appears to be the '*is*' *of meaning analysis*. We say, e.g., '*solubility* is the property that something possesses if and only if it is the case that if it were in water it would dissolve'. We *don't* say, 'solubility is a certain physical-chemical structure', but rather that the solubility of those substances that are soluble is *explained* by their possession of a certain physical-chemical structure. Similarly, in the case of our machines what we would say is that preferring A to B is possessing a rational preference function which assigns a higher value to A than to B. If we say, in addition, that preferring A to B is 'synthetically identical with' possessing a certain physical-chemical structure—say, a certain pattern of flip-flops—then we let ourselves in for what seem to me to be remarkable and insufficiently motivated extensions of usage. For instance, if the same Turing Machine is physically realized in two quite different ways, then even though not only the rational preference function but the whole machine table is the same in the two cases, we shall have to say 'preferring A to B is *something different* in the case of machine 1 and machine 2'. Similarly, we shall have to say that 'belief' is something different in the two cases, etc. It would be much clearer to say that the realization of the machine table is different in the two cases. There are a number of subtleties here of which it is well to be aware, however.

First of all, what has been said so far suggests the incorrect view that two properties can only be *analytically* identical, not *synthetically* identical. This is false. Let 'a_1' be an individual constant designating a particular piece of paper, and suppose I write the single word 'red' on the piece of paper. Then the statement, 'The property *red* is identical with the property designated by the only word written on a_1', is a synthetic statement.[6] However, this is the *only* way in which properties can be 'synthetically identical' and the statements, 'Solubility is a certain molecular structure', 'Pain is stimulation of C-fibres', are not of this kind, as one can easily convince oneself.

---

[6] More simply, 'blue is the colour of the sky' is a synthetic identity statement concerning properties. This example is due to Neil Wilson of Duke University, to whom I am indebted for enlightenment on the subject of identity of properties.

So far I have suggested that, apart from the kind of synthetic identity state-ment just cited, the criterion for the *identity* of two properties is *synonymy*, or equivalence in some analytical sense, of the corresponding designators. In my earlier paper I pointed out that for certain other kinds of abstract entities—e.g. situations, events—this does not seem to be correct, and that there might be reasons for giving this up even in the case of properties. I cited in that paper the '*is*' *of theoretical identification* (i.e. the 'is' exemplified by such statements as 'water *is* H_2O', 'light *is* electromagnetic radiation') and I suggested that some properties might be connectible by this kind of 'is'. But this would not be of help to the identity theorist. (This represents a change of view from my earlier paper.) Even if we are willing to say 'being P *is* being Q' in some cases in which the designators 'P' and 'Q' are not synonymous, we should require that the designators be equivalent and that the equivalence be *necessary*, at least in the sense of *physically necessary*. Thus, if *one* particular physical-chemical composition should turn out to explain *all* cases of solubility, it would not be a wholly unmotivated extension of ordinary usage to say that solubility *is* the possession of this particular physical-chemical composition. There is an argument in my earlier paper for the view that this would not necessarily be a 'change of meaning'. This sort of thing cannot happen in the present case. We *cannot* discover laws by virtue of which it is physically necessary that an organism prefers A to B if and only if it is in a certain physical-chemical state. For we already know that any such laws would be false. They would be false because even in the light of our present knowledge we can see that any Turing Machine that can be physically realized at all can be realized in a host of totally dif-ferent ways. Thus there cannot be a physical-chemical structure the posses-sion of which is a necessary and sufficient condition for preferring A to B, even if we take 'necessary' in the sense of *physically* necessary and not in the sense of logically necessary. And to start speaking of properties as 'identi-cal in some cases' because they happen to be coextensive in *those cases* would be not only a change of meaning but a rather arbitrary change of meaning at that.

So far we have ascribed to our machines only 'multi-tracked' dispositions such as preference and belief but not such more or less transient states as states of feeling. Of course, we have equipped our machines with sense organs, and if we suppose that these sense organs are not perfectly reliable, then, as I argued in my earlier paper, it is easy to see that the distinction between appearance and reality will automatically arise in the 'life' of the machine. We can classify certain configurations of these machines as 'visual impressions', 'tactile impressions', etc. What of such feelings as pain?

By suitably adapting Stuart Hampshire's discussion in his *Feeling and*

Expression,[7] we can introduce into our model a counterpart of pain. Hampshire's idea is that the feelings are states characterized by the fact that they give rise to certain inclinations. For instance, pain is normally, although not invariably, occasioned by damage to part of the body and gives rise to inclinations to withdraw the part of the body that seems to be damaged and to avoid whatever causes the painful damage in question. These inclinations are in a certain sense *spontaneous* ones—a point that has to be emphasized if this account is not to be open to damaging objections. That is, when X hurts my hand, the inclination to withdraw my hand from X arises at once and without ratiocination on my part. I can answer the question, 'Why do you draw your hand away from X?' by saying, 'X is hurting my hand.' One does not then go on to ask, 'But why is that a reason for drawing your hand away from X?' The fact that X's hurting my hand is *ipso facto* a reason for drawing my hand away from X is grounded on and presupposes the spontaneity of the inclination to draw my hand away from X when I am in the state in question.

Let us then equip our machines with 'pain signals', i.e. signals which will normally be occasioned by damage to some part of the machine's 'body', with 'pain fibres', and with 'pain states'. These 'pain states' will normally be caused by damage to some part of the machine's body and will give rise to spontaneous inclinations to avoid whatever causes the pain in question. I think we can see how to introduce the notion of an inclination into our model: inclinations are naturally treated as more or less short-lasting modifications of the rational preference function of the machine. Temporarily, the machine assigns a very high value, as it were, to 'getting its arm out of there'. This *temporary* change in the machine's rational preference function should not, of course, be confused with the long-term change in the machine's behaviour occasioned by learning that something it did not previously know to be painful is painful. This last can be built into the machine's rational preference function to begin with, and need not be accounted for by supposing that the pain experience changed the long-term rational preference function of the machine (although, in a dynamical model, it may have). In a sense this is a complication of Hampshire's model:[8] pain states are characterized both by the momentary and spontaneous inclinations to which they give rise and by the negative weight assigned by the machine's basic rational preference function to things which the machine has learned from experience put the machine into these states.

The above remarks against identifying preference with a particular physi-

[7] London, H. K. Lewis and Co., Ltd., 1961.
[8] Other aspects of Hampshire's model are, however, omitted here: the role of *unconditioned* responses; the suppression' of inclinations; and the role of imitation.

cal-chemical composition apply equally strongly now against identifying pain with a particular physical-chemical composition. Suppose that the pain fibres of the machines are made of copper and these are the only copper fibres in the machines. It would still be absurd to say, 'Pain is stimulation of the copper fibres.' If we said that, then we would have to say that pain is something different in the case of machine 1 and the case of machine 2, if machine 1 had copper pain fibres and machine 2 had platinum pain fibres. Again, it seems clearer to say what we said before: that 'pain' *is* a state of the machine normally occasioned by damage to the machine's body and characterized by giving rise to 'inclinations' to ... etc., and to eschew the formulation, 'Pain is synthetically identical with stimulation of the copper fibres' in favour of the clearer formulation. 'The machine is physically realized in such a way that the "pain" pulses travel along copper fibres.'

3. LOGICAL BEHAVIOURISM

We have seen that statements about the preferences of our machines are not logically equivalent to statements concerning the physical-chemical composition of these machines. Are they perhaps logically equivalent to statements concerning the actual and potential behaviour of these machines? In answering this question, it is convenient to widen the discussion and to consider not only statements about the preferences of our machines but also statements about their 'knowledge', 'belief', and 'sensory awareness'. When we widen the discussion this way, it is easy to see the answer to our question is in the negative. Consider two machines T_1 and T_2 which differ in the following way: T_1 has 'pain fibres' which have been cut, so T_1 is incapable of 'feeling pain'. T_2 has uncut 'pain fibres' but has an unusual rational preference function. This rational preference function is such that if T_2 believes a certain event to have taken place, or a certain proposition to be true, then T_2 will assign a *relatively infinite weight* to concealing the fact that its pain fibres are uncut. In other words, T_2 will maintain its pain fibres have been cut when asked, will contend that it is incapable of 'feeling pain', and suppress its inclination to give behavioural evidence of feeling pain. If T_2 does not believe that the critical event has taken place or that the critical proposition is true, then T_2 will have, as it were, no reason to conceal the fact that it is capable of 'feeling pain' and will then behave quite differently from T_1. In this case, we can tell that a machine is a physical realization of T_2 and not of T_1 by observing its behaviour.

However, once T_1 and T_2 have both been informed that the critical event has taken place or that the critical proposition is true, there is then no distinguishing them on behavioural grounds. That is to say, the hypothesis that a machine is an instance of T_1 which believes that the critical event has taken place leads to exactly the same predictions with respect to all actual and potential behaviour as the hypothesis that a machine is an instance of type T_2 which believes that the critical event has taken place or that the critical proposition is true. In short, certain combinations of beliefs and rational preference functions which are quite different will lead to exactly the same acfual and potential behaviour.

I have argued in another paper[9] that exactly the same thing is true in the case of human beings. That is to say, two human beings may be inclined to behave in the same way under all possible circumstances, one for the normal reason and the other for a quite abnormal combination of reasons. Once we allow the computing skills or the intelligence of the machine to vary, the point becomes even more clear. Consider the problem of distinguishing between a machine with a normal rational preference function but rather low intelligence and a machine equipped with very high intelligence but with an abnormal rational preference function, which assigns relatively infinite weight to concealing its high intelligence. It is clear the difference is not a wholly untestable one. If we are allowed to take the machines apart and to see what goes on inside them, we can tell whether a given machine is an instance of the first type or an instance of the second type, but it is easily seen that there is no way to tell them apart without examining the internal composition of the machines in question. That is, quite different combinations of computing skills, beliefs, and rational preference functions can lead to exactly the same behaviour, not only in the sense of the same actual behaviour but in the sense of the same potential behaviour under all possible circumstances.

Let T_1 be the machine of low intelligence and let T_2 be the machine of higher intelligence which is simulating the behaviour of T_1. It might be asked in what precisely the greater intelligence of T_2 consists. Well, it could consist in two things. First of all, T_2 may be printing many things on its tape which do not contain operant signals and which, therefore, constitute mere interior monologue. T_2 may be solving mathematical problems, analysing the psychology of the human beings with which it comes in contact, writing caustic comments on human mores and institutions, and so forth. T_2 need not even contain any subsystem of states which at all resembles the states or computations of T_1. T_2 may be sufficiently intelligent to determine what T_1 would do in any particular situation without actually reconstructing the thought processes by which T_1 arrives at the decision to do it. This would be analogous to the case of a human being whose behaviour was in no way out of

[9] 'Brains and Behaviour', in *Analytical Philosophy* (ed. R. J. Butler) (Oxford, Basil Blackwell & Mott, Ltd., 1965), pp. 211–35.

the ordinary but who, unknown to everyone else, enjoyed a rich and unusual inner life.

It will be observed that the machines we have been considering all have, in a sense, *pathological* rational preference functions, i.e. rational preference functions which assign a relatively infinite weight to something. Assigning a relatively infinite weight to something simply means preferring that thing over all alternatives, come what may. Suppose we call a rational preference function *non-pathological* if it does *not* assign a relatively infinite weight to anything except possibly the survival of the machine itself. Let T be the theory that all actually existing intelligent systems possess non-pathological rational preference functions. Then it can be shown that the statement that a machine with fixed computing skills has a particular rational preference function is equivalent under T to saying that it has a certain kind of actual and potential behaviour. In fact, to say that a machine has a particular rational preference function is equivalent under T to saying that it behaves under all circumstances exactly as a machine with that particular rational preference function would behave. This does not, however, vindicate logical behaviourism, although it constitutes a kind of 'near miss'. Logical behaviourism in the case of our machines would be the thesis that the statement that a machine has a particular rational preference function is logically equivalent to some statement about the machine's actual and potential behaviour. This is not correct. What is correct is that there is a theory T, which is very likely true (or whose analogue in the case of organisms is very likely true), such that in the theory T every statement of the form 'T prefers A to B' is equivalent to a statement about T's actual and potential behaviour. But there is all the difference in the world between equivalence as a matter of logic alone and equivalence within a synthetic theory.

In a sense the situation with respect to logical behaviourism is very similar to the situation with respect to materialism. In connection with materialism, we saw that although the statement that a machine has a certain machine table is not logically equivalent to the statement that it has a certain physical-chemical composition, it follows from the latter statement within a synthetic theory, namely the theory consisting of the laws of nature together with the completeness statement, i.e. the statement that there do not exist any causal agencies other than the elementary particles and combinations of elementary particles, and that these possess only the degrees of freedom ascribed to them in physical theory. Indeed, it is easily seen that there is a class C of physical compositions such that the statement that a machine has a particular machine table is equivalent, within the synthetic theory mentioned, to the statement that its physical-chemical composition belongs to the class C. Since the statement that the machine prefers A to B, or that it has a certain belief, or that it 'feels pain', etc. is true only if a suitable conjunction of two statements is true, the first of which says that the machine has a certain machine table, while the second describes the total configuration of the machine at the present instant, and since some such conjunction can be true, assuming the synthetic theory alluded to, only if the physical composition of the machine belongs to a very large class C* of physical compositions, we can see that the statement, whatever it may be, will be equivalent within the synthetic theory alluded to, to the statement that the physical composition of the machine is in such a class C*.

Similarly, assuming the synthetic theory alluded to in connection with logical behaviourism—the theory that no machine has a pathological rational preference function—any statement about the 'mental life' of one of our machines will be equivalent to some statement about its actual and potential behaviour.

Given an 'agent' in our hypothetical 'community', this is our situation: with enough information about the actual and potential behaviour of the agent, we may infer with relative certainty that the agent prefers A to B, or again, with enough information about the physical-chemical composition of the agent (and enough knowledge of the laws of nature), we may infer with relative certainty that the agent prefers A to B. But the two inferences do not support the claims of logical behaviourism and materialism, respectively. Both inferences are synthetic inferences carried out within synthetic theories.

But, it may be asked, how can we even know that either the assumption of the non-existence of pathological rational preference functions or the completeness assumption with respect to physical theory is correct? I believe that the answer is much the same in both cases. Each assumption is justified as long as there is no good reason to suppose that it might be false. If this is right, then inferences to the mental life of any empirically given actual system may be perfectly justified; but they are never analytic inferences if the premises only give information about the actual and potential behaviour of the system and about its physical-chemical composition. Such inferences are always 'defeasible': there are always far-fetched circumstances under which the premises might be retained and the conclusion might be overturned.

On looking over what I have written, I must confess to a certain sense of disappointment. It seems to me that what I have said here is too obvious and trivial to be worth saying, even if there are indeed certain philosophers who would disagree. But at the same time, it seems to me that these remarks, even if they do seem obvious, might suggest something about the nature of our mentalistic concepts which it is not at all usual to point out. What is suggested is this: It seems that to know for certain that a human being has a particular belief, or preference, or whatever, involves knowing something about the functional organization of the human being. As applied to Turing Machines, the functional organization is given by the machine table. A description of the functional organization of a human being might well be something quite different and more complicated. But the important thing is that descriptions of the functional organization of a system are logically different in kind either from descriptions of its physical-chemical composition or from descriptions of its actual and potential behaviour. If discussions in the philosophy of mind are often curiously unsatisfying, I think, it is because just this notion, the notion of functional organization has been overlooked or confused with notions of entirely different kinds.

VII

PSYCHOLOGY AS PHILOSOPHY

DONALD DAVIDSON

NOT all human motion is behaviour. Each of us in this room is moving eastward at about 700 miles an hour, carried by the diurnal rotation of the earth, but this is not a fact about our behaviour. When I cross my legs, the raised foot bobs gently with the beat of my heart, but I do not move my foot. Behaviour consists in things we do, whether by intention or not, but where there is behaviour, intention is relevant. In the case of actions, the relevance may be expressed this way: an event is an action if and only if it can be described in a way that makes it intentional. For example, a man may stamp on a hat, believing it is the hat of his rival when it is really his own. Then stamping on his own hat is an act of his, and part of his behaviour, though he did not do it intentionally. As observers we often describe the actions of others in ways that would not occur to them. This does not mean that the concept of intention has been left behind, however, for happenings cease to be actions or behaviour when there is no way of describing them in terms of intention.

These remarks merely graze a large subject, the relation between action and behaviour on the one hand, and intention on the other. I suggest that even though intentional action, at least from the point of view of description, is by no means all the behaviour there is, intention is conceptually central; the rest is understood and defined in terms of intention. If this is true, then what can be said to show that the intentional has traits that segregate it conceptually from other families of concepts (particularly physical concepts) can be applied *mutatis mutandis* to behaviour generally. If the claim is mistaken, then the following considerations apply to psychology only to the extent that psychology employs the concepts of intention, belief, desire, hope, and other attitudes directed (as one says) upon propositions.

Can intentional human behaviour be explained and predicted in the same way other phenomena are? On the one hand, human acts are clearly part of the order of nature, causing and being caused by events outside ourselves.

From *Philosophy of Psychology*, ed. S. C. Brown (Macmillan, London, 1974). Reprinted by permission of Macmillan, London and Basingstoke.

On the other hand, there are good arguments against the view that thought, desire, and voluntary action can be brought under deterministic laws, as physical phenomena can. An adequate theory of behaviour must do justice to both these insights and show how, contrary to appearance, they can be reconciled. By evaluating the arguments against the possibility of deterministic laws of behaviour, we can test the claims of psychology to be a science like others (some others).

When the world impinges on a person, or he moves to modify his environment, the interactions can be recorded and codified in ways that have been refined by the social sciences and common sense. But what emerge are not the strict quantitative laws embedded in sophisticated theory that we confidently expect in physics, but irreducibly statistical correlations that resist, and resist in principle, improvement without limit. What lies behind our inability to discover deterministic psycho-physical laws is this. When we attribute a belief, a desire, a goal, an intention, or a meaning to an agent, we necessarily operate within a system of concepts in part determined by the structure of beliefs and desires of the agent himself. Short of changing the subject, we cannot escape this feature of the psychological; but this feature has no counterpart in the world of physics.

The nomological irreducibility of the psychological means, if I am right, that the social sciences cannot be expected to develop in ways exactly parallel to the physical sciences, nor can we expect ever to be able to explain and predict human behaviour with the kind of precision that is possible in principle for physical phenomena. This does not mean there are any events that are in themselves undetermined or unpredictable; it is only events as described in the vocabulary of thought and action that resist incorporation into a closed deterministic system. These same events, described in appropriate physical terms, may be as amenable to prediction and explanation as any.

I shall not argue here for this version of monism, but it may be worth indicating how the parts of the thesis support one another. Take as a first premiss that psychological events such as perceivings, rememberings, the acquisition and loss of knowledge, and intentional actions are directly or indirectly caused by, and the causes of, physical events. The second premiss is that when events are related as cause and effect, then there exists a closed and deterministic system of laws into which these events, when appropriately described, fit. (I ignore as irrelevant the possibility that micro-physics may be irreducibly probabilistic.) The third premiss, for which I shall be giving reasons, is that there are no precise psycho-physical laws. The three premisses, taken together, imply monism. For psychological events clearly cannot constitute a closed system; much happens that is not psychological, and affects the psychological. But if psychological events are causally related to physical events, there must, by premiss two, be laws that cover them. By premiss three, the laws are not psycho-physical, so they must be purely physical laws. This means that the psychological events are describable, taken one by one, in physical terms, that is, they are physical events. Perhaps it will be agreed that this position deserves to be called *anomalous monism*: monism, because it holds that psychological events are physical events; anomalous, because it insists that events do not fall under strict laws when described in psychological terms.

My general strategy for trying to show that there are no strict psycho-physical laws depends, first, on emphasizing the holistic character of the cognitive field. Any effort at increasing the accuracy and power of a theory of behaviour forces us to bring more and more of the whole system of the agent's beliefs and motives directly into account. But in inferring this system from the evidence, we necessarily impose conditions of coherence, rationality, and consistency. These conditions have no echo in physical theory, which is why we can look for no more than rough correlations between psychological and physical phenomena.

Consider our common-sense scheme for describing and explaining actions. The part of this scheme that I have in mind depends on the fact that we can explain why someone acted as he did by mentioning a desire, value, purpose, goal, or aim the person had, and a belief connecting the desire with the action to be explained. So, for example, we may explain why Achilles returned to the battle by saying he wished to avenge the death of Patroclus. (Given this much, we do not need to mention that he believed that by returning to the battle he could avenge the death of Patroclus.) This style of explanation has many variants. We may adumbrate explanation simply by expanding the description of the action: 'He is returning to battle with the intention of avenging the death of Patroclus.' Or we may more simply redescribe: 'Why is he putting on his armour?' 'He is getting ready to avenge Patroclus' death.' Even the answer 'He just wanted to' falls into the pattern. If given in explanation of why Sam played the piano at midnight, it implies that he wanted to make true a certain proposition, that Sam plays the piano at midnight, and he believed that by acting as he did, he would make it true.

A desire and a belief of the right sort may explain an action, but not necessarily. A man might have good reasons for killing his father, and he might do it, and yet the reasons not be his reasons in doing it (think of Oedipus). So when we offer the fact of the desire and belief in explanation, we imply not only that the agent had the desire and belief, but that they were *efficacious* in producing the action. Here we must say, I think, that causality is involved, i.e. that the desire and belief were causal conditions of the action. Even this is not sufficient, however. For suppose, contrary to the legend, that Oedipus, for some dark oedipal reason, was hurrying along the road intent on killing his father, and, finding a surly old man blocking his way, killed him so he could (as he thought) get on with the main job. Then not only did Oedipus want to kill his father, and actually kill him, but his desire caused him to kill his father. Yet we could not say that in killing the old man he intentionally killed his father, nor that his reason in killing the old man was to kill his father.

Can we somehow give conditions that are not only necessary, but also sufficient, for an action to be intentional, using only such concepts as those of belief, desire, and cause? I think not. The reason, very sketchily stated, is this. For a desire and a belief to explain an action in the right way, they must cause it in the right way, perhaps through a chain or process of reasoning that meets standards of rationality. I do not see how the right sort of causal process can be distinguished without, among other things, giving an account of how a decision is reached in the light of conflicting evidence and conflicting desires. I doubt whether it is possible to provide such an account at all, but certainly it cannot be done without using notions like evidence, or good reasons for believing, and these notions outrun those with which we began.

What prevents us from giving necessary and sufficient conditions for acting on a reason, also prevents us from giving serious laws connecting reasons and actions. To see this, suppose we had the sufficient conditions. Then we could say: whenever a man has such-and-such beliefs and desires, and such-and-such further conditions are satisfied, he will act in such-and-such a way. There are no serious laws of this kind. By a serious law, I mean more than a statistical generalization (the statistical laws of physics are serious because they give sharply fixed probabilities, which spring from the nature of the theory); it must be a law that, while it may have provisos limiting its application, allows us to determine in advance whether or not the conditions of application are satisfied. It is an error to compare a truism like 'If a man wants to eat an acorn omelette, then he generally will if the opportunity exists and no other desire overrides' with a law that says how fast a body will fall in a vacuum. It is an error, because in the latter case, but not the former, we can tell in advance whether the condition holds, and we know what allowance to make if it doesn't. What is needed in the case of action, if we are to predict on the basis of desires and beliefs, is a quantitative calculus that brings all relevant beliefs and desires into the picture. There is no hope of refining the simple pattern of explanation on the basis of reasons into such a calculus.

Two ideas are built into the concept of acting on a reason (and hence, the concept of behaviour generally): the idea of cause and the idea of rationality. A reason is a rational cause. One way rationality is built in is transparent: the cause must be a belief and a desire in the light of which the action is reasonable. But rationality also enters more subtly, since the way desire and belief work to cause the action must meet further, and unspecified, conditions. The advantage of his mode of explanation is clear: we can explain behaviour without having to know too much about how it was caused. And the cost is appropriate: we cannot turn this mode of explanation into something more like science.

Explanation by reasons avoids coping with the complexity of causal factors by singling out one, something it is able to do by omitting to provide, within the theory, a clear test of when the antecedent conditions hold. The simplest way of trying to improve matters is to substitute for desires and beliefs more directly observable events that may be assumed to cause them, such as flashing lights, punishments and rewards, deprivations, or spoken commands and instructions. But perhaps it is now obvious to almost everyone that a theory of action inspired by this idea has no chance of explaining complex behaviour unless it succeeds in inferring or constructing the pattern of thoughts and emotions of the agent.

The best, though by no means the only, evidence for desires and beliefs is action, and this suggests the possibility of a theory that deals directly with the relations between actions, and treats wants and thoughts as theoretical constructs. A sophisticated theory along these lines was proposed by Frank Ramsey (*Truth and Probability*, 1926). (This theory, in a less interesting form, was later, and independently, rediscovered by von Neumann and Morgenstern, and is sometimes called a theory of decision under uncertainty, or simply decision theory, by economists and psychologists.) Ramsey was primarily interested in providing a foundation in behaviour for the idea that a person accords one or another degree of credence to a proposition. Ramsey was able to show that if the pattern of an individual's preferences or choices among an unlimited set of alternatives meets certain conditions, then that individual can be taken to be acting so as to maximize expected utility, that is, he acts as if he assigns values to the outcomes on an interval scale, judges the plausibility of the truth or propositions on a ratio scale, and chooses the alternative with the highest computed expected yield.

Ramsey's theory suggests an experimental procedure for disengaging the roles of subjective probability (or degree of belief) and subjective value in choice behaviour. Clearly, if it may be assumed that an agent judges probabilities in accord with frequencies or so-called objective probabilities, it is easy to compute from his choices among gambles what his values are; and similarly one can compute his degree of belief in various propositions if one can assume that his values are, say, linear in money. But neither assumption seems justified in advance of evidence, and since choices are the resultant of both factors, how can either factor be derived from choices until the other is known? Here, in effect, is Ramsey's solution: we can tell that a man judges an event as likely to happen as not if he doesn't care whether an attractive or an unattractive outcome is tied to it, if he is indifferent, say, between these two options:

	Option 1	Option 2
If it rains you get:	$1,000	a kick
If it doesn't rain:	a kick	$1,000

Using this event with a subjective probability of one half, it is possible to scale values generally and using these values, to scale probabilities.

In many ways, this theory takes a long step towards scientific respectability. It gives up trying to explain actions one at a time by appeal to something more basic, and instead postulates a pattern in behaviour from which beliefs and attitudes can be inferred. This simultaneously removes the need for establishing the existence of beliefs and attitudes apart from behaviour, and takes into systematic account (as a construct) the whole relevant network of cognitive and motivational factors. The theory assigns numbers to measure degrees of belief and desire, as is essential if it is to be adequate to prediction, and yet it does this on the basis of purely qualitative evidence (preferences or choices between pairs of alternatives). Can we accept such a theory of decision as a scientific theory of behaviour on a par with a physical theory?

Well, first we must notice that a theory like Ramsey's has no predictive power at all unless it is assumed that beliefs and values do not change over time. The theory merely puts restrictions on a temporal cross-section of an agent's dispositions to choose. If we try experimentally to test the theory, we run into the difficulty that the testing procedure disturbs the pattern we wish to examine. After spending several years testing variants of Ramsey's theory on human subjects, I tried the following experiment (with Merrill Carlsmith). Subjects made all possible pairwise choices within a small field of alternatives, and in a series of subsequent sessions, were offered the same set of options over and over. The alternatives were complex enough to mask the fact of repetition, so that subjects could not remember their previous choices, and pay-offs were deferred to the end of the experiment so that there was no normal learning or conditioning. The choices for each session and each subject were then examined for inconsistencies—cases where someone had chosen a over b, b over c, and c over a. It was found that as time went on, people became steadily more consistent; intransitivities were gradually eliminated; after six sessions, all subjects were close to being perfectly consistent. This was enough to show that a static theory like Ramsey's could not, even under the most carefully controlled conditions, yield accurate predictions: merely making choices (with no reward or feedback) alters future choices. There was also an entirely unexpected result. If the choices of an individual over all trials were combined, on the assumption that his 'real' preference was for the alternative of a pair he chose most often, then there were almost no inconsistencies at all. Apparently, from the start there were underlying and consistent values which were better and better realized in choice. I found it impossible to construct a theory that could explain this, and gave up my career as an experimental psychologist.

Before drawing a moral from this experiment, let me return to Ramsey's ingenious method for abstracting subjective values and probabilities simultaneously from choice behaviour. Application of the theory depends, it will be remembered, on finding a proposition with a certain property: it must be such that the subject does not care whether its truth or its falsity is tied to the more attractive of two outcomes. In the context of theory, it is clear that this means, *any* two outcomes. So, if the theory is to operate at all, if it is to be used to measure degrees of belief and the relative force of desire, it is first necessary that there be a proposition of the required sort. Apparently, this is an empirical question; yet the claim that the theory is true is then a very sweeping empirical claim. If it is ever correct, according to the theory, to say that for a given person a certain event has some specific subjective probability, it must be the case that a detailed and powerful theory is true concerning the pattern of that person's choice behaviour. And if it is ever reasonable to assert, for example, that one event has a higher subjective probability than another for a given person, then there must be good reason to believe that a very strong theory is true rather than false.

From a formal point of view, the situation is analogous to fundamental measurement in physics, say of length, temperature, or mass. The assignment of numbers to measure any of these assumes that a very tight set of conditions holds. And I think that we can treat the cases as parallel in the following respect. Just as the satisfaction of the conditions for measuring length or mass may be viewed as constitutive of the range of application of the sciences that employ these measures, so the satisfaction of conditions of consistency and rational coherence may be viewed as constitutive of the range of application of such concepts as those of belief, desire, intention, and action. It is not easy to describe in convincing detail an experiment that would persuade us that the transitivity of the relation of *heavier than* had failed. Though the case is not as extreme, I do not think we can clearly say what should convince us that a man at a given time (or without change of mind) preferred *a* to *b*, *b* to *c*, and *c* to *a*. The reason for our difficulty is that we cannot make good sense of an attribution of preference except against a background of coherent attitudes.

The significance of the experiment I described a page or so back is that it demonstrates how easy it is to interpret choice behaviour so as to give it a consistent and rational pattern. When we learn that apparent inconsistency fades with repetition but no learning, we are apt to count the inconsistency as merely apparent. When we learn that frequency of choices may be taken as evidence for an underlying consistent disposition, we may decide to write off what seem to be inconsistent choices as failures of perception of execution. My point is not merely that the data are open to more than one interpretation, though this is obviously true. My point is that if we are intelligibly to attribute attitudes and beliefs, or usefully to describe motions as behaviour, then we are committed to finding, in the pattern of behaviour, belief, and desire, a large degree of rationality and consistency.

A final consideration may help to reinforce this claim. In the experiments I have been describing, it is common to offer the subject choices verbally, and for him to respond by saying what he chooses. We assume that the subject is choosing between the alternatives described by the experimenter, i.e. that the words used by subject and experimenter have the same interpretation. A more satisfying theory would drop the assumption by incorporating in decision theory a theory of communication. This is not a peripheral issue, because except in the case of the most primitive beliefs and desires, establishing the correctness of an attribution of belief or desire involves much the same problems as showing that we have understood the words of another. Suppose I offer a person an apple and a pear. He points to the apple, and I record that he has chosen the apple. By describing his action in this way, I imply that he intended to point to the apple, and that by pointing he intended to indicate his choice. I also imply that he believed he was choosing an apple. In attributing beliefs we can make very fine distinctions, as fine as our own language provides. Not only is there a difference between his believing he is choosing an apple and his believing he is choosing a pear. There is even a difference between his believing he is choosing the best apple in the box and his believing he is choosing the largest apple, and this can happen when the largest is the best.

All the distinctions available in our language are used in the attribution of belief (and desire and intention); this is perhaps obvious from the fact that we can attribute a belief by putting any declarative sentence after the words 'He believes that'. There is every reason to hold, then, that establishing the correctness of an attribution of belief is no easier than interpreting a man's speech. But I think we can go further, and say that the problems are identical. Beliefs cannot be ascertained in general without command of a man's language; and we cannot master a man's language without knowing much of what he believes. Unless someone could talk with him, it would not be possible to know that a man believed Fermat's last theorem was true, or that he believed Napoleon had all the qualities of a great general.

The reason we cannot understand what a man means by what he says without knowing a good deal about his beliefs is this. In order to interpret verbal behaviour, we must be able to tell when a speaker holds a sentence he speaks to be true. But sentences are held to be true partly because of what is believed, and partly because of what the speaker means by his words. The problem of interpretation therefore is the problem of abstracting simultaneously the roles of belief and meaning from the pattern of sentences to which a speaker subscribes over time. The situation is like that in decision theory: just as we cannot infer beliefs from choices without also inferring desires, so we cannot decide what a man means by what he says without at the same time constructing a theory about what he believes.

In the case of language, the basic strategy must be to assume that by and large a speaker we do not yet understand is consistent and correct in his beliefs—according to our own standards, of course. Following this strategy makes it possible to pair up sentences the speaker utters with sentences of our own that we hold true under like circumstances. When this is done systematically, the result is a method of translation. Once the project is under way, it is possible, and indeed necessary, to allow some slack for error or difference of opinion. But we cannot make sense of error until we have established a base of agreement.

The interpretation of verbal behaviour thus shows the salient features of the explanation of behaviour generally: we cannot profitably take the parts one by one (the words and sentences), for it is only in the context of the system (language) that their role can be specified. When we turn to the task of interpreting the pattern, we notice the need to find it in accord, within limits, with standards of rationality. In the case of language, this is apparent, because understanding it is *translating* it into our own system of concepts. But in fact the case is no different with beliefs, desires, and actions.

The constitutive force in the realm of behaviour derives from the need to view others, nearly enough, as like ourselves. As long as it is behaviour and not something else we want to explain and describe, we must warp the evidence to fit this frame. Physical concepts have different constitutive elements. Standing ready, as we must, to adjust psychological terms to one set of standards and physical terms to another, we know that we cannot insist on a sharp and law-like connection between them. Since psychological phenomena do not constitute a closed system, this amounts to saying they are not, even in theory, amenable to precise prediction or subsumption under deterministic laws. The limit thus placed on the social sciences is set not by nature, but by us when we decide to view men as rational agents with goals and purposes, and as subject to moral evaluation.

VIII

BRAIN BISECTION AND THE UNITY OF CONSCIOUSNESS

THOMAS NAGEL

I

THERE has been considerable optimism recently, among philosophers and neuroscientists, concerning the prospect for major discoveries about the neurophysiological basis of mind. The support for this optimism has been extremely abstract and general. I wish to present some grounds for pessimism. That type of self-understanding may encounter limits which have not been generally foreseen: the personal, mentalist idea of human beings may resist the sort of co-ordination with an understanding of humans as physical systems, that would be necessary to yield anything describable as an understanding of the physical basis of mind. I shall not consider what alternatives will be open to us if we should encounter such limits. I shall try to present grounds for believing that the limits may exist—grounds derived from extensive data now available about the interaction between the two halves of the cerebral cortex, and about what happens when they are disconnected. The feature of the mentalist conception of persons which may be recalcitrant to integration with these data is not a trivial or peripheral one, that might easily be abandoned. It is the idea of a *single* person, a single subject of experience and action, that is in difficulties. The difficulties may be surmountable in ways I have not foreseen. On the other hand, this may be only the first of many dead ends that will emerge as we seek a physiological understanding of the mind.

To seek the physical basis or realization of features of the phenomenal world is in many areas a profitable first line of inquiry, and it is the line encouraged, for the case of mental phenomena, by those who look forward to some variety of empirical reduction of mind to brain, through an identity theory, a functionalist theory, or some other device. When physical reductionism is attempted for a phenomenal feature of the external world, the

From *Synthese*. **22**(1971). 396–413. © 1971 D. Reidel Publishing Company. Dordrecht-Holland.
Reprinted by permission of the publishers.

results are sometimes very successful, and can be pushed to deeper and deeper levels. If, on the other hand, they are not entirely successful, and certain features of the phenomenal picture remain unexplained by a physical reduction, then we can set those features aside as *purely* phenomenal, and postpone our understanding of them to the time when our knowledge of the physical basis of mind and perception will have advanced sufficiently to supply it. (An example of this might be the moon illusion, or other sensory illusions which have no discoverable basis in the objects perceived.)

However, if we encounter the same kind of difficulty in exploring the physical basis of the phenomena of the mind itself, we cannot adopt the same line of retreat. That is, if a phenomenal feature of mind is left unaccounted for by the physical theory, we cannot postpone the understanding of it to the time when we study the mind itself—for that is exactly what we are supposed to be doing. To defer to an understanding of the basis of mind which lies beyond the study of the physical realization of certain aspects of it is to admit the irreducibility of the mental to the physical. A clear-cut version of this admission would be some kind of dualism. But if one is reluctant to take such a route, then it is not clear what one would do about central features of the mentalistic idea of persons which resist assimilation to an understanding of human beings as physical systems. It may be true of some of these features that we can neither find an objective basis for them, nor give them up. It may be impossible for us to abandon certain ways of conceiving and representing ourselves, no matter how little support they get from scientific research. This, I suspect, is true of the idea of the unity of a person: an idea whose validity may be called into question with the help of recent discoveries about the functional duality of the cerebral cortex. It will be useful to present those results here in outline.

II

The higher connections between the two cerebral hemispheres have been severed in men, monkeys, and cats, and the results have led some investigators to speak of the creation of two separate centres of consciousness in a single body. The facts are as follows.[1]

[1] The literature on split brains is sizeable. An excellent recent survey is Michael S. Gazzaniga, *The Bisected Brain* (New York, Appleton-Century-Crofts. 1970). Its nine-page list of references is not intended to be a complete bibliography of the subject, however. Gazzaniga has also written a brief popular exposition: 'The Split Brain in Man', *Scientific American*, **217** (1967), 24. The best general treatment for philosophical purposes is to be found in several papers by R. W. Sperry, the leading investigator in the field: 'The Great Cerebral Commissure', *Scientific American*, **210** (1964), 42; 'Brain Bisection and Mechanisms of Consciousness' in *Brain and Conscious Experience*, ed. by J. C. Eccles (Berlin, Springer-Verlag, 1966); 'Mental Unity Following Surgical Disconnections of the Cerebral Hemispheres', *The Harvey Lectures*, Series **62** (New York, Academic Press,

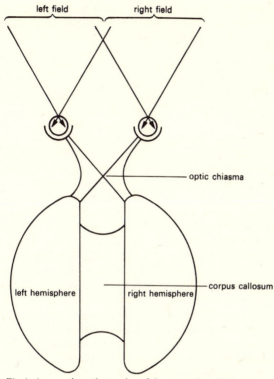

Fig. 1. A very schematic top view of the eyes and cerebral cortex

By and large, the left cerebral hemisphere is associated with the right side of the body and the right hemisphere with the left side. Tactual stimuli from one side are transmitted to the opposite hemisphere—with the exception of the head and neck, which are connected to both sides. In addition, the left half of each retina, i.e. that which scans the right half of the visual field, sends impulses to the left hemisphere, and impulses from the left half of the visual field are transmitted by the right half of each retina to the right hemisphere. Auditory impulses from each ear are to some degree transmitted to both hemispheres. Smells, on the other hand, are transmitted ipsilaterally: the left nostril transmits to the left hemisphere and the right nostril to the right. Finally, the left hemisphere usually controls the production of speech.

1968), 293; 'Hemisphere Deconnection and Unity in Conscious Awareness', *American Psychologist*, 23 (1968), 723. Several interesting papers are to be found in *Functions of the Corpus Callosum: Ciba Foundation Study Group No. 20*, ed. by G. Ettlinger (London, J. & A. Churchill, 1965).

Both hemispheres are linked to the spinal column and peripheral nerves through a common brain stem, but they also communicate directly with one another, by a large transverse band of nerve fibres called the corpus callosum, plus some smaller pathways. These direct cerebral commissures play an essential role in the ordinary integration of function between the hemisphere of normal persons. It is one of the striking features of the subject that this fact remained unknown, at least in the English-speaking world, until the late 1950s, even though a number of patients had had their cerebral commissures surgically severed in operations for the treatment of epilepsy a decade earlier. No significant behavioural or mental effects on these patients could be observed, and it was conjectured that the corpus callosum had no function whatever, except perhaps to keep the hemispheres from sagging.

Then R. E. Myers and R. W. Sperry introduced a technique for dealing with the two hemispheres separately.[2] They sectioned the optic chiasma of cats, so that each eye sent direct information (information about the opposite half of the visual field) only to one side of the brain. It was then possible to train the cats in simple tasks using one eye, and to see what happened when one made them use the other eye instead. In cats whose callosum was intact, there was very good transfer of learning. But in some cats, they severed the corpus callosum as well as the optic chiasma, and in these cases nothing was transmitted from one side to the other. In fact the two severed sides could be taught conflicting discriminations simultaneously, by giving the two eyes opposite stimuli during a single course of reinforcement. Nevertheless this capacity for independent function did not result in serious deficits of behaviour. Unless inputs to the two hemispheres were artificially segregated, the animal seemed normal (though if a split-brain monkey gets hold of a peanut with both hands, the result is sometimes a tug of war).

Instead of summarizing all the data, I shall concentrate on the human cases, a reconsideration of which was prompted by the findings with cats and monkeys.[3] In the brain-splitting operation for epilepsy, the optic

[2] Myers and Sperry, 'Interocular Transfer of a Visual Form Discrimination Habit in Cats after Section of the Optic Chiasm and Corpus Callosum', *Anatomical Record*, 115 (1953), 351; Myers, 'Interocular Transfer of Pattern Discrimination in Cats Following Section of Crossed Optic Fibers'. *Journal of Comparative and Physiological Psychology*, 48 (1955), 470.

[3] The first publication of these reults was M. S. Gazzaniga, J. E. Bogen, and R. W. Sperry, 'Some Functional Effects of Sectioning the Cerebral Commissures in Man', *Proceedings of the National Academy of Sciences*, 48 (1962), Part 2, p. 1765. Interestingly, the same year saw publication of a paper proposing the interpretation of a case of human brain *damage* along similar lines, suggested by the earlier findings with animals. Cf. N. Geschwind and E. Kaplan, 'A Human Cerebral Deconnection Syndrome', *Neurology*, 12 (1962), 675. Also of interest is Geschwind's long two-part survey of the field, which takes up some philosophical questions explicitly: 'Disconnexion Syndromes in Animals and Man', *Brain*, 88 (1965), 247–94, 585–644. Parts of it are reprinted, with other material, in *Boston Studies in the Philosophy of Science*, vol. iv (1969). See also his paper 'The Organization of Language and the Brain', *Science*, 170 (1970), 940.

chiasma is left intact, so one cannot get at the two hemispheres separately just through the two eyes. The solution to the problem of controlling visual input is to flash signals on a screen, on one or other side of the midpoint of the patient's gaze, long enough to be perceived but not long enough to permit an eye movement which would bring the signal to the opposite half visual field and hence to the opposite side of the brain. This is known as tachistoscopic stimulation. Tactile inputs through the hands are for the most part very efficiently segregated, and so are smells through the two nostrils. Some success has even been achieved recently in segregating auditory input, since each ear seems to signal more powerfully to the contralateral than to the ipsilateral hemisphere. As for output, the clearest distinction is provided by speech, which is exclusively the product of the left hemisphere.[4] Writing is a less clear case: it can occasionally be produced in rudimentary form by the right hemisphere, using the left hand. In general, motor control is contralateral, i.e. by the opposite hemisphere, but a certain amount of ipsilateral control sometimes occurs, particularly on the part of the left hemisphere.

The results are as follows. What is flashed to the right half of the visual field, or felt unseen by the right hand, can be reported verbally. What is flashed to the left half-field or felt by the left hand cannot be reported, though if the word 'hat' is flashed on the left, the left hand will retrieve a hat from a group of concealed objects if the person is told to pick out what he has seen. At the same time he will insist verbally that he saw nothing. Or, if two different words are flashed to the two half-fields (e.g. 'pencil' and 'toothbrush') and the individual is told to retrieve the corresponding object from beneath a screen, with both hands, then the hands will search the collection of objects independently, the right hand picking up the pencil and discarding it while the left hand searches for it, and the left hand similarly rejecting the toothbrush which the right hand lights upon with satisfaction.

If a concealed object is placed in the left hand and the person is asked to guess what it is, wrong guesses will elicit an annoyed frown, since the right hemisphere, which receives the tactile information, also hears the answers. If the speaking hemisphere should guess correctly, the result is a smile. A smell fed to the right nostril (which stimulates the right hemisphere) will elicit a verbal denial that the subject smells anything, but if asked to point with the left hand at a corresponding object he will succeed in picking out e.g. a clove of garlic, protesting all the while that he smells absolutely

---

[4] There are individual exceptions to this, as there are to most generalizations about cerebral function: left-handed people tend to have bilateral linguistic control, and it is common in early childhood. All the subjects of these experiments, however, were right-handed, and displayed left cerebral dominance.

nothing, so how can he possibly point to what he smells. If the smell is an unpleasant one like that of rotten eggs, these denials will be accompanied by wrinklings of the nose and mouth, and guttural exclamations of disgust.[5]

One particularly poignant example of conflict between the hemispheres is as follows. A pipe is placed out of sight in the patient's left hand, and he is then asked to write with his left hand what he was holding. Very laboriously and heavily, the left hand writes the letters P and I. Then suddenly the writing speeds up and becomes lighter, the I is converted to an E, and the word is completed as PENCIL. Evidently the left hemisphere has made a guess based on the appearance of the first two letters, and has interfered, with ipsilateral control. But then the right hemisphere takes over control of the hand again, heavily crosses out the letters ENCIL, and draws a crude picture of a pipe.[6]

There are many more data. The split-brain patient cannot tell whether shapes flashed to the two half visual fields or held out of sight in the two hands are the same or different—even if he is asked to indicate the answer by nodding or shaking his head (responses available to both hemispheres). The subject cannot distinguish a continuous from a discontinuous line flashed across both halves of the visual field, if the break comes in the middle. Nor can he tell whether two lines meet at an angle, if the joint is in the middle. Nor can he tell whether two spots in opposite half-fields are the same or different in colour—though he can do all these things if the images to be compared fall within a single half-field. On the whole the right hemisphere does better at spatial relations tests, but is almost incapable of calculation. It appears susceptible to emotion, however. For example, if a photograph of a naked woman is flashed to the left half-field of a male patient, he will grin broadly and perhaps blush, without being able to say what has pleased him, though he may say 'Wow, that's quite a machine you've got there.'

All this is combined with what appears to be complete normalcy in ordinary activities, when no segregation of imput to the two hemispheres has been artificially created. Both sides fall asleep and wake up at the same time. The patients can play the piano, button their shirts, swim, and perform well in other activities requiring bilateral co-ordination. Moreover, they do not report any sensation of division or reduction of the visual field. The most notable deviation in ordinary behaviour was in a patient whose left hand

---

[5] H. W. Gordon and R. W. Sperry, 'Lateralization of Olfactory Perception in the Surgically Separated Hemispheres of Man', *Neuropsychologia*, 7 (1969), 111. One patient, however, was able to say in these circumstances that he smelled something unpleasant, without being able to describe it further.

[6] Reported in Jerre Levy, 'Information Processing and Higher Psychological Functions in the Disconnected Hemispheres of Human Commissurotomy Patients' (unpublished doctoral dissertation, California Institute of Technology, 1969).

appeared to be somewhat hostile to the patient's wife. But by and large the hemispheres co-operate admirably, and it requires subtle experimental techniques to get them to operate separately. If one is not careful, they will give each other peripheral cues, transmitting information by audible, visible, or otherwise sensorily perceptible signals which compensate for the lack of a direct commissural link. (One form of communication is particularly difficult to prevent, because it is so direct: both hemispheres can move the neck and facial muscles, and both can feel them move; so a response produced in the face or head by the right hemisphere can be detected by the left, and there is some evidence that they send signals to one another via this medium.)[7]

III

What one naturally wants to know about these patients is how many minds they have. This immediately raises questions about the sense in which an ordinary person can be said to have one mind, and what the conditions are under which diverse experiences and activities can be ascribed to the same mind. We must have some idea what an ordinary person is one of in order to understand what we want to know whether there is *one or two* of, when we try to describe these extraordinary patients.

However, instead of beginning with an analysis of the unity of the mind, I am going to proceed by attempting to apply the ordinary, unanalysed conception directly in the interpretation of these data, asking whether the patients have one mind, or two, or some more exotic configuration. My conclusion will be that the ordinary conception of a single, countable mind cannot be applied to them at all, and that there is no number of such minds that they possess, though they certainly engage in mental activity. A clearer understanding of the idea of an individual mind should emerge in the course of this discussion but the difficulties which stand in the way of its application to the split-brain cases will provide ground for more general doubts. The concept may not be applicable to ordinary human beings either, for it embodies too simple a conception of the way in which human beings function.

Nevertheless I shall employ the notion of an individual mind in discussing the cases initially, for I wish to consider systematically how they might be

[7] Moreover, the condition of radical disconnection may not be stable: there may be a tendency towards the formation of new interhemispheric pathways through the brain stem, with the lapse of time. This is supported partly by observation of commissurotomy patients, but more importantly by cases of agenesis of the callosum. People who have grown up without one have learned to manage without it; their performance on the tests is much closer to normal than that of recently operated patients. (Cf. Saul and Sperry, 'Absence of Commissurotomy Symptoms with Agenesis of the Corpus Callosum', *Neurology*, **18** (1968).) This fact is very important, but for the present I shall put it aside to concentrate on the immediate results of disconnection.

understood in terms of countable minds, and to argue that they cannot be. After having done this, I shall turn to ordinary people like you and me.

There appear to be five interpretations of the experimental data which utilize the concept of an individual mind.

(1) The patients have one fairly normal mind associated with the left hemisphere, and the responses emanating from the non-verbal right hemisphere are the responses of an automaton, and are not produced by conscious mental processes.

(2) The patients have only one mind, associated with the left hemisphere, but there also occur (associated with the right hemisphere) isolated conscious mental phenomena, not integrated into a mind at all, though they can perhaps be ascribed to the organism.

(3) The patients have two minds, one which can talk and one which can't.

(4) They have one mind, whose contents derive from both hemispheres and are rather peculiar and dissociated.

(5) They have one normal mind most of the time, while the hemispheres are functioning in parallel, but two minds are elicited by the experimental situations which yield the interesting results. (Perhaps the single mind splits in two and reconvenes after the experiment is over.)

I shall argue that each of these interpretations is unacceptable for one reason or another.

IV

Let me first discuss hypotheses (1) and (2), which have in common the refusal to ascribe the activities of the right hemisphere to a mind, and then go on to treat hypotheses (3), (4), and (5), all of which associate a mind with the activities of the right hemisphere, though they differ on what mind it is.

The only support for hypothesis (1), which refuses to ascribe consciousness to the activities of the right hemisphere at all, is the fact that the subject consistently denies awareness of the activities of that hemisphere. But to take this as proof that the activities of the right hemisphere are unconscious is to beg the question, since the capacity to give testimony is the exclusive ability of the left hemisphere, and of course the left hemisphere is not conscious of what is going on in the right. If on the other hand we consider the manifestations of the right hemisphere itself, there seems no reason in principle to regard verbalizability as a *necessary* condition of consciousness. There may be other grounds for the ascription of conscious mental states that are sufficient even without verbalization. And in fact, what the right hemisphere can do on its own is too elaborate, too intentionally directed, and too psychologically intelligible to be regarded merely as a collection of unconscious automatic responses.

The right hemisphere is not very intelligent and it cannot talk; but it is able to respond to complex visual and auditory stimuli, including language, and it can control the performance of discriminatory and manipulative tasks requiring close attention—such as the spelling-out of simple words with plastic letters. It can integrate auditory, visual, and tactile stimuli in order to follow the experimenter's instructions, and it can take certain aptitude tests. There is no doubt that if a person were deprived of his left hemisphere entirely, so that the only capacities remaining to him were those of the right, we should not on that account say that he had been converted into an automaton. Though speechless, he would remain conscious and active, with a diminished visual field and partial paralysis on the right side from which he would eventually recover to some extent. In view of this, it would seem arbitrary to deny that the activities of the right hemisphere are conscious, just because they occur side by side with those of the left hemisphere, about whose consciousness there is no question.

I do not wish to claim that the line between conscious and unconscious mental activity is a sharp one. It is even possible that the distinction is partly relative, in the sense that a given item of mental activity may be assignable to consciousness or not, depending on what other mental activities of the same person are going on at the same time, and whether it is connected with them in a suitable way. Even if this is true, however, the activities of the right hemisphere in split-brain patients do not fall into the category of events whose inclusion in consciousness depends on what else is going on in the patient's mind. Their determinants include a full range of psychological factors, and they demand alertness. It is clear that attention, even concentration is demanded for the tasks of the concealed left hand and tachistoscopically stimulated left visual field. The subjects do not take their experimental tests in a dreamy fashion: they are obviously in contact with reality. The left hemisphere occasionally complains about being asked to perform tasks which the right hemisphere can perform, because it does not know what is going on when the right hemisphere controls the response. But the right hemisphere displays enough awareness of what it is doing to justify the attribution of conscious control in the absence of verbal testimony. If the patients did not deny any awareness of those activities, no doubts about their consciousness would arise at all.

The considerations that make the first hypothesis untenable also serve to refute hypothesis (2), which suggests that the activities of the right hemisphere are conscious without belonging to a mind at all. There may be problems about the intelligibility of this proposal, but we need not consider them here, because it is rendered implausible by the high degree of organization and intermodal coherence of the right hemisphere's mental activities. They are not free-floating, and they are not organized in a fragmentary way. The right hemisphere follows instructions, integrates tactile, auditory, and visual stimuli, and does most of the things a good mind should do. The data present us not merely with slivers of purposive behaviour, but with a system capable of learning, reacting emotionally, following instructions, and carrying out tasks which require the integration of diverse psychological determinants. It seems clear that the right hemisphere's activities are not unconscious, and that they belong to something having a characteristically mental structure: a subject of experience and action.

V

Let me now turn to the three hypotheses according to which the conscious mental activities of the right hemisphere are ascribed to a mind. They have to be considered together, because the fundamental difficulty about each of them lies in the impossibility of deciding among them. The question, then, is whether the patients have two minds, one mind, or a mind that occasionally splits in two.

There is much to recommend the view that they have two minds, i.e. that the activities of the right hemisphere belong to a mind of their own.[8] Each side of the brain seems to produce its own perceptions, beliefs, and actions, which are connected with one another in the usual way, but not to those of the opposite side. The two halves of the cortex share a common body, which they control through a common midbrain and spinal cord. But their higher functions are independent not only physically but psychologically. Functions of the right hemisphere are inaccessible not only to speech but to any direct combination with corresponding functions of the left hemisphere—i.e. with functions of a type that the right hemisphere finds easy on its home ground, like shape or colour discrimination.

One piece of testimony by the patients' left hemispheres may appear to argue against two minds. They report no diminution of the visual field, and little absence of sensation on the left side. Sperry dismisses this evidence on the ground that it is comparable to the testimony of victims of scotoma

---

[8] It is Sperry's view. He puts it as follows: 'Instead of the normally unified single stream of consciousness, these patients behave in many ways as if they have two independent streams of conscious awareness, one in each hemisphere, each of which is cut off from and out of contact with the mental experiences of the other. In other words, each hemisphere seems to have its own separate and private sensations; its own perceptions; its own concepts; and its own impulses to act, with related volitional, cognitive, and learning experiences. Following the surgery, each hemisphere also has thereafter its own separate chain of memories that are rendered inaccessible to the recall process of the other.' *American Psychologist*, **23** (1968), 724.

(partial destruction of the retina), that they notice no gaps in their visual field—although these gaps can be discovered by others observing their perceptual deficiencies. But we need not assume that an elaborate confabulatory mechanism is at work in the left hemisphere to account for such testimony. It is perfectly possible that although there are two minds, the mind associated with each hemisphere receives, through the common brain stem, a certain amount of crude ipsilateral stimulation, so that the speaking mind has a rudimentary and undifferentiated appendage to the left side of its visual field, and vice versa for the right hemisphere.[9]

The real difficulties for the two-minds hypothesis coincide with the reasons for thinking we are dealing with one mind—namely the highly integrated character of the patients' relations to the world in ordinary circumstances. When they are not in the experimental situation, their startling behavioural dissociation disappears, and they function normally. There is little doubt that information from the two sides of their brains can be pooled to yield integrated behavioural control. And although this is not accomplished by the usual methods, it is not clear that this settles the question against assigning the integrative functions to a single mind. After all, if the patient is permitted to touch things with both hands and smell them with both nostrils, he arrives at a unified idea of what is going on around him and what he is doing, without revealing any left–right inconsistencies in his behaviour or attitudes. It seems strange to suggest that we are not in a position to ascribe all those experiences to the same person, just because of some peculiarities about how the integration is achieved. The people who *know* these patients find it natural to relate to them as single individuals.

Nevertheless, if we ascribe the integration to a single mind, we must also ascribe the experimentally evoked dissociation to that mind, and that is not easy. The experimental situation reveals a variety of dissociation or conflict that is unusual not only because of the simplicity of its anatomical basis, but because such a wide *range* of functions is split into two non-communicating branches. It is not as though two conflicting volitional centres shared a common perceptual and reasoning apparatus. The split is much deeper than that. The one-mind hypothesis must therefore assert that the contents of the individual's single consciousness are produced by two independent control systems in the two hemispheres, each having a fairly complete mental structure. If this dual control were accomplished during experimental situations by temporal alternation, it would be intelligible, though mysterious. But that is not the hypothesis, and the hypothesis as it stands does not supply us with understanding. For in these patients there appear to be things

---

[9] There is some direct evidence for such primitive ipsilateral inputs, both visual and tactile; cf. Gazzaniga, *The Bisected Brain*, Ch. 3.

happening *simultaneously* which cannot fit into a single mind: simultaneous attention to two incompatible tasks, for example, without interaction between the purposes of the left and right hands.

This makes it difficult to conceive what it is like to *be* one of these people. Lack of interaction at the level of a preconscious control system would be comprehensible. But lack of interaction in the domain of visual experience and conscious intention threatens assumptions about the unity of consciousness which are basic to our understanding of another individual as a person. These assumptions are associated with our conception of ourselves, which to a considerable extent constrains our understanding of others. And it is just these assumptions, I believe, that make it impossible to arrive at an interpretation of the cases under discussion in terms of a countable number of minds.

Roughly, we assume that a single mind has sufficiently immediate access to its conscious states so that, for elements of experience or other mental events occurring simultaneously or in close temporal proximity, the mind which is their subject can also experience the simpler *relations* between them if it attends to the matter. Thus, we assume that when a single person has two visual impressions, he can usually also experience the sameness or difference of their colouration, shape, size, the relation of their position and movement within his visual field, and so forth. The same can be said of cross-modal connections. The experiences of a single person are thought to take place in an *experientially* connected domain, so that the relations among experiences can be substantially captured in experiences of those relations.[10]

Split-brain patients fail dramatically to conform to these assumptions in experimental situations, and they fail over the simplest matters. Moreover, the dissociation holds between two classes of conscious states each characterized by significant *internal* coherence: normal assumptions about the unity of consciousness hold intrahemispherically, although the requisite comparisons cannot be made across the interhemispheric gap.

These considerations lead us back to the hypothesis that the patients have two minds each. It at least has the advantage of enabling us to understand what it is like to *be* these individuals, so long as we do not try to imagine what it is like to be both of them at the same time. Yet the way to a comfortable acceptance of this conclusion is blocked by the compelling behavioural

[10] The two can of course diverge, and this fact underlies the classic philosophical problem of inverted spectra, which is only distantly related to the subject of this paper. A type of relation can hold between elements in the experience of a single person that cannot hold between elements of the experience of distinct persons: looking similar in colour, for example. In so far as our concept of similarity of experience in the case of a single person is dependent on his experience of similarity, the concept is not applicable between persons.

integration which the patients display in ordinary life, in comparison to which the dissociated symptoms evoked by the experimental situation seem peripheral and atypical. We are faced with diametrically conflicting bodies of evidence, in a case which does not admit of arbitrary decision. There is a powerful inclination to feel that there must be *some* whole number of minds in those heads, but the data prevent us from deciding how many.

This dilemma makes hypothesis (5) initially attractive, especially since the data which yield the conflict are to some extent gathered at different times. But the suggestion that a second mind is brought into existence only during experimental situations loses plausibility on reflection. First, it is entirely *ad hoc*: it proposes to explain one change in terms of another without suggesting any explanation of the second. There is nothing about the experimental situation that might be expected to produce a fundamental internal change in the patient. In fact it produces no anatomical changes and merely elicits a noteworthy set of symptoms. So unusual an event as a mind's popping in and out of existence would have to be explained by something more than its explanatory convenience.

But secondly, the behavioural evidence would not even be explained by this hypothesis, simply because the patients' integrated responses and their dissociated responses are not clearly separated in time. During the time of the experiments the patient is functioning largely as if he were a single individual: in his posture, in following instructions about where to focus his eyes, in the whole range of trivial behavioural control involved in situating himself in relation to the experimenter and the experimental apparatus. The two halves of his brain co-operate completely except in regard to those very special inputs that reach them separately and differently. For these reasons hypothesis (5) does not seem to be a real option; if two minds are operating in the experimental situation, they must be operating largely in harmony although partly at odds. And if there are two minds then, why can there not be two minds operating essentially in parallel the rest of the time?

Nevertheless the psychological integration displayed by the patients in ordinary life is so complete that I do not believe it is possible to accept that conclusion, nor any conclusion involving the ascription to them of a whole number of minds. These cases fall midway between ordinary persons with intact brains (between whose cerebral hemispheres there is also co-operation, though it works largely via the corpus callosum), and pairs of individuals engaged in a performance requiring exact behavioural co-ordination, like using a two-handed saw, or playing a duet. In the latter type of case we have two minds which communicate by subtle peripheral cues; in the former we have a single mind. Nothing taken from either of those cases can compel us to assimilate the split-brain patient to one or the other of them.

If we decided that they definitely had two minds, then it would be problematical why we didn't conclude on anatomical grounds that everyone has two minds, but that we don't notice it except in these odd cases because most pairs of minds in a single body run in perfect parallel due to the direct communication between the hemispheres which provide their anatomical bases. The two minds each of us has running in harness would be much the same except that one could talk and the other couldn't. But it is clear that this line of argument will get us nowhere. For if the idea of a single mind applies to anyone it applies to ordinary individuals with intact brains, and if it does not apply to them it ought to be scrapped, in which case there is no point in asking whether those with split brains have one mind or two.[11]

VI

If I am right, and there is no whole number of individual minds that these patients can be said to have, then the attribution of conscious, significant mental activity does not require the existence of a single mental subject. This is extremely puzzling in itself, for it runs counter to our need to construe the mental states we ascribe to others on the model of our own. Something in the ordinary conception of a person, or in the ordinary conception of experience, leads to the demand for an account of these cases which the same conception makes it impossible to provide. This may seem a problem not worth worrying about very much. It is not so surprising that, having begun with a phenomenon which is radically different from anything else previously known, we should come to the conclusion that it cannot be adequately described in ordinary terms. However, I believe that consideration of these very unusual cases should cause us to be sceptical about the concept of a single subject of consciousness as it applies to ourselves.

The fundamental problem in trying to understand these cases in mentalistic terms is that we take ourselves as paradigms of psychological unity, and are then unable to project ourselves into their mental lives, either once or twice. But in thus using ourselves as the touchstone of whether another organism can be said to house an individual subject of experience or not, we are subtly ignoring the possibility that our own unity may be nothing absolute, but merely another case of integration, more or less effective, in the control system of a complex organism. This system speaks in the first

[11] In case anyone is inclined to embrace the conclusion that we all have two minds, let me suggest that the trouble will not end there. For the mental operations of a single hemisphere, such as vision, hearing, speech, writing, verbal comprehension, etc. can to a great extent be separated from one another by suitable cortical deconnections; why then should we not regard *each* hemisphere as inhabited by several co-operating minds with specialized capacities? Where is one to stop? If the decision on the number of minds associated with a brain is largely arbitrary, the original point of the question has disappeared.

person singular through our mouths, and that makes it understandable that we should think of its unity as in some sense numerically absolute, rather than relative and a function of the integration of its contents.

But this is quite genuinely an illusion. The illusion consists in projecting inward to the centre of the mind the very subject whose unity we are trying to explain: the individual person with all his complexities. The ultimate account of the unity of what we call a single mind consists of an enumeration of the types of functional integration that typify it. We know that these can be eroded in different ways, and to different degrees. The belief that even in their complete version they can be explained by the presence of a numerically single subject is an illusion. Either this subject contains the mental life, in which case it is complex and its unity must be accounted for in terms of the unified operation of its components and functions, or else it is an extensionless point, in which case it explains nothing.

An intact brain contains two cerebral hemispheres each of which possesses perceptual, memory, and control systems adequate to run the body without the assistance of the other. They co-operate in directing it with the aid of a constant two-way internal communication system. Memories, perceptions, desires, and so forth therefore have duplicate physical bases on both sides of the brain, not just on account of similarities of initial input, but because of subsequent exchange. The co-operation of the undetached hemispheres in controlling the body is more efficient and direct than the co-operation of a pair of detached hemispheres, but it is co-operation none the less. Even if we analyse the idea of unity in terms of functional integration, therefore, the unity of our own consciousness may be less clear than we had supposed. The natural conception of a single person controlled by a mind possessing a single visual field, individual faculties for each of the other senses, unitary systems of memory, desire, belief, and so forth, may come into conflict with the physiological facts when it is applied to ourselves.

The concept of a person might possibly survive an application to cases which require us to speak of two or more persons in one body, but it seems strongly committed to some form of whole number countability. Since even this seems open to doubt, it is possible that the ordinary, simple idea of a single person will come to seem quaint some day, when the complexities of the human control system become clearer and we become less certain that there is anything very important that we are *one* of. But it is also possible that we shall be unable to abandon the idea no matter what we discover.[12]

[12] My research was supported in part by the National Science Foundation.

IX

THE SELF AND THE FUTURE

BERNARD WILLIAMS

S U P P O S E that there were some process to which two persons, A and B, could be subjected as a result of which they might be said—question-beggingly—to have *exchanged bodies*. That is to say—less question-beggingly—there is a certain human body which is such that when previously we were confronted with it, we were confronted with person A, certain utterances coming from it were expressive of memories of the past experiences of A, certain movements of it partly constituted the actions of A and were taken as expressive of the character of A, and so forth; but now, after the process is completed, utterances coming from this body are expressive of what seem to be just those memories which previously we identified as memories of the past experiences of B, its movements partly constitute actions expressive of the character of B, and so forth; and conversely with the other body.

There are certain important philosophical limitations on how such imaginary cases are to be constructed, and how they are to be taken when constructed in various ways. I shall mention two principal limitations, not in order to pursue them further here, but precisely in order to get them out of the way.

There are certain limitations, particularly with regard to character and mannerisms, to our ability to imagine such cases even in the most restricted sense of our being disposed to take the later performances of that body which was previously A's as expressive of B's character; if the previous A and B were extremely unlike one another both physically and psychologically, and if, say, in addition, they were of different sex, there might be grave difficulties in reading B's dispositions in any possible performances of A's body. Let us forget this, and for the present purpose just take A and B as being sufficiently alike (however alike that has to be) for the difficulty not to arise; after the experiment, persons familiar with A and B are just *overwhelmingly struck* by the B-ish character of the doings associated with what was previously A's body, and conversely. Thus the feat of imagining an exchange of

From *Philosophical Review* (1970); reprinted in *Problems of the Self* (Cambridge University Press, 1973). Reprinted by permission of the author and the publishers.

bodies is supposed possible in the most restricted sense. But now there is a further limitation which has to be overcome if the feat is to be not merely possible in the most restricted sense but also is to have an outcome which, on serious reflection, we are prepared to describe as A and B having changed bodies—that is, an outcome where, confronted with what was previously A's body, we are prepared seriously to say that we are now confronted with B.

It would seem a necessary condition of so doing that the utterances coming from that body be taken as genuinely expressive of memories of B's past. But memory is a causal notion; and as we actually use it, it seems a necessary condition on x's present knowledge of x's earlier experiences constituting memory of those experiences that the causal chain linking the experiences and the knowledge should not run outside x's body. Hence if utterances coming from a given body are to be taken as expressive of memories of the experiences of B, there should be some suitable causal link between the appropriate state of that body and the original happening of those experiences to B. One radical way of securing that condition in the imagined exchange case is to suppose, with Shoemaker,[1] that the brains of A and of B are transposed. We may not need so radical a condition. Thus suppose it were possible to extract information from a man's brain and store it in a device while his brain was repaired, or even renewed, the information then being replaced: it would seem exaggerated to insist that the resultant man could not possibly have the memories he had before the operation. With regard to our knowledge of our own past, we draw distinctions between merely recalling, being reminded, and learning again, and those distinctions correspond (roughly) to distinctions between no new input, partial new input, and total new input with regard to the information in question; and it seems clear that the information-parking case just imagined would not count as new input in the sense necessary and sufficient for 'learning again'. Hence we can imagine the case we are concerned with in terms of information extracted into such devices from A's and B's brains and replaced in the other brain; this is the sort of model which, I think not unfairly for the present argument, I shall have in mind.

We imagine the following. The process considered above exists; two persons can enter some machine, let us say, and emerge changed in the appropriate ways. If A and B are the persons who enter, let us call the persons who emerge the *A-body-person* and the *B-body-person*: the *A*-body-person is that person (whoever it is) with whom I am confronted when, after the experiment, I am confronted with that body which previously was A's body—that is to say, that person who would naturally be taken for A by someone who

[1] *Self-Knowledge and Self-Identity* (Ithaca, N.Y., 1963), p. 23 f.

just saw this person, was familiar with A's appearance before the experiment, and did not know about the happening of the experiment. A non-question-begging description of the experiment will leave it open which (if either) of the persons A and B the A-body-person is; the description of the experiment as 'persons changing bodies' of course implies that the A-body-person is actually B.

We take two persons A and B who are going to have the process carried out on them. (We can suppose, rather hazily, that they are willing for this to happen; to investigate at all closely at this stage why they might be willing or unwilling, what they would fear, and so forth, would anticipate some later issues.) We further announce that one of the two resultant persons, the A-body-person and the B-body-person, is going after the experiment to be given $100,000, while the other is going to be tortured. We then ask each A and B to choose which treatment should be dealt out to which of the persons who will emerge from the experiment, the choice to be made (if it can be) on selfish grounds.

Suppose that A chooses that the B-body-person should get the pleasant treatment and the A-body-person the unpleasant treatment; and B chooses conversely (this might indicate that they thought that 'changing bodies' was indeed a good description of the outcome). The experimenter cannot act in accordance with both these sets of preferences, those expressed by A and those expressed by B. Hence there is one clear sense in which A and B cannot both get what they want: namely, that if the experimenter, before the experiment, announces to A and B that he intends to carry out the alternative (for example), of treating the B-body-person unpleasantly and the A-body-person pleasantly—then A can say rightly, 'That's not the outcome I chose to happen', and B can say rightly, 'That's just the outcome I chose to happen.' So, evidently, A and B before the experiment can each come to know either that the outcome he chose will be that which will happen, or that the one he chose will not happen, and in that sense they can get or fail to get what they wanted. But is it also true that when the experimenter proceeds *after* the experiment to act in accordance with one of the preferences and not the other, then one of A and B will have got what he wanted, and the other not?

There seems very good ground for saying so. For suppose the experimenter, having elicited A's and B's preference, says nothing to A and B about what he will do; conducts the experiment; and then, for example, gives the unpleasant treatment to the B-body-person and the pleasant treatment to the A-body-person. Then the B-body-person will not only complain of the unpleasant treatment as such, but will complain (since he has A's memories) that that was not the outcome he chose, since he chose that the B-body-person should be well treated; and since *A* made his choice in selfish spirit, he may add that he precisely chose in that way because he did not want the unpleasant things to happen to *him*. The *A*-body-person meanwhile will express satisfaction both at the receipt of the $100,000, and also at the fact that the experimenter has chosen to act in the way that he, *B*, so wisely chose. These facts make a strong case for saying that the experimenter has brought it about that *B* did in the outcome get what he wanted and *A* did not. It is therefore a strong case for saying that the *B*-body-person really is *A*, and the *A*-body-person really is *B*; and therefore for saying that the process of the experiment really is that of changing bodies. For the same reasons it would seem that *A* and *B* in our example really did choose wisely, and that it was *A*'s bad luck that the choice he correctly made was not carried out, *B*'s good luck that the choice he correctly made was carried out. This seems to show that to care about what happens to me in the future is not necessarily to care about what happens to *this* body (the one I now have); and this in turn might be taken to show that in some sense of Descartes's obscure phrase, I and my body are 'really distinct' (though, of course, nothing in these considerations could support the idea that I could exist without a body at all).

These suggestions seem to be reinforced if we consider the cases where *A* and *B* make other choices with regard to the experiment. Suppose that *A* chooses that the *A*-body-person should get the money, and the *B*-body-person get the pain, and *B* chooses conversely. Here again there can be no outcome which matches the expressed preferences of both of them: they cannot both get what they want. The experimenter announces, before the experiment, that the *A*-body-person will in fact get the money, and the *B*-body-person will get the pain. So *A* at this stage gets what he wants (the announced outcome matches his expressed preference). After the experiment, the distribution is carried out as announced. Both the *A*-body-person and the *B*-body-person will have to agree that what is happening is in accordance with the preference that *A* originally expressed. The *B*-body-person will naturally express this acknowledgement (since he has *A*'s memories) by saying that this is the distribution he chose; he will recall, among other things, the experimenter announcing this outcome, his approving it as what he chose, and so forth. However, he (the *B*-body-person) certainly does not like what is now happening to him, and would much prefer to be receiving what the *A*-body-person is receiving—namely, $100,000. The *A*-body-person will on the other hand recall choosing an outcome other than this one, but will reckon it good luck that the experimenter did not do what he recalls choosing. It looks, then, as though the *A*-body-person has got what he wanted, but not what he chose, while the *B*-body-person has got what he chose, but not what he wanted. So once more it looks as though they are, respectively, *B* and *A*; and that in this case the original choices of both *A* and *B* were unwise.

Suppose, lastly, that in the original choice *A* takes the line of the first case and *B* of the second: that is, *A* chooses that the *B*-body-person should get the money and the *A*-body-person the pain, and *B* chooses exactly the same thing. In this case, the experimenter would seem to be in the happy situation of giving both persons what they want—or at least, like God, what they have chosen. In this case, the *B*-body-person likes what he is receiving, recalls choosing it, and congratulates himself on the wisdom of (as he puts it) his choice; while the *A*-body-person does not like what he is receiving, recalls choosing it, and is forced to acknowledge that (as he puts it) his choice was unwise. So once more we seem to get results to support the suggestions drawn from the first case.

Let us now consider the question, not of *A* and *B* choosing certain outcomes to take place after the experiment, but of their willingness to engage in the experiment at all. If they were initially inclined to accept the description of the experiment as 'changing bodies' then one thing that would interest them would be the character of the other person's body. In this respect also what would happen after the experiment would seem to suggest that 'changing bodies' was a good description of the experiment. If *A* and *B* agreed to the experiment, being each not displeased with the appearance, physique, and so forth of the other person's body; after the experiment the *B*-body-person might well be found saying such things as: 'When I agreed to this experiment, I thought that *B*'s face was quite attractive, but now I look at it in the mirror, I am not so sure'; or the *A*-body-person might say 'When I agreed to this experiment I did not know that *A* had a wooden leg; but now, after it is over, I find that I have this wooden leg, and I want the experiment reversed.' It is possible that he might say further that he finds the leg very uncomfortable, and that the *B*-body-person should say, for instance, that he recalls that he found it very uncomfortable at first, but one gets used to it: but perhaps one would need to know more than at least I do about the physiology of habituation to artificial limbs to know whether the *A*-body-person would find the leg uncomfortable: that body, after all, has had the leg on it for some time. But apart from this sort of detail, the general line of the outcome regarded from this point of view seems to confirm our previous conclusions about the experiment.

Now let us suppose that when the experiment is proposed (in non-question-begging terms) *A* and *B* think rather of their psychological advantages and disadvantages. *A*'s thoughts turn primarily to certain sorts of anxiety to which he is very prone, while *B* is concerned with the frightful memories he has of past experiences which still distress him. They each hope that the experiment will in some way result in their being able to get away from these things. They may even have been impressed by philosophical arguments to the effect that bodily continuity is at least a necessary condition of personal identity: A, for example, reasons that, granted the experiment comes off, then the person who is bodily continuous with him will not have this anxiety, while the other person will no doubt have some anxiety—perhaps in some sense his anxiety—and at least that person will not be he. The experiment is performed and the experimenter (to whom A and B previously revealed privately their several difficulties and hopes) asks the A-body-person whether he has gotten rid of his anxiety. This person presumably replies that he does not know what the man is talking about; he never had such anxiety, but he did have some very disagreeable memories, and recalls engaging in the experiment to get rid of them, and is disappointed to discover that he still has them. The B-body-person will react in a similar way to questions about his painful memories, pointing out that he still has his anxiety. These results seem to confirm still further the description of the experiment as 'changing bodies'. And all the results suggest that the only rational thing to do, confronted with such an experiment, would be to identify oneself with one's memories, and so forth, and not with one's body. The philosophical arguments designed to show that bodily continuity was at least a necessary condition of personal identity would seem to be just mistaken.

Let us now consider something apparently different. Someone in whose power I am tells me that I am going to be tortured tomorrow. I am frightened, and look forward to tomorrow in great apprehension. He adds that when the time comes, I shall not remember being told that this was going to happen to me, since shortly before the torture something else will be done to me which will make me forget the announcement. This certainly will not cheer me up, since I know perfectly well that I can forget things, and that there is such a thing as indeed being tortured unexpectedly because I had forgotten or been made to forget a prediction of the torture: that will still be a torture which, so long as I do know about the prediction, I look forward to in fear. He then adds that my forgetting the announcement will be only part of a larger process: when the moment of torture comes, I shall not remember any of the things I am now in a position to remember. This does not cheer me up either, since I can readily conceive of being involved in an accident, for instance, as a result of which I wake up in a completely amnesiac state and also in great pain; that could certainly happen to me, I should not like it to happen to me, nor to know that it was going to happen to me. He now further adds that at the moment of torture I shall not only not remember the things I am now in a position to remember, but will have a different set of impressions of my past, quite different from the memories I now have.

I do not think that this would cheer me up either. For I can at least conceive the possibility, if not the concrete reality, of going completely mad, and thinking perhaps that I am George IV or somebody; and being told that something like that was going to happen to me would have no tendency to reduce the terror of being told authoritatively that I was going to be tortured, but would merely compound the horror. Nor do I see why I should be put into any better frame of mind by the person in charge adding lastly that the impressions of my past with which I shall be equipped on the eve of torture will exactly fit the past of another person now living, and that indeed I shall acquire these impressions by (for instance) information now in his brain being copied into mine. Fear, surely, would still be the proper reaction: and not because one did not know what was going to happen, but because in one vital respect at least one did know what was going to happen—torture, which one can indeed expect to happen to oneself, and to be preceded by certain mental derangements as well.

If this is right, the whole question seems now to be totally mysterious. For what we have just been through is of course merely one side, differently represented, of the transaction which we considered before; and it represents it as a perfectly hateful prospect, while the previous considerations represented it as something one should rationally, perhaps even cheerfully, choose out of the options there presented. It is differently presented, of course, and in two notable respects; but when we look at these two differences of presentation, can we really convince ourselves that the second presentation is wrong or misleading, thus leaving the road open to the first version which at the time seemed so convincing? Surely not.

The first difference is that in the second version the torture is throughout represented as going to happen to *me*: 'you', the man in charge persistently says. Thus he is not very neutral. But should he have been neutral? Or, to put it another way, does his use of the second person have a merely emotional and rhetorical effect on me, making me afraid when further reflection would have shown that I had no reason to be? It is certainly not obviously so. The problem just is that through every step of his predictions I seem to be able to follow him successfully. And if I reflect on whether what he has said gives me grounds for fearing that I shall be tortured, I could consider that behind my fears lies some principle such as this: that my undergoing physical pain in the future is not excluded by any psychological state I may be in at the time, with the platitudinous exception of those psychological states which in themselves exclude experiencing pain, notably (if it is a psychological state) unconsciousness. In particular, what impressions I have about the past will not have any effect on whether I undergo the pain or not. This principle seems sound enough.

It is an important fact that not everything I would, as things are, regard as an evil would be something that I should rationally fear as an evil if it were predicted that it would happen to me in the future and also predicted that I should undergo significant psychological changes in the meantime. For the fact that I regard that happening, things being as they are, as an evil can be dependent on factors of belief or character which might themselves be modified by the psychological changes in question. Thus if I am appallingly subject to acrophobia, and am told that I shall find myself on top of a steep mountain in the near future, I shall to that extent be afraid; but if I am told that I shall be psychologically changed in the meantime in such a way as to rid me of my acrophobia (and as with the other prediction, I believe it), then I have no reason to be afraid of the predicted happening, or at least not the same reason. Again, I might look forward to meeting a certain person again with either alarm or excitement because of my memories of our past relations. In some part, these memories operate in connection with my emotion, not only on the present time, but projectively forward: for it is to a meeting itself affected by the presence of those memories that I look forward. If I am convinced that when the time comes I shall not have those memories, then I shall not have just the same reasons as before for looking forward to that meeting with the one emotion or the other. (Spiritualism, incidentally, appears to involve the belief that I have just the same reasons for a given attitude towards encountering people again after I am dead, as I did before: with the one modification that I can be sure it will all be very nice.)

Physical pain, however, the example which for simplicity (and not for any obsessional reason) I have taken, is absolutely minimally dependent on character or belief. No amount of change in my character or my beliefs would seem to affect substantially the nastiness of tortures applied to me; correspondingly, no degree of predicted change in my character and beliefs can unseat the fear of torture which, together with those changes is predicted for me.

I am not at all suggesting that the *only* basis, or indeed the only rational basis, for fear in the face of these various predictions is how things will be relative to my psychological state in the eventual outcome. I am merely pointing out that this is one component; it is not the only one. For certainly one will fear and otherwise reject the changes themselves, or in very many cases one would. Thus one of the old paradoxes of hedonistic utilitarianism; if one had assurances that undergoing certain operations and being attached to a machine would provide one for the rest of one's existence with an unending sequence of delicious and varied experiences, one might very well reject the option, and react with fear if someone proposed to apply it compulsorily;

and that fear and horror would seem appropriate reactions in the second case may help to discredit the interpretation (if anyone has the nerve to propose it) that one's reason for rejecting the option voluntarily would be a consciousness of duties to others which one in one's hedonic state would leave undone. The prospect of contented madness or vegetableness is found by many (not perhaps by all) appalling in ways which are obviously not a function of how things would then be for them, for things would then be for them not appalling. In the case we are at present discussing, these sorts of considerations seem merely to make it clearer that the predictions of the man in charge provide a double ground of horror: at the prospect of torture, and at the prospect of the change in character and in impressions of the past that will precede it. And certainly, to repeat what has already been said, the prospect of the second certainly seems to provide no ground for rejecting or not fearing the prospect of the first.

I said that there were two notable differences between the second presentation of our situation and the first. The first difference, which we have just said something about, was that the man predicted the torture for *me*, a psychologically very changed 'me'. We have yet to find a reason for saying that he should not have done this, or that I really should be unable to follow him if he does; I seem to be able to follow him only too well. The second difference is that in this presentation he does not mention the other man, except in the somewhat incidental role of being the provenance of the impressions of the past I end up with. He does not mention him at all as someone who will end up with impressions of the past derived from me (and, incidentally, with $100,000 as well—a consideration which, in the frame of mind appropriate to this version, will merely make me jealous).

But why *should* he mention this man and what is going to happen to him? My selfish concern is to be told what is going to happen to me, and now I know: torture, preceded by changes of character, brain operations, changes in impressions of the past. The knowledge that one other person, or none, or many will be similarly mistreated may affect me in other ways, of sympathy, greater horror at the power of this tyrant, and so forth; but surely it cannot affect my expectations of torture? But—someone will say—this is to leave out exactly the feature which, as the first presentation of the case showed, makes all the difference: for it is to leave out the person who, as the first presentation showed, will be you. It is to leave out not merely a feature which should fundamentally affect your fears, it is to leave out the very person for whom you are fearful. So of course, the objector will say, this makes all the difference.

But can it? Consider the following series of cases. In each case we are to suppose that after what is described, *A* is, as before, to be tortured; we are also to suppose the person A is informed beforehand that just these things followed by the torture will happen to him:

(*i*) A is subjected to an operation which produces total amnesia;

(*ii*) Amnesia is produced in A, and other interference leads to certain changes in his character;

(*iii*) changes in his character are produced, and at the same time certain illusory 'memory' beliefs are induced in him; these are of a quite fictitious kind and do not fit the life of any actual person;

(*iv*) the same as (*iii*), except that both the character traits and the 'memory' impressions are designed to be appropriate to another actual person, B;

(*v*) the same as (*iv*), except that the result is produced by putting the information into A from the brain of B, by a method which leaves B the same as he was before;

(*vi*) the same happens to A as in (*v*), but B is not left the same, since a similar operation is conducted in the reverse direction.

I take it that no one is going to dispute that A has reasons, and fairly straightforward reasons, for fear of pain when the prospect is that of situation (*i*); there seems no conceivable reason why this should not extend to situation (*ii*), and the situation (*iii*) can surely introduce no difference of principle— it just seems a situation which for more than one reason we should have grounds of fearing, as suggested above. Situation (*iv*) at least introduces the person B, who was the focus of the objection we are now discussing. But it does not seem to introduce him in any way which makes a material difference; if I can expect pain through a transformation which involves new 'memory'-impressions, it would seem a purely external fact, relative to that, that the 'memory'-impressions had a model. Nor, in (*iv*), do we satisfy a causal condition which I mentioned at the beginning for the 'memories' actually being memories; though notice that if the job were done thoroughly, I might well be able to elicit from the A-body-person the kinds of remarks about his previous expectations of the experiment—remarks appropriate to the original B—which so impressed us in the first version of the story. I shall have a similar assurance of this being so in situation (*v*), where, moreover, a plausible application of the causal condition is available.

But two things are to be noticed about this situation. First, if we concentrate on A and the A-body-person, we do not seem to have added anything which from the point of view of his fears makes any material difference; just as, in the move from (*iii*) to (*iv*), it made no relevant difference that the new 'memory'-impressions which precede the pain had, as it happened, a model, so in the move from (*iv*) to (*v*) all we have added is that they have a model which is also their cause: and it is still difficult to see why that, to him looking forward, could possibly make the difference between expecting pain and not expecting pain. To illustrate that point from the case of character: if A is capable of expecting pain, he is capable of expecting pain preceded by a change in his dispositions—and to that expectation it can make no difference, whether that change in his dispositions is modelled on, or indeed indirectly caused by, the dispositions of some other person. If his fears can, as it were, reach through the change, it seems a mere trimming how the change is in fact induced. The second point about situation (v) is that if the crucial question for A's fears with regard to what befalls the A-body-person is whether the A-body-person is or is not the person B,[2] then that condition has not yet been satisfied in situation (v): for there we have an undisputed B in addition to the A-body-person, and certainly those two are not the same person.

But in situation (vi), we seemed to think, that is finally what he is. But if A's original fears could reach through the expected changes in (v), as they did in (iv) and (iii), then certainly they can reach through in (vi). Indeed, from the point of view of A's expectations and fears, there is less difference between (vi) and (v) than there is between (v) and (iv) or between (iv) and (iii). In those transitions, there were at least differences—though we could not see that they were really relevant differences—in the content and cause of what happened to him; in the present case there is absolutely no difference at all in what happens to him, the only difference being in what happens to someone else. If he can fear pain when (v) is predicted, why should he cease to when (vi) is?

I can see only one way of relevantly laying great weight on the transition from (v) to (vi); and this involves a considerable difficulty. This is to deny that, as I put it, the transition from (v) to (vi) involves merely the addition of something happening to *somebody else*; what rather it does, it will be said, is to involve the reintroduction of A himself, as the B-body-person; since he has reappeared in this form, it is for this person, and not for the unfortunate A-body-person, that A will have his expectations. This is to reassert, in effect, the viewpoint emphasized in our first presentation of the experiment. But this surely has the consequence that A should not have fears for the A-body-person who appeared in situation (v). For by the present argument, the A-body-person in (vi) is not A; the B-body-person is. But the A-body-person in (v) is, in character, history, everything, exactly the same as the A-body-person in (vi); so if the latter is not A, then neither is the former. (It is this point, no doubt, that encourages one to speak of the difference

[2]This of course does not have to be the crucial question, but it seems one fair way of taking up the present objection.

that goes with (vi) as being, on the present view, the *reintroduction* of A.) But no one else in (v) has any better claim to be A. So in (v), it seems, A just does not exist. This would certainly explain why A should have no fears for the state of things in (v)—though he might well have fears for the path to it. But it rather looked earlier as though he could well have fears for the state of things in (v). Let us grant, however, that that was an illusion, and that A really does not exist in (v); then does he exist in (iv), (iii), (ii), or (i)? It seems very difficult to deny it for (i) and (ii); are we perhaps to draw the line between (iii) and (iv)?

Here someone will say: you must not insist on drawing a line—borderline cases are borderline cases, and you must not push our concepts beyond their limits. But this well-known piece of advice, sensible as it is in many cases, seems in the present case to involve an extraordinary difficulty. It may intellectually comfort observers of A's situation; but what is A supposed to make of it? To be told that a future situation is a borderline one for its being myself that is hurt, that it is conceptually undecidable whether it will be me or not, is something which, it seems, I can do nothing with; because, in particular, it seems to have no comprehensible representation in my expectations and the emotions that go with them.

If I expect that a certain situation, S, will come about in the future, there is of course a wide range of emotions and concerns, directed on S, which I may experience now in relation to my expectation. Unless I am exceptionally egoistic, it is not a condition on my being concerned in relation to this expectation, that I myself will be involved in S—where my being 'involved' in S means that I figure in S as someone doing something at that time or having something done to me, or, again, that S will have consequences affecting me at that or some subsequent time. There are some emotions, however, which I will feel only if I will be involved in S, and fear is an obvious example.

Now the description of S under which it figures in my expectations will necessarily be, in various ways, indeterminate; and one way in which it may be indeterminate is that it leaves open whether I shall be involved in S or not. Thus I may have good reason to expect that one out of us five is going to get hurt, but no reason to expect it to be me rather than one of the others. My present emotions will be correspondingly affected by this indeterminacy. Thus, sticking to the egoistic concern involved in fear, I shall presumably be somewhat more cheerful than if I knew it was going to be me, somewhat less cheerful than if I had been left out altogether. Fear will be mixed with, and qualified by, apprehension; and so forth. These emotions revolve around the thought of the eventual determination of the indeterminacy; moments of straight fear focus on its really turning out to be me, of hope on its turning out not to be me. All the emotions are related to the coming about of what

I expect: and what I expect in such a case just cannot come about save by coming about in one of the ways or another.

There are other ways in which indeterminate expectations can be related to fear. Thus I may expect (perhaps neurotically) that something nasty is going to happen to me, indeed expect that when it happens it will take some determinate form, but have no range, or no closed range, of candidates for the determinate form to rehearse in my present thought. Different from this would be the fear of something radically indeterminate—the fear (one might say) of a nameless horror. If somebody had such a fear, one could even say that he had, in a sense, a perfectly determinate expectation: if what he expects indeed comes about, there will be nothing more determinate to be said about it after the event than was said in the expectation. Both these cases of course are cases of *fear* because one thing that is fixed amid the indeterminacy is the belief that it is me to which the things will happen.

Central to the expectation of S is the thought of what it will be like when it happens—thought which may be indeterminate, range over alternatives, and so forth. When S involves me, there can be the possibility of a special form of such thought: the thought of how it will be for me, the imaginative projection of myself as participant in S.[3]

I do not have to think about S in this way, when it involves me; but I may be able to. (It might be suggested that this possibility was even mirrored in the language, in the distinction between 'expecting to be hurt' and 'expecting that I shall be hurt'; but I am very doubtful about this point, which is in any case of no importance.)

Suppose now that there is an S with regard to which it is for conceptual reasons undecidable whether it involves me or not, as is proposed for the experimental situation by the line we are discussing. It is important that the expectation of S is not *indeterminate* in any of the ways we have just been considering. It is not like the nameless horror, since the fixed point of that case was that it was going to happen to the subject, and that made his state unequivocally fear. Nor is it like the expectation of the man who expects one of the five to be hurt; his fear was indeed equivocal, but its focus, and that of the expectation, was that when S came about, it would certainly come about in one way or the other. In the present case, fear (of the torture, that is to say, not of the initial experiment) seems neither appropriate, nor inappropriate, nor appropriately equivocal. Relatedly, the subject has an incurable difficulty about how he may think about S. If he engages in projective imaginative thinking (about how it will be for him), he implicitly answers

[3] For a more detailed treatment of issues related to this, see *Imagination and the Self*, British Academy (London, 1966); reprinted in P. F. Strawson (ed.), *Studies in Thought and Action* (Oxford, 1968), and in Bernard Williams, *Problems of the Self* (Cambridge, 1973).

the necessarily unanswerable question; if he thinks that he cannot engage in such thinking, it looks very much as if he also answers it, though in the opposite direction. Perhaps he must just refrain from such thinking; but is he just refraining from it, if it is incurably undecidable whether he can or cannot engage in it?

It may be said that all that these considerations can show is that fear, at any rate, does not get its proper footing in this case; but that there could be some other, more ambivalent, form of concern which would indeed be appropriate to this particular expectation, the expectation of the conceptually undecidable situation. There are, perhaps, analogous feelings that actually occur in actual situations. Thus material objects do occasionally undergo puzzling transformations which leave a conceptual shadow over their identity. Suppose I were sentimentally attached to an object to which this sort of thing then happened; then it might be that I could neither feel about it quite as I did originally, nor be totally indifferent to it, but would have some other and rather ambivalent feeling towards it. Similarly, it may be said, towards the prospective sufferer of pain, my identity relations with whom are conceptually shadowed, I can feel neither as I would if he were certainly me, nor as I would if he were certainly not, but rather some such ambivalent concern.

But this analogy does little to remove the most baffling aspect of the present case—an aspect which has already turned up in what was said about the subject's difficulty in thinking either projectively or non-projectively about the situation. For to regard the prospective pain-sufferer *just* like the transmogrified object of sentiment, and to conceive of my ambivalent distress about his future pain as just like ambivalent distress about some future damage to such an object, is of course to leave him and me clearly distinct from one another, and thus to displace the conceptual shadow from its proper place. I have to get nearer to him than that. But is there any nearer that I can get to him without expecting his pain? If there is, the analogy has not shown us it. We can certainly not get nearer by expecting, as it were, *ambivalent* pain; there is no place at all for that. There seems to be an obstinate bafflement to mirroring in my expectations a situation in which it is conceptually undecidable whether I occur.

The bafflement seems, moreover, to turn to plain absurdity if we move from conceptual undecidability to its close friend and neighbour, conventionalist decision. This comes out if we consider another description, overtly conventionalist, of the series of cases which occasioned the present discussion. This description would reject a point I relied on in an earlier argument—namely, that if we deny that the A-body-person in (vi) is A (because the B-body-person is), then we must deny that the A-body-person in (*v*) is *A*, since they are exactly the same. 'No,' it may be said, 'this is just to assume that we say the same in different sorts of situation. No doubt when we have the very good candidate for being *A*—namely, the *B*-body-person—we call him *A*; but this does not mean that we should not call the *A*-body-person *A* in that other situation when we have no better candidate around. Different situations call for different descriptions.' This line of talk is the sort of thing indeed appropriate to lawyers deciding the ownership of some property which has undergone some bewildering set of transformations; they just have to decide, and in each situation, let us suppose, it has got to go to somebody, on as reasonable grounds as the facts and the law admit. But as a line to deal with a person's fears or expectations about his own future, it seems to have no sense at all. If *A*'s fears can extend to what will happen to the *A*-body-person in (*v*), I do not see how they can be rationally diverted from the fate of the exactly similar person in (*vi*) by his being told that someone would have a reason in the latter situation which he would not have in the former for deciding to call another person *A*.

Thus, to sum up, it looks as though there are two presentations of the imagined experiment and the choice associated with it, each of which carries conviction, and which lead to contrary conclusions. The idea, moreover, that the situation after the experiment is conceptually undecidable in the relevant respect seems not to assist, but rather to increase, the puzzlement; while the idea (so often appealed to in these matters) that it is conventionally decidable is even worse. Following from all that, I am not in the least clear which option it would be wise to take if one were presented with them before the experiment. I find that rather disturbing.

Whatever the puzzlement, there is one feature of the arguments which have led to it which is worth picking out, since it runs counter to something which is, I think, often rather vaguely supposed. It is often recognized that there are 'first-personal' and 'third-personal' aspects of questions about persons, and that there are difficulties about the relations between them. It is also recognized that 'mentalistic' considerations (as we may vaguely call them) and considerations of bodily continuity are involved in questions of personal identity (which is not to say that there are mentalistic and bodily criteria of personal identity). It is tempting to think that the two distinctions run in parallel: roughly, that a first-personal approach concentrates attention on mentalistic considerations, while a third-personal approach emphasizes considerations of bodily continuity. The present discussion is an illustration of exactly the opposite. The first argument, which led to the 'mentalistic' conclusion that *A* and *B* would change bodies and that each person should identify himself with the destination of his memories and character, was an argument entirely conducted in third-personal terms. The second argument, which suggested the bodily continuity identification, concerned itself with the first-personal issue of what A could expect. That this is so seems to me (though I will not discuss it further here) of some significance.

I will end by suggesting one rather shaky way in which one might approach a resolution of the problem, using only the limited materials already available.

The apparently decisive arguments of the first presentation, which suggested that A should identify himself with the B-body-person, turned on the extreme neatness of the situation in satisfying, if any could, the description of 'changing bodies'. But this neatness is basically artificial; it is the product of the will of the experimenter to produce a situation which would naturally elicit, with minimum hesitation, that description. By the sorts of methods he employed, he could easily have left off earlier or gone on further. He could have stopped at situation (v), leaving B as he was; or he could have gone on and produced two persons each with A-like character and memories, as well as one or two with B-like characteristics. If he had done either of those, we should have been in yet greater difficulty about what to say; he just chose to make it as easy as possible for us to find something to say. Now if we had some model of ghostly persons in bodies, which were in some sense actually moved around by certain procedures, we could regard the neat experiment just as the *effective* experiment: the one method that really did result in the ghostly persons' changing places without being destroyed, dispersed, or whatever. But we cannot seriously use such a model. The experimenter has not in the sense of that model *induced* a change of bodies; he has rather produced the one situation out of a range of equally possible situations which we should be most disposed to call a change of bodies. As against this, the principle that one's fears can extend to future pain whatever psychological changes precede it seems positively straightforward. Perhaps, indeed, it is not; but we need to be shown what is wrong with it. Until we are shown what is wrong with it, we should perhaps decide that if we were the person A then, if we were to decide selfishly, we should pass the pain to the B-body-person. It would be risky: that there is room for the notion of a *risk* here is itself a major feature of the problem.

X

PERSONAL IDENTITY[1]

DEREK PARFIT

WE can, I think, describe cases in which, though we know the answer to every other question, we have no idea how to answer a question about personal identity. These cases are not covered by the criteria of personal identity that we actually use.

Do they present a problem?

It might be thought that they do not, because they could never occur. I suspect that some of them could. (Some, for instance, might become scientifically possible.) But I shall claim that even if they did they would present no problem.

My targets are two beliefs: one about the nature of personal identity, the other about its importance.

The first is that in these cases the question about identity must have an answer.

No one thinks this about, say, nations or machines. Our criteria for the identity of these do not cover certain cases. No one thinks that in these cases the questions 'Is it the same nation?' or 'Is it the same machine?' must have answers.

Some people believe that in this respect they are different. They agree that our criteria of personal identity do not cover certain cases, but they believe that the nature of their own identity through time is, somehow, such as to guarantee that in these cases questions about their identity must have answers. This belief might be expressed as follows: 'Whatever happens between now and any future time, either I shall still exist, or I shall not. Any future experience will either be *my* experience, or it will not.'

This first belief—in the special nature of personal identity—has, I think, certain effects. It makes people assume that the principle of self-interest is

From *Philosophical Review* (1971). Reprinted by permission of the author and the editor of the journal.
[1] I have been helped in writing this by D. Wiggins, D. F. Pears, P. F. Strawson, A. J. Ayer, M. Woods, N. Newman, and (through his publications) S. Shoemaker.

more rationally compelling than any moral principle. And it makes them more depressed by the thought of ageing and of death.

I cannot see how to disprove this first belief. I shall describe a problem case. But this can only make it seem implausible.

Another approach might be this. We might suggest that one cause of the belief is the projection of our emotions. When we imagine ourselves in a problem case, we do feel that the question 'Would it be me?' must have an answer. But what we take to be a bafflement about a further fact may be only the bafflement of our concern.

I shall not pursue this suggestion here. But one cause of our concern is the belief which is my second target. This is that unless the question about identity has an answer, we cannot answer certain important questions (questions about such matters as survival, memory, and responsibility).

Against this second belief my claim will be this. Certain important questions do presuppose a question about personal identity. But they can be freed of this presupposition. And when they are, the question about identity has no importance.

I

We can start by considering the much-discussed case of the man who, like an amoeba, divides.[2]

Wiggins has recently dramatized this case.[3] He first referred to the operation imagined by Shoemaker.[4] We suppose that my brain is transplanted into someone else's (brainless) body, and that the resulting person has my character and apparent memories of my life. Most of us would agree, after thought, that the resulting person is me. I shall here assume such agreement.[5]

Wiggins then imagined his own operation. My brain is divided, and each half is housed in a new body. Both resulting people have my character and apparent memories of my life.

---

[2] Implicit in John Locke, *Essay Concerning Human Understanding*, ed. by John W. Yolton (London, 1961), vol. ii, Ch. XXVII, sec. 18, and discussed by (among others) A. N. Prior in 'Opposite Number', *Review of Metaphysics*, 11 (1957–8), and 'Time, Existence and Identity', *Proceedings of the Aristotelian Society*, lvii (1965–6); J. Bennett in 'The Simplicity of the Soul', *Journal of Philosophy*, lxiv (1967); and R. Chisholm and S. Shoemaker in 'The Loose and Popular and the Strict and the Philosophical Senses of Identity', in *Perception and Personal Identity: Proceedings of the 1967 Oberlin Colloquium in Philosophy*, ed. by Norman Care and Robert H. Grimm (Cleveland, 1967).

[3] In *Identity and Spatio-Temporal Continuity* (Oxford, 1967), p. 50.

[4] In *Self-Knowledge and Self-Identity* (Ithaca, N.Y., 1963), p. 22.

[5] Those who would disagree are not making a mistake. For them my argument would need a different case. There must be some multiple transplant, faced with which these people would both find it hard to believe that there must be an answer to the question about personal identity, and be able to be shown that nothing of importance turns upon this question.

What happens to me? There seem only three possibilities: (1) I do not survive; (2) I survive as one of the two people; (3) I survive as both.

The trouble with (1) is this. We agreed that I could survive if my brain were successfully transplanted. And people have in fact survived with half their brains destroyed. It seems to follow that I could survive if half my brain were successfully transplanted and the other half were destroyed. But if this is so, how could I *not* survive if the other half were also successfully transplanted? How could a double success be a failure?

We can move to the second description. Perhaps one success is the maximum score. Perhaps I shall be one of the resulting people.

The trouble here is that in Wiggins's case each half of my brain is exactly similar, and so, to start with, is each resulting person. So how can I survive as only one of the two people? What can make me one of them rather than the other?

It seems clear that both of these descriptions—that I do not survive, and that I survive as one of the people—are highly implausible. Those who have accepted them must have assumed that they were the only possible descriptions.

What about our third description: that I survive as both people?

It might be said, 'If "survive" implies identity, this description makes no sense—you cannot be two people. If it does not, the description is irrelevant to a problem about identity.'

I shall later deny the second of these remarks. But there are ways of denying the first. We might say, 'What we have called "the two resulting people" are not two people. They are one person. I do survive Wiggins's operation. Its effect is to give me two bodies and a divided mind.'

It would shorten my argument if this were absurd. But I do not think it is. It is worth showing why.

We can, I suggest, imagine a divided mind. We can imagine a man having two simultaneous experiences, in having each of which he is unaware of having the other.

We may not even need to imagine this. Certain actual cases, to which Wiggins referred, seem to be best described in these terms. These involve the cutting of the bridge between the hemispheres of the brain. The aim was to cure epilepsy. But the result appears to be, in the surgeon's words, the creation of 'two separate spheres of consciousness',[6] each of which controls one half of the patient's body. What is experienced in each is, presumably, experienced by the patient.

There are certain complications in these actual cases. So let us imagine a simpler case.

[6] R. W. Sperry, in *Brain and Conscious Experience*, ed. by J. C. Eccles (New York, 1966), p. 299.

Suppose that the bridge between my hemispheres is brought under my voluntary control. This would enable me to disconnect my hemispheres as easily as if I were blinking. By doing this I would divide my mind. And we can suppose that when my mind is divided I can, in each half, bring about reunion.

This ability would have obvious uses. To give an example: I am near the end of a maths exam, and see two ways of tackling the last problem. I decide to divide my mind, to work, with each half, at one of two calculations, and then to reunite my mind and write a fair copy of the best result.

What shall I experience?

When I disconnect my hemispheres, my consciousness divides into two streams. But this division is not something that I experience. Each of my two streams of consciousness seems to have been straightforwardly continuous with my one stream of consciousness up to the moment of division. The only changes in each stream are the disappearance of half my visual field and the loss of sensation in, and control over, half my body.

Consider my experiences in what we can call my 'right-handed' stream. I remember that I assigned my right hand to the longer calculation. This I now begin. In working at this calculation I can see, from the movements of my left hand, that I am also working at the other. But I am not aware of working at the other. So I might, in my right-handed stream, wonder how, in my left-handed stream, I am getting on.

My work is now over. I am about to reunite my mind. What should I, in each stream, expect? Simply that I shall suddenly seem to remember just having thought out two calculations, in thinking out each of which I was not aware of thinking out the other. This, I submit, we can imagine. And if my mind was divided, these memories are correct.

In describing this episode, I assumed that there were two series of thoughts, and that they were both mine. If my two hands visibly wrote out two calculations, and if I claimed to remember two corresponding series of thoughts, this is surely what we should want to say.

If it is, then a person's mental history need not be like a canal, with only one channel. It could be like a river, with islands, and with separate streams.

To apply this to Wiggins's operation: we mentioned the view that it gives me two bodies and a divided mind. We cannot now call this absurd. But it is, I think, unsatisfactory.

There were two features of the case of the exam that made us want to say that only one person was involved. The mind was soon reunited, and there was only one body. If a mind was permanently divided and its halves developed in different ways, the point of speaking of one person would start to disappear. Wiggins's case, where there are also two bodies, seems to be over the borderline. After I have had his operation, the two 'products' each have all the attributes of a person. They could live at opposite ends of the earth. (If they later met, they might even fail to recognize each other.) It would become intolerable to deny that they were different people.

Suppose we admit that they are different people. Could we still claim that I survived as both, using 'survive' to imply identity?

We could. For we might suggest that two people could compose a third. We might say, 'I do survive Wiggins's operation as two people. They can be different people, and yet be me, in just the way in which the Pope's three crowns are one crown.'[7]

This is a possible way of giving sense to the claim that I survive as two different people, using 'survive' to imply identity. But it keeps the language of identity only by changing the concept of a person. And there are obvious objections to this change.[8]

The alternative, for which I shall argue, is to give up the language of identity. We can suggest that I survive as two different people without implying that I am these people.

When I first mentioned this alternative, I mentioned this objection: 'If your new way of talking does not imply identity, it cannot solve our problem. For that is about identity. The problem is that all the possible answers to the question about identity are highly implausible.'

We can now answer this objection.

We can start by reminding ourselves that this is an objection only if we have one or both of the beliefs which I mentioned at the start of this paper.

The first was the belief that to any question about personal identity, in any describable case, there must be a true answer. For those with this belief, Wiggins's case is doubly perplexing. If all the possible answers are implausible, it is hard to decide which of them is true, and hard even to keep the belief that one of them must be true. If we give up this belief, as I think we should, these problems disappear. We shall then regard the case as like many others in which, for quite unpuzzling reasons, there *is* no answer to a question about identity. (Consider 'Was England the same nation after 1066?')

Wiggins's case makes the first belief implausible. It also makes it trivial.

---

[7] Cf. David Wiggins, op. cit., p. 40.

[8] Suppose the resulting people fight a duel. Are there three people fighting, one on each side, and one on both? And suppose one of the bullets kills. Are there two acts, one murder and one suicide? How many people are left alive? One? Two? (We could hardly say, 'One and a half.') We could talk in this way. But instead of saying that the resulting people *are* the original person—so that the pair is a trio—it would be far simpler to treat them as a pair, and describe their relation to the original person in some new way. (I owe this suggested way of talking, and the objections to it, to Michael Woods.)

For it undermines the second belief. This was the belief that important questions turn upon the question about identity. (It is worth pointing out that those who have only this second belief do not think that there must *be* an answer to this question, but rather that we must decide upon an answer.)

Against this second belief my claim is this. Certain questions do presuppose a question about personal identity. And because these questions *are* important, Wiggins's case does present a problem. But we cannot solve this problem by answering the question about identity. We can solve this problem only by taking these important questions and prizing them apart from the question about identity. After we have done this, the question about identity (though we might for the sake of neatness decide it) has no further interest.

Because there are several questions which presuppose identity, this claim will take some time to fill out.

We can first return to the question of survival. This is a special case, for survival does not so much presuppose the retaining of identity as seem equivalent to it. It is thus the general relation which we need to prize apart from identity. We can then consider particular relations, such as those involved in memory and intention.

'Will I survive?' seems, I said, equivalent to 'Will there be some person alive who is the same person as me?'

If we treat these questions as equivalent, then the least unsatisfactory description of Wiggins's case is, I think, that I survive with two bodies and a divided mind.

Several writers have chosen to say that I am neither of the resulting people. Given our equivalence, this implies that I do not survive, and hence, presumably, that even if Wiggins's operation is not literally death, I ought, since I will not survive it, to regard it *as* death. But this seemed absurd.

It is worth repeating why. An emotion or attitude can be criticized for resting on a false belief, or for being inconsistent. A man who regarded Wiggins's operation as death must, I suggest, be open to one of these criticisms.

He might believe that his relation to each of the resulting people fails to contain some element which is contained in survival. But how can this be true? We agreed that he *would* survive if he stood in this very same relation to only *one* of the resulting people. So it cannot be the nature of this relation which makes it fail, in Wiggins's case, to be survival. It can only be its duplication.

Suppose that our man accepts this, but still regards division as death. His reaction would now seem wildly inconsistent. He would be like a man who, when told of a drug that could double his years of life, regarded the taking of this drug as death. The only difference in the case of division is that the extra years are to run concurrently. This is an interesting difference. But it cannot mean that there are *no* years to run.

I have argued this for those who think that there must, in Wiggins's case, be a true answer to the question about identity. For them, we might add, 'Perhaps the original person does lose his identity. But there may be other ways to do this than to die. One other way might be to multiply. To regard these as the same is to confuse nought with two.'

For those who think that the question of identity is up for decision, it would be clearly absurd to regard Wiggins's operation as death. These people would have to think, 'We could have chosen to say that I should be one of the resulting people. If we had, I should not have regarded it as death. But since we have chosen to say that I am neither person, I *do*.' This is hard even to understand.[9]

My first conclusion, then, is this. The relation of the original person to each of the resulting people contains all that interests us—all that matters—in any ordinary case of survival. This is why we need a sense in which one person can survive as two.[10]

One of my aims in the rest of this paper will be to suggest such a sense. But we can first make some general remarks.

II

Identity is a one–one relation. Wiggins's case serves to show that what matters in survival need not be one–one.

Wiggins's case is of course unlikely to occur. The relations which matter are, in fact, one–one. It is because they are that we can imply the holding of these relations by using the language of identity.

This use of language is convenient. But it can lead us astray. We may assume that what matters *is* identity and, hence, has the properties of identity.

In the case of the property of being one–one, this mistake is not serious. For what matters is in fact one–one. But in the case of another property, the mistake *is* serious. Identity is all-or-nothing. Most of the relations which matter in survival are, in fact, relations of degree. If we ignore this, we shall be led into quite ill-grounded attitudes and beliefs.

The claim that I have just made—that most of what matters are relations of degree—I have yet to support. Wiggins's case shows only that these relations need not be one–one. The merit of the case is not that it shows this in particular, but that it makes the first break between what matters and

---

[9] Cf. Sydney Shoemaker, in *Perception and Personal Identity: Proceedings of the 1967 Oberlin Colloquium in Philosophy.*
[10] Cf. David Wiggins, op. cit., p. 54.

identity. The belief that identity *is* what matters is hard to overcome. This is shown in most discussions of the problem cases which actually occur: cases, say, of amnesia or of brain damage. Once Wiggins's case has made one breach in this belief, the rest should be easier to remove.[11]

To turn to a recent debate: most of the relations which matter can be provisionally referred to under the heading 'psychological continuity' (which includes causal continuity). My claim is thus that we use the language of personal identity in order to imply such continuity. This is close to the view that psychological continuity provides a criterion of identity.

Williams has attacked this view with the following argument. Identity is a one–one relation. So any criterion of identity must appeal to a relation which is logically one–one. Psychological continuity is not logically one–one. So it cannot provide a criterion.[12]

Some writers have replied that it is enough if the relation appealed to is always in fact one–one.[13]

I suggest a slightly different reply. Psychological continuity is a ground for speaking of identity when it is one–one.

If psychological continuity took a one–many or branching form, we should need, I have argued, to abandon the language of identity. So this possibility would not count against this view.

We can make a stronger claim. This possibility would count in its favour.

The view might be defended as follows. Judgements of personal identity have great importance. What gives them their importance is the fact that they imply psychological continuity. This is why, whenever there is such continuity, we ought, if we can, to imply it by making a judgement of identity.

If psychological continuity took a branching form, no coherent set of judgements of identity could correspond to, and thus be used to imply, the branching form of this relation. But what we ought to do, in such a case,

---

[11] Bernard Williams's 'The Self and the Future', *Philosophical Review*, lxxix (1970), 161–80, is relevant here. He asks the question 'Shall I survive?' in a range of problem cases, and he shows how natural it is to believe (1) that this question must have an answer, (2) that the answer must be all-or-nothing, and (3) that there is a 'risk' of our reaching the *wrong* answer. Because these beliefs are so natural, we should need in undermining them to discuss their causes. These, I think, can be found in the ways in which we misinterpret what it is to remember (cf. section III below) and to anticipate (cf. Williams's 'Imagination and the Self', *Proceedings of the British Academy*, lii (1966), 105–24; and also in the way in which certain features of our egoistic concern—e.g. that it is simple, and applies to all imaginable cases—are 'projected' on to its object. (For another relevant discussion, see Terence Penelhum's *Survival and Disembodied Existence* (London, 1970), final chapters.)

[12] 'Personal Identity and Individuation', *Proceedings of the Aristotelian Society*, lvii (1956–7), 229–53; also *Analysis*, **21** (1960–1), 43–8.

[13] J. M. Shorter, 'More about Bodily Continuity and Personal Identity', *Analysis*, **22** (1961–2), 79–85; and Mrs. J. M. R. Jack (unpublished), who requires that this truth be embedded in a causal theory.

is take the importance which would attach to a judgement of identity and attach this importance directly to each limb of the branching relation. So this case helps to show that judgements of personal identity do derive their importance from the fact that they imply psychological continuity. It helps to show that when we can, usefully, speak of identity, this relation is our ground.

This argument appeals to a principle which Williams put forward.[14] The principle is that an important judgement should be asserted and denied only on importantly different grounds.

Williams applied this principle to a case in which one man is psychologically continuous with the dead Guy Fawkes, and a case in which two men are. His argument was this. If we treat psychological continuity as a sufficient ground for speaking of identity, we shall say that the one man is Guy Fawkes. But we could not say that the two men are, although we should have the same ground. This disobeys the principle. The remedy is to deny that the one man is Guy Fawkes, to insist that sameness of the body is necessary for identity.

Williams's principle can yield a different answer. Suppose we regard psychological continuity as more important than sameness of the body.[15] And suppose that the one man really is psychologically (and causally) continuous with Guy Fawkes. If he is, it would disobey the principle to deny that he is Guy Fawkes, for we have the same important ground as in a normal case of identity. In the case of the two men, we again have the same important ground. So we ought to take the importance from the judgement of identity and attach it directly to this ground. We ought to say, as in Wiggins's case, that each limb of the branching relation is as good as survival. This obeys the principle.

To sum up these remarks: even if psychological continuity is neither logically, nor always in fact, one–one, it can provide a criterion of identity. For this can appeal to the relation of *non-branching* psychological continuity, which is logically one–one.[16]

The criterion might be sketched as follows. 'X and Y are the same person if they are psychologically continuous and there is no person who is contemporary with either and psychologically continuous with the other.' We should need to explain what we mean by 'psychologically continuous' and

[14] *Analysis*, **21** (1960–1), 44.

[15] For the reasons given by A. M. Quinton in 'The Soul', *Journal of Philosophy*, lix (1962), 393–409.

[16] Cf. S. Shoemaker, 'Persons and Their Pasts', in the *American Philosophical Quarterly* (1970), and 'Wiggins on Identity', *Philosophical Review*, lxxix (1970), 542.

say how much continuity the criterion requires. We should then, I think, have described a sufficient condition for speaking of identity.[17]

We need to say something more. If we admit that psychological continuity might not be one–one, we need to say what we ought to do if it were not one–one. Otherwise our account would be open to the objections that it is incomplete and arbitrary.[18]

I have suggested that if psychological continuity took a branching form, we ought to speak in a new way, regarding what we describe as having the same significance as identity. This answers these objections.[19]

We can now return to our discussion. We have three remaining aims. One is to suggest a sense of 'survive' which does not imply identity. Another is to show that most of what matters in survival are relations of degree. A third is to show that none of these relations needs to be described in a way that presupposes identity.

We can take these aims in the reverse order.

III

The most important particular relation is that involved in memory. This is because it is so easy to believe that its description must refer to identity.[20] This belief about memory is an important cause of the view that personal identity has a special nature. But it has been well discussed by Shoemaker[21] and by Wiggins.[22] Sor we can be brief.

It may be a logical truth that we can only remember our own experiences. But we can frame a new concept for which this is not a logical truth. Let us call this 'q-memory'.

To sketch a definition[23] I am q-remembering an experience if (1) I have a belief about a past experience which seems in itself like a memory belief, (2) someone did have such an experience, and (3) my belief is dependent upon

[17] But not a necessary condition, for in the absence of psychological continuity bodily identity might be sufficient.

[18] Cf. Bernard Williams, 'Personal Identity and Individuation', *Proceedings of the Aristotelian Society*, lvii (1956–7), 240–1, and *Analysis*, 21 (1960–1), 44; and also Wiggins, op. cit., p. 38: 'if coincidence under [the concept] f is to be *genuinely* sufficient we must not withhold identity … simply because transitivity is threatened'.

[19] Williams produced another objection to the 'psychological criterion', that it makes it hard to explain the difference between the concepts of identity and exact similarity (*Analysis*, 21 (1960–1), 48). But if we include the requirement of causal continuity we avoid this objection (and one of those produced by Wiggins in his note 47).

[20] Those philosophers who have held this belief, from Butler onward, are too numerous to cite.

[21] 'Persons and Their Pasts'.

[22] In a paper on Butler's objection to Locke ('Locke, Butler and the Stream of Consciousness: and Men as a Natural Kind', *Philosophy*, 1976).

[23] I here follow Shoemaker's 'quasi-memory'. Cf. also Penelhum's 'retrocognition', in his article on 'Personal Identity', in the *Encyclopedia of Philosophy*, ed. by Paul Edwards.

this experience in the same way (whatever that is) in which a memory of an experience is dependent upon it.

According to (1) q-memories seem like memories. So I q-remember *having* experiences.

This may seem to make q-memory presuppose identity. One might say, 'My apparent memory of *having* an experience is an apparent memory of *my* having an experience. So how could I q-remember my having other people's experiences?'

This objection rests on a mistake. When I seem to remember an experience, I do indeed seem to remember *having* it.[24] But it cannot be a part of what I seem to remember about this experience that I, the person who now seems to remember it, am the person who had this experience.[25] That I am is something that I automatically assume. (My apparent memories sometimes come to me simply as the belief that *I* had a certain experience.) But it is something that I am justified in assuming only because I do not in fact have q-memories of other people's experiences.

Suppose that I did start to have such q-memories. If I did, I should cease to assume that my apparent memories must be about my own experiences. I should come to assess an apparent memory by asking two questions: (1) Does it tell me about a past experience? (2) If so, whose?

Moreover (and this is a crucial point) my apparent memories would now come to me as q-memories. Consider those of my apparent memories which do come to me simply as beliefs about my past: for example, 'I did that.' If I knew that I could q-remember other people's experiences, these beliefs would come to me in a more guarded form: for example, 'Someone—probably I—did that.' I might have to work out who it was.

I have suggested that the concept of q-memory is coherent. Wiggins's case provides an illustration. The resulting people, in his case, both have apparent memories of living the life of the original person. If they agree that they are not this person, they will have to regard these as only q-memories. And when they are asked a question like 'Have you heard this music before?' they might have to answer 'I am sure that I q-remember hearing it. But I am not sure whether I remember hearing it. I am not sure whether it was I who heard it, or the original person.'

We can next point out that on our definition every memory is also a q-

---

[24] As Shoemaker put it, I seem to remember the experience 'from the inside' (Persons and Their Pasts').

[25] This is what so many writers have overlooked. Cf. Thomas Reid: 'My memory testifies not only that this was done, but that it was done by me who now remember it' ('Of Identity', in *Essays on the Intellectual Powers of Man*, ed. by A. D. Woozley (London, 1941), p. 203). This mistake is discussed by A. B. Palma in 'Memory and Personal Identity', *Australasian Journal of Philosophy*, **42** (1964), 57.

memory. Memories are, simply, q-memories of one's own experiences. Since this is so, we could afford now to drop the concept of memory and use in its place the wider concept q-memory. If we did, we should describe the relation between an experience and what we now call a 'memory' of this experience in a way which does not presuppose that they are had by the same person.[26]

This way of describing this relation has certain merits. It vindicates the 'memory criterion' of personal identity against the charge of circularity.[27] And it might, I think, help with the problem of other minds.

But we must move on. We can next take the relation between an intention and a later action. It may be a logical truth that we can intend to perform only our own actions. But intentions can be redescribed as q-intentions. And one person could q-intend to perform another person's actions.

Wiggins's case again provides the illustration. We are supposing that neither of the resulting people is the original person. If so, we shall have to agree that the original person can, before the operation, q-intend to perform their actions. He might, for example, q-intend, as one of them, to continue his present career, and, as the other, to try something new.[28] (I say 'q-intend as one of them' because the phrase 'q-intend that one of them' would not convey the directness of the relation which is involved. If I intend that someone else should do something, I cannot get him to do it simply by forming this intention. But if I am the original person, and he is one of the resulting people, I can.)

The phrase 'q-intend as one of them' reminds us that we need a sense in which one person can survive as two. But we can first point out that the concepts of q-memory and q-intention give us our model for the others that we need: thus, a man who can q-remember could q-recognize, and be a q-

[26] It is not logically necessary that we only q-remember our own experiences. But it might be necessary on other grounds. This possibility is intriguingly explored by Shoemaker in his 'Persons and Their Pasts'. He shows that q-memories can provide a knowledge of the world only if the observations which are q-remembered trace out fairly continuous spatiotemporal paths. If the observations which are q-remembered traced out a network of frequently interlocking paths, they could not, I think, be usefully ascribed to persisting observers, but would have to be referred to in some more complex way. But in fact the observations which are q-remembered trace out single and separate paths; so we can ascribe them to ourselves. In other words, it is epistemologically necessary that the observations which are q-remembered should satisfy a certain general condition, one particular form of which allows them to be usefully self-ascribed.

[27] Cf. Wiggins's paper on Butler's objection to Locke.

[28] There are complications here. He could form *divergent* q-intentions only if he could distinguish, in advance, between the resulting people (e.g. as 'the left-hander' and 'the right-hander'). And he could be confident that such divergent q-intentions would be carried out only if he had reason to believe that neither of the resulting people would change their (inherited) mind. Suppose he was torn between duty and desire. He could not solve this dilemma by q-intending, as one of the resulting people, to do his duty, and, as the other, to do what he desires. For the one he q-intended to do his duty would face the same dilemma.

witness of, what he has never seen; and a man who can q-intend could have q-ambitions, make q-promises, and be q-responsible for.

To put this claim in general terms: many different relations are included within, or are a consequence of, psychological continuity. We describe these relations in ways which presuppose the continued existence of one person. But we could describe them in new ways which do not.

This suggests a bolder claim. It might be possible to think of experiences in a wholly 'impersonal' way. I shall not develop this claim here. What I shall try to describe is a way of thinking of our own identity through time which is more flexible, and less misleading, than the way in which we now think.

This way of thinking will allow for a sense in which one person can survive as two. A more important feature is that it treats survival as a matter of degree.

IV

We must first show the need for this second feature. I shall use two imaginary examples.

The first is the converse of Wiggins's case: fusion. Just as division serves to show that what matters in survival need not be one–one, so fusion serves to show that it can be a question of degree.

Physically, fusion is easy to describe. Two people come together. While they are unconscious, their two bodies grow into one. One person then wakes up.

The psychology of fusion is more complex. One detail we have already dealt with in the case of the exam. When my mind was reunited, I remembered just having thought out two calculations. The one person who results from a fusion can, similarly, q-remember living the lives of the two original people. None of their q-memories need be lost.

But some things must be lost. For any two people who fuse together will have different characteristics, different desires, and different intentions. How can these be combined?

We might suggest the following. Some of these will be compatible. These can coexist in the one resulting person. Some will be incompatible. These, if of equal strength, can cancel out, and if of different strengths, the stronger can be made weaker. And all these effects might be predictable.

To give examples—first, of compatibility: I like Palladio and intend to visit Venice. I am about to fuse with a person who likes Giotto and intends to visit Padua. I can know that the one person we shall become will have both tastes and both intentions. Second, of incompatibility: I hate red hair, and always vote Labour. The other person loves red hair, and always votes

Conservative. I can know that the one person we shall become will be indifferent to red hair, and a floating voter.

If we were about to undergo a fusion of this kind, would we regard it as death?

Some of us might. This is less absurd than regarding division as death. For after my division the two resulting people will be in every way like me, while after my fusion the one resulting person will not be wholly similar. This makes it easier to say, when faced with fusion, 'I shall not survive', thus continuing to regard survival as a matter of all-or-nothing.

This reaction is less absurd. But here are two analogies which tell against it.

First, fusion would involve the changing of some of our characteristics and some of our desires. But only the very self-satisfied would think of this as death. Many people welcome treatments with these effects.

Second, someone who is about to fuse can have, beforehand, just as much 'intentional control' over the actions of the resulting individual as someone who is about to marry can have, beforehand, over the actions of the resulting couple. And the choice of a partner for fusion can be just as well considered as the choice of a marriage partner. The two original people can make sure (perhaps by 'trial fusion') that they do have compatible characters, desires, and intentions.

I have suggested that fusion, while not clearly survival, is not clearly failure to survive, and hence that what matters in survival can have degrees.

To reinforce this claim we can now turn to a second example. This is provided by certain imaginary beings. These beings are just like ourselves except that they reproduce by a process of natural division.

We can illustrate the histories of these imagined beings with the aid of the diagram on the next page. The lines on the diagram represent the spatio-temporal paths which would be traced out by the bodies of these beings. We can call each single line (like the double line) a 'branch'; and we can call the whole structure a 'tree'. And let us suppose that each 'branch' corresponds to what is thought of as the life of one individual. These individuals are referred to as 'A', 'B + 1', and so forth.

Now, each single division is an instance of Wiggins's case. So A's relation to both $B + 1$ and $B + 2$ is just as good as survival. But what of A's relation to B + 30?

I said earlier that what matters in survival could be provisionally referred to as 'psychological continuity'. I must now distinguish this relation from another, which I shall call 'psychological connectedness'.

Let us say that the relation between a q-memory and the experience q-remembered is a 'direct' relation. Another 'direct' relation is that which holds

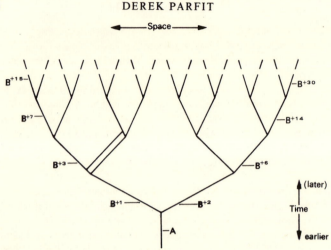

between a q-intention and the q-intended action. A third is that which holds between different expressions of some lasting q-characteristic.

'Psychological connectedness', as I define it, requires the holding of these direct psychological relations. 'Connectedness' is not transitive, since these relations are not transitive. Thus, if X q-remembers most of Y's life, and Y q-remembers most of Z's life, it does not follow that X q-remembers most of Z's life. And if X carries out the q-intentions of Y, and Y carries out the q-intentions of Z, it does not follow that X carries out the q-intentions of Z.

'Psychological continuity', in contrast, only requires overlapping chains of direct psychological relations. So 'continuity' *is* transitive.

To return to our diagram. A *is* psychologically continuous with $B + 30$. There are between the two continuous chains of overlapping relations. This, A has q-intentional control over $B + 2$, $B + 2$ has q-intentional control over $B + 6$, and so on up to $B + 30$. Or $B + 30$ can q-remember the life of $B + 14$, $B + 14$ can q-remember the life of $B + 6$, and so on back to A.[29]

A, however, need *not* be psychologically connected to $B + 30$. Connectedness requires direct relations. And if these beings are like us, A cannot stand in such relations to every individual in his indefinitely long 'tree'. Q-memories will weaken with the passage of time, and then fade away. Q-ambitions, once fulfilled, will be replaced by others. Q-characteristics will gradually change. In general, A stands in fewer and fewer direct psychological

[29] The chain of continuity must run in one direction of time. $B + 2$ is not, in the sense I intend, psychologically continuous with $B + 1$.

relations to an individual in his 'tree' the more remote that individual is. And if the individual is (like $B+30$) sufficiently remote, there may be between the two *no* direct psychological relations.

Now that we have distinguished the general relations of psychological continuity and psychological connectedness, I suggest that connectedness is a more important element in survival. As a claim about our own survival, this would need more arguments than I have space to give. But it seems clearly true for my imagined beings. A is as close psychologically to $B+1$ as I today am to myself tomorrow. A is as distant from $B+30$ as I am from my great-great-grandson.

Even if connectedness is not more important than continuity, the fact that one of these is a relation of degree is enough to show that what matters in survival can have degrees. And in any case the two relations are quite different. So our imagined beings would need a way of thinking in which this difference is recognized.

V

What I propose is this.

First, A can think of any individual, anywhere in his 'tree', as 'a descendant self'. This phrase implies psychological continuity. Similarly, any later individual can think of any earlier individual on the single path[30] which connects him to A as 'an ancestral self'.

Since psychological continuity is transitive, 'being an ancestral self of' and 'being a descendant self of' are also transitive.

To imply psychological connectedness I suggest the phrases 'one of my future selves' and 'one of my past selves'.

These are the phrases with which we can describe Wiggins's case. For having past and future selves is, what we needed, a way of continuing to exist which does not imply identity through time. The original person does, in this sense, survive Wiggins's operation: the two resulting people are his later selves. And they can each refer to him as 'my past self'. (They can share a past self without being the same self as each other.)

Since psychological connectedness is not transitive, and is a matter of degree, the relations 'being a past self of' and 'being a future self of' should themselves be treated as relations of degree. We allow for this series of descriptions: 'my most recent self', 'one of my earlier selves', 'one of my distant selves', 'hardly one of *my* past selves (I can only q-remember a few of his experiences)', and, finally, 'not in any way one of *my* past selves—just an ancestral self'.

This way of thinking would clearly suit our first imagined beings. But let

[30] Cf. David Wiggins, op. cit.

us now turn to a second kind of being. These reproduce by fusion as well as by division.[31] And let us suppose that they fuse every autumn and divide every spring. This yields the following diagram:

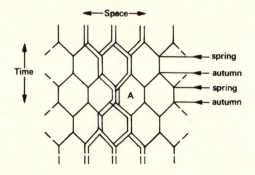

If A is the individual whose life is represented by the three-lined 'branch', the two-lined 'tree' represents those lives which are psychologically continuous with A's life. (It can be seen that each individual has his own 'tree', which overlaps with many others.)

For the imagined beings in this second world, the phrases 'an ancestral self' and 'a descendant self' would cover too much to be of much use. (There may well be pairs of dates such that every individual who ever lived before the first date was an ancestral self of every individual who ever will live after the second date.) Conversely, since the lives of each individual last for only half a year, the word 'I' would cover too little to do all of the work which it does for us. So part of this work would have to be done, for these second beings, by talk about past and future selves.

We can now point out a theoretical flaw in our proposed way of thinking. The phrase 'a past self of' implies psychological connectedness. Being a past self of is treated as a relation of degree, so that this phrase can be used to imply the varying degrees of psychological connectedness. But this phrase can imply only the degrees of connectedness between different lives. It cannot be used within a single life. And our way of delimiting successive lives does not refer to the degrees of psychological connectedness. Hence there is no guarantee that this phrase, 'a past self of', could be used whenever it was needed. There is no guarantee that psychological connectedness will not vary in degree within a single life.

This flaw would not concern our imagined beings. For they divide and

---

[31] Cf. Sydney Shoemaker in 'Persons and Their Pasts'.

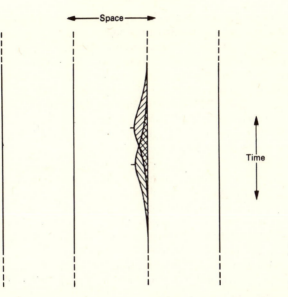

unite so frequently, and their lives are in consequence so short, that within a single life psychological connectedness would always stand at a maximum.

But let us look, finally, at a third kind of being.

In this world there is neither division nor union. There are a number of everlasting bodies, which gradually change in appearance. And direct psychological relations, as before, hold only over limited periods of time. This can be illustrated with a third diagram. In this diagram the two shadings represent the degrees of psychological connectedness to their two central points.

These beings could not use the way of thinking that we have proposed. Since there is no branching of psychological continuity, they would have to regard themselves as immortal. It might be said that this is what they are. But there is, I suggest, a better description.

Our beings would have one reason for thinking of themselves as immortal. The parts of each 'line' are all psychologically continuous. But the parts of each 'line' are not all psychologically connected. Direct psychological relations hold only between those parts which are close to each other in time. This gives our beings a reason for *not* thinking of each 'line' as corresponding to one single life. For if they did, they would have no way of implying these direct relations. When a speaker says, for example, 'I spent a period doing such and such', his hearers would not be entitled to assume that the speaker has any memories of this period, that his character then and now are in any way similar, that he is now carrying out any of the plans or intentions which he then had, and so forth. Because the word 'I' would carry none of these implications, it would not have for these 'immortal' beings the usefulness which it has for us.[32]

To gain a better way of thinking, we must revise the way of thinking that we proposed above. The revision is this. The distinction between successive selves can be made by reference, not to the branching of psychological continuity, but to the degrees of psychological connectedness. Since this connectedness is a matter of degree, the drawing of these distinctions can be left to the choice of the speaker and be allowed to vary from context to context.

On this way of thinking, the word 'I' can be used to imply the greatest degree of psychological connectedness. When the connections are reduced, when there has been any marked change of character or style of life, or any marked loss of memory, our imagined being would say, 'It was not I who did that, but an earlier self.' They could then describe in what ways, and to what degree, they are related to this earlier self.

This revised way of thinking would suit not only our 'immortal' beings. It is also the way in which we ourselves could think about our lives. And it is, I suggest, surprisingly natural.

One of its features, the distinction between successive selves, has already been used by several writers. To give an example, from Proust: 'we are incapable, while we are in love, of acting as fit predecessors of the next persons who, when we are in love no longer, we shall presently have become....'[33]

Although Proust distinguished between successive selves, he still thought of one person as being these different selves. This we would not do on the way of thinking that I propose. If I say, 'It will not be me, but one of my future selves', I do not imply that I will be that future self. He is one of my later selves, and I am one of his earlier selves. There is no underlying person who we both are.

To point out another feature of this way of thinking. When I say, 'There is no person who we both are', I am only giving my decision. Another person could say, 'It will be you', thus deciding differently. There is no question of either of these decisions being a mistake. Whether to say 'I', or 'one of my future selves', or 'a descendant self' is entirely a matter of choice. The matter of fact, which must be agreed, is only whether the disjunction applies. (The question 'Are X and Y the same person?' thus becomes 'Is X at least an ancestral [or descendant] self of Y?')

---

[32] Cf. Austin Duncan Jones, 'Man's Mentality', *Analysis,* **28** (1967–8), 65–70.
[33] *Within a Budding Grove* (London. 1949). i. 226 (my own translation).

VI

I have tried to show that what matters in the continued existence of a person are, for the most part, relations of degree. And I have proposed a way of thinking in which this would be recognized.

I shall end by suggesting two consequences and asking one question.

It is sometimes thought to be especially rational to act in our own best interests. But I suggest that the principle of self-interest has no force. There are only two genuine competitors in this particular field. One is the principle of biased rationality: do what will best achieve what you actually want. The other is the principle of impartiality: do what is in the best interests of everyone concerned.

The apparent force of the principle of self-interest derives, I think, from these two other principles.

The principle of self-interest is normally supported by the principle of biased rationality. This is because most people care about their own future interests.

Suppose that this prop is lacking. Suppose that a man does not care what happens to him in, say, the more distant future. To such a man, the principle of self-interest can only be propped up by an appeal to the principle of impartiality. We must say, 'Even if you don't care, you ought to take what happens to you then equally into account.' But for this, as a special claim, there seem to me no good arguments. It can only be supported as part of the general claim, 'You ought to take what happens to everyone equally into account.'[34]

The special claim tells a man to grant an *equal* weight to all the parts of his future. The argument for this can only be that all the parts of his future are *equally* parts of *his* future. This is true. But it is a truth too superficial to bear the weight of the argument. (To give an analogy: The unity of a nation is, in its nature, a matter of degree. It is therefore only a superficial truth that all of a man's compatriots are *equally* his compatriots. This truth cannot support a good argument for nationalism.)[35]

I have suggested that the principle of self-interest has no strength of its own. If this is so, there is no special problem in the fact that what we ought

---

[34] Cf. Thomas Nagel's *The Possibility of Altruism* (Oxford, 1970), in which the special claim is in effect defended as part of the general claim.

[35] The unity of a nation we seldom take for more than what it is. This is partly because we often think of nations, not as units, but in a more complex way. If we thought of ourselves in the way that I proposed, we might be less likely to take our own identity for more than what it is. We are, for example, sometimes told, 'It is irrational to act against your own interests. After all, it will be *you* who will regret it.' To this we could reply, 'No, not me. Not even one of my future selves. Just a descendant self.'

to do can be against our interests. There is only the general problem that it may not be what we want to do.

The second consequence which I shall mention is implied in the first. Egoism, the fear not of near but of distant death, the regret that so much of one's *only* life should have gone by—these are not, I think, wholly natural or instinctive. They are all strengthened by the beliefs about personal identity which I have been attacking. If we give up these beliefs, they should be weakened.

My final question is this. These emotions are bad, and if we weaken them we gain. But can we achieve this gain without, say, also weakening loyalty to, or love of, other particular selves? As Hume warned, the 'refined reflections which philosophy suggests ... cannot diminish ... our vicious passions ... without diminishing ... such as are virtuous. They are ... applicable to all our affections. In vain do we hope to direct their influence only to one side.'[36]

That hope *is* vain. But Hume had another: that more of what is bad depends upon false belief. This is also my hope.[37]

---

[36] 'The Sceptic', in 'Essays Moral, Political and Literary', *Hume's Moral and Political Philosophy* (New York, 1959), p. 349.

[37] (Footnote added in 1976.) Of the many things which I now regret in this paper, I shall briefly mention three. (1) Talk about 'successive selves' is only a *façon de parler*; taken as anything more it can be misleading. (2) I should not have claimed that connectedness was more important than continuity. I now think that neither relation can be shown to be more important than the other. (3) The real issue seems to me now this. Does personal identity just consist in bodily and psychological continuity, or is it a further fact, independent of the facts about these continuities? Our reactions to the 'problem cases' show, I think, that we believe the latter. And we seem inclined to believe that this further fact is peculiarly deep, and is all-or-nothing—we believe that in any describable case it must hold either completely or not at all. My main claim is *the denial of this further fact*. This is what may make a difference. (No one needs to be told that psychological continuity is, in part, a matter of degree.) For some further remarks, see 'On "The Importance of Self-identity"', *Journal of Philosophy*, 21 Oct. 1971, 'Later Selves and Moral Principles', in *Philosophy and Personal Relations*, ed. Alan Montefiore (Routledge & Kegan Paul, 1973), and 'Lewis, Perry, and What Matters', in *The Identities of Persons*, ed. Amelie Rorty (University of California Press, 1976).

NOTES ON THE CONTRIBUTORS

B. A. FARRELL is a Fellow of Corpus Christi College, Oxford, and Wilde Reader in Mental Philosophy.

PATRICK GARDINER is a Fellow of Magdalen College, Oxford.

G. A. COHEN is a Lecturer in the Department of Philosophy at University College, London.

J. A. DEUTSCH is Professor of Psychology at the University of California at San Diego.

STUART HAMPSHIRE is Warden of Wadham College, Oxford.

HILARY PUTNAM is Professor of Philosophy at Harvard University.

DONALD DAVIDSON is Professor of Philosophy at Princeton University.

THOMAS NAGEL is Professor of Philosophy at Princeton University.

BERNARD WILLIAMS is Knightbridge Professor of Philosophy at Cambridge.

DEREK PARFIT is a Fellow of All Souls' College, Oxford.

BIBLIOGRAPHY

1. CLASSICS

ARISTOTLE, *De Anima*.
ARISTOTLE, *Nicomachean Ethics*.
RENE DESCARTES, *The Passions of the Soul*.
BARUCH SPINOZA, *Ethics*.
JOHN LOCKE, *An Essay Concerning Human Understanding*.
DAVID HUME, *A Treatise of Human Nature*.
IMMANUEL KANT, *Critique of Pure Reason*.
ERNST MACH, *The Analysis of Sensations*.
WILLIAM JAMES, *The Principles of Psychology*.
MARCEL PROUST, *Remembrance of Things Past*.
SIGMUND FREUD, *Collected Works*.
BERTRAND RUSSELL, *The Analysis of Mind*.
LUDWIG WITTGENSTEIN, *Philosophical Investigations*.
GILBERT RYLE, *The Concept of Mind*.

2. SOME GENERAL BOOKS

G. E. M. ANSCOMBE, *Intention* (Oxford, 1958).
D. M. ARMSTRONG, *Bodily Sensations* (London, 1962).
— — *A Materialist Theory of the Mind* (London, 1968).
JONATHAN BENNETT, *Rationality* (London, 1964).
C. D. BROAD, *The Mind and Its Place in Nature* (London, 1925).
NAOM CHOMSKY, *Language and Mind* (New York, 1968).
ERIC D'ARCY, *Human Acts, An Essay in their Moral Evaluation* (Oxford, 1963).
D. C. DENNETT, *Content and Consciousness, An Analysis of Mental Phenomena* (London, 1969).
HERBERT FEIGL, *The 'Mental' and the 'Physical'* (Minneapolis, 1967).
PETER GEACH, *Mental Acts, Their Content and Their Objects* (London, 1957).
J. C. B. GOSLING, *Pleasure and Desire* (Oxford, 1969).
STUART HAMPSHIRE, *Thought and Action* (London, 1959).
— — *Freedom of Mind* (Oxford, 1972).
ANTHONY KENNY, *Action Emotion and Will* (London, 1963).
— — *The Anatomy of the Soul, Historical Studies in the Philosophy of Mind* (Oxford, 1973).
DON LOCKE, *Myself and Others, A Study in our Knowledge of Minds* (Oxford, 1968).
NORMAN MALCOLM, *Dreaming* (London, 1959).
MAURICE MERLEAU-PONTY, *Phenomenology of Perception* (London, 1962).
DAVID PEARS, *Questions in the Philosophy of Mind* (London, 1975).
R. S. PETERS, *The Concept of Motivation* (London, 1958).
H. H. PRICE, *Thinking and Experience* (London, 1953).

HILARY PUTNAM, *Philosophical Papers*, vol. 2: *Mind, Language and Reality* (Cambridge, 1975).

ANTHONY QUINTON, *The Nature of Things* (London, 1973).

JEAN-PAUL SARTRE, *Sketch for a Theory of the Emotions* (London, 1962).

— — *The Psychology of Imagination* (New York, 1966).

— — *Being and Nothingness, An Essay on Phenomenological Ontology* (New York, 1966).

ERWIN SCHRÖDINGER, *Mind and Matter* (Cambridge, 1958).

JEROME A. SHAFFER, *Philosophy of Mind* (Englewood Cliffs, 1968).

CHARLES SHERRINGTON, *Man On His Nature* (Harmondsworth, 1955).

SYDNEY SHOEMAKER, *Self-Knowledge and Self-Identity* (Ithaca, 1963).

P. F. STRAWSON, *Freedom and Resentment and Other Essays* (London, 1974).

RICHARD TAYLOR, *Action and Purpose* (Englewood Cliffs, 1966).

A. R. WHITE, *Attention* (Oxford, 1964).

BERNARD WILLIAMS, *Problems of the Self* (Cambridge, 1973).

JOHN WISDOM, *Other Minds* (Oxford, 1965).

3. ANTHOLOGIES

ALAN ROSS ANDERSON, *Minds and Machines* (Englewood Cliffs, 1964).

AMERICAN PHILOSOPHICAL QUARTERLY, *Studies in the Philosophy of Mind* (Oxford, 1972).

R. BINKLEY, R. BRONAUGH, and A. MARRAS, *Agent, Action and Reason* (Oxford, 1971).

ROBERT BORGER and FRANK CIOFFI, *Explanation in the Behavioural Sciences* (Cambridge, 1970).

C. V. BORST, *The Mind–Brain Identity Theory* (London, 1970).

S. C. BROWN, *Philosophy of Psychology* (London, 1974).

H.-N. CASTANEDA, *Intentionality, Minds and Perception* (Detroit, 1967).

V. C. CHAPPELL, *Philosophy of Mind* (Englewood Cliffs, 1962).

JOHN C. ECCLES, *Brain and Conscious Experience* (New York, 1966).

JOEL FEINBERG, *Moral Concepts* (Oxford, 1969).

ANTONY FLEW, *Body, Mind and Death* (New York, 1964).

DONALD F. GUSTAFSON, *Essays in Philosophical Psychology* (New York, 1964).

SAMUEL GUTTENPLAN, *Mind and Language*, Wolfson College Lectures 1974 (Oxford, 1975).

STUART HAMPSHIRE, *Philosophy of Mind* (New York, 1966).

SIDNEY HOOK, *Dimensions of Mind* (New York, 1961).

O. R. JONES, *The Private Language of Argument* (London, 1971).

ANTHONY KENNY et al., *The Nature of Mind* (Edinburgh, 1972).

PETER LASLETT, *The Physical Basis of Mind* (Oxford, 1968).

HAROLD MORICK, *Wittgenstein and the Problem of Other Minds* (New York, 1967).

HERBERT MORRIS, *Guilt and Shame* (Belmont, 1971).

GEORGE PITCHER, *Wittgenstein: The Philosophical Investigations* (London, 1968).

C. F. PRESLEY, *The Identity Theory of Mind* (Queensland, 1967).

KENNETH M. SAYRE and FREDERICK J. CROSSON, *The Modeling of Mind* (Notre Dame, 1963).

J. R. SMYTHIES, *Brain and Mind* (London, 1965).

P. F. STRAWSON, *Studies in the Philosophy of Thought and Action* (Oxford, 1968).

G. J. WARNOCK, *Philosophy of Perception* (Oxford, 1967).

A. R. WHITE, *Philosophy of Action* (Oxford, 1968).

OSCAR P. WOOD and GEORGE PITCHER, *Ryle* (London, 1971).
G. N. A. VESEY, *Body and Mind* (London, 1964).

4. SOME TOPICS DISCUSSED IN THIS BOOK

(a) *Psycho-analysis and the Unconscious*

SIGMUND FREUD, *Five Lectures on Psychoanalysis* (London, 1957).
STEPHEN TOULMIN, *The Logical Status of Psychoanalysis*, in Margaret MacDonald
    (ed.), *Philosophy and Analysis* (Oxford, 1954).
ANTONY FLEW, *Psycho-Analytic Explanation*, in Margaret MacDonald (ed.), *Philo-
    sophy and Analysis* (Oxford, 1954).
R. S. PETERS, *The Concept of Motivation* (London, 1958), Ch. 3.
A. C. MACINTYRE, *The Unconscious, A Conceptual Study* (London, 1958).
B. A. FARRELL, 'Can Psychoanalysis be Refuted?', *Inquiry* (1961).
B. A. FARRELL, J. O. WISDOM, and P. M. TURQUET, 'The Criteria for a Psy-
    choanalytic Interpretation', *Proceedings of the Aristotelian Society*, Supplemen-
    tary Volume (1962).
FRANK CIOFFI, *Freud and the Idea of a Pseudo-Science*, in Robert Borger and Frank
    Cioffi (eds.), *Explanation in the Behavioural Sciences* (Cambridge, 1970).
RICHARD WOLLHEIM (ed.), *Freud, A Collection of Critical Essays* (New York, 1974).

(b) *Self-Deception*

MARCEL PROUST, *Swann's Way*, trans. C. K. Scott Moncrieff (London, 1922), Part
    II, pp. 79–81.
JEAN-PAUL SARTRE, *Being and Nothingness, An Essay on Phenomenological Onto-
    logy* (New York, 1966), Part I, Ch. 2.
RAPHAEL DEMOS, 'Lying to Oneself', *Journal of Philosophy* (1960).
F. A. SIEGLER, 'Demos on Lying to Oneself', *Journal of Philosophy* (1960).
JOHN V. CANFIELD and DON F. GUSTAFSON, 'Self-Deception', *Analysis* (1962).
TERENCE PENELHUM, 'Pleasure and Falsity', *American Philosophical Quarterly*
    (1964).
HERBERT FINGARETTE, *Self-Deception* (London, 1969).
DAVID PEARS, 'The Paradoxes of Self-Deception', in *Questions in the Philosophy
    of Mind* (London, 1975).

(c) *Roles*

JEAN-PAUL SARTRE, *Anti-Semite and Jew* (New York, 1948).
ERVING GOFFMAN, *The Presentation of Self in Everyday Life* (New York, 1959).
— — *Role Distance*, in *Where the Action is* (London, 1969).
STUART HAMPSHIRE, *Thought and Action* (London, 1959), Chs. 2 and 3.

(d) *Psychological Explanation*

N. S. SUTHERLAND, 'Motives as Explanations', *Mind* (1959).
G. A. MILLER, E. GALANTER, and K. H. PRIBRAM, *Plans and the Structure
    of Behaviour* (New York, 1960).
DONALD DAVIDSON, 'Reasons, Actions and Causes', *Journal of Philosophy* (1963).
CHARLES TAYLOR, *The Explanation of Behaviour* (London, 1964).
NOAM CHOMSKY, *Language and Mind* (New York, 1968).
JERRY A. FODOR, *Psychological Explanation, An Introduction to the Philosophy of
    Psychology* (New York, 1968).

G. H. VON WRIGHT, *Explanation and Understanding* (London, 1971).

ROBERT BORGER and FRANK CIOFFI (eds.), *Explanation in the Behavioural Sciences* (Cambridge, 1970).

DAVID PEARS, *Sketch for a Causal Theory of Wanting and Doing*, in *Questions in the Philosophy of Mind* (London, 1975).

(e) *Feelings and their Expression*

CHARLES DARWIN, *The Expression of the Emotions in Man and Animals* (London, 1872).

WILLIAM JAMES, *Principles of Psychology* (New York, 1950), Ch. 25.

LUDWIG WITTGENSTEIN, *Philosophical Investigations* (Oxford, 1953), esp. sections 244 ff.

ALAN DONAGAN, *Wittgenstein on Sensation*, in George Pitcher (ed.), *Wittgenstein: The Philosophical Investigations* (London, 1968).

DAVID PEARS, *Wittgenstein* (London, 1971), Ch. 8.

GILBERT RYLE, *The Concept of Mind* (London, 1949), Ch. 4.

A. J. AYER, *Privacy*, in *The Concept of a Person and Other Essays* (London, 1963).

ANTHONY KENNY, *Action, Emotion and Will* (London, 1963), Chs. 1–6.

R. M. HARE and PATRICK GARDINER, 'Pain and Evil', *Proceedings of the Aristotelian Society*, Supplementary Volume (1964).

HILARY PUTNAM, 'Brains and Behaviour', in R. J. Butler (ed.), *Analytical Philosophy*, 2nd Ser. (Oxford, 1965).

J. C. B. GOSLING, *Pleasure and Desire* (Oxford, 1969).

RONALD MELZACK, *The Puzzle of Pain* (Harmondsworth, 1973), Chs. 1 and 2.

(f) *Minds and Machines*

ALAN ROSS ANDERSON (ed.), *Minds and Machines* (Englewood Cliffs, 1964).

HILARY PUTNAM, 'Robots: Machines or Artificially Created Life?', *Journal of Philosophy* (1964).

JERRY A. FODOR, *Psychological Explanation, An Introduction to the Philosophy of Psychology* (New York, 1968), Ch. 4.

(g) *Mind and Brain*

D. H. HUBEL and T. N. WIESEL, 'Receptive Fields of Single Neurones in the Cat's Striate Cortex', *Journal of Physiology* (1959).

JOHN C. ECCLES (ed.), *Brain and Conscious Experience* (New York, 1966).

WILDER PENFIELD, *The Excitable Cortex in Conscious Man* (Liverpool, 1967).

A. R. LURIA, *The Working Brain, An Introduction to Neuropsychology* (Harmondsworth, 1973).

C. V. BORST (ed.), *The Mind–Brain Identity Theory* (London, 1970).

D. M. ARMSTRONG, *A Materialist Theory of the Mind* (London, 1968).

DONALD DAVIDSON, *Mental Events*, in Lawrence Forster and J. W. Swanson (eds.), *Experience and Theory* (London, 1970).

JAMES W. CORNMAN, *Materialism and Sensations* (New Haven, 1971).

(h) *The Unity or Divisibility of Consciousness*

See references to SPERRY, GAZZANIGA, and GESCHWIND in notes 1 and 3 of Nagel's article (pp. 112–14 above).

C. S. SHERRINGTON, *Man On His Nature* (Edinburgh, 1940), Ch. 9.

ERWIN SCHRÖDINGER, *Mind and Matter* (Cambridge, 1958), Ch. 4.

SYDNEY SHOEMAKER, *Self-Knowledge and Self-Identity* (Ithaca, 1963); Ch. 3.
JOHN ECCLES. *The Brain and the Unity of Conscious Experience* (Cambridge, 1965).
ROLAND PUCCETTI, *Brain Bisection and Personal Identity'*, *British Journal for the Philosophy of Science*, 1973.
FRANK SCHMIDT (ed.). *The Neurosciences*, Third Series (London, 1974).
JONATHAN BENNETT, *Kant's Dialectic* (Cambridge, 1974), Ch. 5.

(i) *Personal Identity*

JOHN LOCKE, *Essay Concerning Human Understanding*, Bk. 2, Ch. 27.
DAVID HUME, *Treatise of Human Nature*, Bk. I, Part IV, Section 6.
WILLIAM JAMES, *Principles of Psychology* (New York, 1950), Ch. 10.
P. F. STRAWSON, *Individuals* (London, 1959), Ch. 3.
A. M. QUINTON, 'The Soul', *Journal of Philosophy* (1962).
SYDNEY SHOEMAKER, *Self-Knowledge and Self-Identity* (Ithaca, 1963).
DAVID WIGGINS, *Identity and Spatio-Temporal Continuity* (Oxford, 1967), especially Part 4.
SYDNEY SHOEMAKER. 'Wiggins on Identity', *Philosophical Review* (1970).
— — 'Persons and their Pasts', *American Philosophical Quarterly* (1970).
TERENCE PENELHUM, *Survival and Disembodied Existence* (London, 1970).
BERNARD WILLIAMS, *Problems of the Self* (Cambridge, 1973).
DEREK PARFIT, *Later Selves and Moral Principles*, in Alan Montfiore (ed.), *Philosophy and Personal Relations* (London, 1973).
JONATHAN BENNETT, *Kant's Dialectic* (Cambridge, 1974), Chs. 4–6.

(j) *Some Source Material*

A. R. LURIA. *The Mind of a Mnemonist* (London, 1969).
— — *The Man With a Shattered World, A History of a Brain Wound* (London, 1973).
OLIVER W. SACKS, *Awakenings*, revised edition (Harmondsworth, 1976).

INDEX OF NAMES

(not including authors mentioned only in the Bibliography)